The Independent Study Catalog

NUCEA's Guide to Independent Study Through Correspondence Instruction

Fourth Edition

Editors
John H. Wells
Barbara C. Ready

The Catalog Committee of the Division of Independent Study, NUCEA

Norman Loewenthal, University of North Carolina; Chair
Mary Beth Almeda, University of California Extension
James Andrews, University of Florida
Dennis DeFrain, Weber State College
Diane Leos, Pennsylvania State University
Suzanne Logan, Texas Tech University
Morris Sammons, University of Illinois
Clair Woodward, Indiana State University
Arlene Glover, University of North Carolina; Secretary to the Committee

Division of Independent Study Officers

Hal Markowitz, University of Florida; Chair
Von Pittman, University of Iowa; Chair-Elect
Mary Beth Almeda, University of California Extension; Immediate Past
   Chair
Joyce Nielsen, Western Illinois University; Secretary
Phyllis Luebke, Oklahoma State University; Treasurer

Division of Independent Study Administrative Committee

Robert Batchellor, University of Illinois
Ernestine Copas, University of Georgia
Charles Feasly, Oklahoma State University
Hugh Harris, University of Oklahoma
Norman Loewenthal, University of North Carolina
Suzanne Logan, Texas Tech University
Monty McMahon, University of Nebraska–Lincoln
David Mercer, Pennsylvania State University
Morris Sammons, University of Illinois
Marvin Van Kekerix, University of Nebraska–Lincoln

A Peterson's Publication for the National University Continuing Education Association

Published by Peterson's Guides for the National University Continuing Education Association

Copyright ©1989 by the National University Continuing Education Association, One Dupont Circle, Washington, D.C.

Previous editions copyright 1983, 1986

Previously published as *Guide to Independent Study Through Correspondence Instruction,* copyright 1980, 1977

ISBN 0-87866-757-1
ISSN 0733-6020

Composition and design by Peterson's Guides

Printed in the United States of America

Members of the National University Continuing Education Association (NUCEA) include accredited, degree-granting institutions of higher education and comparable nonprofit organizations with a substantial involvement in postsecondary continuing higher education. Through continuing education programs, NUCEA members make the resources of their institutions available to youth, adults, volunteer organizations, professional bodies, government, labor, and private business and industry.

10   9   8   7   6   5   4   3   2   1

CONTENTS

In parentheses following each institution's name is each division of instruction offered by the institution for courses listed in this Guide, as follows: E = Elementary, H = High School, C = College, G = Graduate, NC = Noncredit.

Contents

Correspondence study, which is also commonly referred to as "independent study," "home study," or any of a variety of similar terms, is individual instruction by mail. It is flexible, convenient, and personalized. Students can enroll at any time, study at home, and set their own pace. Work is typically done on a one-to-one basis with faculty experts who design the instructional materials, guide the study of individual students as they proceed through the course, and prepare specific responses to the submitted work.

The Nature of Correspondence Study

Correspondence study helps a wide range of people meet their educational needs and objectives. Individuals who are unable to come to the classroom, or who prefer to study at their own pace, can earn credit toward a degree or toward a professional certificate. Adults with work and family responsibilities can gain new job skills and learn about new subjects for personal enrichment or satisfaction. With an increased choice of courses, students seeking academic degrees can:

- Gain advanced standing upon admission
- Solve campus scheduling problems
- Meet course prerequisites
- Explore new subjects
- Study while away from campus
- Accelerate their programs
- Restore academic eligibility

Credit courses are offered for every academic level from elementary school (including preschool) through graduate work, although the emphasis is on high school and undergraduate courses.

Noncredit courses and courses offered for certification purposes are also available from most NUCEA institutions.

Additional study opportunities for off-campus students include telecourses, group study, credit by examination, and external degree programs. (See the sections on "Special Study Opportunities" and "External Degree Programs," pages 6 and 7.)

The Study Skills Required

Correspondence study is demanding. Since the printed word and written exchanges are the principal learning media, it is essential that students have reasonably strong reading and writing skills. While the flexibility of correspondence study is one of its distinct advantages, it is also one of its greatest hazards. Many people who enroll in correspondence courses do not finish them. Being on their own, unsupported by the discipline of the traditional classroom, correspondence students *must* have the initiative and self-reliance to develop good study habits, work independently, and establish and maintain a regular schedule of study.

In general, students who complete correspondence courses feel that they have learned as much as—if not more than—they would have in a traditional course, but they also feel that the experience has been more rigorous. Those who are able to take responsibility for their own education find correspondence study rewarding and satisfying. Anyone contemplating enrollment in correspondence study should give careful consideration to both the advantages and drawbacks of the correspondence study method before enrolling.

The Institutions in this Guide: An Assurance of Quality

This Guide includes only those institutions whose correspondence programs meet a high standard of quality and accessibility. Institutions are selected on the basis of these criteria:

1. The institution must be a member of the National University Continuing Education Association (NUCEA). In all cases but one, institutions hold full institutional membership in NUCEA; the only exception is explained below under "Accreditation and NUCEA Membership."

2. The institution must be accredited by a regional accrediting association, unless special considerations warrant the acceptance of the institution on the basis of accreditation by some other recognized body. Again, the exceptions are described below.

3. The institution must affirm that it accepts and supports the published Standards of NUCEA's Independent Study Division. The Standards are guidelines for conducting

effective programs of independent study and improving their quality. They are also intended to assist units of independent study in the internal and external evaluation of their program. The Standards serve as goals toward which independent study programs should strive, and they address all aspects of program operation: mission, instruction, services, faculty, administration, staff, and research and evaluation.

4. The institution must affirm that its correspondence program offers study opportunities that are free of the time and place constraints that are typical of most other forms of instruction. In general, this means that the institution's correspondence courses are open to students residing anywhere, that the courses do not include any requirements to attend classes, and that credits earned in the correspondence program may be transferred to other regionally accredited institutions.

5. The institution must be represented in NUCEA's Independent Study Division by at least one individual employed within its correspondence unit.

Accreditation and NUCEA Membership

One of the principal ways of assuring readers of the quality of institutions in this Guide is through their accreditation and their affiliation with the National University Continuing Education Association (NUCEA). Members of NUCEA are primarily degree-granting institutions of higher education accredited by one of the six regional accrediting associations that hold membership in the Council on Postsecondary Accreditation (COPA) or, with the approval of the Board of Directors, by another accrediting agency that holds membership in COPA. In addition, member institutions must have substantial programs in continuing education.

NUCEA embraces some 370 colleges and universities devoted to continuing higher education and public service. All of the programs and courses of these institutions, including those offered through correspondence instruction, are covered by the accreditation of the institution.

With two exceptions, all of the institutions included in this directory are accredited by one of the six regional accrediting associations. Home Study International is accredited by the National Home Study Council, which is recognized by COPA but is not a regional accrediting association. However, HSI is affiliated with Columbia Union College, which is accredited by the Middle States Association of Colleges and Schools. This affiliation is approved by the Middle States Association and the Maryland State Board of Higher Education. The North Dakota Division of Independent Study is accredited by the North Dakota Department of Public Instruction rather than by a regional accrediting association. It is under the supervision of the North Dakota State Board of Public School Education. Because of this accreditation status, the Division is an affiliate member of NUCEA rather than a full institutional member.

The six U.S. regional accrediting associations that hold membership in COPA are the New England Association of Schools and Colleges, the Middle States Association of Colleges and Schools, the North Central Association of Colleges and Schools, the Northwest Association of Schools and Colleges, the Southern Association of Colleges and Schools, and the Western Association of Schools and Colleges. The National Home Study Council, which also holds membership in COPA, is the specialized accrediting body for institutions and organizations that have been established primarily to offer programs for home study.

In addition to the accreditation of NUCEA institutions by these bodies, approval by state educational agencies is conferred separately on some high school correspondence courses offered by NUCEA members.

Admission

In general, correspondence study courses listed in this Guide are open to all individuals, regardless of age, place of residence, or educational background. Applications are usually accepted without entrance examinations or proof of prior educational experience. However, some institutions may impose certain requirements before they will accept correspondence study credit, and some courses or programs may require previous study or experience. *Students should determine the requirements of the resident institution or of the particular program for which they intend to earn credit before enrolling in a correspondence study course.* An institution's catalog will list both general admission requirements and prerequisites for individual courses.

Usually, to enroll in a correspondence course, the student simply fills in the registration form provided by the institution and sends a check or money order to cover tuition and fees, as listed in the catalog.

After reviewing the course names shown in this Guide, prospective students may obtain registration forms and catalogs, providing descriptions of the courses, from all NUCEA member institutions listed in this Guide. In addition, some institutions offer detailed information about individual courses, such as a course outline, which will be sent upon request. To obtain these materials, the contact name and address or telephone number shown at the top of each institution's entry in the "Institutions and Correspondence Courses Offered" section should be used.

Enrollment, Registration Forms, and Catalogs

Courses are not limited by traditional academic schedules. Students can enroll at their convenience and work at their own pace. An enrollment is valid for a certain period, often for twelve months, and most institutions provide for extensions of time. Some institutions, however, do have regulations prohibiting rapid completion of a course to ensure the validity of the learning experience and to enable the instructor to respond to the student's work before the final examination. Such regulations are listed in the institutional catalog. Within these broad limits, students determine the time it will take to complete their program of study.

The institutional catalog should also be consulted for specific policies and time limitations pertaining to withdrawals, refunds, transfers, and renewal periods.

Time Requirements

While each institution has somewhat different policies and procedures, the details of which are contained in the institutional catalog, correspondence study generally follows the pattern outlined below.

The Mechanics of Correspondence Study

1. **Study Materials.** A study guide that includes a list of required textbooks and materials, supplementary information, lecture notes and discussion of course content, specific learning assignments, and all other details necessary for successful completion of the course is sent to a student as soon as the enrollment process is complete.

2. **Textbooks.** The required textbooks and other course materials may be obtained in a number of ways, depending upon the procedures of the particular institution. They are ordered at the time of enrollment and sent at the same time as the study guide, ordered from a designated bookstore after the receipt of the study guide, or obtained from local sources. Audiovisual materials, if any, are usually sent with the study guide, and charges for these are indicated in the catalogs of the individual institutions.

3. **Study Assignments.** The study guide divides the course into segments, usually called "lessons" or "assignments." Each lesson directs certain study activities, such as readings, self-check exercises, occasional field trips, interviews, and any other activities that are appropriate to the subject area of the course. These are done in preparation for the successful completion of the next step.

4. **Assignments for Evaluation.** After the study activities in each lesson are completed, a written assignment is submitted for evaluation. This varies widely from course to course, and sometimes even within the same course. A written assignment may consist of prescribed objective or essay questions, a report, a paper, or any other example of written work. In some instances, the student has the opportunity to submit an audiocassette, answering questions or performing orally.

   These assignments are evaluated by the instructor and returned as soon as possible. The instructor evaluates the assignment and usually provides comments and suggestions as well as a grade.

5. **Examinations.** Credit courses usually require one or two examinations that must be taken under the supervision of an authorized proctor. Generally, students are able to arrange for supervision of the examination at an institution near their home. In some cases, noncredit courses also require final examinations. Examination forms are sent directly to the proctor, and the completed examination is returned to the institution by the

proctor after it has been administered to the student. Specific details are given in the catalog or the study guide of the enrolling institution.

6. **Records and Transcripts.** A record of a completed correspondence course is maintained by each institution. For credit courses, the student's grade is recorded, and transcripts of the credit earned may be requested from the institution. Generally, a small charge is assessed for each transcript. For noncredit and certificate courses, some institutions award a certificate of completion or Continuing Education Units (CEUs).

Credit

Limits of Correspondence Study Credit. Students who wish to apply credit earned through correspondence study to a college degree or a high school diploma should consult the resident institution **before enrolling in a correspondence study course.** Most institutions have limitations on the number and kinds of correspondence study credits that they will accept.

Some accredited colleges and universities offer a college degree or high school diploma mainly or entirely by correspondence. Students interested in external degree or diploma programs should contact the institution of their choice and inquire whether such a program is available.

College Credit. Academic credit is measured in semester or quarter hours. The equivalent value of semester and quarter hours that is generally employed is as follows:

1⅓ semester hours	=	2 quarter hours
2 semester hours	=	3 quarter hours
2⅔ semester hours	=	4 quarter hours
3 semester hours	=	4½ quarter hours
3⅓ semester hours	=	5 quarter hours
4 semester hours	=	6 quarter hours

You may wish to consult with the institution(s) to which you are transferring credits, because some institutions use different systems of conversion or do not accept partial hours of credit.

Grades and Transcripts for College Courses. Each institution follows its regular grading policies in evaluating the work of independent students. When a course is completed, a grade report is sent to the student, the grade is recorded at the institution, and a transcript will be sent to any address designated by the student in a written request. Some institutions use special designations to indicate courses that have been taken by correspondence. Most institutions charge for additional transcripts.

Transfer of Credit. Credit earned in correspondence study courses taken from a regionally accredited institution is normally transferable from one institution to another; however, since policies and degree requirements vary among universities and colleges, students are urged to consult appropriate officials of the institution from which they expect to receive a degree to ascertain whether credit is transferable. If course work is taken from an institution that is not regionally accredited, the transferability of the course work for credit to another institution may be more difficult.

High School Credit. Most institutions offering credit for high school courses tailor their credit units to coincide with the method most common in the state system they serve. Generally, courses are offered for one-half unit of credit (equal to one semester of course work in a regular classroom) or for one-quarter credit, depending on the state system.

High schools that offer a diploma by correspondence award credit on a semester basis of one-half unit of credit per course. Prior approval of correspondence work should be obtained from the resident high school to ensure acceptance of the credit.

Enrollment in Credit Courses on a Noncredit Basis. Most NUCEA member universities and colleges accept enrollment in credit courses on a noncredit basis and take special interest in students who are studying for personal satisfaction without regard to credit.

The Continuing Education Unit or CEU. The Continuing Education Unit (CEU) is used to recognize and measure achievement in noncredit courses. The CEU is defined as 10 contact hours of participation in an organized continuing education experience under responsible sponsorship, capable direction, and qualified instruction. Individuals interested in receiving CEUs for noncredit courses listed in this Guide should request information from the institutions offering the courses.

Financial Considerations

The costs associated with taking a correspondence course vary from course to course and from one college or university to another. Each institution sets its own pricing structure, based upon the expenses associated with a course and the institution's overall fee policies.

In general, a person can expect direct charges for tuition, textbooks, and other necessary course materials, and sometimes for postage and handling.

Tuition. Tuition for college and university credit courses is most often figured on the basis of a set amount per credit hour, regardless of whether the institution uses the semester or quarter unit of measurement. (Example: Accounting 101 offered for 3 credits at $50 per credit requires a tuition of $150, to be sent with the registration: 3 x $50 = $150.)

Tuition for noncredit and high school courses is usually stated as a flat fee for the course rather than in terms of a set amount per credit hour. For such courses, no computation is needed in completing a registration form.

Tuition rates for college credit courses at NUCEA member institutions ranged from a low of $24 to a high of $208 per credit unit at the time this Guide was printed. Rates for high school and noncredit courses also vary widely and change frequently. Before enrolling, any interested person should check the catalog of the individual institution for current rates.

Textbooks. In most cases, the cost of textbooks is not included in the cost of the course, and students must purchase their own books. The catalog of the enrolling institution or the study guide that is mailed to a student who enrolls will indicate exactly how the texts can be obtained and the exact or approximate cost. The cost can vary widely, depending upon the number and kinds of texts. In a few instances, the study guide also serves as the text.

Course Materials. Course materials always include a study guide, which is usually provided as part of the initial cost. In addition, workbooks, procedure manuals, kits, audiocassette tapes, phonograph records, filmstrips or slides, photographs, or various other audiovisual materials may be required, in which case the cost is borne by the student. Although these items are sometimes quite expensive, they often cost only a few dollars. In some cases, the material is loaned to the student, who pays a deposit that is partially refunded when the material is returned. Details about costs for course materials will be listed in the institution's catalog or in the study guide.

Postage. In all cases, students bear the cost for postage on items that they mail. Some institutions levy a postage fee for items mailed to their students, such as course materials and returned assignments. Rates for domestic postage are not high, but rates for postage to foreign countries can be a major expense. When possible, students going to foreign countries should enroll before they leave the United States, taking their textbooks and course materials with them in order to avoid both postage and tariff expenses. An institution's catalog will identify policies and costs for foreign enrollments.

Handling and Special Fees. Some institutions charge a handling fee to help them defray the cost of processing materials and registration. In addition, rental fees, usually small, are sometimes charged for special course materials. Special fees are usually charged for course transfers and renewals and sometimes for enrollment by out-of-state residents.

Payment Plans. Most institutions require at the time of registration full payment of all charges due. The preferred method of payment is a check or money order. In a few instances, textbooks are paid for separately. Some institutions accept charge cards, and a few have some form of partial or deferred payment plan, but the number of institutions that offer these options is small. It is necessary to examine the catalog or bulletin of the institution to determine its payment policies.

Financial Aid

Financial aid is not as readily available for correspondence study students as it is for traditional classroom students. However, the sources listed below can occasionally provide some financial aid, and students who require aid should explore all applicable possibilities.

Employers. Many employers provide educational benefits to their employees. These are generally administered through the personnel or benefits department of the organization. Teachers and other public school personnel may be able to receive reimbursement of fees taken for college credit; they should contact the coordinator of staff development within their district for further information.

Unions. Unions often negotiate educational benefits into their contracts. The union's business manager would be the person to provide information.

Veterans' and Military Benefits. All of the federal veterans' assistance acts have had provisions for financial assistance for college and university correspondence study, usually under the term independent study. The amount and type of assistance varies, and it is best to check with a local Veterans Administration office for specific details.

Active-duty military personnel, including members of the National Guard and Armed Forces Reserve, have two options available to them for financial assistance. The first consists of "in-service" benefits through the Veterans Administration. The second is "tuition assistance," which comes from the military person's respective service and is administered by DANTES (Defense Activity for Non-Traditional Educational Support). In either case, the Educational Service Officer of the base, post, or ship can provide information.

In addition to the federal government's tuition assistance plans, some states have educational benefits for veterans and military personnel. Questions and inquiries should be directed to the state veterans or military affairs offices.

Other Federal Programs. Although most federal programs providing grants or loans are oriented to the resident student, some are applicable to the correspondence student as well. Under certain conditions, for example, Pell Grants may be available to persons studying by correspondence. Because eligibility is limited to degree candidates, students should contact the financial aid office of the institution from which they are seeking their degree.

Vocational Rehabilitation. Nearly all states provide financial benefits for the education of persons with some form of handicap. A number of states include correspondence study in the forms of education allowable for benefits. Any inquiries should be directed to a state's department of vocational rehabilitation.

Institutional Aid. A small number of colleges and universities have a limited amount of financial aid available for correspondence study. Guide users should carefully examine the catalogs of the institutions for financial aid information or consult the office of financial aid.

Special Study Opportunities

While the focus of this Guide is on correspondence courses, other related opportunities are frequently offered by independent study programs. To obtain details, you will need to contact an institution's independent study office.

Some institutions use periodic or regular transmission of televised material by broadcast, cablecast, or other means to supplement independent study instruction. Courses having radio components are also occasionally offered. These courses are generally limited both by time of offering and by geographical area. Some correspondence courses also use audiocassette tape recordings, laboratory kits, and computer programs as instructional tools. Videocassette recordings are becoming a more common feature of correspondence courses. Some programs have begun to use the **computer disk** or the **interactive capabilities of personal computers,** linked by telephone lines, to serve as the means by which information is conveyed between student and instructor.

Such opportunities as **credit by examination, tutorial study,** and **directed study** are also available at some institutions. Credit by examination allows students to receive degree credit for successful scores on the various tests of the College-Level Examination Program (CLEP) or the ACT Proficiency Examination Program (PEP), on Advanced Placement tests, or on institutionally administered tests. Tutorial study makes it possible for students to arrange for correspondence instruction in courses not otherwise offered by the correspondence method. Directed study allows the student to substitute special projects or submissions for the assignments usually required in a course. Some correspondence courses include **optional class meetings.** Others lend themselves well to **group study** projects for the benefit of friends or associates who wish to study the same subject. In some instances such projects may include visits with the instructor or other experts. These variations of the traditional correspondence format are especially helpful for students with special needs.

In many states correspondence courses serve as a way of meeting requirements for **professional certification** or certification renewal. Teachers constitute one major group that has benefited in this way, though persons in other professions should also determine if correspondence study might allow them to complete requirements in their fields. Some institutions offer entire **series of correspondence courses** in specific subject areas, sometimes in relation to vocational or professional requirements. Often a certificate of completion is awarded to individuals who complete the full series.

External Degree Programs

Related in concept to correspondence courses are **external degree programs,** which are now offered by numerous colleges and universities in the United States. These flexible programs make it possible for students to complete all degree requirements with little or no attendance on campus. Correspondence courses are one of several ways that requirements toward an external degree may be met. A useful directory of external degree programs is the American Council on Education's *Guide to External Degree Programs in the United States.* Check for this and other references at your local library or bookstore. Care should be taken to verify that the external degree program is accredited by a recognized accrediting agency.

Special Advice and Counseling

As a prospective nontraditional student in correspondence study, you face three major questions that institutions have helped traditional students answer but to which you must find the answers yourself: (1) Why am I taking this course? (2) What options are available to me for completing the requirements of taking this course? (3) How do I study?

Anyone contemplating independent study should determine the answers to these questions before enrolling in a correspondence course. In some instances, the correspondence study offices of the colleges and universities can answer a few questions, particularly in reference to their own institution. However, it is best to get official information from the admissions office, the academic department in which you wish to take a course, or the counseling service of the college or university. In addition, it is vitally important that you seek formal counseling and advice from the institution's counseling service, particularly when academic credit is involved. Very few of the correspondence study offices have the personnel to answer questions or to advise you, and in many cases they are not authorized to do so.

The section below offers you help in finding answers to the three basic questions.

Question 1. Why am I taking this course?

If the course is for college or high school credit, you must ask:
a. Will any college or high school accept the course credit and apply it toward my graduation?
b. How many credits by correspondence will be accepted toward graduation?
c. Will my institution accept credit for correspondence work transferred from another institution?
d. Will credits earned by correspondence be accepted in my area of concentration?

If the course is being taken for certification and not for degree purposes, you should ask:

a. What are the certification requirements?
b. Will the course be acceptable to the certifying agency?
c. How many credits can be earned or how much work can be done by correspondence?

Question 2. **What options are available to me for completing course requirements?**

Some institutions offer optional ways of taking their courses or of earning degree credit. For these, you should ask:

a. Is the pass-fail option acceptable to my college or certifying agency?
b. Is credit by examination acceptable?
c. Is credit for experiential learning available and acceptable?
d. Are the external degree programs that some institutions offer by correspondence acceptable to other colleges, employers, and certifying agencies?

Question 3. **How do I study?**

Since successful correspondence study requires really good study habits, you should take the time to evaluate your own approach to studying before you enroll. Assess your study habits and decide, with as much objectivity as possible, how well you think you can study on your own.

Schedule. It is extremely important to set aside a regularly scheduled time for study. If you have not been involved in academic pursuits recently, you may find that your career, family, hobbies, or social and civic commitments leave little time for studying. In order to make room for study in your schedule, you may have to sacrifice other activities. To help you decide how to do this, keep a record for a week or two of how you spend your time, and see what you are willing to give up. Since you won't have the built-in pacing of classes and preestablished deadlines set by instructors, you may find it hard to make progress unless you set up a definite study schedule.

Try to schedule this study for a time when you will be mentally fresh and able to devote at least one hour to your work. Think of the hour as "reserved time," but don't get discouraged if you can't always keep the schedule. After all, one of the advantages of correspondence study is its flexibility. Just keep in mind that regularly scheduled study is the ideal, and make it your goal. If you miss too many study periods, revise your schedule.

Where to Study. You'll find it easier to focus on your work if you arrange an appropriate environment for study. You will need a place that is quiet and free from reminders of other responsibilities. You might consider a public library if your home does not offer a suitable place.

Reading Skills. The abilities to read with comprehension and to retain what you read are necessary for real learning to take place, especially in correspondence study. These skills can be developed by concentrating on what you read and by taking frequent pauses to organize and review the material in your mind. At the end of a study session, you should review everything you have read, making special notes of important points learned in that session.

Writing Skill. Writing is also an essential skill. Written assignments provide the main channel of communication between you and your instructor. In your written assignments, you collect and synthesize what you've learned, demonstrating to your instructor that you are progressing according to plan. An elementary skill in writing is prerequisite to taking a correspondence course, but it is also a skill that is developed further in most courses.

In preparing written assignments, you must pay careful attention to instructions and be sure you understand what is being asked. Are you willing to work at preparing a good answer? You may need to develop a brief outline of your responses or draft your answer and check it over before preparing a final copy. Organization, grammar, and writing style are important in most correspondence study courses. If your skills in these areas need improvement, you may need to do extra work in a writing handbook.

If you do not understand some point, inquiries can be made only by mail. Responses to your instructor's comments on your lessons, requests for clarification of comments, and all other exchanges between you and your instructor will take time. This written interaction with your instructor can be very rewarding, but you must be willing to take the initiative, and you must have a great deal of patience in order to make it worthwhile.

Completing a correspondence course is not always easy. It requires a great deal of self-discipline and work. However, the benefits you derive can also be great. In addition to the mastery of subject matter, the study skills you develop should help you to undertake other difficult educational tasks with more confidence.

Division of Independent Study, NUCEA

The Division of Independent Study is one of six divisions within the Council for Continuing Education Delivery Systems and Formats of the National University Continuing Education Association (NUCEA). Over 70 of the Association's members offer correspondence study programs, and the Division of Independent Study provides the professional base for the various staff members of these programs.

The primary purposes of the Division of Independent Study are to provide a means of evolving guidelines for programs of high quality and to offer professional development for staff members. The Division also acts to promote the concept of correspondence study, encourage research, offer a forum for the exchange of information, and conduct a variety of programs to strengthen university-based distance education.

This book, *The Independent Study Catalog: NUCEA's Guide to Independent Study Through Correspondence Instruction,* is one of the major projects of the Division. The intent of the book is to offer a composite picture of the college- and university-based correspondence study opportunities that are currently available through more than 70 of the NUCEA member institutions. The Guide provides in convenient form the title and course number, sponsoring department, credit value, level of instruction, and special instructional feature of each correspondence course.

The National University Continuing Education Association is the premier national association concerned with postsecondary continuing higher education in the United States. It currently comprises some 370 colleges, universities, and other educational institutions, all of which have a commitment to the part-time student.

The mission of NUCEA is:

1. To promote excellence and the highest standards of college and university continuing education
2. To represent the broad interests of continuing higher education before governmental bodies and all other appropriate forums
3. To foster cooperation with relevant organizations in the public and private sectors in order to advance the interests of continuing higher education
4. To facilitate the exchange of ideas among continuing higher education professionals
5. To develop and disseminate timely information and research of particular relevance to continuing higher education professionals
6. To enable continuing higher education leaders to serve the needs of diverse publics by providing frequent and varied professional development opportunities

HOW TO USE THIS GUIDE

The Independent Study Catalog: NUCEA's Guide to Independent Study Through Correspondence Instruction is just that, a "guide" to colleges and universities providing correspondence instruction and to the courses offered by those institutions. There are three ways of using the Guide:

Finding Courses

1. **Finding Courses from a Particular Institution.** If you have already decided to study through a particular institution listed in this book, simply find the institution's page number in the Contents, turn to its entry in the "Institutions and Correspondence Courses Offered" section, and review the courses offered.

   Each institution's entry lists elementary school courses, if any, first, followed by high school, college, graduate, and noncredit courses offered; these five kinds of courses are discussed on page 11. For each kind of course, course names are grouped together by academic or subject-matter area. To the right of each course name is the department offering the course, the number of the course, the number of credits earned by its successful completion, the level of instruction, and a special feature (if the course offers one of the five supportive instructional technologies that may be noted here). The codes for credits, levels of instruction, and special feature are explained on page 12. A list of department abbreviations and the names they stand for begins on page 13.

2. **Finding Courses Through the Index.** To locate a course in a particular category, turn to the Index. Listed there alphabetically are broad subject-matter areas (given 2-digit **NCES numbers**), representing major academic disciplines, with more specific areas grouped under them in two levels of subordination (assigned 4-digit and 6-digit NCES numbers). The name of an area is followed by the **code number of each institution** offering one or more courses in that area, plus a **code letter for each kind of course** the institution offers in that area (E = Elementary, H = High School, C = College, G = Graduate, N = Noncredit; see the following section entitled "Kinds of Courses"). Institutional code numbers and their corresponding institutional names are listed numerically and alphabetically in the Contents, on the inside back flap, and on the pages in the "Institutions and Correspondence Courses Offered" section of this book.

   After finding a subject-matter area of interest in the Index, make a note of its 4-digit or 6-digit **NCES number** (to left of area name) and the code number of each institution offering a course in that area. Note also the code letter, indicating the kind of course offered, that is attached to an institution's number. Then turn directly to the institution's entry in the "Institutions and Correspondence Courses Offered" section, where the code numbers and corresponding institutional names are listed numerically and alphabetically at the beginning of institutional entries and—in dictionary fashion—at the top of pages. When using the Index, you may wish to keep the back cover foldout open, in order to quickly identify the institution corresponding to a given code number and the kind of course indicated by the code letter.

   To find the specific course name(s) in an institution's entry, locate the section for the kind of course indicated by the code letter, then run down the numerical listing of NCES numbers (first column) until you find the one that corresponds to the subject-matter area of interest. You will find the name of each course offered by the institution in that category, the department offering it, the number of the course, the number of credits earned by its successful completion, the level of instruction, and, in the case of some courses, a special feature (any one of five supplemental instructional technologies). The abbreviations used for department names are explained on page 13.

3. **Finding a Specific Subject-Matter Area.** If you have difficulty locating a subject-matter area in the Index, refer to the Alphabetical Listing of Subject-Matter Areas, which precedes the Index. Then turn to the Index and follow the instructions above.

This Guide does not and cannot provide all of the information needed to actually enroll in a course. To do that, the prospective student must use the address at the top of an institution's entry to request a copy of the correspondence study catalog and specific information about enrolling. Some institutions offer detailed information about individual courses, such as an outline of the course, which will be sent upon request.

In general, course selection should follow an assessment of the purpose for which the course is needed: (1) for credit to apply toward a degree or diploma; (2) for personal development, without regard to credit; or (3) for certification in a professional program.

Students who expect to apply credit earned through correspondence study to a degree or a diploma should contact the resident institution for counseling and advice in order to ensure that the credit will be accepted. (See the sections on "Credit," page 4, and "Special Advice and Counseling," page 7.)

Kinds of Courses

Five kinds of correspondence study courses are listed in this Guide:

1. **Elementary School Courses.** One institution (Home Study International) offers correspondence courses for the elementary grades.

2. **High School Courses.** Courses covering virtually every area of high school study are offered by NUCEA member institutions. A few institutions offer high school diplomas by correspondence, but in most cases correspondence credit is accepted by the local high school, which issues the diploma. Students should have approval from the diploma-granting institution before enrolling in a correspondence study course.

3. **College Courses.** A great variety of courses offering undergraduate credit are provided.

4. **Graduate Courses.** Only a few institutions offer courses for graduate credit only, although some offer courses that are applicable toward credit at either the upper-division collegiate **or** graduate level. Some institutions will not accept correspondence study courses as credit toward a graduate degree.

5. **Noncredit Courses.** Courses designed to meet the job-related, professional, cultural, or personal needs of individuals who do not desire credit are offered by most NUCEA institutions. In addition, most courses that are offered for credit can **also** be taken on a noncredit basis.

In addition to offering single courses, some institutions offer complete programs of courses to meet certification, vocational, or professional needs. Students should consult an institution's catalog to obtain specific information.

In general, vocational courses are not listed in the Guide. Individuals who are interested in this type of study can secure information about such courses from institutions that are members of the National Home Study Council. The NHSC is the accrediting association for private, proprietary correspondence schools and publishes the **Directory of Accredited Home Study Schools.** A free copy of this directory can be obtained from the National Home Study Council, 1601 Eighteenth Street, NW, Washington, D.C. 20009. Send the Council a postcard stating your request, with your name, address, and zip code printed clearly on it.

Course Information and Abbreviations

All information in the section entitled "Institutions and Correspondence Courses Offered" has been supplied by the institutions themselves in response to a 1988 NUCEA survey. If any part of the usual data does not appear with a course listing, it was not supplied by the college or university, and students are advised to write directly to the institution for further information.

NCES Code Numbers. The first number appearing on a line with the name of a course in an institution's entry is the National Center for Education Statistics (NCES) number, as determined by the institution offering the course. This number derives from the taxonomy, or system of numerical classification, of educational subject matter prepared by the National Center for Education Statistics and published as **A Classification of Educational Subject Matter** by the U.S. Government Printing Office in 1978. This taxonomy is also used as a basis for the alphabetical listing of subject-matter areas and the subject-matter index in the Guide, although only those portions of it that relate to courses in this book are shown.

01 = Agriculture and renewable natural resources
02 = Architecture and environmental design
03 = Arts, visual and performing
04 = Business

05 = Communication
06 = Computer science and data processing
07 = Education
08 = Engineering and engineering technology
09 = Health care and health sciences
10 = Home economics
11 = Industrial arts, trades, and technology
12 = Language, linguistics, and literature
13 = Law
14 = Libraries and museums
15 = Life sciences and physical sciences
16 = Mathematical sciences
17 = Military sciences
18 = Philosophy, religion, and theology
19 = Physical education, health education, and leisure
20 = Psychology
21 = Public administration and social services
22 = Social sciences and social studies

Course Names and Numbers. Wherever possible, course names have been written in full, with the name of the department offering the course and the course number appearing to the right. However, because of space limitations, it has been necessary to abbreviate long course names. If there is any question about the specific content of a course, students should write directly to the institution offering the course, referring to the department and course number.

Credit Code. The credits earned by successful completion of courses listed in this Guide are indicated by the number of credits followed, usually, by S or Q to indicate the specific number of semester or quarter credit hours. (Example: 2S = 2 semester hours.) One or more of the following codes may also be used:

TN = Tenth unit
QT = Quarter unit
TH = Third unit
HF = Half unit
2T = Two-thirds unit
TQ = Three-quarters unit
1U = One unit
NC = Noncredit
CV = Credit varies

Level of Instruction. The level of instruction for each course listed in this Guide is indicated by one of the following codes:

L = Lower-division collegiate
U = Upper-division collegiate
B = Upper-division collegiate **or** graduate
G = Graduate
V = Vocational certificate
D = Developmental or remedial
H = High school
E = Elementary

Special Feature. If a course offers one of the five supplemental instructional technologies listed below, this is indicated by the corresponding code. (Because of limited space, no more than one feature is noted for any course.)

AC = Audiocassette
CI = Computer-aided instruction
LK = Lab kits
SL = Slides
VC = Videocassette

Department Name Abbreviations. The name of the department offering a course has usually been abbreviated and is shown to the right of the course name, although the names of some departments are written in full (e.g., Art = Art). The following list defines abbreviations appearing in this Guide:

A&Soc	Anthropology and Sociology
AAC	Athletic Administration and Coaching
Acctg	Accounting
AcDir	Activities Directors Series
ACS	American Cultural Studies
AdJus	Administration of Justice
Admn	Administration
AdmSc	Administrative Science
AdmSt	Administrative Studies
AduEd	Adult Education
Advt	Advertising
AEdSF	Adult Education and Social Foundations
AerAE	Aerospace and Aeronautical Engineering
Aero	Aerospace
AeroE	Aeronautical Engineering
AerSc	Aeronautical Science
AeSpE	Aerospace Engineering
AfAmS	Afro-American Studies
AFMgt	Aviation Flight Management
AfrSt	African Studies
AgEcB	Agriculture, Economics, and Business
AgEco	Agricultural Economics
AgEd	Agricultural Education
AgEng	Agricultural Engineering
Agri	Agriculture
Agron	Agronomy
AgSci	Agricultural Science
AInSt	American Indian Studies
Alcho	Alcoholism
Algbr	Algebra
AllHC	Allied Health Careers
AllHl	Allied Health
AmCul	American Culture
AmGvt	American Government
AmHis	American History
AmLit	American Literature
AMrch	Applied Merchandising
AmSt	American Studies
AMTec	Aviation Maintenance Technology
AnHis	Ancient History
AnSci	Animal Sciences
Anthr	Anthropology
AOM	Administrative Office Management
AppSt	Applied Studies
Ar&Sc	Arts and Sciences
Arab	Arabic
Arch	Architecture
ArchE	Architectural Engineering
Archy	Archaeology
ArHis	Art History
ArPlg	Architecture and Planning
ArsIn	Arson Investigation
Art	Art
ArtEd	Art Education
ASBE	Administrative Systems and Business Education
Asian	Asian Languages and Literature

AsiSt	Asian Studies
Astro	Astronomy
Athl	Athletics
AtmSc	Atmospheric Sciences
ATS	Advanced Technical Studies
Aviat	Aviation
AvTec	Avionics Technology
Bact	Bacteriology
BCEd	Business Career and Education
Bdcst	Broadcasting
BDEOA	Business–Distributive Education and Office Administration
BEOA	Business Education and Office Administration
BGS	Bachelor of General Studies Program
BiMet	Biometeorology
Bio	Biology
Bioch	Biochemistry
BioSc	Biological Sciences
Bkpng	Bookkeeping
BlgIn	Building Inspection
BlkSt	Black Studies
BMT	Business Management Technology
BOAdm	Business Office Administration
BOEd	Business and Office Education
Botny	Botany
BPAdm	Business and Public Administration
BTWri	Business and Technical Writing
Bu&Ec	Business and Economics
BuCom	Business Communications
BuLaw	Business Law
BuLog	Business Logistics
BuMgt	Business Management
BuPol	Business Policy
Bus	Business
BusAd	Business Administration
BusAr	Business Arithmetic
BusEc	Business Economics
BusEd	Business Education
BusEn	Business English
BusHS	Business, High School Level
BusMa	Business Mathematics
BVEd	Business and Vocational Education
C&HE	Consumer and Homemaking Education
CA&Sc	Communication Arts and Sciences
CAC	Computer-assisted Courses
CaPlg	Career Planning
CarEd	Career Education
CaRes	Career Resources
CESHP	Continuing Education, Science/Health Professions
CET	Civil Engineering Technology
ChDev	Child Development
ChEd	Child Education
Chem	Chemistry
ChemE	Chemical Engineering
ChFam	Child and Family Studies
Chin	Chinese
ChiSt	Chinese Studies

ChPsy	Child Psychology
Citz	Citizenship
Civcs	Civics
CivEE	Civil and Environmental Engineering
CivlE	Civil Engineering
CJC	Criminal Justice and Criminology
Class	Classics
ClCiv	Classical Civilization
ClCul	Classical Culture
CLEE	Corrections and Law Enforcement Education
ClLL	Classical Languages and Literature
ClLSc	Clinical Laboratory Science
ClPsy	Clinical Psychology
ClrPr	Clerical Practice
ClTex	Clothing and Textiles
CmpSc	Computer Science
CmpuE	Computer Engineering
COAS	College of Arts and Sciences
ComDi	Communicative Disorders
Comm	Commerce
Commu	Communications
Comp	Composition and Communication
CompL	Comparative Literature
ComSt	Communication Studies
Condo	Condominium Management
ConEc	Consumer Economics
ConEd	Continuing Education
ConSc	Consumer Sciences
ConsT	Construction Technology
CorLa	Correlated Language Arts
CpScM	Computer Science and Mathematics
Crim	Criminology
CrJus	Criminal Justice
CrWri	Creative Writing
CSA	Coaching and Sports Administration
CSLP	Civil Service License Preparation
CuIns	Curriculum and Instruction
Curr	Curriculum
Dan	Danish
Dance	Dance
DAsst	Dental Assisting
DCT	Dental Chairside Techniques
Dem	Democracy
DenCh	Dental Charting
DePsy	Developmental Psychology
DisEd	Distributive Education
DLT	Dental Laboratory Technology
DOP	Dental Office Procedures
DP	Data Processing
DRad	Dental Radiology
Drama	Drama
DrvEd	Driver Education
Dsgn	Design
DsgnT	Design Technology
DSM	Dietetic Food Systems Management
DtMgt	Diet Management
DySc	Dairy Science

EAsLL	East Asian Languages and Literature
Econ	Economics
EdAdm	Educational Administration
EdED	Education: Emotional Disorders
EdFA	Educational Foundations and Administration
EdFdn	Educational Foundations
EdGS	Educational Guidance Counseling and Student Services
EdPAd	Educational Policies and Administration
EdPSF	Educational Psychology and Social Foundations
EdPsy	Educational Psychology
EdRes	Educational Research
EdSE	Education: Special Education
EdThP	Educational Theory and Policy
Educ	Education
EduM	Educational Studies–Media
EdVI	Education: Visually Impaired
EEngl	Elementary-Level English
EHist	Elementary-Level History
EHlth	Elementary-Level Health
Elec	Electronics
ElecE	Electrical Engineering
ElecT	Electronics Technology
ElEd	Elementary Education
EMath	Elementary-Level Math
EMech	Engineering Mechanics
EMSci	Earth and Mineral Science
EngAS	Engineering and Applied Science
EngGr	Engineering Graphics
EngHS	English, High School Level
Engin	Engineering
Engl	English
EngLL	English Language and Literature
EnglL	English Literature
EngSc	Engineering Science
EnTec	Engineering Technology
Entom	Entomology
EntSc	Entomological Science
EnvD	Environmental Design
EnvEn	Environmental Engineering
EnvSc	Environmental Science
EnvSt	Environmental Studies
EPR	Educational Psychology and Research
ERlgn	Elementary-Level Religion
ErSci	Earth Science
Esk	Eskimo
ESLR	Educational Systems and Learning Resources
ESS	Exercise and Sport Science
Etiq	Etiquette
ETypg	Elementary-Level Typing
EuHis	European History
ExtEd	Extension Education
FamDC	Family Day Care
FamEc	Family Economics
FamHS	Family Studies, High School Level
Famil	Family
FamLC	Family Living Center
FamRM	Family Resource Management
FamSc	Family Science
FCMed	Family and Community Medicine
FdNut	Food and Nutrition

FdSci	Food Science
FdScN	Food Science and Nutrition
FdSHA	Food Service and Housing Administration
FdSHN	Food Science and Human Nutrition
FdSS	Food Services for Supervisors
FdSt	Food Studies
Film	Film
Finan	Finance
Finn	Finnish
FLHS	Family and Local History Studies
FMHCS	Family Management and Housing and Consumer Science
FnArt	Fine Arts
FND	Food, Nutrition, and Dietetics
FNIM	Food, Nutrition, and Institution Management
Folkl	Folklore
FOM	Fundamentals of Mathematics
Foren	Forensics
ForES	Forestry and Environmental Studies
Fores	Forestry
ForLg	Foreign Languages
ForLL	Foreign Languages and Literature
ForMg	Forestry Management
FrCul	Fruit Culture
FrEng	Freshman English
Frnch	French
FrPro	Fire Protection
FrSci	Fire Science
FrTrn	Fireman Training
FSA	Fire Services Administration
FSocS	Family Social Service
FuelE	Fuels Engineering
GBAdm	General Business Administration
GBio	General Biology
GblSt	Global Studies
GColl	General College
GComp	General Computers
GEB	General Education B (Science)
GEC	General Education C (Social Sciences)
GED	General Education D (Communication)
GEDev	General Educational Development
GeGe	Geography/Geology
GenBs	General Business
Genea	Genealogy
GenEn	General Engineering
Genet	Genetics
GenSc	General Science
GenSt	General Studies
GeoEn	Geological Engineering
Geog	Geography
Geol	Geology
Geom	Geometry
GeoSc	Geological Science
Geosc	Geosciences
Germn	German
Geron	Gerontology
GIBM	Growth in Basic Mathematics
GnHum	General Humanities
GnKno	General Knowledge
GnMth	General Mathematics
GnTec	General Technology

GovIS	Government and International Studies
Govt	Government
Graph	Graphic Arts/Design
GrBks	Great Books
Greek	Greek
GSoSc	General Social Science
Guida	Guidance
H&Rec	Hobbies and Recreation
H&SS	Health & Sport Science
HCA	Health Care Administration
HDFL	Human Development and Family Life
Hebr	Hebrew
HFL	Home and Family Life
HFS	Hotel and Food Service/Housing and Food Service
HFT	Hospitality, Food, and Tourism
Hist	History
Hl&HS	Health and Human Services
Hl&Sf	Health and Safety
HlEd	Health Education
HlSci	Health Sciences
Hlth	Health
HmMgt	Home Management
HNFd	Human Nutrition and Foods
HNFSM	Human Nutrition and Food Service Management
HoAdm	Hotel Administration
HomEc	Home Economics
HomLv	Home Living
HomSt	Home Study
Hort	Horticulture
HPA	Health Planning and Administration
HPE&R	Health, Physical Education, and Recreation
HPSc	History and Philosophy of Science
HRA	Hotel and Restaurant Administration
HRIM	Hotel, Restaurant, and Institutional Management
HRM	Human Resource Management
HSArt	High School Art
HSBus	High School Business
HSCSc	High School Computer Science
HSEng	High School English
HsHCA	Hospital and Health Care Administration
HSHE	High School Home Economics
HSLng	High School Languages
HSMgt	Health Systems Management
HSMth	High School Mathematics
HSMus	High School Music
HSSci	High School Science
HSSpn	High School Spanish
HSSSt	High School Social Studies
HSStS	High School Study Skills
HSTec	Human Services Technology
HSU	Health Science Unit
HuDev	Human Development
Hum	Humanities
HuNut	Human Nutrition
ICS	Intercultural Studies
IEOR	Industrial Engineering/Operations Research
IFS	Individual and Family Studies
IMSE	Industrial and Management Systems Engineering
InArt	Industrial Arts

InCom	Interpersonal Communication
InDec	Interior Decoration
IndEd	Industrial Education
IndEn	Industrial Engineering
InDes	Interior Design
IndRe	Industrial Relations
IndSt	Individual Study
IndTc	Industrial Technology
InMed	Instructional Media
InSci	Instructional Science
Insur	Insurance
IntBu	International Business
IntEn	Interior Environment
IntRe	International Relations
IntSt	Interdisciplinary Studies
Irrig	Irrigation
ISA	International Society of Appraisers
Ital	Italian
IVE	Industrial and Vocational Education
Japan	Japanese
JMC	Journalism and Mass Communications
Journ	Journalism
JrEng	Junior English
JusAd	Justice Administration
JusSt	Justice Studies
Just	Justice
JwSt	Jewish Studies
Kines	Kinesiology
LabSt	Labor Studies
LAEP	Landscape Architecture and Environmental Planning
Lang	Languages
LanHS	Languages, High School Level
LArch	Landscape Architecture
LatAm	Latin American Studies
Latin	Latin
Law	Law, Preparation for
LawEn	Law Enforcement
LEA	Law Enforcement Administration
LegSt	Legal Studies
LeiSt	Leisure Studies
LET	Law Enforcement Technology
LfSci	Life Sciences
LgRl	Legal Relations
LibAr	Liberal Arts
LibIn	Library and Information Sciences
LibSc	Library Sciences
LibSt	Liberal Studies
LibSv	Library Service
Ling	Linguistics
LIRel	Labor and Industrial Relations
Lit	Literature
LitSt	Literary Studies
LMT	Library Media Technology
LrnSk	Learning Skills
MAF	Marriage and Family
MarSc	Marine Science
Math	Mathematics

MatHS	Mathematics, High School Level
MCE	Mathematics and Consumer Economics
MComm	Mass Communications
MdTrm	Medical Terminology
MdvSt	Medieval Studies
MEAS	Mathematics, Engineering, and Applied Sciences
MecEn	Mechanical Engineering
Mech	Mechanics
MetEn	Metallurgical Engineering
Meteo	Meteorology
Mgmt	Management
MGS	Master of General Studies Program
MgtEc	Management Economics
MgtFn	Management/Finance
MgtSc	Management Science
Micro	Microbiology
Milit	Military Sciences
Mktg	Marketing
MLang	Modern Languages
MLS	Medical Laboratory Science
MrinE	Marine Engineering
Multi	Multidisciplinary Studies
Museo	Museology
Music	Music
MWPE	Men/Women Physical Education
NatSc	Natural Sciences
NCRE	Noncredit Real Estate
NELL	Near Eastern Languages and Literature
NFS	Nutrition and Food Science
Norw	Norwegian
Nrsng	Nursing
Nu&Fd	Nutrition and Foods
NucEg	Nuclear Energy
NucEn	Nuclear Engineering
NucSc	Nuclear Science
Nutri	Nutrition
NutSc	Nutritional Sciences
OccTh	Occupational Therapy
Ocean	Oceanography
OE	Organization and Environment
OfAdm	Office Administration
OfPro	Office Procedures
OrgB	Organizational Behavior
OrStu	Oriental Studies
PAIR	Personnel Administration and Industrial Relations
PBM	Personal Business Management
PCD	Principles of Curriculum Design
PCG	Psychology, Counseling and Guidance
PeerC	Peer Counseling
PerDv	Personal Development
Persi	Persian
Petro	Petroleum
Pharm	Pharmacology, Pharmacy
Philo	Philosophy
Photo	Photography
Phycs	Physics
PhyEd	Physical Education
PhySc	Physical Sciences

PlEd	Paralegal Education
PlSci	Plant Sciences
Plsh	Polish
PMR	Physical, Medical Rehabilitation
PNG	Petroleum and Natural Gas
PolAd	Police Administration
Polic	Police Science
Polit	Politics
PolSc	Political Science
POM	Production/Operations Management
Port	Portuguese
PPath	Plant Pathology
PrArt	Practical Arts
PreS	Preschool
PrPM	Procurement and Property Management
PSS	Plant and Soil Science
PstCn	Pest Control
Psych	Psychology
PsyGS	Psychology (General Studies)
PsyPe	Psychology of Personality
PTher	Physical Therapy
PubAd	Public Administration
PubAf	Public Affairs
PubHl	Public Health
PubRe	Public Relations
PvMed	Preventive Medicine
QBA	Quantitative Business Analysis
QMB	Quantitative Methods of Business
QMeth	Quantitative Methods
R&SL	Russian and Slavic Languages
Radio	Radio
RadTV	Radio/Television
Rd&St	Reading and Study Skills
RdTec	Radiology/Radiologic Technology
Re&Fn	Research and Foundations
Read	Reading
Rec	Recreation
RecEd	Recreation Education
RecLe	Recreation and Leisure
RecPA	Recreation and Park Administration
RecPk	Recreation and Parks
Rehab	Rehabilitation Studies
REIns	Real Estate and Insurance
Relig	Religion (Religious Studies)
Res	Resources
Rhet	Rhetoric
RHIM	Restaurant, Hotel, and Institutional Management
RlEst	Real Estate
RngSc	Range Science
RNR	Renewable Natural Resources
RomLg	Romance Languages
Rus	Russian
RuSoc	Rural Sociology
SAcct	High School–Level Accounting
Sales	Salesmanship
SAT	SAT Review
SBio	High School–Level Biology
Scand	Scandinavian Languages

SChem	High School–Level Chemistry
Sci	Science
SciEd	Science Education
SciHS	Science, High School Level
SEAS	Southeast Asian Studies
SecEd	Secondary Education
SecLP	Security and Loss Prevention
SecTr	Secretarial Training
SelfD	Self-Development
SEngl	High School–Level English
SFren	High School–Level French
SFS	School Food Services
SftEd	Safety Education
Sfty	Safety
SHist	High School–Level History
SHlth	High School–Level Health
SHmEc	High School–Level Home Economics
SHSci	Speech and Hearing Sciences
Shthd	Shorthand
Slav	Slavic Languages and Literature
SMath	High School–Level Mathematics
SMT	Social Management of Technology
SMusc	High School–Level Music
SocAn	Sociology/Anthropology
SocHS	Sociology, High School Level
Socio	Sociology
SocSt	Social Studies
SocWk	Social Work
SoEng	Sophomore English
SoilS	Soil Science
SoJus	Society and Justice
SOP	Secretarial Office Procedure
SoPsy	Social Psychology
SoSci	Social Science
SouSt	Southern Studies
SoWel	Social Welfare
Span	Spanish
Spch	Speech
SpDrA	Speech and Dramatic Arts
SPEA	School of Public and Environmental Affairs
SpeCm	Speech Communication
SplEd	Special Education
SrEng	Senior English
SRlgn	High School–Level Religion
Srvyg	Surveying
SSpan	High School–Level Spanish
SST	Security Safety Technology
Stat	Statistics
STC	School of Technical Careers
StSkl	Study Skills
STypg	High School–Level Typing
Suprv	Supervision
Swed	Swedish
T&TE	Teaching and Teacher Education
TAM	Theoretical and Applied Mechanics
TchEd	Teacher Education
Tech	Technology
ThArt	Theater Arts
Theat	Theater
Theo	Theology

Ther	Therapy
Tlcom	Telecommunications
TMTec	Tool and Manufacturing Technology
Trans	Transportation
Trig	Trigonometry
TrSaf	Traffic Safety
TV	Television
Typg	Typewriting
UColl	University College
UConj	University Conjoint Courses
UnStu	University Studies
UrbPl	Urban Planning
USGov	United States Government
USHis	United States History
VetSc	Veterinary Sciences
VisAr	Visual Arts
VocEd	Vocational Education
VoTec	Vocational Technology
VTIE	Vocational, Trade, and Industrial Education
WCiv	Western Civilization
WGS	World Geography Studies
WHS	World History Studies
WlfSc	Wildlife Science
WomSt	Women's Studies
Writ	Writing
WshMg	Watershed Management
WtrTr	Water Treatment
WWTrt	Wastewater Treatment
YthLd	Youth Leadership
Zoolg	Zoology

INSTITUTIONS AND CORRESPONDENCE COURSES OFFERED

① ADAMS STATE COLLEGE

Mr. Phillip Gore
Director of Extension, Colorado Consortium for Independent Study
  via Correspondence
Office of Extension and Field Service
Adams State College
Alamosa, Colorado 81102
Phone: 303-589-7671

Telecourses are offered. Enrollment on a noncredit basis accepted in credit courses. High school students may enroll in undergraduate courses for credit. Overseas enrollment not accepted. Institution offers special arrangements to take courses not listed in this Catalog. Maximum period for course completion is one year.

NCES No.	Course Title	Dept.	Course No.	Cred.	Lev.	Specl. Feat.
	High School courses					
160301	Arithmetic	Math	095-3	3S	H	
160302	Algebra	Math	099-3	3S	H	
	College courses					
070516	Math for elem teachers	Math	108-3	3S	L	
070516	Math for elem teachers	Math	109-3	3S	L	
081399	Toxic chemicals	EnvSc	325	3S	U	
081399	Environmental control	EnvSc	431	2S	U	
160406	Differential equations	Math	327	3S	U	
200406	Success psychology	Psych	179	3S	L	
200504	Human development	Psych	205	3S	L	
200603	Psychological testing	Psych	445	3S	U	
220426	Spain	Hist	346	3S	U	
220426	Women in European history	Hist	379	3S	U	
220427	Mexico	Hist	357	3S	U	
220699	Formation of self-concept	Socio	240	2S	L	

② ARIZONA STATE UNIVERSITY

Ms. Shari I. Westbrook
Administrative Assistant
Correspondence Study Office
Off-Campus Academic Services, Farmer 404
Arizona State University
Tempe, Arizona 85287-1811
Phone: 602-965-6563

Overseas enrollment accepted. Military personnel may enroll through the DANTES program. Minimum period for course completion is 1 week per credit hour. Maximum period for course completion is 1 year.

NCES No.	Course Title	Dept.	Course No.	Cred.	Lev.	Specl. Feat.
	College courses					
040601	Business communications	Bus	GN233	3S	L	
040604	Business report writing	Bus	GN431	3S	U	
040904	Principles of management	Mgmt	MG301	3S	U	
049900	Elmnts of bus enterprise	Bus	GN101	3S	L	
049900	Business law	Bus	BL305	3S	U	
049900	Business law	Bus	BL306	3S	U	
051102	Elmnts of intculturl comm	Commu	CO263	3S	L	
051199	Urban communication	Commu	CO494	3S	U	
051199	Intercultural communicats	Commu	CO363	3S	U	
051199	Crisis communication	Commu	CO414	3S	U	
051199	Death and dying	Commu	CO494	3S	U	
051199	Woman and communications	Commu	CO316	3S	U	
051199	Communication and aging	Commu	CO417	3S	U	
051199	Medical communication	Commu	CO494	3S	U	
051299	Nonverbal communication	Commu	CO275	3S	U	
051299	Sktch skls for spch clncn	SHSci	SH294	1S	L	
070302	Dev of lang as commu bhvr	Commu	CO472	3S	U	
070302	Elem school org and manag	ElEd	ED334	3S	U	
070302	Home-school relations	ElEd	ED498	3S	U	
070303	Prin & curr of sec schls	Educ	SE311	3S	U	
070520	Educational psychology	Educ	ED310	3S	U	
070520	St: principles of beh mod	EdPsy	ED494	3S	U	
070610	Reading in content areas	Educ	RD467	2S	U	
070610	Practicum rdg in content	Educ	RD480	1S	U	
070800	Orientation to ed ex chil	SplEd	SP311	3S	U	
070805	Intro to learnng disabilt	SplEd	SP361	3S	U	
070805	Mthds of rmdtng lrng dsab	SplEd	SP494	3S	U	
070806	Mental retardation	Educ	SP312	3S	U	

NCES No.	Course Title	Dept.	Course No.	Cred.	Lev.	Specl. Feat.
070811	Natr of fluency disorders	SHSci	431	2S	U	
100313	Human nutrition	HomEc	FO141	3S	L	
100602	Family relationships	HomEc	FA331	3S	U	
120299	Books for children	LibSc	LI494	3S	U	
121000	Elementary French	Frnch	FR101	4S	L	
121000	Elementary French	Frnch	FR102	4S	L	
121000	Intermediate French	Frnch	FR201	4S	L	
121000	Intermediate French	Frnch	FR202	4S	L	
121000	French literature	Frnch	FR321	3S	U	
121000	French literature	Frnch	FR322	3S	U	
121100	Elementary German	Germn	GE101	4S	L	
121100	Elementary German	Germn	GE102	4S	L	
121100	Intermediate German	Germn	GE201	4S	L	
121100	Intermediate German	Germn	GE202	4S	L	
122500	Elementary Spanish	Span	SP101	4S	L	
122500	Elementary Spanish	Span	SP102	4S	L	
122500	Intermediate Spanish	Span	SP201	4S	L	
122500	Intermediate Spanish	Span	SP202	4S	L	
122500	Spanish conversation	Span	SP313	3S	U	
160302	Intermediate algebra	Math	MA106	3S	L	
160302	College algebra	Math	MA117	3S	L	
160401	Brief calculus	Math	MA210	3S	L	
160602	Plane trigonometry	Math	MA118	3S	L	
200501	Abnormal psychology	PsyGS	PG466	3S	U	
209900	Intro to psychology	Psych	PG100	3S	L	
220201	Prin of macroeconomics	Econ	EC111	3S	L	
220201	Prin of microeconomics	Econ	EC112	3S	L	
220423	Japan	Hist	HI477	3S	U	
220423	Japan	Hist	HI478	3S	U	
220423	Asian civilizations	Hist	HI305	3S	U	
220423	Asian civilizations	Hist	HI306	3S	U	
220426	Hitler—man and legend	Hist	HI434	3S	U	
220432	United States history	Hist	HI103	3S	L	
220432	United States history	Hist	HI104	3S	L	
220433	Western civilization	Hist	HI102	3S	L	
220453	Modern American cltrl his	Hist	HI304	3S	U	
220453	Contemporary America	Hist	HI411	3S	U	
220501	American national govt	PolSc	PO310	3S	U	
220501	AZ constitution and govt	PolSc	PO311	2S	U	
220505	The US and Japan	Hist	HI471	3S	U	
220602	The justice system	JusSt	JU100	3S	U	
220602	The police function	JusSt	JU306	3S	U	
220602	Rsrch in justice studies	JusSt	JU301	3S	U	
220602	Basic stats analysis-just	JusSt	JU302	3S	U	
220602	The adjudication function	JusSt	JU308	3S	U	
220602	Comm relatns in just sys	JusSt	JU320	3S	U	
220605	Courtship and marriage	Socio	SO305	3S	U	
220615	Women's roles	Socio	SO464	3S	U	
220615	Women and society	WomSt	WS100	3S	L	
220615	Women and contemp society	WomSt	WS300	3S	U	
220699	Socio of deviant behavior	Socio	SO340	3S	U	
220699	Intro to sociology	Socio	SO101	3S	L	

③ BALL STATE UNIVERSITY

Dr. M. Edward Ratliff
Director, Independent Study
Carmichael Hall, School of Continuing Education
Ball State University
Muncie, Indiana 47306
Phone: 317-285-1581
      800-872-0369

External degree available through the program. Credit by examination is available. Telecourses are offered. Enrollment on a noncredit basis accepted in credit courses. High school students may enroll in undergraduate courses for credit. Overseas enrollment not accepted. Minimum period for course completion is one month. Maximum period for course completion is one year. Most courses require three months to complete.

NCES No.	Course Title	Dept.	Course No.	Cred.	Lev.	Specl. Feat.
	College courses					
030400	Intro to theater	ThArt	100	3S	L	
040100	Elem of acctg 1	Acctg	201	3S	L	
040107	Elem of acctg 2	Acctg	202	3S	L	
040203	Records administration	BEOA	353	3S	L	
040700	Prin of insurance	Insur	370	3S	U	
040903	Intro operations mgt	MgtSc	251	3S	L	

NCES No.	Course Title	Dept.	Course No.	Cred.	Lev.	Specl. Feat.
040904	Management principles	MgtSc	200	3S	L	
041103	Personnel & supervision	MgtSc	261	3S	L	
050102	Intro to advertising	Journ	250	3S	L	
050600	Mass media in society	Journ	101	3S	L	
100206	Personal finance	Finan	110	3S	L	
120201	World literature	Engl	205	3S	L	
120300	English composition 1	Engl	103	3S	L	
120300	English composition 2	Engl	104	3S	L	
150100	Mysteries of the sky	Astro	100	3S	L	
150201	Climate	Geog	331	3S	U	
150202	Weather 1	Geog	230	3S	L	
150501	Geomorphology	Geol	240	3S	L	
150599	Historical geology	Geol	102	3S	L	
150702	Intro to energy space sci	Phycs	100	3S	L	
160802	Elem statistics	Psych	241	3S	L	
180301	Ethics	Philo	202	3S	L	
180400	Intro to philosophy	Philo	100	3S	L	
190303	Intro to sport in Am life	IntSt	205	3S	L	
200103	General psychology	Psych	100	3S	L	
210300	Intro Am crim justice	CJC	101	3S	L	
210301	Institutional corrections	CJC	360	3S	L	
210301	Community corrections	CJC	361	3S	U	
210304	Data and theory crim deli	CJC	210	3S	L	
210304	Proc adult and juven offe	CJC	211	3S	L	
210304	Policing in Amer society	CJC	300	3S	L	
220200	Elements macroeconomics	Econ	202	3S	L	
220200	Elements microeconomics	Econ	201	3S	L	
220201	Survey of econ ideas	Econ	116	3S	L	
220300	Global geog for teachers	Geog	111	3S	L	
220300	Global geography	Geog	150	3S	L	
220305	Phy geog earth sci teache	Geog	111	3S	L	
220306	Geography of Indiana	Geog	353	3S	L	
220306	Geog of US and Canada	Geog	350	3S	U	
220399	Earth sea & sky geol view	Geog	101	3S	L	
220400	Intro hist bus in US	Hist	110	3S	L	
220409	Hist Am popular cultures	Hist	222	3S	L	
220421	American hist 1492-1876	Hist	201	3S	L	
220422	The world in recent times	Hist	153	3S	L	
220426	World civilization 2	Hist	152	3S	L	
220427	The Spanish borderlands	Hist	327	3S	U	
220428	History of Indiana	Hist	415	3S	U	
220432	American history	Hist	202	3S	L	
220432	Recent US hist 1945-pres	Hist	413	3S	U	
220432	Indians in US history	Hist	421	3S	U	
220452	World civilization I	Hist	151	3S	L	
220499	Western civilization I	Hist	150	3S	L	
220501	American national govt	PolSc	130	3S	L	
220501	Urban government in US	PolSc	238	3S	L	
220509	Public opinion pol proces	PolSc	370	3S	U	
220511	State and local politics	PolSc	237	3S	L	
220511	Metropolitan problems	PolSc	438	3S	U	
220600	Prin of sociology	Socio	100	3S	L	
220605	The family	Socio	424	3S	U	
220610	Soc of deviant behavior	Socio	241	3S	L	
220613	Social problems	Socio	242	3S	L	
220699	Social gerontology	Socio	431	3S	U	

④ BRIGHAM YOUNG UNIVERSITY

Mr. Ralph Rowley
Director
Independent Study
206 Harmon Continuing Education Building
Brigham Young University
Provo, Utah 84602
Phone: 801-378-2868

External degree available through the program. Telecourses are offered. Enrollment on a noncredit basis accepted in credit courses. High school students may enroll in undergraduate courses for credit. Overseas enrollment accepted. Military personnel may enroll through the DANTES program. Institution offers special arrangements to take courses not listed in this Catalog. Minimum period for course completion is one and one half semester hours/week. Maximum period for course completion is one year. Students must have the instructor's approval to submit more than three lessons per week.

NCES No.	Course Title	Dept.	Course No.	Cred.	Lev.	Specl. Feat.
	High School courses					
020103	Inter design & decoration	HomLv	6	HF	H	
030302	Beginning guitar pt 1	Music	3	HF	H	AC
030302	Beginning guitar pt 2	Music	4	HF	H	AC
030403	Intro to the theater	EngLL	47	HF	H	
030599	Calligraphy	Art	4	HF	H	
040104	Bookkeeping 1 pt 1	Bus	2	HF	H	
040104	Bookkeeping 1 pt 2	Bus	3	HF	H	
040114	Understanding 1989 taxes	Bus	6	HF	H	
040199	Business law pt 1	Bus	11	HF	H	
040199	Business law pt 2	Bus	12	HF	H	
040205	Shorthand: Gregg Pt 1	Bus	8	HF	H	
040205	Shorthand: Gregg Pt 2	Bus	9	HF	H	
040207	Beginning typing Pt 1	Bus	4	HF	H	
040207	Beginning typing Pt 2	Bus	5	HF	H	
040300	Finance and credit	Bus	35	HF	H	
040502	Starting your own busnss	Bus	29	HF	H	
040502	Ldg and supv in busnss	Bus	32	HF	H	
040999	Work experience	Bus	1	HF	H	
041001	Merchandising	Bus	17	HF	H	
041001	Gen merchandise retailing	Bus	38	HF	H	
041001	General marketing pt 1	Bus	15	HF	H	
041001	General marketing pt 2	Bus	16	HF	H	
041003	Basic salesmanship	Bus	19	HF	H	
041100	Developing life skills	SoSci	23	HF	H	
041300	Real estate	Bus	40	HF	H	
050100	Advertising services	Bus	33	HF	H	
050101	Advertising	Bus	21	HF	H	
050199	Communications in mrktng	Bus	25	HF	H	
050499	Man & mass media pt 1	EngLL	36	HF	H	
050900	Psych & hum rel in mrktng	Bus	27	HF	H	
051107	Intro to pub speaking 1	EngLL	45	HF	H	
060199	Basic programming pt 1	CmpSc	2	HF	H	
060199	Basic programming pt 2	CmpSc	3	HF	H	
061101	Computer literacy	CmpSc	1	HF	H	
061101	Computer literacy	CmpSc	1	HF	H	
079900	Study skills	SoSci	25	HF	H	AC
090101	General health	HlSci	1	HF	H	
090272	Home nursing pt 1	HomLv	14	HF	H	
090403	The drug scene	Sci	5	HF	H	
090999	General health	Hlth	1	HF	H	
100100	Fashion merchandising	Bus	34	HF	H	
100103	Clothing: fashion fund	HomLv	4	QT	H	
100104	Basic clothg constr pt 1	HomLv	1	HF	H	
100300	Food marketing	Bus	36	HF	H	
100309	Food services	Bus	37	HF	H	
100311	Guide to modern meals	HomLv	5	HF	H	
100401	Practical decision making	SoSci	22	HF	H	
100601	Child development pt 1	HomLv	7	HF	H	
100601	Child development pt 2	HomLv	8	HF	H	
100699	Preprg fr resp parenthood	HomLv	16	HF	H	
110104	House wiring	IndEd	4	HF	H	
110205	Leathercraft	IndEd	1	HF	H	LK
110406	Upholstery repair	IndEd	2	HF	H	
110412	Small engine repair	IndEd	6	HF	H	
110413	Auto fundamentals pt 1	IndEd	7	HF	H	
110413	Auto fundamentals pt 2	IndEd	8	HF	H	
110413	Auto body repair	IndEd	5	HF	H	
110503	Keys to drawing accuracy	Art	3	HF	H	
110504	General photography	Art	5	HF	H	
110599	General art pt 1	Art	1	HF	H	
110599	General art pt 2	Art	2	HF	H	
120305	9th grade English pt 1	EngLL	1	HF	H	
120305	9th grade English pt 2	EngLL	2	HF	H	
120305	Business English	EngLL	9	HF	H	
120305	Basic spelling skills	EngLL	42	HF	H	
120307	The year 2100	EngLL	18	QT	H	
120307	Self-esteem	EngLL	12	QT	H	
120307	Bible as literature	EngLL	22	HF	H	
120307	Steps to reading literatu	EngLL	10	HF	H	
120308	12th-grade English pt 2	EngLL	8	HF	H	
120308	Remedial developt reading	EngLL	26	HF	H	
120308	Recreational reading	EngLL	27	HF	H	
120308	Reading comprehension	EngLL	23	HF	H	
120308	Analytical reading	EngHS	21	HF	H	
120310	10th-grade English pt 1	EngLL	3	HF	H	
120310	10th-grade English pt 2	EngLL	4	HF	H	
120310	11th-grade English pt 1	EngLL	5	HF	H	
120310	12th-grade English pt 1	EngLL	7	HF	H	
120310	Comp expo writing	EngLL	31	HF	H	

NCES No.	Course Title	Dept.	Course No.	Cred.	Lev.	Specl. Feat.
120310	Comp narr description	EngLL	32	HF	H	
120310	Creative writing	EngLL	33	HF	H	
120310	College writing pt 1	EngLL	34	HF	H	
120310	Editing & proofreading	EngLL	43	HF	H	
120310	11th-grade English pt 2	EngLL	6	HF	H	
120399	Review of fundamentals	EngLL	20	HF	H	
120700	Beginng Chinese Mandarin	ForLg	7	HF	H	AC
122500	Spanish pt 1	ForLg	3	HF	H	AC
122500	Spanish pt 2	ForLg	4	HF	H	AC
150300	Human physiology/anatomy	Sci	4	HF	H	
150301	Biology pt 1	Sci	1	HF	H	
150301	Biology pt 2	Sci	2	HF	H	
150304	Ecology pt 1	Sci	3	HF	H	
150324	Taxidermy	Sci	6	HF	H	
150401	Chemistry pt 1	Sci	16	HF	H	
150401	Chemistry pt 2	Sci	17	HF	H	
150799	Nonmath physics pt 1	Sci	9	HF	H	
150799	Nonmath physics pt 2	Sci	10	HF	H	
150900	Earth & space sci pt 1	Sci	13	HF	H	
150900	Earth & space sci pt 2	Sci	14	HF	H	
160301	Remedial arithmetic pt 1	Math	1	HF	H	
160301	Remedial arithmetic pt 2	Math	2	HF	H	
160301	Rem arith using a cal pt1	Math	18	HF	H	
160302	1st course algebra pt 1	Math	5	HF	H	
160302	1st course algebra pt 2	Math	6	HF	H	
160302	2nd course algebra pt 1	Math	7	HF	H	
160302	2nd course algebra pt 2	Math	8	HF	H	
160399	Computerized rem math 1	Math	13	HF	H	CI
160399	Computerized rem math 2	Math	14	HF	H	CI
160401	Calculus with anal geomet	Math	15	HF	H	
160401	Differential calculus	Math	16	HF	H	VC
160401	Integral calc w/analyt ge	MatHS	17	HF	H	VC
160601	Plane geometry pt 1	Math	9	HF	H	
160601	Plane geometry pt 2	Math	10	HF	H	
160602	Trigonometry pt 1	Math	11	HF	H	
160602	Trigonometry pt 2	Math	12	HF	H	
161101	Mathematics in marketing	Bus	26	HF	H	
161201	Bus & consumer math pt 1	Math	3	HF	H	
161201	Bus & consumer math pt 2	Math	4	HF	H	
190102	Fitness for living	PhyEd	3	HF	H	
190102	Jogging	PhyEd	7	HF	H	
190102	Aerobic dance	PhyEd	6	HF	H	AC
190103	Tennis	PhyEd	4	HF	H	
190103	Bowling	PhyEd	5	HF	H	
190603	Driver education	DrvEd	1	HF	H	
200100	Elements of psychology	SoSci	31	QT	H	
200499	Undstdg & improvg memory	SoSci	26	HF	H	AC
200502	Educ & career planning	SoSci	20	HF	H	
200799	Dating—romance & reason	SoSci	16	HF	H	
209900	Project self-discovery	SoSci	39	HF	H	
220201	Economics Amer free enter	SoSci	19	HF	H	
220208	Consumer economics	SoSci	18	HF	H	
220306	World geography	SoSci	29	HF	H	
220426	World hist: Europe & Russ	SoSci	10	HF	H	
220432	US history—foreign polic	SoSci	5	QT	H	
220432	US history—government	SoSci	6	QT	H	
220432	American government pt 1	SoSci	12	HF	H	
220432	American government pt 2	SoSci	13	HF	H	
220432	US hist: liberty/soc chng	SoSci	1	HF	H	
220432	US hist: Amer chrt/ec	SoSci	2	HF	H	
220432	US hist: consti/demo gov	SoSci	3	HF	H	
220433	World hist-modern era	SoSci	7	QT	H	
220433	World hist: Europe/Asia	SoSci	8	HF	H	
220433	World hist: Western Hemis	SoSci	9	HF	H	
220499	How to climb yr fam tree	SoSci	21	HF	H	
220499	Current events	SoSci	38	HF	H	
220601	Sociology 1	SoSci	27	HF	H	
220615	Sociology 2	SoSci	28	HF	H	
220699	Pers freedom: life contro	SoSci	14	HF	H	

College courses

NCES No.	Course Title	Dept.	Course No.	Cred.	Lev.	Specl. Feat.
010602	Heredity	Bio	276	3S	L	
020103	Intro to interior design	InDes	102	3S	L	
030403	Intro to the theatre	ThArt	115	3S	L	
030403	Playwriting	ThArt	378R	3S	U	
030499	Playwriting	Theat	378R	3S	U	
030502	19th-century European art	ArHis	309	3S	U	
030502	Survey of western art 1	ArHis	211	3S	L	
030502	Survey of western art 2	ArHis	212	3S	L	
030603	Modern art	Art	310	3S	U	
039900	Intro to the humanities	Hum	101	3S	L	AC
040108	Elementary accounting	Acctg	201	3S	L	

NCES No.	Course Title	Dept.	Course No.	Cred.	Lev.	Specl. Feat.
040108	Elementary accounting	Acctg	202	3S	L	
040311	Financial management	Bus	301	3S	U	
040601	Business communications	IVE	320	3S	U	
040602	Intro to info management	IVE	210	3S	L	
041004	Marketing management	Bus	341	3S	U	
050605	Magazine writing	Commu	427	3S	U	
050608	News writing	Commu	211	3S	L	
051102	Analysis of communication	Commu	201	2S	L	
051107	Public speaking	Commu	150	3S	L	
051107	Debate & argumnt strategy	Commu	353	4S	U	
059900	Intro to mass communicati	Commu	101	3S	L	
060103	Elem computer application	CmpSc	103	2S	L	
060799	Intro comp programming	CmpSc	142	2S	L	
070199	Youth agencies & organiza	RecEd	344	2S	U	
070199	Yth mtgs, activts & con	RecEd	371	2S	U	
070299	The professional teacher	ElEd	452	1S	U	
070299	The professional teacher	ElEd	452	1S	U	
070301	Early chil learn experien	ElEd	515R9	2S	U	
070401	5 stps to effctv tutoring	ElEd	51520	2S	U	
070402	Creativity in the classrm	SecEd	37611	1S	U	
070402	Improv student behavior	SecEd	37634	1S	U	
070402	Form useful instruc objec	SecEd	37645	1S	U	
070402	Questions that turn stdts	SecEd	37646	1S	U	AC
070402	Test and measurement theo	EdPsy	501	3S	U	
070402	Teaching reading	SecEd	37652	1S	U	
070404	How to teach concepts	EdPsy	515R3	2S	U	
070512	Children's literature	ElEd	340	3S	U	
070512	Apply struc tutor mod rdg	ElEd	51522	2S	U	
070512	Apply struc tutor adv rdg	ElEd	51524	2S	U	
070512	Shakespeare	Engl	232	3S	L	
070512	Am lit since 1914	Engl	363	3S	L	
070516	Apply struc mod bsc math	InSci	51525	2S	U	
070516	Metric measurements	ElEd	515R8	1S	U	
070599	Equity in education	EdPsy	51516	2S	U	
070602	Life plan & decision makg	CarEd	115	2S	L	
070602	Managing life/car transit	CarEd	317	2S	U	
070610	Companion rdg program	InSci	51518	1S	U	
070611	Struc tut tchg Eng 2d lan	InSci	51531	2S	U	
070613	Org adm driver safety ed	HlSci	444	2S	U	
070613	Drvr & safety ed workshop	Hlth	502R	CV	U	
070701	Resolving studt hostility	EdPsy	515R5	2S	U	AC
070701	Obtaining stu coop class	EdPsy	51543	1S	U	
070701	Intro to coun and guidanc	EdPsy	600	3S	U	
070803	Educ of exceptional child	EdPsy	204	2S	L	
070803	Behav mod tech tchr exce	EdPsy	51550	2S	U	
070806	Ed of intel handicapped	EdPsy	519	3S	U	
070899	Implem public law ed hand	EdPsy	51551	1S	U	
070902	Community relationships	RecEd	332	2S	U	
071101	Simulation and games	SecEd	37656	1S	U	
071103	Evaluating stud learning	SecEd	37635	1S	U	
071199	Impro stud attit learn	SecEd	37620	1S	U	
080704	Eng mech/mech of material	CivlE	203	3S	L	
080707	Structural analysis	CivlE	321	3S	U	
081000	Intro to engineering grph	Dsgn	111	3S	L	
081104	Eng mechanics/dynamics	CivlE	204	3S	L	
081104	Eng mech - vector statics	CivlE	103	3S	L	
090272	Family health management	Nrsng	288	2S	L	
090403	Drug use and addict behav	HlSci	460	2S	U	
090504	First aid & safety instr	HlSci	121	2S	L	
090504	School hlth for ele tchrs	HlSci	361	2S	U	
090504	School hlth for sec tchrs	HlSci	362	2S	U	
090702	Consumer health	HlSci	370	2S	U	
090702	Community health	HlSci	451	2S	U	AC
090799	Safety education	HlSci	325	2S	U	
090902	Health and lifestyle mgmt	HlSci	129	1S	L	
090902	Health and lifestyle mgmt	HlSci	130	2S	L	
090999	Health crisis interventio	Hlth	465	2S	U	
099900	Hlth & the aging process	Hlth	563	2S	U	
100101	General textiles	ClTex	260	3S	L	LK
100104	Flat pattern designing	ClTex	145	2S	L	
100206	Personal finance	Bus	200	2S	L	
100302	Intro to human nutrition	FdScN	115	2S	L	
100399	Special problems food sci	FdScN	494R	CV	U	
100601	Child development	FamSc	210	3S	L	
100601	Parenting	FamSc	303	3S	U	
100601	Developing parenting skil	FamSc	395R2	3S	U	
110104	Basic electricity	InArt	209	2S	L	
110599	Intro to hand lettering	Art	109	2S	L	
120201	Intro to Spanish lit	Span	339	3S	U	
120201	Survey of Spanish lit	Span	441	3S	U	
120204	Shakespeare	Engl	382	3S	U	
120305	Vocabulary building	Engl	225	2S	L	

NCES No.	Course Title	Dept.	Course No.	Cred.	Lev.	Specl. Feat.
120305	Modern American usage	Engl	322	3S	U	
120305	Study in English grammars	Engl	328	3S	U	
120305	Trad grammar and usage	Engl	325	3S	U	
120307	Fundmntls of literature	Engl	251	3S	L	AC
120307	Vital themes in Amer lit	Engl	235	3S	L	
120307	The English novel	Engl	333	3S	U	
120307	The American novel	Engl	336	3S	U	
120307	Modern poetry	Engl	366	2S	U	
120307	Engl lit from 1780-1832	Engl	374	3S	U	
120307	Lit for adolescents	Engl	420	2S	U	
120307	Bible as literature	Engl	350	3S	U	
120307	The short story	Engl	359	3S	U	
120307	Children's nonfiction lit	ElEd	515R6	1S	U	
120307	Fiction drama poetry	Engl	230	3S	L	
120307	Eminent authors	Engl	395R	3S	U	
120308	Wrtg for chldrn & adolesc	Engl	217	2S	L	
120308	College reading	Engl	114	2S	L	
120310	Creative writing	Engl	218	3S	L	
120310	Writing personal history	Engl	220	3S	L	
120310	Critical & interprtv wrtg	Engl	312	3S	U	
120310	Exposition & report wrtg	Engl	315	3S	U	
120310	Technical writing	Engl	316	3S	U	
120310	Writing of fiction	Engl	318R	3S	U	
120310	Writing of poetry	Engl	319R	3S	U	
120310	College writing	Engl	113	2S	L	
120310	Critical wrtng & research	Engl	252	3S	L	
120399	Study habits	GenSt	111	1S	L	
120399	Expanded literacy	Engl	105	3S	L	
120399	Freshman English	Engl	115	4S	L	
120399	Analytical reading	GenSt	214R	1S	L	
121000	Interm French read & conv	Frnch	201	4S	L	AC
121100	German lit periods & mvmt	Germn	440R	3S	U	
121100	Third-yr Ger grammar-comp	Germn	320	3S	U	
121300	First-yr biblical Hebrew	Hebr	131	4S	L	AC
121300	First-year biblical Heb	Hebr	132	4S	L	
121300	Intermediate biblical Heb	Hebr	133	2S	L	
121600	Latin for genealogists	Latin	121	3S	L	
122500	Third-yr Span gram & comp	Span	321	3S	U	
122500	Third-yr Span gram & comp	Span	322	3S	U	
122500	Introductory Spanish	Span	100A	2S	L	AC
122500	Survey of Hispanic Am lit	Span	451	3S	U	
122500	Second-yr Spanish	Span	201	4S	L	AC
129900	American Sign Lang interp	Ling	431	4S	U	
140199	How to use the library	LibSc	111	1S	L	
150100	Descriptive astronomy	Phycs	127	3S	L	
150302	Principles of biology	Bio	100	3S	L	
150304	Conservation of nat rescs	Botny	400	2S	U	
150311	General microbiology	Micro	221	3S	U	
150399	Plant kingdom	Botny	105	3S	L	
150399	Principles of biology	Bio	100	3S	L	
150401	Elementary coll chemistry	Chem	100	3S	L	
150504	Life of the past	Geol	103	3S	L	
150599	Intro to geology	Geol	101	3S	L	
150800	Physical science	PhySc	100	3S	L	
160101	Math & the humanities	Math	307	3S	U	
160102	History of mathematics	Math	300	3S	U	
160301	Concepts of mathematics	Math	306	3S	U	
160301	Basic concepts of math	Math	305	4S	U	
160302	Intermediate algebra	Math	100	2S	L	
160302	Finite math for teachers	Math	301	3S	U	
160302	College algebra	Math	110	3S	L	
160302	College algebra	Math	110	3S	L	
160306	Elements of linear algebr	Math	114	2S	L	
160401	Calculus I	Math	112	4S	L	
160401	Calculus II	Math	113	4S	L	
160401	Multivariate calculus	Math	214	3S	L	
160403	Introdtry multivrt calc	Math	215	2S	L	
160406	Intro ordinary diffent eq	Math	321	2S	U	
160412	Intro to calculus	Math	119	4S	L	
160600	Topics in geometry	Math	451R	3S	U	
160602	Trigonometry	Math	111	2S	L	
160699	Survey of geometry	Math	302	3S	U	
160706	Elementary probability	Stat	341	3S	U	
160801	Prin of statistics 1	Stat	221	3S	L	
160801	Prin of statistics 2	Stat	222	4S	L	
160801	Prin of statistics 3	Stat	223	1S	L	
160802	Applied social statistics	Socio	205	3S	L	
160803	Elements of math stats	Stat	321	3S	U	
161108	Psychological statistics	Psych	301	4S	U	
180199	Arts & lttrs wstrn civ 2	Hum	202	3S	L	
180401	Intro to philosophy	Philo	110	3S	L	
180504	Intro to logic	Philo	205	3S	L	
181202	The New Testament	Relig	211	2S	L	
181202	The New Testament	Relig	212	2S	L	
181202	The Old Testament	Relig	301	2S	U	
181202	The Old Testament	Relig	302	2S	U	
181202	The doctrine & covenants	Relig	324	2S	U	
181202	The doctrine & covenants	Relig	325	2S	U	
181299	The pearl of great price	Relig	327	2S	U	
181299	Writings of Isaiah	Relig	304	2S	U	
181299	Intro to Book of Mormon	Relig	122	2S	L	
181299	Intro to Book of Mormon	Relig	121	2S	L	
181304	LDS history since 1900	Relig	393R5	1S	U	
181603	Doctrines of the Gospel	Relig	231	2S	L	
181603	Intro to genealogy	Relig	261	2S	U	
181603	Teach of the living proph	Relig	333	2S	U	
181603	LDS chrch hist after 1844	Relig	342	2S	U	
181603	LDS church hist to 1844	Relig	341	2S	U	
181603	The writings of John	Relig	392R1	1S	U	
181603	Spec topics in chur hist	Relig	540R	3S	U	
181603	The international church	Relig	344	2S	U	
181603	Gspl prin in youth progrm	Relig	393R1	1S	U	VC
181603	Presidents of the church	Relig	393R2	1S	U	VC
181603	Fam hist & the LDS fmly	Relig	393R3	1S	U	
181607	Principles of chrch admin	Relig	393R3	1S	U	
181608	Sharing the Gospel	Relig	130	2S	L	VC
189900	Senior seminar in relig	Relig	491	1S	U	
189900	Senior seminar in relig	Relig	492	1S	U	
190102	Fitness for living	PhyEd	129	HF	L	
190102	Jogging	PhyEd	139	HF	L	
190102	Intermediate swimming	PhyEd	172	HF	L	
190108	Mgt of athletic intra pro	PhyEd	351	3S	U	
190199	Sociology & psych of spor	PhyEd	450	2S	U	
190401	Social dance: beginning	PhyEd	180	HF	L	VC
190499	Aerobic dance	PhyEd	130	HF	L	
190512	Sex roles in fam & societ	Psych	306	3S	U	
190705	Family recreation	RecEd	314	2S	U	
200104	General psychology	Psych	111	3S	L	
200199	Understnd & improv memry	Psych	495R1	1S	U	AC
200199	Psychology statistics	Psych	301	4S	U	
200300	Environmental psychology	Psych	359	3S	U	
200404	How to motivate students	EdPsy	515R4	1S	U	
200406	Early childhood lrng expr	FamSc	395R1	2S	U	VC
200504	Child psychology	Psych	320	3S	U	
200504	Adolescent psychology	Psych	321	3S	U	
200504	Adult psychology	Psych	322	3S	U	
200505	Personal & social adjust	Psych	240	3S	L	
200505	Developing hlthy slf imag	Psych	495R2	2S	U	AC
200507	Exceptional children	Psych	346	3S	U	
200508	Single adult in fam & soc	FamSc	305	3S	U	
200509	Personality	Psych	341	3S	U	
200599	Emotional cont/self-consl	EdPsy	515R2	1S	U	
200599	Leadership development	Psych	358	3S	U	
200701	Develop hlthy self-image	Psych	495R2	2S	U	
200702	Interprsnl growth group	Psych	357	3S	U	
200702	Interprsnl growth group	Socio	357	3S	U	
200703	Organizational psychology	Psych	330	3S	U	
200799	Intro to social psychol	Psych	350	3S	U	
200799	Intro sociology	Socio	111	3S	L	
200804	The community educ philos	RecEd	585	2S	U	
210101	Intro public admin	PolSc	330	3S	U	
220109	The Africans: introductio	Anthr	390R	3S	U	
220206	Econmy, society & pub pol	Econ	110	3S	L	
220216	Economics of market syst	MgtEc	200	3S	L	
220299	Macroecon for bus decsn	MgtEc	301	3S	U	
220303	Geog and world affairs	Geog	120	3S	L	
220306	North America	Geog	450	3S	U	
220307	Trvl plng rates & tariffs	Geog	350	3S	U	
220399	Intro to geography	Geog	101	3S	L	
220399	Travel & tourism patterns	Geog	250	3S	L	
220399	Tour operation	Geog	352	3S	U	
220406	American cultural history	Hist	390R1	3S	U	
220424	England to 1689	Hist	335	3S	U	
220424	England and Wales 1538	Hist	391R4	3S	U	
220424	Brtsh resch Scotlnd/Ireld	Hist	391R6	3S	U	
220426	19th-century Europe	Hist	322	3S	U	
220426	The European family	Hist	326	3S	U	
220428	Utah	Hist	366	3S	U	
220431	USSR	Hist	331	3S	U	
220432	The United States to 1877	Hist	120	3S	L	
220432	The United States fr 1877	Hist	121	3S	L	
220432	California	Hist	365	2S	U	
220432	American heritage	SoSci	100	3S	L	
220432	Northeast US and Canada	Hist	391R1	3S	U	

NCES No.	Course Title	Dept.	Course No.	Cred.	Lev.	Specl. Feat.
220432	Southern states	Hist	391R2	3S	U	
220432	Middle states	Hist	391R3	3S	U	
220432	Practicum	Hist	480R1	2S	U	
220432	Seminar	Hist	480R2	2S	U	
220432	Writing family history	Hist	397R1	3S	U	
220432	Oral hist interviewing	Hist	422	3S	U	AC
220433	Wrld civilization to 1500	Hist	201	3S	L	
220433	World civ since 1500	Hist	202	3S	L	
220499	Directed readings	Hist	498R	CV	U	
220499	Cultural hist of the US	Hist	390R1	3S	U	
220499	Cultural hist Scotld/Irel	Hist	390R2	3S	U	
220499	Paleography/English	Hist	400R1	2S	U	
220501	Amer govt and politics	PolSc	110	3S	L	
220509	Moral foundations of poli	PolSc	302	3S	U	
220511	State-local govt politics	PolSc	311	3S	U	
220605	Developing parenting skls	FamSc	395R2	3S	U	VC
220607	Intro to social psycholog	Socio	350	3S	U	
220613	Soc aspects of mental hlt	Socio	389	3S	U	
220613	Modern social problems	Socio	112	3S	U	
220699	Mthds of rsch in sociolog	Socio	300	3S	U	
220699	Stress & coping behavior	Socio	390R3	1S	U	
220699	Sociology of aging	Socio	365	2S	U	
229900	Social services for aging	SocWk	367	2S	U	

Graduate courses

NCES No.	Course Title	Dept.	Course No.	Cred.	Lev.	Specl. Feat.
070404	Improving your teaching	EdPsy	515R7	1S	G	AC
070404	Using structured tutoring	SecEd	51532	2S	G	
070404	Tchnq to improve std disc	SecEd	51534	1S	G	AC
070404	Evaltng student learning	SecEd	51535	1S	G	
070404	Simulation and games	SecEd	51536	1S	G	
070404	Creativity in classroom	SecEd	51537	1S	G	
070404	Improving student attitud	SecEd	51538	1S	G	
070404	Formltng useful inst obj	SecEd	51545	1S	G	
070404	Qstns that turn stdnts on	SecEd	51546	1S	G	AC
070404	Intro to couns & guidance	EdPsy	600	3S	G	
070610	Tchng rdng in contnt area	SecEd	51552	CV	G	
070610	Reading-teach decodng skl	ElEd	51511	1S	G	
070610	Reading-tchng comp skills	ElEd	51512	2S	G	
120308	Comp reading program	ElEd	51517	2S	G	
181605	Christian rites & liturgy	Relig	540R1	3S	G	
200599	Aging and leisure	RecEd	570	2S	G	

Noncredit courses

NCES No.	Course Title	Dept.	Course No.	Cred.	Lev.	Specl. Feat.
030301	Organ certification	FnArt	70	NC		
030302	Fun guitar for all part 1	FnArt	76	NC		AC
030302	Fun guitar for all part 2	FnArt	77	NC		AC
030599	Calligraphy	FnArt	73	NC		
040902	Way to become success mgr	Bus	70	NC		
041004	Salesmanship for managers	Bus	73	NC		
041004	Improving manager skills	Bus	74	NC		
041102	Personnel management	Bus	75	NC		
049900	Interviewing: improving	Bus	71	NC		
049900	Legal decision, law & emp	Bus	72	NC		
049900	Employment strategy	Bus	80	NC		
070610	Rdng for speed & comp	PerDv	78	NC		
070701	Changing undesired emotio	PerDv	72	NC		
100206	Understanding taxes	Bus	81	NC		
100401	Practical decision making	PerDv	70	NC		
100401	Help teen make career dec	Famil	76	NC		
100601	Early child lrng exp home	Famil	71	NC		AC
100601	Nurt childs nat curiosity	Famil	72	NC		VC
100601	Prep child to succ in sch	Famil	70	NC		
100604	Help yourself: self-impro	PerDv	74	NC		
100604	Handle conflict at home	PerDv	75	NC		AC
100604	Slim chance in a fat wrld	Hlth	70	NC		AC
110599	Keys to drawing accuracy	Graph	72	NC		
120308	Tutor child: rdg skills 1	Famil	73	NC		
120308	Tutor child: rdg skills 2	Famil	74	NC		
120310	Remedial spelling	GenSt	15R1	NC	D	
120310	Remedial grammar	GenSt	15R2	NC	D	
120310	Children's creative writ	Famil	75	NC		
120399	English at home part 1	Lang	85-1	NC		AC
120399	English at home part 2	Lang	85-2	NC		AC
120399	English at home part 3	Lang	85-3	NC		AC
120399	Building your vocabulary	PerDv	77	NC		
120700	Comp intro Mandar Chinese	CAC	75	NC		
121500	Comp intro Japanese	CAC	76	NC		
122500	Intro Spanish	Lang	80	NC		AC
160199	Review of basic math	Math	99	NC	L	
160301	Computerized rem math pt1	CAC	13	NC		CI
160301	Computerized rem math pt2	CAC	14	NC		CI
160302	Beginning algebra	Math	98	NC	L	

NCES No.	Course Title	Dept.	Course No.	Cred.	Lev.	Specl. Feat.
190102	Hooked on aerobics	Hlth	71	NC		AC
200599	Spirit roots human relats	PerDv	76	NC		AC
220424	British rsch 1: survey	Genea	73-1	NC		
220424	British rsch 1: Brit pt 1	Genea	73-2	NC		
220424	Brit rsch 2: Scot rsch 1	Genea	74-1	NC		
220424	Brit rsch 2: Irish rsch 1	Genea	74-3	NC		
220427	Mexican research English	Genea	81-1	NC		
220427	Mexican research Spanish	Genea	81-2	NC		
220432	N Am rsch 2: NE states Ca	Genea	72-1	NC		
220432	N Am rsch 2: midwest sts	Genea	72-3	NC		
220432	8 steps to find your root	Genea	70	NC		

⑤ **CENTRAL MICHIGAN UNIVERSITY**

Ms. Ann Marie Bridges
Director, Office of Independent Study
Continuing Education and Community Services
Rowe Hall 125
Central Michigan University
Mt. Pleasant, Michigan 48859
Phone: 517-774-7140

Enrollment on a noncredit basis accepted in credit courses. Overseas enrollment accepted. Military personnel may enroll through the DANTES program. Minimum period for course completion is six weeks. Maximum period for course completion is nine months. Telecourses are offered, but enrollment is limited to the local PBS broadcast area in the state of Michigan.

College courses

NCES No.	Course Title	Dept.	Course No.	Cred.	Lev.	Specl. Feat.
030599	Understanding art	Art	125	2S	L	
040101	Financial accounting	Acctg	201	3S	L	
040101	Managerial accounting	Acctg	221	3S	L	
051103	Persuasion	InCom	365	3S	L	
051108	Foundations comm theory	InCom	251	3S	L	
120101	Contrastive appl linguist	ForLL	510	3S	U	
120307	English literature	EnglLL	235	3S	L	
120307	English literature	EnglLL	236	3S	L	
120307	American literature	EnglLL	251	3S	L	
120307	American literature	EnglLL	252	3S	L	
121000	Intermediate French I	Frnch	201	4S	L	
121000	Intermediate French II	Frnch	202	4S	L	
121100	Elementary German	Germn	101	4S	L	
150304	Ecology	Bio	340	3S	L	
150316	Nature study	Bio	229	3S	L	
150799	Physics for poets	Phycs	100	3S	L	
160102	Hist of elementary math	Math	253	2S	U	
160102	History of mathematics	Math	573	3S	U	
160302	College algebra	Math	107	3S	L	
160602	Plane trigonometry	Math	106	3S	L	
160801	Intro to statistics	Math	282	3S	L	
190502	Community health	HlEd	317	3S	L	
190509	Personal health	HlEd	106	3S	L	
190511	Safety education	HlEd	209	2S	L	
190701	Admin of recreation parks	Rec	505	3S	U	
190702	Community recreation prog	RecLe	540	3S	U	
220106	Physical anthropology	Anthr	171	3S	L	
220201	Principles of economics 1	Econ	201	3S	L	
220201	Principles of economics 2	Econ	202	3S	L	
220301	Cultures of the world	Geog	121	3S	L	
220301	Environment and man	Geog	120	3S	L	
220432	Westward movement in Amer	Hist	322	3S	L	
220432	United States to 1865	Hist	111	3S	L	
220432	United States 1865-presen	Hist	112	3S	L	
220499	Western civilization	Hist	101	3S	L	
220499	Western civilization	Hist	102	3S	L	
220501	Intro: Am govt & politics	PolSc	105	3S	L	
220503	Comparative politics: Eur	PolSc	240	3S	L	
220503	World politics	PolSc	150	3S	L	
220599	Intro to political sci	PolSc	100	3S	L	
220604	Juvenile delinquency	Socio	222	3S	L	
220605	The family	Socio	411	3S	L	
220606	Introductory sociology	Socio	100	3S	L	
220607	Social psychology	Socio	201	3S	L	
220615	Minorities	Socio	323	3S	L	
220699	Intro to human sexuality	Socio	213	3S	L	
220699	Religion in society	Socio	319	3S	L	

⑥ COLORADO STATE UNIVERSITY

Mr. Richard Thomas
Coordinator, Distance Learning
Division of Continuing Education
Telecommunications Extended Studies, Spruce Hall
Colorado State University
Fort Collins, Colorado 80523
Phone: 303-491-5608
          800-525-4950 (out of state)

Enrollment on a noncredit basis accepted in credit courses. High school students may enroll in undergraduate courses for credit. Overseas enrollment accepted. Students have one calendar year from the date of registration in which to complete the course requirements. The minimum time for completing a course is eight weeks. Fall semester begins in early September and ends in mid-December; spring semester begins in late January and ends in mid-May; summer session begins in mid-June and ends in early August. All course work must be completed five to six weeks prior to the end of a semester or the summer session if grades are to be recorded for a particular semester.

NCES No.	Course Title	Dept.	Course No.	Cred.	Lev.	Specl. Feat.
	College courses					
010406	Poultry science & prod	AnSci	AN200	2S	L	
010407	Basic nutrition for pets	AnSci	AN322	2S	U	
010505	Ind study/turfgrass	Agri	A495	3S	U	
010603	Ind study/pesticides	Agri	A495	3S	U	
010603	Ind study/stored grain	Agri	A495	1S	U	
010603	Ind study/wood preserv	Agri	A495	2S	U	
011000	Found of forest recreatn	RecPk	OR435	1S	B	
011000	Needs-rec resource users	RecPk	OR435	1S	U	
011000	RIM syst-special uses	RecPk	OR435	2S	U	
011000	Facilit design/oper/maint	RecPk	OR435	3S	U	
011000	Recreation planning	RecPk	OR435	3S	U	
011000	Plan/mgmt unique areas	RecPk	OR435	2S	U	
011000	Mgmt of wilderness	RecPk	OR435	2S	U	
011299	Hunter educ for instructr	Fores	FW355	2S	U	
060102	Ind study/autocad fund	IndTc	IS495	3S	U	
070309	Ind study/adult education	Educ	AD495	CV	B	
070899	Educational psychology	Educ	ED355	3S	U	
070899	Exceptionality & hum rel	Educ	ED428	3S	U	
070900	Evaluation of achievement	Educ	ED452	2S	B	
100313	Nutrition & preschool chl	HomEc	FN160	2S	L	
100401	Decision making: pers/fam	HomEc	HC330	3S	U	
100601	Play behavior	HomEc	HD430	2S	B	
100601	Prof skill dev-child dev	HomEc	H0376	2S	U	
100602	Ind & family development	HomEc	HD101	3S	L	
100699	Practicum I	HomEc	HD286	2S	L	
100699	Adm of human dvlpmt ctrs	HomEc	HD438	3S	B	
120299	Western American lit	Engl	E179	3S	L	
190108	Beg phys ed-tennis	PhyEd	EX100	1S	L	
220431	Imperial Russia	Hist	HY440	3S	B	
220470	Afro-Amer hist 1619-1865	Hist	HY250	3S	L	
	Graduate courses					
050602	Seminar: grantsmanship	InArt	IS592	3S	G	
060102	Ind study/adv autocad	IndTc	IS695	2S	G	
070309	Adult education	Educ	AD520	3S	G	
070799	Guidnce:multicult &sp pop	Educ	ED551	3S	G	
070899	Educ exceptional student	Educ	ED528	2S	G	
	Noncredit courses					
010407	Basic nutrition for pets	AnSci	CE112	NC		
010505	Mgmt-ctrl turfgrass pests	Agri	CE105	NC		
010603	Pesticides: how & why	Agri	CE102	NC		
010603	Mgmt stored-grain pests	Agri	CE103	NC		
010603	Wood preservatives	Agri	CE104	NC		
011000	Forest recreation	RecPk	CE140	NC		
011000	Needs-rec resource users	RecPk	CE141	NC		
011000	RIM syst-special uses	RecPk	CE142	NC		
011000	Facilit design/oper/maint	RecPk	CE143	NC		
011000	Recreation planning	RecPk	CE144	NC		
011000	Plan/mgmt unique areas	RecPk	CE145	NC		
011000	Mgmt of wilderness	RecPk	CE146	NC		
060102	Autocad fundamentals	IndTc	CE798	NC		
060102	Adv autocad	IndTc	CE799	NC		
070309	Program development	Educ	3107	NC		
070309	Administration	Educ	3108	NC		
070309	Adult development	Educ	3109	NC		
070309	Adult basic education	Educ	3111	NC		
070309	Adult learner	Educ	3112	NC		

NCES No.	Course Title	Dept.	Course No.	Cred.	Lev.	Specl. Feat.
070309	Adult teaching	Educ	3113	NC		
110413	Motor vehicle emissions	VTIE	CE880	NC		

⑦ EASTERN KENTUCKY UNIVERSITY

Marion Ogden
Director, Division of Extended Programs
Coats Box 27-A
Eastern Kentucky University
Richmond, Kentucky 40475-3101
Phone: 606-622-2001

Credit by examination is available. Telecourses are offered. Enrollment on a noncredit basis accepted in credit courses. High school students may enroll in undergraduate courses for credit. Overseas enrollment accepted. Institution offers special arrangements to take courses not listed in this Catalog. Minimum period for course completion is five weeks. Maximum period for course completion is one year.

NCES No.	Course Title	Dept.	Course No.	Cred.	Lev.	Specl. Feat.
	High School courses					
120305	English grammar	Engl	11	HF	H	
120305	English grammar	Engl	12	HF	H	
120307	American literature	Engl	11A	HF	H	
120307	American literature	Engl	11B	HF	H	
120307	British literature	Engl	12A	HF	H	
120307	British literature	Engl	12B	HF	H	
190502	Personal/community health	Hlth	1	HF	H	
220201	Economics	Econ	12	HF	H	
220399	World geography	Geog	10A	HF	H	
220399	World geography	Geog	10B	HF	H	
220432	American history	Hist	11A	HF	H	
220432	American history	Hist	11B	HF	H	
220433	World history	Hist	10A	HF	H	
220433	World history	Hist	10B	HF	H	
220501	Government	Govt	12	HF	H	
220502	Civics	Civcs	9	HF	H	
220606	Sociology	Socio	12	HF	H	
	College courses					
030302	Enjoyment of music	Music	271	3S	L	AC
040299	Introduction to business	OfAdm	101	3S	L	
040299	Business communications	OfAdm	201	3S	L	
040299	Bus & office calculations	BOEd	254	3S	L	
040308	Money and banking	Econ	324	3S	U	
040904	Principles of management	Mgmt	300	3S	U	
040999	Intro to management	Mgmt	220	3S	L	
041001	Marketing	Mktg	300	3S	U	
041099	Intro to marketing	Mktg	200	3S	L	
041099	Consumer behavior	Mktg	450	3S	U	
041303	Real estate principles	RIEst	310	3S	U	
041306	Real estate finance	RIEst	330	3S	U	
041308	Real estate law	RIEst	320	3S	U	
041399	Real estate marketing	RIEst	350	3S	U	
050199	Advertising	Mktg	320	3S	U	
060000	Computers and modern wld	CmpSc	102	3S	U	CI
060599	Intro to comp info systms	CmpSc	212	3S	L	CI
090703	Envrnmtl & indus toxiclgy	PubHl	440	3S	U	
090799	Industrial hygiene	PubHl	340	3S	U	
120201	Survey of world lit 1	Engl	211	3S	L	
120201	Survey of world lit 2	Engl	212	3S	L	
120305	English composition 1	Engl	101	3S	L	
120305	English composition 2	Engl	102	3S	L	
120307	American literature 1	Engl	350	3S	U	
130700	Legal environ of business	BuLaw	204	3S	L	
150399	Economic plants	Bio	300	3S	U	
160199	Understanding arithmetic	Math	201	3S	L	
160302	College algebra	Math	107	3S	L	
160602	Trigonometry	Math	108	3S	L	
180199	Beginning philosophy	Philo	110	3S	L	
181199	World religions	Relig	301	3S	L	
190502	Personal/community health	Hlth	281	2S	L	
190511	Safety and first aid	Hlth	202	2S	L	
200199	Psychology as a social sc	Psych	202	3S	L	
200501	Abnormal psychology	Psych	308	3S	U	
200504	Life span devel psych	Psych	311	3S	L	
210300	Police administration	PolAd	101	3S	L	
210300	Prin & proc in admin jus	PolAd	110	3S	U	
210300	Delinq & juv jus system	PolAd	311	3S	U	

NCES No.	Course Title	Dept.	Course No.	Cred.	Lev.	Specl. Feat.
210300	Introduction to security	SecLP	110	3S	U	
210300	Alcohol and other drugs	TrSaf	232	3S	U	
210300	Introduction to security	PolAd	110	3S	U	
210301	Crim justice in a democ	CrJus	101	3S	L	
210301	Intro to corrections	CLEE	120	3S	L	
210305	Legl envirn protectv serv	SST	215	3S	L	
220201	Principles of economics 1	Econ	230	3S	L	
220201	Principles of economics 2	Econ	231	3S	L	
220302	Economic geography	Geog	330	3S	U	
220399	Cons, technol & env probl	Geog	302	3S	U	
220399	Intro to geography	Geog	101	3S	L	
220405	History of science	Sci	310	3S	U	
220432	American civiliz to 1877	Hist	202	3S	L	
220432	American civ since 1877	Hist	203	3S	L	
220433	Preindustrial world civ	GSoSc	246	3S	L	
220433	Industrialism in wrld civ	GSoSc	247	3S	L	
220499	Kentucky history	Hist	516	3S	U	
220501	Intro to American govt	PolSc	101	3S	L	
220511	Amer state & local govt	PolSc	333	3S	L	
220599	Government of Kentucky	PolSc	332	3S	U	
220605	Sociology of the family	Socio	245	3S	L	
220606	Introductory sociology	Socio	131	3S	L	

---

⑧ **EASTERN MICHIGAN UNIVERSITY**

Mr. Michael J. McPhillips
Director, Independent Study
Division of Continuing Education
329 Goodson Hall
Eastern Michigan University
Ypsilanti, Michigan 48197
Phone: 313-487-1081

High school students may enroll in undergraduate courses for credit. Overseas enrollment accepted. Minimum period for course completion is five weeks. Maximum period for course completion is one year. Students may enroll anytime. Any course may be taken on a noncredit basis at a reduced rate. VISA and MasterCard are accepted.

NCES No.	Course Title	Dept.	Course No.	Cred.	Lev.	Specl. Feat.
	College courses					
040601	Business communication	Mgmt	202	3S	L	
041106	Basic supervision	Mgmt	281	3S	L	
110299	Wire manufact technology	Tech	479	3S	U	
120299	Children's literature	Engl	207	3S	L	
120302	History English language	Engl	421	3S	B	AC
120305	Modern English syntax	Engl	402	3S	B	
120308	Reading of literature	EngLL	100	3S	L	VC
120310	Expository writing	Engl	325	3S	L	
160302	Intermediate algebra	Math	104	3S	L	AC
220432	US history to 1877	Hist	123	3S	L	AC
220432	US history-1877-present	Hist	124	3S	L	AC
220606	Introduction to sociology	Socio	105	3S	L	
220612	Basic technolog/concept	Tech	150	3S	L	
	Noncredit courses					
100206	Financial plan & invest	Finan	N/C	NC		

---

⑨ **EMBRY-RIDDLE AERONAUTICAL UNIVERSITY**

Thomas W. Pettit
Director
Department of Independent Studies
Embry-Riddle Aeronautical University
Daytona Beach, Florida 32014
Phone: 904-239-6397

External degree available through the program. Credit by examination is available. Enrollment on a noncredit basis accepted in credit courses. Overseas enrollment accepted. Military personnel may enroll through the DANTES program. Institution offers special arrangements to take courses not listed in this Catalog. Maximum period for course completion is twelve weeks. Professional degrees in aeronautics and aviation business administration are offered. Transfer credits are accepted for courses completed at an accredited institution with a grade of C or better.

NCES No.	Course Title	Dept.	Course No.	Cred.	Lev.	Specl. Feat.
	College courses					
040100	Accounting	MgtSc	110	3S	L	AC
040400	Business info systems	MgtSc	320	3S	U	AC
040904	Principles of management	MgtSc	201	3S	L	
040999	Analysis methods for mgt	MgtSc	350	3S	U	AC
040999	Mgt planning and control	MgtSc	401	3S	U	AC
041001	Marketing	MgtSc	311	3S	U	AC
060100	Intro to comp in aviation	CmpSc	105	3S	L	
080100	Airport dev and operation	AerSc	401	3S	U	AC
080101	Basic aerodynamics	AerSc	309	3S	U	AC
080101	Aircraft performance	AerSc	310	3S	U	AC
120310	Eng comp and lit I	Hum	122	3S	L	
120310	Tech report writing	Hum	221	3S	L	AC
139900	Aviation law	AerSc	405	3S	U	
150799	Explorations in physics	PhySc	102	3S	L	AC
160399	College math for aviation	Math	111	3S	L	AC
160899	Statistics with avia apps	Math	211	3S	L	VC
180599	Intro to logic	Hum	250	3S	L	AC
220201	Microeconomics	Econ	210	3S	L	AC
220201	Macroeconomics	Econ	211	3S	L	AC
220499	Hist/regulation of aviat	AerSc	253	3S	L	AC

---

⑩ **GOVERNORS STATE UNIVERSITY**

Mr. Richard Venneri
Dean, Special Programs and Continuing Education
Office of Extended Learning
Governors State University
University Parkway
University Park, Illinois 60466
Phone: 312-534-5000

External degree available through the program. Credit by examination is available. Overseas enrollment accepted. Military personnel may enroll through the DANTES program. Maximum period for course completion is one trimester. U.S. citizens only (military) book service is offered through the GSU bookstore. Registration for courses follows the on-campus semester timetable. A free catalog may be requested from the Independent Study by Correspondence Office.

NCES No.	Course Title	Dept.	Course No.	Cred.	Lev.	Specl. Feat.
	College courses					
040312	Public finance	Econ	404	3U	B	
040903	Organizational behavior	Mgmt	401	3U	B	
059900	Concepts in communication	Commu	310	3U	B	
120310	Writing principles	Engl	310	3U	B	
150900	Human evolution	Bio	308	3U	B	
190501	Alchlm: stdy of addiction	Alcho	340	3U	B	
210100	Intro to public administr	PubAd	301	3U	B	
220614	Principles of urban studi	Socio	310	3U	B	
229900	Survey of social science	SoSci	311	3U	B	
	Graduate courses					
120307	Black literature	Engl	512	3U	G	
190501	Alchlm employe assist pgm	Alcho	52A	3U	G	
220409	Family history legacies	Socio	52A	3U	G	AC
220420	African civilization	ICS	548	3U	G	
220428	Hist of Il & its constitu	Hist	50A	3U	G	
220431	Russian hist since 1900	Hist	53A	3U	G	
220470	Hispanic experience in US	ICS	540	3U	G	
220472	Women in American history	Hist	550	3U	G	
220599	Urban politics	PolSc	538	3U	G	
229900	Urban dynamics	SocWk	530	3U	G	
229900	Ethnic culture & politics	ICS	541	3U	G	

---

⑪ **HOME STUDY INTERNATIONAL**

George P. Babcock
President
Home Study International
6940 Carroll Avenue
Takoma Park, Maryland 20912
Phone: 202-722-6572

Enrollment on a noncredit basis accepted in credit courses. High school students may enroll in undergraduate courses for credit. Overseas enrollment accepted. Military personnel may enroll through the DANTES program. Maximum period for course completion is one year. HSI is accredited by the National Home Study Council and affiliated with Columbia Union College, which is accredited by the Middle States Association.

NCES No.	Course Title	Dept.	Course No.	Cred.	Lev.	Specl. Feat.
Elementary courses						
040207	Elementary typing	ETypg	6		E	
040207	Elementary typing	ETypg	7		E	
040207	Elementary typing	ETypg	8		E	
090000	Science health 1st sem	EHlth	71		E	
090000	Science health 2nd sem	EHlth	72		E	
090000	Science health 1st sem	EHlth	81		E	
090000	Science health 2nd sem	EHlth	82		E	
120399	Language 1st sem	EEngl	71		E	
120399	Language 2nd sem	EEngl	72		E	
120399	Language 1st sem	EEngl	81		E	
120399	Language 2nd sem	EEngl	82		E	
161199	Mathematics 1st sem	EMath	71		E	
161199	Mathematics 2nd sem	EMath	72		E	
161199	Mathematics 1st sem	EMath	81		E	
161199	Mathematics 2nd sem	EMath	82		E	
189900	Bible 1st sem	ERlgn	71		E	
189900	Bible 2nd sem	ERlgn	72		E	
189900	Bible 1st sem	ERlgn	81		E	
189900	Bible 2nd sem	ERlgn	82		E	
220432	United States history 1s	EHist	81		E	
220432	United States history 2s	EHist	82		E	
229900	Social studies 1st sem	EHist	71		E	
229900	Social studies 2nd sem	EHist	72		E	
High School courses						
030302	Music apprec 1st sem	SMusc	15	HF	H	
030302	Music apprec 2nd sem	SMusc	15	HF	H	
040102	Bookkpng & acctg 1st sem	SAcct	3	HF	H	
040102	Bookkpng & acctg 2nd sem	SAcct	4	HF	H	
040207	Typing 1st sem	STypg	7	HF	H	AC
040207	Typing 2nd sem	STypg	8	HF	H	
100104	Clothing construction	SHmEc	16	HF	H	
100503	Home planning	SHmEc	18	HF	H	
100702	Foods	SHmEc	17	HF	H	
120299	Adventist literature	SEngl	13	HF	H	
120305	English I 1st sem	SEngl	1	HF	H	
120305	English I 2nd sem	SEngl	2	HF	H	
120305	English II 1st sem	SEngl	3	HF	H	AC
120305	English II 2nd sem	SEngl	4	HF	H	AC
120307	American lit 1st sem	SEngl	9	HF	H	
120307	American lit 2nd sem	SEngl	10	HF	H	
120307	English lit 1st sem	SEngl	11	HF	H	
120307	English lit 2nd sem	SEngl	12	HF	H	
120399	Structure of writing	SEngl	8	HF	H	
121000	French I 1st sem	SFren	1	HF	H	AC
121000	French I 2nd sem	SFren	2	HF	H	AC
122500	Spanish I 1st sem	SSpan	13	HF	H	AC
122500	Spanish I 2nd sem	SSpan	14	HF	H	AC
122500	Spanish II 1st sem	SSpan	15	HF	H	AC
122500	Spanish II 2nd sem	SSpan	16	HF	H	AC
150300	Biology 1st sem	SBio	5	HF	H	SL
150300	Biology 2nd sem	SBio	6	HF	H	LK
150400	Chemistry 1st sem	SChem	7	HF	H	LK
150400	Chemistry 2nd sem	SChem	8	HF	H	LK
160302	Algebra I 1st sem	SMath	5	HF	H	
160302	Algebra I 2nd sem	SMath	6	HF	H	
160302	Algebra II	SMath	11	1U	H	
160601	Geometry 1st sem	SMath	7	HF	H	
160601	Geometry 2nd sem	SMath	8	HF	H	
161202	Consumer math 1st sem	SMath	3	HF	H	
161202	Consumer math 2nd sem	SMath	4	HF	H	
189900	Breakthru w God 1st sem	SRlgn	1	HF	H	
189900	Breakthru w God 2nd sem	SRlgn	2	HF	H	
189900	God's church 1st sem	SRlgn	5	HF	H	
189900	God's church 2nd sem	SRlgn	6	HF	H	
189900	God's Word	SRlgn	9	HF	H	
189900	God's Word	SRlgn	10	HF	H	
189900	God's world	SRlgn	13	HF	H	
189900	God's world	SRlgn	14	HF	H	
190515	Health	SHlth	15	HF	H	AC
220432	American hist 1st sem	SHist	7	HF	H	
220432	American hist 2nd sem	SHist	8	HF	H	
220433	World history 1st sem	SHist	3	HF	H	

NCES No.	Course Title	Dept.	Course No.	Cred.	Lev.	Specl. Feat.
220433	World history 2nd sem	SHist	4	HF	H	
220501	American govt 1st sem	SHist	9	HF	H	
220501	American govt 2nd sem	SHist	10	HF	H	
College courses						
030302	Music appreciation	Music	204	3S	L	AC
040101	Prin of accounting sem 1	Acctg	101	3S	L	
040101	Prin of accounting sem 2	Acctg	102	3S	L	
040207	Typing 1st sem	SecTr	105	2S	L	AC
040207	Typing 2nd sem	SecTr	106	2S	L	
070509	Health education	Educ	260	3S	L	
070516	Math in elementary school	Educ	355	3S	U	
070522	Teach social studies	Educ	340	3S	U	
070599	The teaching of reading	Educ	354	3S	U	
071103	Evaluation in teaching	Educ	360	3S	U	
100313	Nutrition	HomEc	300	3S	U	
100601	Child development	Psych	242	3S	L	
120299	American lit 1st sem	Engl	221	3S	L	
120299	American lit 2nd sem	Engl	222	3S	L	
120307	English lit 1st sem	Engl	241	3S	L	
120307	English lit 2nd sem	Engl	242	3S	L	
120310	Freshman comp 1st sem	Engl	101	3S	L	
120310	Freshman comp 2nd sem	Engl	102	3S	L	
121000	French I 1st sem	Frnch	101	2S	L	AC
121000	French I 2nd sem	Frnch	102	2S	L	AC
121100	Intermed German 1st sem	Germn	201	3S	L	AC
121100	Intermed German 2nd sem	Germn	202	3S	L	AC
121200	Greek I 1st sem	Greek	201	2S	L	
121200	Greek I 2nd sem	Greek	202	2S	L	
121200	Intermed Greek 1st sem	Greek	311	3S	U	
121200	Intermed Greek 2nd sem	Greek	312	3S	U	
121200	Greek II 1st sem	Greek	203	2S	L	
121200	Greek II 2nd sem	Greek	204	2S	L	
122500	Spanish I 1st sem	Span	101	2S	L	AC
122500	Spanish I 2nd sem	Span	102	2S	L	AC
122500	Spanish II 1st sem	Span	103	2S	L	AC
122500	Spanish II 2nd sem	Span	104	2S	L	AC
150300	Scientfc stdy of creation	Bio	311	2S	U	AC
160302	College algebra	Math	121	3S	L	
180999	Bible doctrines 1st sem	Relig	321	2S	U	
180999	Bible doctrines 2nd sem	Relig	322	2S	U	
180999	World religions	Relig	300	2S	U	
180999	Adventist history	Relig	230	3S	L	
181202	Daniel	Relig	311	2S	U	
181202	Acts and the Epistles	Relig	350	3S	U	
181202	Bible survey 1st semester	Relig	101	2S	L	
181202	Bible survey 2nd semester	Relig	102	2S	L	
181202	Corinthian Epistles	Relig	340	2S	U	
181202	Revelation	Relig	312	2S	U	
181406	Life & tchngs of Jesus 1s	Relig	201	2S	L	
181406	Life & tchngs of Jesus 2s	Relig	202	2S	L	
189900	Old Testmt prophets-early	Relig	335	3S	U	
189900	Old Testmt prophets-later	Relig	336	3S	U	
189900	Philos of Adventist educ	Educ	210	3S	L	
189900	Prophetic guidance	Relig	360	2S	U	AC
189900	Science & Chrstian belief	Relig	314	1S	U	
190599	Health principles	Hlth	100	3S	L	
200100	General psychology	Psych	120	3S	L	
200406	Psychology of learning	Psych	365	3S	U	
209900	General psychology	Psych	120	3S	L	
220301	Cultural geography 1st sm	Geog	351	2S	U	
220301	Cultural geography 2nd sm	Geog	352	2S	U	
220408	Adventist history	Hist	304	3S	U	
220423	Asian backgrounds	Hist	305	2S	U	
220432	US history 1st semester	Hist	201	3S	L	
220432	US history 2nd semester	Hist	202	3S	L	
220499	Church history 1st sem	Hist	311	3S	U	
220499	Church history 2nd sem	Hist	312	3S	U	
220499	Hist of West civiliz 1 sm	Hist	104	3S	L	
220499	Hist of West civiliz 2 sm	Hist	105	3S	L	
220501	Govt in the United States	Hist	203	3S	L	
220699	Sociology	Socio	204	3S	L	
Noncredit courses						
189900	Work of the Bible instruc	AduEd		NC		
189900	Literature evangelism	AduEd		NC		

(12) INDIANA STATE UNIVERSITY

Dr. Clair D. Woodward
Director of Independent Study
Alumni Center 124
Indiana State University
Terre Haute, Indiana 47809
Phone: 812-237-2555
800-234-1639 ext. 2555

Enrollment on a noncredit basis accepted in credit courses. High school students may enroll in undergraduate courses for credit. Overseas enrollment accepted. Minimum period for course completion is two and a half months. Maximum period for course completion is one year. Six-month and additional extensions are available. Afro-American Studies 499N contains both audio and video required components: 'Eyes on the Prize,' available at many public and university libraries. Journalism 270 (ConEd J-270) requires a 35mm camera.

NCES No.	Course Title	Dept.	Course No.	Cred.	Lev.	Specl. Feat.
	College courses					
030502	Art appreciation	Art	100	2S	L	
030502	Visual arts in civilizatn	Art	151	3S	L	
040707	Life & health insurance	Finan	341	3S	U	
040708	Risk and insurance	Finan	340	3S	U	
050605	Magazine writing	Journ	318	3S	U	
050608	Newswriting	Journ	116	3S	L	
050609	Intro to photojournalism	Journ	270	3S	L	
051099	Survey of broadcasting	Commu	218	3S	L	
051106	Parliamentary procedures	Commu	251	1S	L	
051303	Writing for brdcst media	Commu	290	3S	L	
070604	Intr sys/desgn mktng educ	ASBE	396	2S	L	
070604	Intro to marketing educ	ASBE	397	2S	L	
120305	English grammar	Engl	310	3S	U	
120307	Intro to literature	Engl	130	2S	L	
120307	Intro to literature	Engl	130	3S	L	
120307	Intro to the short story	Engl	231	2S	L	
120307	Lit for younger children	Engl	280	3S	L	
120307	The Bible as literature	Engl	334	3S	U	
120310	Intro to fiction writing	Engl	220	3S	L	
120310	Expository writing	Engl	305	2S	U	
120310	Technical writing	Engl	305T	2S	U	
160301	Basic elementary math I	Math	104	3S	L	
160301	Basic elementary math III	Math	304	3S	U	
160302	Intermediate algebra	Math	111	3S	L	
160801	Principles of statistics	Math	241	3S	L	
161101	Math of finance	Math	212	3S	L	
161199	Fundamentals & applicatns	Math	201	3S	L	
161199	Fund & applic of calculus	Math	301	3S	U	
181002	World religions	Hum	250	3S	U	AC
190104	Hist & principles of PE	MWPE	201	2S	U	
190106	Org & admin of phys educ	MWPE	441	3S	U	
190509	Pers hlth behav & wellnes	HI&Sf	111	3S	L	
190511	Intro to general safety	HI&Sf	323	3S	L	
190599	Ath trng & emer first aid	MWPE	292	3S	L	
190699	Traffic & transp safety	HI&Sf	325	3S	U	
200199	General psychology	Psych	101	3S	L	
200501	Abnormal psychology	Psych	368	3S	U	
200504	Developmental psychology	EdPsy	221	3S	L	
200504	Adolescent psychology	EdPsy	422	3S	U	
200799	Intro to social psycholgy	Socio	240	3S	L	
210304	Retail security	Crim	202	3S	L	
220301	Political geography	Geog	432	3S	U	
220301	Global geography	Geog	330	3S	U	
220305	Man's physical environmnt	Geog	111	3S	L	
220305	Intro to earth & sky sci	Geog	113	3S	L	
220308	Urban geography	Geog	431	3S	U	
220399	Conservation of nat resrs	Geog	433	3S	U	
220432	The US since 1865	Hist	202	3S	L	
220433	Studies in world civlztn	Hist	101	3S	L	
220433	Studies in world civlztn	Hist	102	3S	L	
220470	Eyes on the Prize	AfAmS	499N	3S	U	VC
220602	Criminology	Crim	200	3S	L	
220602	Correctional institutions	Crim	430	3S	U	
220602	Criminal investigations	Crim	435	3S	U	
220604	Juvenile delinquency	Crim	423	3S	U	
220606	Principles of sociology	Socio	120	3S	L	
220613	Contemporary soc problems	Socio	220	3S	L	
220613	Social conflict	Socio	322	3S	U	VC
	Noncredit courses					
050605	Magazine writing	ConEd	J-318	NC		
050609	Intro to photojournalism	ConEd	J-270	NC		
120310	Intro to fiction writing	ConEd	E-220	NC		

(13) INDIANA UNIVERSITY

Mr. Frank R. DiSilvestro
Associate Director of Extended Studies for Independent Study
Division of Extended Studies, Owen Hall 001
Indiana University
Bloomington, Indiana 47405
Phone: 812-855-3693

External degree available through the program. Enrollment on a noncredit basis accepted in credit courses. High school students may enroll in undergraduate courses for credit. Overseas enrollment accepted. Military personnel may enroll through the DANTES program. Maximum period for course completion is one year.

NCES No.	Course Title	Dept.	Course No.	Cred.	Lev.	Specl. Feat.
	High School courses					
010600	Plant science 1st sem	Sci	21H	HF	H	
010600	Plant science 2nd sem	Sci	22H	HF	H	
030501	Drawing and storytelling	Art	23A	HF	H	
030501	Basic art level 1	Art	03A	HF	H	
030502	Art history & appreciatn	Art	31H	HF	H	
040108	Beginning accounting 1	BusEd	21B	HF	H	
040108	Beginning accounting 2	BusEd	22B	HF	H	
040205	Beginning shorthand sem 1	BusEd	25S	HF	H	
040207	Typewriting 1st sem	BusEd	21T	HF	H	
040207	Typewriting 2nd sem	BusEd	22T	HF	H	
040299	Office procedures	BusEd	31P	HF	H	
040601	Business English	BusEd	31E	HF	H	
049900	General business 1st sem	BusEd	11G	HF	H	
049900	General business 2nd sem	BusEd	12G	HF	H	
049900	Salesmanship	DisEd	31S	HF	H	
049900	Gen merchandising retail	DisEd	31M	HF	H	
050699	Journalism	Engl	01J	HF	H	
051103	Speech	Engl	09S	HF	H	AC
059900	Mass media	Engl	01M	HF	H	
060705	Intr BASIC programming 1	Multi	33C	HF	H	
060705	Intr BASIC programming 2	Multi	34C	HF	H	
061101	Computer literacy	Multi	01C	HF	H	
061104	Information processing	BusEd	31D	HF	H	
070703	Vocational information	Multi	01V	HF	H	
070703	Voc info self-discovery	Multi	02V	HF	H	
090901	Family health care	Hlth	12H	HF	H	
090999	Health & safety I	HIEd	11B	HF	H	
100202	Consumer education	C&HE	41C	HF	H	
100313	Begin food and nutrition	C&HE	11N	HF	H	
100402	Family management	C&HE	02F	HF	H	
100503	Housing & interior design	C&HE	41H	HF	H	
100601	Begin child development	C&HE	31C	HF	H	
100699	Adjustment marr/family	C&HE	01F	HF	H	
110503	Drafting 1st semester	InArt	11M	HF	H	
110503	Drafting 2nd semester	InArt	12M	HF	H	
110503	Architectural drafting	InArt	21A	HF	H	
120299	Experience of drama II	Engl	31D	HF	H	
120305	Basic vocabulary	Engl	01V	HF	H	
120305	English 11 grammar & comp	Engl	30W	HF	H	
120305	Adv grammar & composition	Engl	51R	HF	H	
120307	Freshman English 1st sem	Engl	11E	HF	H	
120307	English 9 second semester	Engl	12E	HF	H	
120307	English 10 first semester	Engl	21E	HF	H	
120307	English 10 second sem	Engl	22E	HF	H	
120307	American lit 1st sem	Engl	31L	HF	H	
120307	American lit 2nd sem	Engl	32L	HF	H	
120307	Women writers	Engl	33L	HF	H	
120307	English lit 1st sem	Engl	41L	HF	H	
120307	English lit 2nd sem	Engl	42L	HF	H	
120307	Four American novels	Engl	73L	QT	H	
120307	Children's literature	Engl	81K	QT	H	
120307	Literature of the future	Engl	82L	QT	H	
120307	Mythology	Engl	83L	QT	H	
120307	Mysteries	Engl	84L	QT	H	
120307	The short story	Engl	81L	QT	H	
120308	Developmental reading	Engl	01R	HF	H	
120310	Senior-year composition	Engl	41W	HF	H	
120310	Creative writing-fiction	Engl	05W	HF	H	

NCES No.	Course Title	Dept.	Course No.	Cred.	Lev.	Specl. Feat.
120310	Basic composition	Engl	81W	QT	H	
120310	Advanced composition	Engl	91W	QT	H	
120310	Writing for beginners	Engl	02W	HF	H	
120399	Vocabulary improvement	Engl	81V	QT	H	
120399	How to study in college	Engl	91S	QT	H	
121000	French level I 1st sem	Frnch	11F	HF	H	AC
121000	French level I 2nd sem	Frnch	12F	HF	H	AC
121000	French level II 1st sem	Frnch	21F	HF	H	AC
121000	French level II 2nd sem	Frnch	22F	HF	H	AC
121100	German level I 1st sem	Germn	11G	HF	H	AC
121100	German level 1 2nd sem	Germn	12G	HF	H	AC
121100	German level II 1st sem	Germn	21G	HF	H	AC
121100	German level II 2nd sem	Germn	22G	HF	H	AC
121600	Latin level I 1st sem	Latin	11L	HF	H	
121600	Latin level I 2nd sem	Latin	12L	HF	H	
121600	Latin level II 1st sem	Latin	21L	HF	H	
121600	Latin level II 2nd sem	Latin	22L	HF	H	
122500	Spanish level I 1st sem	Span	11S	HF	H	AC
122500	Spanish level I 2nd sem	Span	12S	HF	H	AC
122500	Spanish level II 1st sem	Span	21S	HF	H	AC
122500	Spanish level II 2nd sem	Span	22S	HF	H	AC
130799	Business law	BusEd	31L	HF	H	
149900	Library & research skills	Engl	23L	HF	H	
150399	General biology 1st sem	Sci	21B	HF	H	
150399	General biology 2nd sem	Sci	22B	HF	H	
150401	Phys sci-introd chemistry	Sci	21P	HF	H	
150700	Phys sci-introd physics	Sci	22P	HF	H	
150799	Physics level I 1st sem	Sci	41P	HF	H	
150799	Physics level I 2nd sem	Sci	42P	HF	H	
150900	Int erth/spce sc I 1st sm	Sci	11E	HF	H	
150900	Int erth/spce sc I 2nd sm	Sci	12E	HF	H	
160199	Basic math 1st sem	Math	11M	HF	H	
160199	Basic math 2nd sem	Math	12M	HF	H	
160302	Algebra level I 1st sem	Math	11A	HF	H	
160302	Algebra level I 2nd sem	Math	12A	HF	H	
160302	Algebra level II 1st sem	Math	21A	HF	H	
160302	Algebra level II 2nd sem	Math	22A	HF	H	
160401	Calculus 1st sem	Math	41C	HF	H	
160601	Geometry 1st sem	Math	21G	HF	H	
160601	Geometry 2nd sem	Math	22G	HF	H	
160602	Trigonometry	Math	41T	HF	H	
161201	Business mathematics	Math	11B	HF	H	
161202	Consumer mathematics	Math	03C	HF	H	
200199	Psychology	SocSt	01P	HF	H	
200406	Understand-improve memory	Engl	81S	HF	H	
220201	Economics	SocSt	41E	HF	H	
220399	World geography 1st sem	SocSt	21G	HF	H	
220399	World geography 2nd sem	SocSt	22G	HF	H	
220432	US history 1st sem	SocSt	31A	HF	H	
220432	US history 2nd sem	SocSt	32A	HF	H	
220433	World history 1st sem	SocSt	11W	HF	H	
220433	World history 2nd sem	SocSt	12W	HF	H	
220501	US government 1st sem	SocSt	41G	HF	H	
220501	US government 2nd sem	SocSt	42G	HF	H	
220699	Sociology	SocSt	01S	HF	H	
220699	Males & females in Am soc	SocSt	05S	HF	H	
229900	Intro to social science	SocSt	11X	HF	H	

College courses

NCES No.	Course Title	Dept.	Course No.	Cred.	Lev.	Specl. Feat.
030399	Music for the listener	Music	M174	3S	L	AC
030501	Textiles	AMrch	H203	3S	L	
030502	Intro to African art	FnArt	A250	3S	L	SL
030603	Ancient & medieval art	FnArt	A101	4S	L	
040101	Intro to accounting I	Bus	A201	3S	L	
040101	Intro to accounting II	Bus	A202	3S	L	
040101	Intermediate accounting I	Bus	A311	3S	U	
040101	Intermediate accountng II	Bus	A312	3S	U	
040106	Cost accounting	Bus	A325	3S	U	
040109	Prins of hospital acctg	Bus	A203	3S	L	
040109	Intermed hospital acctg	Bus	A233	3S	L	
040109	Hosp budget & cost analys	Bus	A333	3S	U	
040109	Fund accounting	Bus	A335	3S	U	
040114	Intro to taxation	Bus	A328	3S	U	
040114	Advanced income tax	Bus	A339	3S	U	
040302	Personal finance	Bus	F260	3S	L	
040312	Bus enterprise & pub pol	Bus	G406	3S	U	
040601	Business communications	Bus	X204	3S	L	
040708	Prin of risk & insurance	Bus	N300	3S	U	
040800	Intro to internat'l bus	Bus	D300	3S	U	
040800	Environ anal for int bus	Bus	D419	3S	U	
040902	Retail management	Bus	M419	3S	U	
040903	Org behav & leadership	Bus	Z300	3S	U	
040903	Org behav & ldrship-hosp	Bus	Z300H	3S	U	
040904	Financial management	Bus	F301	3S	U	
040904	Operations management	Bus	P301	3S	U	
041001	Intro to marketing	Bus	M300	3S	U	
041303	Prins of real estate	Bus	R300	3S	U	
049900	Business admin: intro	Bus	X100	3S	L	
049900	Job search techniques	Bus	X425	1S	U	
049900	Basic career development	COAS	Q294	1S	L	
049900	Principles of urban econ	Bus	G330	3S	U	
050605	Writing for publication	Journ	C327	3S	U	
051103	Interpersonal communicatn	Spch	S122	2S	L	AC
051103	Public speaking	Spch	S121	2S	L	AC
059900	Intro to mass communicats	Journ	C200	3S	L	
059900	Citizen and the news	Journ	C300	3S	U	AC
060705	COBOL & file processing	CmpSc	C203	3S	L	CI
060705	COBOL programming	CmpSc	C303	1S	U	CI
060707	Foundations digital comp	CmpSc	C251	3S	L	
060799	Intr to computer programg	CmpSc	C201	4S	L	CI
070401	Math in elementary school	Educ	E343	3S	U	
070503	Self-instruction in art	Educ	M135	1S	L	
070503	Self-instruction in art	Educ	M135	2S	L	
070503	Self-instruction in art	Educ	M135	3S	L	
070503	Self-instruction in art	Educ	M135	4S	L	
070503	Self-instruction in art	Educ	M135	5S	L	
070516	Math for elem teachers 1	Math	T101	3S	L	
070516	Math for elem teachers 2	Math	T102	3S	L	
070516	Math for elem teachers 3	Math	T103	3S	L	
070704	Human dev opps college st	Educ	U205	3S	L	
070899	Intr to exceptional child	Educ	K205	3S	L	
090115	Nutrition for hlth profes	Nrsng	B215	3S	L	
090118	Nursing pharmacology	Nrsng	B216	3S	L	
090255	Health promo in community	Nrsng	H430	3S	U	
090699	Leadership in nursing	Nrsng	L473	3S	U	
090999	Med terms from Greek-Lat	Class	C209	2S	L	AC
100313	Human nutrition	HPE&R	N231	3S	L	
100313	Basic nutrition	HPE&R	N220	3S	U	
100699	Marriage & family interac	HPE&R	F258	3S	L	
110699	Prins of transportation	Bus	T300	3S	U	
120199	Intro to study of lang	Ling	L103	3S	L	
120201	Introduction to film	CompL	C190	3S	L	
120201	Mod lit & other arts: int	CompL	C255	3S	L	AC
120204	Literary interpretation	Engl	L202	3S	L	
120204	English lit to 1700	Engl	L211	3S	L	
120204	English lit since 1700	Engl	L212	3S	L	
120204	Literary interpretation	Engl	L202A	3S	U	
120204	Science fiction	Engl	L230	3S	L	
120204	Engl lit from 1600-1800	Engl	L298	3S	U	
120305	Intro to the English lang	Engl	G205	3S	L	
120305	English grammar review	Engl	W202	1S	L	
120305	English lang improvement	Ling	L100	3S	L	
120307	Classical mythology	Class	C205	3S	L	
120307	Introduction to drama	Engl	L203	3S	L	
120307	Introduction to fiction	Engl	L204	3S	L	
120307	Introduction to poetry	Engl	L205	3S	L	
120307	Intro to Shakespeare	Engl	L220	3S	L	
120307	Late plays of Shakespeare	Engl	L314	3S	U	
120307	American fiction to 1900	Engl	L355	3S	U	
120307	American drama	Engl	L363	3S	U	
120307	Children's literature	Engl	L390	3S	U	
120307	19th-century Brit fiction	Engl	L348	3S	U	
120307	20th-century Amer fiction	Engl	L358	3S	U	
120307	Women and literature	Engl	L207	3S	L	
120308	Manag resources for lrng	Educ	X150	1S	D	
120308	Read/learn techs 3: human	Educ	X152A	1S	D	
120308	Read/learn tech 3: soc sc	Educ	X152B	1S	D	
120308	Literary masterpieces I	Engl	L213	3S	L	
120308	Literary masterpieces II	Engl	L214	3S	L	
120308	Amer lit since 1914	Engl	L354	3S	U	
120309	Bus & prof communication	Spch	S223	3S	L	
120309	Freedom of speech	Spch	S339	3S	U	
120310	Elementary composition I	Engl	W131	3S	L	
120310	Prof writing skills	Engl	W231	3S	L	
120310	Advanced expository writg	Engl	W350	3S	U	
120310	Creative writing: poetry	Engl	W203A	3S	L	
120310	Creative writing: prose	Engl	W203B	3S	L	
120310	Creative wrtg: poet/prose	Engl	W203C	3S	L	
120310	Intro creative writing	Engl	W103	3S	L	
120310	Crit review writing-film	Engl	W119	1S	L	
120310	Advanced expository wrtng	Engl	W350A	3S	U	
120399	Intr wrtg & lit I	Engl	L141	4S	L	
120399	Intr wrtg & lit II	Engl	L142	4S	L	
120399	Intr wrtg & lit I: murder	Engl	L141A	4S	L	

NCES No.	Course Title	Dept.	Course No.	Cred.	Lev.	Specl. Feat.
120399	Vocabulary acquisition	Engl	W205	1S	L	
121000	Elementary French I	Frnch	F100	4S	L	AC
121000	Elem Frnch II lang & cult	Frnch	F150	3S	U	AC
121400	Elementary Italian I	Ital	M100	4S	L	AC
121400	Elementary Italian II	Ital	M150	3S	L	AC
121600	Elementary Latin I	Class	L100	4S	L	
121600	Elementary Latin II	Class	L150	4S	L	
122500	2nd yr Spanish reading I	Span	S216	3S	L	
122500	2nd yr Spanish reading II	Span	S266	3S	L	
122500	Elementary Spanish I	Span	S100	4S	L	
122500	Elementary Spanish II	Span	S150	4S	L	
130299	Leg environment of bus	Bus	L201	3S	L	
130299	Commercial law II	Bus	L303	3S	U	
130403	Amer juvenile justice sys	CrJus	P475	3S	U	
131004	Occupationl hlth & safety	LabSt	L240	3S	L	
131099	Labor law	LabSt	L201	3S	L	
131099	Grievance representation	LabSt	L220	3S	U	
131099	Grievance arbitration	LabSt	L320	3S	U	
131099	Topics lab st: phil/work	LabSt	L490	3S	U	
150102	The solar system	Astro	A100	3S	L	
150103	Stellar astronomy	Astro	A105	3S	L	
150199	Introduction to astronomy	Astro	A110	3S	L	
150201	Weather and climate	Geog	G109	3S	L	
150399	Contemporary biology	Bio	N100	3S	L	
150599	Earth sci: matls/process	Geol	G103	3S	L	
150799	Physics in modern world I	Phycs	P101	4S	L	
150799	Energy	Phycs	P110	2S	L	
150799	Energy and technology	Phycs	P120	3S	L	
160199	Excursions into math	Math	M110	3S	L	
160203	Finite mathematics	Math	M118	3S	L	
160302	Basic algebra	Math	M014	4S	D	
160399	Pre-calculus mathematics	Math	M125	3S	L	
160401	Brief surv of calculus I	Math	M119	3S	L	
160602	Trigonometric functions	Math	M126	2S	L	
160603	Analyt geom & calc I	Math	M215	5S	L	
160603	Analyt geom & calc II	Math	M216	5S	L	
160899	Statistical techniques	Psych	K300	3S	U	
180399	Elementary ethics	Philo	P140	3S	L	
180401	Ancient Greek philosophy	Philo	P201	3S	L	
180499	Women in phil thought	Philo	P282	3S	L	
180700	Philosophy of work	Philo	P337	3S	U	
180800	Intro to philosophy	Philo	P100	3S	L	
180902	Crstn chrch/New Test time	Relig	R220	3S	U	
181104	Intro to relig in West	Relig	R152	3S	L	
190106	Org & curr str phy e K-12	HPE&R	P497	3S	U	
190502	Health probs in community	HPE&R	C366	3S	U	
190509	Personal health	HPE&R	H363	3S	U	
190702	Semnr rec & pks-arm frces	HPE&R	R317	3S	U	
190702	Special recreation srvcs	HPE&R	R270	3S	U	
190703	Recreation and leisure	HPE&R	R160	3S	L	
190703	Recreational sports progr	HPE&R	R324	3S	U	
190704	Rec act & ldrshp methods	HPE&R	R272	3S	U	
190704	Dynamics of camp ldrshp	HPE&R	R275	3S	U	
190799	Research & evaluation	HPE&R	R490	3S	U	
200199	Introd psychology I	Psych	P101	3S	L	
200199	Introd psychology II	Psych	P102	3S	L	
200501	Abnormal psychology	Psych	P324	3S	U	
200508	Psy: childhood & adolesc	Psych	P316	3S	U	
200509	Psychology of personality	Psych	P319	3S	U	
200799	Social psychology	Psych	P320	3S	U	
200804	Psych measurement-schools	Educ	P407	3S	U	
210103	Personnel mgt in pub sect	SPEA	V373	3S	U	
210199	Policy in state govt	SPEA	V445	3S	U	
210304	Fndtns criminal investig	CrJus	P320	3S	U	
220101	Human origins & prehist	Anthr	A105	3S	L	
220102	Intro to cultures/Africa	Anthr	E310	3S	U	
220102	Culture and society	Anthr	E105	3S	L	
220201	Intro to microeconomics	Econ	E103	3S	L	
220201	Intro to macroeconomics	Econ	E104	3S	L	
220206	Public finance: survey	Econ	E360	3S	U	
220213	Intro to managerial econ	Bus	G300	3S	U	
220299	Intro stat theory ec/bus	Econ	E270	3S	L	
220301	Intro to human geography	Geog	G110	3S	L	
220305	Phys systems–environment	Geog	G107	3S	L	
220306	World regional geography	Geog	G120	3S	L	
220399	Environmental conservatn	Geog	G315	3S	U	
220399	Meteorology & climatology	Geog	G304	3S	U	
220409	Mod Am soc/intellect hist	Hist	A317	3S	U	
220420	History of Africa II	Hist	E432	3S	U	
220421	American colonial history	Hist	A301	3S	U	
220423	Mod East Asian civiliz	Hist	H207	3S	L	
220426	Europe in 20th century I	Hist	B361	3S	U	

NCES No.	Course Title	Dept.	Course No.	Cred.	Lev.	Specl. Feat.
220426	Europe in 20th century II	Hist	B362	3S	U	
220426	French Rev & Napoleon	Hist	B356	3S	U	
220426	Europe: Renaissance/Napol	Hist	H103	3S	L	
220426	Europe: Napoleon/present	Hist	H104	3S	L	
220427	Lat-Am culture & civiliz	Hist	H211	3S	L	
220428	Survey Indiana history	Hist	A363	3S	U	
220428	History of Indiana I	Hist	A333	2S	U	
220432	American history I	Hist	H105	3S	L	
220432	American history II	Hist	H106	3S	L	
220432	Unted States 1789-1865 II	Hist	A304	3S	U	
220433	World in 20th century I	Hist	H101	3S	L	
220450	Ancient Greek culture	Class	C101	3S	L	
220450	Roman culture	Class	C102	3S	L	
220470	Hist of Black Americans	Hist	A364	3S	U	
220472	Topic: women in Amer hist	Hist	T226	3S	L	
220499	The American West	Hist	A318	3S	U	
220499	American military history	Hist	H220	3S	L	
220499	American labor history	LabSt	L101	3S	L	
220499	Directed labor study	LabSt	L495	CV	U	
220499	Sports in history	Hist	H233	3S	U	
220507	Pol parties & int groups	PolSc	Y301	3S	U	
220509	Intro to Amer politics	PolSc	Y103	3S	L	
220510	Intro to political theory	PolSc	Y105	3S	L	
220511	Urban politics	PolSc	Y308	3S	U	
220599	Labor & political system	LabSt	L203	3S	L	
220599	Union govt & organization	LabSt	L270	3S	U	
220599	Sex discrimination & law	PolSc	Y200	3S	L	
220599	Black politics	PolSc	Y325	3S	U	
220599	Intro to world politics	Polit	Y109	3S	L	
220601	The community	Socio	S309	3S	U	
220602	Intro to criminal justice	CrJus	P100	3S	L	
220603	Population & human ecol	Socio	S305	3S	U	
220605	Sociology of the family	Socio	S316	3S	U	
220606	Soc analysis of society	Socio	S100	3S	L	
220606	Principles of sociology	Socio	S161	3S	L	
220606	Social theory	Socio	S340	3S	U	
220610	Deviant bhvr/soc control	Socio	S320	3S	U	
220610	Theor of crime & deviance	CrJus	P200	3S	L	
220612	Social change	Socio	S215	3S	L	
220612	Social organization	Socio	S210	3S	L	
220613	Social problems	Socio	R121	3S	L	
220614	Urban sociology	Socio	S361	3S	U	
220699	Society & the individual	Socio	S230	3S	L	
220699	Sociology of religion	Socio	S313	3S	U	
220699	Sociology of work	Socio	S315	3S	U	
220699	Sociology of sex roles	Socio	S338	3S	U	
220699	Sociology of law	Socio	S326	3S	U	
229900	Introduction to folklore	Folkl	F101	3S	L	AC
229900	Intro to Amer folklore	Folkl	F220	3S	L	AC
229900	Intro to philos of sci	HPSc	X303	3S	U	
229900	Scientific reasoning	HPSc	X200	3S	L	
229900	Topics: interdisciplinary	Folkl	F404	3S	U	AC

Noncredit courses

NCES No.	Course Title	Dept.	Course No.	Cred.	Lev.	Specl. Feat.
030599	Appraisal antique furn	ISA	ISA3	NC		
030599	Appraisal deprec res cont	ISA	ISA6	NC		
030599	Appraisal of oriental art	ISA	ISA12	NC		
030599	Appraisal ltd ed prints	ISA	ISA1	NC		
030599	Appraisal oriental rugs	ISA	ISA4	NC		
030599	Appraisal apprec res cont	ISA	ISA5	NC		
030599	Appraisal paintings	ISA	ISA7	NC		
030599	Appraisal antique jewelry	ISA	ISA10	NC		
040306	Securities & investing	Bus	PF1	NC		
060700	Intro computer literacy	CmpSc	Comp1	NC		CI
060800	Intro BASIC programming 1	CmpSc	Comp2	NC		CI
060800	Intro BASIC programming 2	CmpSc	Comp3	NC		CI
090308	Ther rec act bdrdn/handcp	AcDir	CP6	NC		
090399	Motivating nurs home res	AcDir	CP7	NC		
090399	Soc servs health care fac	AcDir	CP11	NC		
120305	Adv grammar & composition	LrnSk	RS3	NC		
120399	Understndg/improvg memory	LrnSk	RS4	NC		
160199	Overcoming math anxiety	MatHS	GIBM3	NC		
160399	Arithmetic for algebra I	MatHS	GIBM1	NC		
160399	Arithmetic for algebra II	MatHS	GIBM2	NC		
190311	Pressure defense basketba	H&Rec	Ath 1	NC		
190703	Plan soc rec act old adul	AcDir	CP3	NC		
199900	Intro to collectibles	H&Rec	H&R2	NC		
220502	English & government	Citz	CIT1	NC		
220502	Our Constitution & govt	Citz	CIT2	NC		

(14) **LOUISIANA STATE UNIVERSITY**

Dr. Don Hammons
Director
Office of Independent Study
Louisiana State University
Baton Rouge, Louisiana 70803
Phone: 504-388-3171
        800-225-5578 ext. 3171

Enrollment on a noncredit basis accepted in credit courses. High school students may enroll in undergraduate courses for credit. Overseas enrollment accepted. Minimum period for course completion is six weeks. Maximum period for course completion is nine months. One 3-month extension is available at end of the maximum enrollment period. Accept three lessons per week.

NCES No.	Course Title	Dept.	Course No.	Cred.	Lev.	Specl. Feat.
	High School courses					
030599	Art	Art	121	HF	H	
030599	Art	Art	122	HF	H	
040104	Bookkeeping	Bus	231	HF	H	
040104	Bookkeeping	Bus	232	HF	H	
040205	Shorthand	Bus	221	HF	H	
040207	Typewriting	Bus	211	HF	H	
040207	Typewriting	Bus	212	HF	H	
040299	Clerical practice	Bus	241	HF	H	
040299	Data processing	Bus	251	HF	H	
049900	General business	Bus	201	HF	H	
049900	General business	Bus	202	HF	H	
061101	Computer literacy	Math	171	HF	H	
081000	Drafting technology	InArt	161	HF	H	
100202	Consumer education	HomEc	153	HF	H	
100312	Nutrition education	HomEc	155	HF	H	
100699	Home and family	HomEc	151	HF	H	
120399	English I	Engl	311	HF	H	
120399	English I	Engl	312	HF	H	
120399	English II	Engl	321	HF	H	
120399	English II	Engl	322	HF	H	
120399	English III	Engl	331	HF	H	
120399	English III	Engl	332	HF	H	
120399	English IV	Engl	341	HF	H	
120399	English IV	Engl	342	HF	H	
120399	Business English	Engl	351	HF	H	
120399	Business English	Engl	352	HF	H	
121000	French I	Frnch	141	HF	H	VC
121000	French I	Frnch	142	HF	H	VC
121000	French II	Frnch	143	HF	H	VC
121000	French II	Frnch	144	HF	H	VC
121600	Latin I	Latin	191	HF	H	
121600	Latin I	Latin	192	HF	H	
121600	Latin II	Latin	193	HF	H	
121600	Latin II	Latin	194	HF	H	
122500	Spanish I	Span	145	HF	H	VC
122500	Spanish I	Span	146	HF	H	VC
122500	Spanish II	Span	147	HF	H	VC
122500	Spanish II	Span	148	HF	H	VC
150300	Biology	Bio	511	HF	H	
150300	Biology	Bio	512	HF	H	
150899	General science	Sci	501	HF	H	
150899	General science	Sci	502	HF	H	
160301	Mathematics I	Math	401	HF	H	
160301	Mathematics I	Math	402	HF	H	
160301	Mathematics II	Math	441	HF	H	
160301	Mathematics II	Math	442	HF	H	
160302	Algebra I	Math	411	HF	H	
160302	Algebra I	Math	412	HF	H	
160302	Algebra II	Math	431	HF	H	
160302	Algebra II	Math	432	HF	H	
160602	Trigonometry	Math	451	HF	H	
161201	Business math	Math	421	HF	H	
161201	Business math	Math	422	HF	H	
161202	Consumer mathematics	Math	461	HF	H	
161202	Consumer mathematics	Math	462	HF	H	
190599	Health	HlEd	131	HF	H	
190599	Health	HlEd	132	HF	H	
220100	Anthropology	Anthr	691	HF	H	
220299	Free enterprise	SoSci	661	HF	H	
220399	World geography	SoSci	601	HF	H	
220399	World geography	SoSci	602	HF	H	
220432	American history	SoSci	641	HF	H	
220432	American history	SoSci	642	HF	H	
220433	World history	SoSci	621	HF	H	
220501	American government	SoSci	631	HF	H	
220501	American government	SoSci	632	HF	H	
220611	Sociology	SoSci	651	HF	H	
220612	Sociology	SoSci	652	HF	H	
229900	Civics	SoSci	611	HF	H	
229900	Civics	SoSci	612	HF	H	
	College courses					
010199	Coop in agriculture	Agri	4020C	3S	U	
010406	Elements of dairying	DySc	1048C	3S	U	
020902	Home planning	InDes	3721C	3S	U	
030399	Music appreciation	Music	1751C	3S	L	
030399	Music appreciation	Music	1752C	3S	L	
030399	Music history	Music	4451C	2S	U	
030399	Music history	Music	4450	2S	U	
030499	Introduction to theater	Spch	1020C	3S	L	
040101	Intro financial acctg	Acctg	2001C	3S	L	
040101	Intermediate acctg pt I	Acctg	2021C	3S	L	
040101	Intermediate acctg pt II	Acctg	3021C	3S	U	
040101	Advanced accounting	Acctg	4022C	3S	U	
040101	Intermediate acctg pt III	Acctg	3023C	3S	U	
040103	Auditing	Acctg	3222C	3S	U	
040106	Cost analysis & control	Acctg	3121C	3S	U	
040111	Intro managerial acctg	Acctg	2101C	3S	L	
040111	Income-tax accounting	Acctg	3221C	3S	U	
040201	Office management	OfAdm	3400C	3S	U	
040203	Records management	BusAd	3200C	3S	U	
040205	Beginning shorthand	OfAdm	2100C	3S	L	
040207	Beginning typewriting	OfAdm	2000C	3S	L	
040207	Intermediate typing	OfAdm	2001C	3S	L	
040207	Advanced typing	OfAdm	3000C	3S	U	
040301	Basic business finance	Finan	3715C	3S	U	
040308	Money and banking	Econ	2035C	3S	L	
040399	Business law	Finan	3201C	3S	U	
040399	Commercial transactions	Finan	3203C	3S	U	
040399	Principles of real estate	Finan	3351C	3S	U	
040601	Business communication	BuCom	2071C	3S	L	
040601	Business communication	BuCom	2071C	3S	U	
040901	Mgmt prin & policies	Mgmt	3159C	3S	U	
040901	Bus policies & problems	Mgmt	3190C	3S	U	
040903	Human behavior in orgn	Mgmt	4164C	3S	U	
040999	Operations & info systems	Mgmt	3115C	3S	U	
041001	Principles of marketing	Mktg	3401C	3S	U	
041004	Retailing management	Mktg	3431C	3S	U	
041099	Consumer anal & behavior	Mktg	3411C	3S	U	
041099	Marketing research	Mktg	3413C	3S	U	
041099	Mkt comm selling & advtg	Mktg	3421C	3S	U	
041104	Management organized labr	Mgmt	3126C	3S	U	
041107	Personnel-human resources	Mgmt	4167C	3S	U	
041299	Operations & info systems	QMeth	3115C	3S	U	
049900	Intro to business	Bus	1001C	3S	L	
051103	Interpersonal communicatn	SpeCm	2010C	3S	L	
051199	Argumentation & debate	SpeCm	2063C	3S	L	
060701	COBOL programming	CmpSc	2270C	3S	L	
060701	Intro to Pascal programng	CmpSc	1248C	3S	L	
070514	School libraries	Educ	3553C	3S	U	
070514	Bks/AV mat yng ad res ctr	Educ	3100C	3S	U	
070599	Books & AV for children	Educ	3000C	3S	U	
070801	Char of excep children	Educ	3700C	3S	U	
071199	Evaluation of instruction	Educ	3200C	2S	U	
081000	Engineering graphics	Engin	1001C	2S	L	
081000	Machine drawing	Engin	2162C	2S	L	
081104	Dynamics	MecEn	3133C	3S	U	
100312	Intro to human nutrition	HomEc	1010C	3S	L	
119900	Intro to voc education	VTIE	2070C	3S	L	
120305	English grammar	Engl	2210C	3S	L	
120307	English lit to 1798	Engl	2020C	3S	L	
120307	English lit 1798-present	Engl	2022C	3S	L	
120310	English composition	Engl	1001C	3S	L	
120310	English composition	Engl	1002C	3S	L	
120310	Advanced composition	Engl	2001C	3S	L	
120310	Technical writing	Engl	3002C	3S	L	
120310	Business writing	Engl	2002C	3S	L	
120399	Intro to fiction	Engl	2025C	3S	L	
120399	Intro to drama & poetry	Engl	2027C	3S	L	
120399	Major American writers	Engl	2070C	3S	L	
121000	Elementary French	Frnch	1001C	5S	L	
121000	Intermediate French	Frnch	2051C	5S	L	
121000	Intermediate French	Frnch	2053C	3S	L	
121100	Intermediate German	Germn	2053C	3S	L	VC
121100	Reading in German lit	Germn	2055	3S	L	VC

NCES No.	Course Title	Dept.	Course No.	Cred.	Lev.	Specl. Feat.
121600	Elementary Latin	Latin	1001C	5S	L	
121600	Intermediate Latin	Latin	2051C	5S	L	
121600	Greek and Roman mythology	Latin	2090C	3S	L	
122500	Elementary Spanish	Span	1001C	5S	L	VC
122500	Intermediate Spanish	Span	2051C	5S	L	VC
122500	Intermediate Spanish	Span	2053C	3S	L	
122500	Readings in Spanish lit	Span	2055C	3S	L	
150103	Stellar astronomy	Astro	1102C	3S	L	
150199	The solar system	Astro	1101C	3S	L	
150300	Human physiology	Bio	2160C	3S	L	
150399	General biology	Bio	1001C	3S	L	
150399	General biology	Bio	1002C	3S	L	
150599	Geology-physical	Geol	1001C	3S	L	
150599	Geology-historical	Geol	1003C	3S	L	
150799	General physics	Phycs	2001C	3S	L	
150799	General physics	Phycs	2002C	3S	L	
150899	Physical science	PhySc	1001C	3S	L	
150899	Physical science	PhySc	1002C	3S	L	
160302	Algebra	Math	1021C	3S	L	
160302	Algebra and applications	Math	1015C	3S	L	
160302	Linear algebra	Math	2085C	3S	L	
160305	Introductory coll math I	Math	1009C	3S	L	
160305	Introductory coll math II	Math	1010C	3S	L	
160401	Analyt geom & calculus II	Math	1452C	5S	L	
160401	Multidimensional calculus	Math	2057C	3S	L	
160602	Plane trigonometry	Math	1022C	3S	L	
160603	Analyt geom & calculus I	Math	1450C	5S	L	
160801	Statistcl methods/models	QMeth	2000C	3S	L	
160802	Intro to business science	QMeth	2001C	3S	L	
160802	Statistical analysis	QMeth	3001C	3S	U	
160803	Foun for operations resch	QMeth	3002C	3S	U	
161103	Calculus with bus & econ	Math	1431C	3S	L	
161103	Finite math—bus & econ	Math	1435C	3S	L	
180301	Intro to philosophy	Philo	1011C	3S	L	
180502	Elementary logic	Philo	1021C	3S	L	
180502	Intro to logic theory	Philo	2010C	3S	L	
190502	Personal & comm health	HPE&R	1600C	2S	L	
190511	Occupational safety	IndEd	2051C	3S	L	
190512	Human sexuality	HPE&R	2600C	3S	L	
190599	Community safety educ	HPE&R	4602C	3S	U	
200199	Intro to psychology	Psych	2000C	3S	L	
200505	Psychology of adjustment	Psych	2004C	3S	L	
200599	Child psychology	Psych	2076C	3S	L	
200599	Adolescent psychology	Psych	2078C	3S	L	
200804	Educational psychology	Psych	2060C	3S	L	
220102	Cultural anthropology	Anthr	1003C	3S	L	
220106	Physical anthropology	Anthr	1001C	3S	L	
220201	Econ prins & problems	Econ	2010C	3S	L	
220201	Econ prins & problems	Econ	2020C	3S	L	
220201	Economic principles	Econ	2030C	3S	L	
220209	Dev of econ system in US	Econ	1010C	3S	L	
220212	Economics of consumption	Econ	3310C	3S	U	
220299	Macroecon anal & policy	Econ	2035C	3S	L	
220299	Econ of govt regulation	Econ	4440C	3S	U	
220301	Human geography	Geog	1001C	3S	L	
220301	Human geography	Geog	1003C	3S	L	
220406	History of Western civ	Hist	1001C	3S	L	
220406	History of Western civ	Hist	1003C	3S	L	
220421	Colonial Amer 1607-1763	Hist	4051C	3S	U	
220421	The American Revolution	Hist	4052C	3S	U	
220424	English history	Hist	2012C	3S	L	
220424	English history	Hist	2011C	3S	L	
220428	History of Louisiana	Hist	2071C	3S	L	
220432	American history	Hist	2055C	3S	L	
220432	American history	Hist	2057C	3S	L	
220501	American government	PolSc	2051C	3S	L	
220503	Intro to comparative pol	PolSc	2053C	3S	L	
220507	Pol parties in the US	PolSc	4031C	3S	U	
220602	Criminology	Socio	4461C	3S	U	
220605	Marriage and family relat	Socio	2505C	3S	L	
220608	Rural sociology	Socio	2351C	3S	L	
220613	Current social problems	Socio	2501C	3S	L	
220699	Introductory sociology	Socio	2001C	3S	L	

Noncredit courses

NCES No.	Course Title	Dept.	Course No.	Cred.	Lev.	Specl. Feat.
040101	Basic accounting	Acctg	42	NC	V	
040101	Basic accounting part II	Acctg	43	NC	V	
061101	Computer literacy	CmpSc	44	NC	D	
061101	BASIC programming	CmpSc	45	NC	V	
120305	Review of English grammar	Engl	55	NC	V	
120305	Engl for law enforcement	Engl	51	NC	V	
120310	English composition	Engl	0001C	NC	L	

NCES No.	Course Title	Dept.	Course No.	Cred.	Lev.	Specl. Feat.
150300	Physiology for social wk	Bio	81	NC	V	
150704	Electricity–alt current	InArt	0002	NC	V	
150704	Electricity–dir current	InArt	0001	NC	V	
160301	Refresher math	Math	0000	NC	D	
160301	Arithmetic for college	Math	0091C	NC	D	
160302	Intro to college algebra	Math	0092C	NC	D	
210302	Firefighter I	FrTrn	I	NC	V	
210302	Firefighter II	FrTrn	II	NC	V	
210302	Firefighter III	FrTrn	III	NC	V	
210302	Fire service inspector I	FrTrn	0000	NC	V	
210302	Fire service officer	FrTrn	32	NC	V	

(15) MISSISSIPPI STATE UNIVERSITY

Dr. C. K. Lee
Director, Independent Study Program by Correspondence
Mississippi State University
P.O. Drawer 5247
Mississippi State, Mississippi 39762
Phone: 601-325-3473

Enrollment on a noncredit basis accepted in credit courses. Overseas enrollment accepted. Minimum period for course completion is thirty days. Maximum period for course completion is one year.

NCES No.	Course Title	Dept.	Course No.	Cred.	Lev.	Specl. Feat.
	High School courses					
049900	Business dynamics	Bus		1U	H	
061101	Computer literacy	CmpSc		HF	H	
070515	General science	Sci		1U	H	
090100	Health education I	Sci		HF	H	
090100	Health education II	Sci		HF	H	
100699	Family livng & parenthood	HomEc		HF	H	
120307	English I	Engl		1U	H	
120307	English II	Engl		1U	H	
120307	English III	Engl		1U	H	
120307	English IV	Engl		1U	H	
121000	French III pt 1	ForLg		HF	H	
121000	French III pt 2	ForLg		HF	H	
121600	Latin I	ForLg		1U	H	
121600	Latin II	ForLg		1U	H	
122500	Spanish III	ForLg		1U	H	
122500	Spanish IV	ForLg		1U	H	
150300	Fundamentals of biology I	Sci		HF	H	
150300	Fundamentals of biology 2	Sci		HF	H	
160199	General mathematics I	Math		1U	H	
160199	General mathematics II	Math		1U	H	
160199	Senior math	Math		1U	H	
160302	Algebra I	Math		1U	H	
160302	Algebra II	Math		1U	H	
160601	Unified geometry	Math		1U	H	
160602	Trigonometry	Math		HF	H	
161202	Consumer math	Math		1U	H	
220201	Economics	SocSt		HF	H	
220399	World geography	SocSt		HF	H	
220428	Mississippi history	SocSt		HF	H	
220432	US history	SocSt		1U	H	
220433	World history	SocSt		1U	H	
220501	US government	SocSt		HF	H	
220511	MS state & local govt	SocSt		HF	H	
220599	Problems in American demo	SocSt		HF	H	
	College courses					
040101	Accounting principles I	Acctg	1413	3S	L	
040101	Accounting principles II	Acctg	1423	3S	L	
040106	Cost accounting	Acctg	2213	3S	L	
040206	Secretarial procedures	Bus	3113	3S	U	
040299	Office management	Bus	3133	3S	U	
040301	Business finance	Bus	2223	3S	U	
040308	Money and banking	Bus	2113	3S	U	
041001	Principles of marketing	Mktg	2313	3S	U	
041099	Retailing	Mktg	2223	3S	U	
060100	Basic comp concepts & app	CmpSc	1103	3S	L	
070516	Tcng math: elem & jr high	ElEd	5453	3S	U	
070520	Learning theories classrm	Psych	4133	3S	U	
070701	Basic course in counselng	Guida	4103	3S	U	
070705	Devmtl cnsIng & mntl hlth	Guida	4113	3S	U	
070800	Psy & ed of excp ch & yth	SplEd	4223	3S	U	
070899	Work/parents of excpt ch	SplEd	5113	3S	U	

NCES No.	Course Title	Dept.	Course No.	Cred.	Lev.	Specl. Feat.
070899	Tchg the disadvantaged ch	SplEd	5123	3S	U	
071199	Measurement & evaluation	Psych	4313	3S	U	
090114	Elem microbiology	Bio	1113	3S	L	
090199	Science of public health	Bio	1123	3S	L	
100399	Indiv & family nutrition	HomEc	3213	3S	U	
100799	Purch food & equip instit	HomEc	5293	3S	U	
121000	Intermediate French	Lang	1133	3S	L	
121000	Intermediate French	Lang	1143	3S	L	
122500	Intermediate Spanish	Lang	1133	3S	L	
122500	Intermediate Spanish	Lang	1143	3S	L	
150199	Descriptive astronomy	Phycs	1063	3S	L	
150899	Physical science survey	Phycs	1013	3S	L	
150899	Physical science survey	Phycs	1023	3S	L	
160202	Structure real number sys	Math	1513	3S	L	
160204	Informal geometry & meas	Math	1523	3S	L	
160302	College algebra	Math	1153	3S	L	
160401	Finite math & intro calcu	Math	1263	3S	L	
160401	Calculus I	Math	1713	3S	L	
160401	Calculus II	Math	1723	3S	L	
160602	Trigonometry	Math	1253	3S	L	
160899	Intro to business statist	Bus	1513	3S	L	
180302	Intro to ethics	Philo	1123	3S	L	
180302	Intro to Old Testament	Relig	1213	3S	L	
180302	Intro to New Testament	Relig	1223	3S	L	
180302	World religions I	Relig	2203	3S	U	
180302	World religions II	Relig	2213	3S	U	
181101	Intro to philosophy	Philo	1103	3S	L	
190199	Prin of elem health & PE	PhyEd	3123	3S	U	
190502	Community recreation	PhyEd	3362	2S	U	
190502	Community hygiene	PubHl	1003	3S	L	
190503	Consumer health	PhyEd	2163	3S	U	
190504	Communicable disease	PubHl	2003	3S	U	
190504	Foodborne-disease control	PubHl	2013	3S	U	
190504	Vectorborne-disease cntrl	PubHl	2023	3S	U	
190504	Waterborne-disease cntrl	PubHl	2033	3S	U	
190511	General safety methods	PhyEd	3433	3S	U	
190599	Health education	PhyEd	3233	3S	U	
200000	General psychology	Psych	1013	3S	L	
200504	Human growth & developmt	Psych	1053	3S	L	
200599	Psychology of adolescence	Psych	1073	3S	L	
200804	Prin of educational psych	Psych	2123	3S	U	
220201	Prin of economics I	Econ	1113	3S	L	
220201	Prin of economics II	Econ	1123	3S	L	
220428	Mississippi history	Hist	3333	3S	U	
220432	Early US history	Hist	1063	3S	L	
220432	Modern US history	Hist	1073	3S	L	
220499	Early Western world	Hist	1013	3S	L	
220499	Modern Western world	Hist	1023	3S	L	
220501	American government	Govt	1013	3S	L	
220502	Comparative government	Govt	1513	3S	L	
220505	International relations	Govt	1313	3S	L	
220605	Marriage and family	Socio	1503	3S	L	
220606	Intro to sociology	Socio	1003	3S	L	

(16) MURRAY STATE UNIVERSITY

Mr. Stanley L. Groppel
Director, Bachelor of Independent Studies Program
Center for Continuing Education, Sparks Hall
Murray State University
Murray, Kentucky 42071
Phone: 502-762-4159

External degree available through the program. Credit by examination is available. Telecourses are offered. Overseas enrollment not accepted. Minimum period for course completion is six weeks. Maximum period for course completion is one year.

NCES No.	Course Title	Dept.	Course No.	Cred.	Lev.	Specl. Feat.
	College courses					
010400	Animal science	Agri	100	3S	L	
010400	Poultry science	Agri	121	3S	L	
010400	Swine science	Agri	326	3S	U	
010600	Crop science	Agri	240	3S	L	
010900	Introduction to forestry	Agri	269	3S	L	
040101	Prin of accounting I	Acctg	200	3S	L	
040101	Prin of accounting II	Acctg	201	3S	L	
040114	Federal income tax	Acctg	302	3S	U	
040200	Prin of office administra	OfAdm	360	3S	U	

NCES No.	Course Title	Dept.	Course No.	Cred.	Lev.	Specl. Feat.
040203	Records management	OfAdm	235	3S	L	
040299	Admin supervision	OfAdm	260	3S	L	
120310	Composition I	Engl	101	3S	L	
120310	Composition II	Engl	102	3S	L	
120310	Tech writing/ind technol	Engl	225	3S	L	
130700	Business law I	LegSt	240	3S	L	
130700	Business law II	LegSt	540	3S	U	
160302	College algebra	Math	140	4S	L	
160302	Trigonometry	Math	145	3S	L	
180500	Logic	Philo	103	3S	L	
190100	Intro to phys education	PhyEd	175	3S	L	
200100	General psychology	Psych	180	3S	L	
210500	Personal health	Hlth	191	2S	L	
210500	First aid and safety	Hlth	195	2S	L	
210500	School health	Hlth	598	3S	U	
210500	Intro to recreation	Rec	101	3S	L	
220400	Civil War and Reconstruc	Hist	534	3S	U	
220400	Modern Europe	Hist	201	3S	L	
220400	Amer experience to 1865	Hist	221	3S	L	
220400	Amer experience snc 1865	Hist	222	3S	L	
220426	Europe since 1914	Hist	503	3S	U	
220500	American national govt	Polit	140	3S	L	
220500	State and local govt	Polit	240	3S	L	
220600	Introductory sociology	Socio	133	3S	L	
220600	Social problems	Socio	231	3S	L	
220600	The family	Socio	331	3S	L	

(17) NEW YORK INSTITUTE OF TECHNOLOGY

Dr. Andrew Sass
Director
American Open University
New York Institute of Technology, Building #66
211 Carlton Avenue
Central Islip, New York 11722
Phone: 516-348-3300
        800-222-NYIT (out of state)

Credit by examination is available. Telecourses are offered. Enrollment on a noncredit basis accepted in credit courses. High school students may enroll in undergraduate courses for credit. Overseas enrollment accepted. Military personnel may enroll through the DANTES program. Institution offers special arrangements to take courses not listed in this Catalog. Maximum period for course completion is six months. Three external degrees are offered. The B.S. in general studies, the B.S. in business administration, and the B.S. in behavioral sciences entail no on-campus requirements, and students may transfer in up to 90 credits. One hundred thirty courses are offered. Study by correspondence or computer conferencing. Call or write for catalog.

NCES No.	Course Title	Dept.	Course No.	Cred.	Lev.	Specl. Feat.
	College courses					
040108	Accounting I	Acctg	3511	3S	U	
040108	Accounting II	Acctg	3521	3S	U	
040300	Commercial banking	Econ	2074	3S	U	
040301	Corporate finance	Finan	3630	3S	U	
040306	Principles of investments	Finan	3640	3S	U	
040308	Money and banking	Econ	2072	3S	U	
040399	Financial management	Finan	3631	3S	U	
040400	Intro to EDP in business	Bus	3801	3S	U	
040400	Intro to mgt info systems	Bus	3811	3S	U	
040800	Intro to internatl busns	IntBu	3907	3S	U	
040900	Small business management	BuMgt	3905	3S	U	
040900	Sales management	Mgmt	3401	3S	U	
040999	Retailing management	Mgmt	3403	3S	U	
040999	Management of promotion	Mgmt	3405	3S	U	
041000	New product management	Bus	3904	3S	U	
041001	Introduction to marketing	Mktg	3400	3S	U	
041099	Marketing research	Mktg	3406	3S	U	
041100	Businss organzatn & admin	Bus	3900	3S	U	
041100	Personnel administration	PAIR	3901	3S	U	
041104	Colectv bargn & labor rel	Bus	3902	3S	U	
041200	Statistics	Stat	3802	3S	U	
041202	Quant appli/mangerl decis	Bus	3803	3S	U	
060100	Computer concepts	CmpSc	5641	3S	U	
060500	Operations management	IndEn	7011	3S	U	
069900	Intro to comp confrncing	CmpSc	1008	3S	U	
080900	Communication circuits	Tech	5316	4S	U	

NCES No.	Course Title	Dept.	Course No.	Cred.	Lev.	Specl. Feat.
120200	The art of drama	Lit	1053	3S	U	
120200	The art of fiction	Lit	1054	3S	U	
120200	Art of prose:sci/tech lit	Lit	1056	3S	U	
120300	Basic writing and reading	Engl	1007	5S	U	
120300	College composition I	Engl	1010	3S	U	
120300	College composition II	Engl	1020	3S	U	
120300	Basic speech communicatn	Spch	1023	3S	U	
120300	Business writing	BusEn	1042	3S	U	
120300	Technical writing	Writ	1043	3S	U	
120300	Report writing	Writ	1044	3S	U	
120300	Adv sci & tech writing	Writ	1048	3S	U	
130701	Business law I	BuLaw	3529	3S	U	
130702	Business law II	BuLaw	3532	3S	U	
130703	Business law III	BuLaw	3533	3S	U	
130801	Politics of tech assistnc	SoSci	2732	3S	U	
130803	Amer soc & judicial behvr	SoSci	2740	3S	U	
131000	The law of labor relatns	LabSt	3908	3S	U	
150400	Engineering chemistry I	Chem	4500	4S	U	
150700	Introductory physics	Phycs	4003	3S	U	
150800	Surv of the physical scis	PhySc	4005	3S	U	
150900	Environmental sciences	EnvSc	9500	3S	U	
159900	Intro to life & hlth scis	LfSci	4420	3S	U	
160200	Finite mathematics	Math	3010	3S	U	
160300	College algebra and trig	Algbr	3011	3S	U	
160300	Technical mathematics I	Math	3310	4S	U	
160700	Intro concepts of math	Math	3015	3S	U	
160700	Intro to probability	Math	3017	3S	U	
160900	Quantitative methods	QMeth	3019	3S	U	
180300	Ethics and social philos	Philo	1530	3S	U	
180499	Philos & hist of science	Philo	1541	3S	U	
189900	Problems of philosophy	Philo	1510	3S	U	
200100	Introductory psychology	Psych	2401	3S	U	
200104	Learning theory	Psych	2413	3S	U	
200400	Measurement concepts	Psych	2421	3S	U	
200500	Child psychology	ChPsy	2439	3S	U	
200500	Adolescent psychology	Psych	2441	3S	U	
200500	Psych of adlthood & aging	Psych	2442	3S	U	
200501	Abnormal psychology	Psych	2465	3S	U	
200509	Theories of personality	PsyPe	2445	3S	U	
200700	Social stratification	Psych	2438	3S	U	
200700	Occupational psychology	Psych	2452	3S	U	
200700	The institutnl community	Psych	2453	3S	U	
200700	Job satisfac & job stress	Psych	2456	3S	U	
200700	Commu & interviewing tech	Psych	2460	3S	U	
200700	Intro to effective commun	Psych	2461	3S	U	
200702	Grp dynmcs/intrprsnl proc	Psych	2466	3S	U	
200799	Social psychology	Psych	2415	3S	U	
200800	Rehabilitation psychology	Rehab	2496	3S	U	
200800	Introduction to counselng	Psych	2497	3S	U	
200801	Community mental health	Psych	2454	3S	U	
200801	Community psychology	Psych	2495	3S	U	
200804	Educational psychology	EdPsy	2423	3S	U	
200900	Behavioral sci in mktg	Psych	2451	3S	U	
200900	Psych of salesmanship	Psych	2468	3S	U	
200900	Intro resrch meth for BES	Psych	2470	3S	U	
200904	Organizational behavior	Psych	2458	3S	U	
210100	Political sociology	PolSc	2478	3S	U	
210100	Anthropology	Anthr	2405	3S	U	
220200	Principles of economics I	Econ	2010	3S	U	
220200	Basic economics	Econ	2011	3S	U	
220200	Principles of economcs II	Econ	2020	3S	U	
220200	Bus cycles & forecasting	Econ	2075	3S	U	
220204	Physiolgcl basis of behvr	Psych	2421	3S	U	
220204	Monetary theory & policy	Econ	2073	3S	U	
220432	American history I	AmHis	2500	3S	U	
220432	American history II	AmHis	2510	3S	U	
220433	World history I	WHS	2521	3S	U	
220433	World history II	WHS	2531	3S	U	
220500	Government and business	Govt	2708	3S	U	
220501	American govt & politics	AmGvt	2700	3S	U	
220503	Comparative government	Govt	2710	3S	U	
220511	Govt & metropolitan probs	Govt	2705	3S	U	
220600	Legl concpts & admin just	SoSci	2730	3S	U	
220600	Intro to sociologcl thery	SoPsy	2448	3S	U	
220600	Medical sociology	Socio	2476	3S	U	
220600	Occupations	Psych	2493	3S	U	
220600	Intro to social work	SocWk	2494	3S	U	
220600	Social work II	SocWk	2498	3S	U	
220602	Law of evidence	CrJus	2300	3S	U	
220602	Criminal law & proceedngs	CrJus	2301	3S	U	
220602	Police administration	PolAd	2305	3S	U	
220602	Patrol function	Polic	2310	3S	U	

NCES No.	Course Title	Dept.	Course No.	Cred.	Lev.	Specl. Feat.
220602	Crim invest & forensc sci	CrJus	2315	3S	U	
220602	Police & communty relatns	CrJus	2320	3S	U	
220602	Crsis intrvn pub sfty per	CrJus	2325	3S	U	
220602	Crm prevntn: systm apprch	CrJus	2340	3S	U	
220602	Physical security strateg	CrJus	2341	3S	U	
220602	Security & protection mgt	CrJus	2342	3S	U	
220602	Probation and parole	CrJus	2350	3S	U	
220602	Correction administration	CrJus	2355	3S	U	
220602	Principles of correction	CrJus	2360	3S	U	
220602	Contemporary police servc	CrJus	2393	3S	U	
220602	The American court system	CrJus	2397	3S	U	
220602	Contemporary corrections	CrJus	2398	3S	U	
220602	Prvt sec: concpts & strat	CrJus	2399	3S	U	
220602	Criminology	Crim	2477	3S	U	
220603	Environmental psychology	Psych	2482	3S	U	
220604	Juvenile delinquency	Psych	2473	3S	U	
220605	Marriage and the family	Psych	2425	3S	U	
220606	Introduction to sociology	Socio	2411	3S	U	
220609	Quant meth for behvrl sci	Psych	2428	3S	U	
220611	Social policy	Socio	2479	3S	U	
220613	Social problems	Psych	2475	3S	U	
220614	American urban minorities	Psych	2435	3S	U	
220614	Urban society	Psych	2455	3S	U	

(18) **NORTH DAKOTA DIVISION OF INDEPENDENT STUDY**

Robert R. Stone Jr.
Director
North Dakota Division of Independent Study
Box 5036
State University Station
Fargo, North Dakota 58105
Phone: 701-237-7182

Credit by examination is available. Enrollment on a noncredit basis accepted in credit courses. Overseas enrollment accepted. Maximum period for course completion is one year. Students can earn a high school diploma through the Division. Spanish is available with a video series, which can also be used with the computer-assisted version of the Spanish courses. The Division's program is accredited through the North Dakota Department of Public Instruction.

NCES No.	Course Title	Dept.	Course No.	Cred.	Lev.	Specl. Feat.
High School courses						
010107	Farm management	Agri		HF	H	
010399	Farm power and machinery	Agri		HF	H	
010406	Livestock production	Agri		HF	H	
010407	Feeding farm animals	Agri		HF	H	
010703	Conservatn of nat resrces	Sci		HF	H	
011202	Wildlife management	Sci		HF	H	
019900	General agriculture	Agri		HF	H	
020103	Interior design	Art		HF	H	
030302	Beginning piano	Music		HF	H	
030302	Fundamentals of music	Music		HF	H	
030399	Music appreciation	Music		HF	H	AC
030502	Basic drawing	Art		HF	H	
030502	Beginning painting	Art		HF	H	
030503	Knowing about art	Art		HF	H	
030603	Art craft	Art		HF	H	
030603	Calligraphy	Art		HF	H	
040101	Accounting I	Bus		HF	H	CI
040101	Accounting II	Bus		HF	H	CI
040205	Shorthand I	Bus		HF	H	AC
040205	Shorthand II	Bus		HF	H	AC
040207	Keyboarding/typewriting I	Bus		HF	H	CI
040207	Keyboarding/typewritng II	Bus		HF	H	CI
040299	Office procedures	Bus		HF	H	
049900	General business I	Bus		HF	H	
049900	General business II	Bus		HF	H	
050600	Journalism	Engl		HF	H	
061103	Intro to computers I	CmpSc		HF	H	CI
061103	Intro to computers II	CmpSc		HF	H	CI
081000	Mechanical drawing	Mech		HF	H	
100105	Fashion design	Art		HF	H	
100202	Dollars and sense	HomEc		HF	H	
100314	Creative cooking	HomEc		HF	H	
100400	Housng & home furnishings	HomEc		HF	H	
100601	Child development	HomEc		HF	H	

NCES No.	Course Title	Dept.	Course No.	Cred.	Lev.	Specl. Feat.
100602	Family relations	HomEc		HF	H	
100604	Personal management	HomEc		HF	H	
109900	Etiquette	HomEc		HF	H	
110104	Basic electricity	Mech		HF	H	
110104	Home wiring	Mech		HF	H	
110119	Arc welding	Mech		HF	H	
110119	Welding processes	Mech		HF	H	
110412	Small engines	Mech		HF	H	
110413	Automotive chassis	Mech		HF	H	
110413	Automotive engines	Mech		HF	H	
110504	Photography	Photo		HF	H	
110599	Lettering & poster design	Art		HF	H	
110601	Aviation	Mech		HF	H	
120305	Developmental English	Engl		HF	H	
120305	Freshman language	Engl		HF	H	
120305	Sophomore language	Engl		HF	H	
120305	Junior language	Engl		HF	H	
120305	Senior language	Engl		HF	H	
120307	Freshman literature	Engl		HF	H	
120307	Sophomore literature	Engl		HF	H	
120307	American literature	Engl		HF	H	
120307	English literature	Engl		HF	H	
120307	The novel	Engl		HF	H	
120307	World literature	Engl		HF	H	
120310	Creative writing	Engl		HF	H	
120399	Business English	Engl		HF	H	
121000	First year French I	Frnch		HF	H	VC
121000	First year French II	Frnch		HF	H	VC
121000	Second year French I	Frnch		HF	H	AC
121000	Second year French II	Frnch		HF	H	AC
121100	First year German I	Germn		HF	H	AC
121100	First year German II	Germn		HF	H	AC
121100	Second year German I	Germn		HF	H	AC
121100	Second year German II	Germn		HF	H	AC
121600	First year Latin I	Latin		HF	H	AC
121600	First year Latin II	Latin		HF	H	
121600	Second year Latin I	Latin		HF	H	
121600	Second year Latin II	Latin		HF	H	
121800	First year Norwegian I	Norw		HF	H	AC
121800	First year Norwegian II	Norw		HF	H	AC
122000	First year Russian I	Rus		HF	H	VC
122000	First year Russian II	Rus		HF	H	VC
122500	Second year Spanish II	Span		HF	H	CI
122500	First year Spanish I	Span		HF	H	CI
122500	First year Spanish II	Span		HF	H	CI
122500	Second year Spanish I	Span		HF	H	CI
130799	Business law	Bus		HF	H	
150300	Biology I	Sci		HF	H	
150300	Biology II	Sci		HF	H	
150327	Entomology	Sci		HF	H	
150331	Ornithology	Sci		HF	H	
150401	Chemistry I	Sci		HF	H	LK
150401	Chemistry II	Sci		HF	H	LK
150700	Physics I	Sci		HF	H	
150700	Physics II	Sci		HF	H	
150800	Physical science I	Sci		HF	H	
150800	Physical science II	Sci		HF	H	
160301	General math I	Math		HF	H	
160301	General math II	Math		HF	H	
160302	Algebra I	Math		HF	H	
160302	Algebra II	Math		HF	H	
160302	Advanced algebra I	Math		HF	H	
160302	Advanced algebra II	Math		HF	H	
160401	Precalculus I	Math		HF	H	
160401	Precalculus II	Math		HF	H	
160601	Geometry I	Math		HF	H	
160601	Geometry II	Math		HF	H	
160602	Trigonometry	Math		HF	H	
161201	Business math	Bus		HF	H	
161202	Consumer math I	Math		HF	H	
161202	Consumer math II	Math		HF	H	
180902	Old Testament	Relig		HF	H	
180902	New Testament	Relig		HF	H	
190100	First aid and nutrition	PhyEd		HF	H	
190312	Individual & team sports	PhyEd		HF	H	
190501	Alcohol, tobacco, drugs	PhyEd		HF	H	
190506	Everyday nursing	HomEc		HF	H	
190509	Modern health	PhyEd		HF	H	
200100	Psychology	SocSt		HF	H	VC
209900	Project self discovery	SocSt		HF	H	
220201	Economics	SocSt		HF	H	
220300	World geography I	SocSt		HF	H	

NCES No.	Course Title	Dept.	Course No.	Cred.	Lev.	Specl. Feat.
220300	World geography II	SocSt		HF	H	
220428	Local history	SocSt		HF	H	VC
220428	North Dakota history	SocSt		HF	H	VC
220432	US history I	SocSt		HF	H	
220432	US history II	SocSt		HF	H	
220433	World history I	SocSt		HF	H	
220433	World history II	SocSt		HF	H	
220470	Minorities in America	SocSt		HF	H	
220501	American government	SocSt		HF	H	
220501	Problems of democracy I	SocSt		HF	H	
220501	Problems of democracy II	SocSt		HF	H	
220503	Comparative government	SocSt		HF	H	
220505	International relations	SocSt		HF	H	
220511	North Dakota government	SocSt		HF	H	
220600	Sociology	SocSt		HF	H	
	Noncredit courses					
190699	Driver education	DrvEd		NC	H	

⑲ OHIO UNIVERSITY

Dr. Richard W. Moffitt
Director of Independent Study
302 Tupper Hall
Ohio University
Athens, Ohio 45701-2979
Phone: 614-593-2910
    800-444-2910

Credit by examination is available. Enrollment on a noncredit basis accepted in credit courses. High school students may enroll in undergraduate courses for credit. Overseas enrollment accepted. Military personnel may enroll through the DANTES program. Institution offers special arrangements to take courses not listed in this Catalog. Maximum period for course completion is one year. Students may enroll in individual courses or complete selected two- or four-year degrees through the Independent Study External Student Program.

NCES No.	Course Title	Dept.	Course No.	Cred.	Lev.	Specl. Feat.
	College courses					
030302	Jazz history	Music	428	3Q	U	AC
030502	History of art	ArHis	211	4Q	L	
040101	Financial accounting	Acctg	201	4Q	L	
040101	Financial acctg procedure	Acctg	103	3Q	L	
040101	Financial acctg procedure	Acctg	104	3Q	L	
040111	Managerial accounting	Acctg	202	4Q	L	
040301	Managerial finance	Finan	325	4Q	U	
040502	Small-business administra	BusAd	445	4Q	U	
040601	Business communications	Mgmt	325J	4Q	U	
040604	Business report writing	BMT	260	4Q	L	
040902	Management	Mgmt	300	4Q	U	
040902	Managing finance in bus	BMT	210	4Q	L	
040903	Introd to management	Mgmt	200	4Q	L	
040903	Organizational behavior	Mgmt	340	4Q	U	
040999	Production/ops management	POM	310	4Q	U	
041004	Marketing principles	Mktg	301	4Q	U	
041099	Consumer surv in mktplace	Mktg	101	4Q	L	
041100	Human resource management	HRM	420	4Q	U	
041106	Elements of supervision	BMT	150	3Q	L	
041108	Occup safety and health	SST	120	3Q	L	
049900	Bus and its environment	BusAd	101	4Q	L	
051103	Fund of human communicatn	InCom	101	3Q	L	AC
051108	Intro to communica theory	InCom	234	5Q	L	
051202	Deaf language & culture	HSTec	290C	3Q	L	VC
051300	Intro to telecommunicatns	Tlcom	106	4Q	L	
059900	Intro to mass communicatn	Journ	105	4Q	L	
060503	Info and data systems sec	SST	230	3Q	L	
070509	Teaching of health	HlSci	379	5Q	U	
070512	Children's literature	Educ	321L	4Q	U	
070516	Elem topics in math	Math	121	3Q	L	
070516	Elem topics in math	Math	120	4Q	L	
070703	Career & life planning	EdGS	201	3Q	L	VC
070799	Life & career exper analy	EdGS	102	4Q	L	
079900	Effective study skills	UColl	110	2Q	L	
080102	Priv pilot ground instruc	Aviat	110	4Q	L	
080102	Comm pilot ground instruc	Aviat	310	4Q	U	
080102	Instrument ground instruc	Aviat	350	4Q	U	

NCES No.	Course Title	Dept.	Course No.	Cred.	Lev.	Specl. Feat.
090704	Bio and the future of man	Zoolg	390H	5Q	U	
090705	Occup safety and health	SST	120	3Q	L	
090904	Law of health care	BuLaw	360	4Q	U	
100202	Family consumer economics	HomEc	390	3Q	U	
100299	Consumer surv in mktplace	Mktg	101	4Q	L	
100313	Intro to nutrition	HomEc	128	4Q	L	
120201	Hum: Great Bks: ancient	Hum	107	4Q	L	
120201	Hum: Great Bks: med & ren	Hum	108	4Q	L	
120201	Hum: Great Bks: modern	Hum	109	4Q	L	
120201	Intro to mod intl lit III	Engl	206	5Q	L	
120201	Spanish lit in English	Span	336A	4Q	U	
120201	Spanish lit in English	Span	336B	4Q	U	
120202	Interpretation of fiction	Engl	201	4Q	L	
120202	Interpretation of poetry	Engl	202	4Q	L	
120202	Interpretation of drama	Engl	203	4Q	L	
120202	Shakespeare—histories	Engl	301	5Q	U	
120202	Shakespeare—comedies	Engl	302	5Q	U	
120202	Shakespeare—tragedies	Engl	303	5Q	U	
120202	Med and Ren English lit	Engl	312	5Q	U	
120202	Res and neoclass Engl lit	Engl	313	5Q	U	
120202	Am lit to the Civil War	Engl	321	5Q	U	
120202	Am lit since the Civil Wr	Engl	322	5Q	U	
120202	20th-cent Brit and Am lit	Engl	331	5Q	U	
120202	Romantic & Victorian lit	Engl	314	5Q	U	
120202	Intro to literature	Engl	200	4Q	L	
120307	Women & men in literature	Engl	153A	5Q	L	
120308	Speed readg & comprehensn	UColl	112	2Q	L	
120310	Fundamental usage skills	Engl	150	4Q	L	
120310	Frsh comp:writing/reading	Engl	152	5Q	L	
120310	Advanced composition	Engl	308J	4Q	U	
120310	Creative writing–poetry	Engl	309A	5Q	U	
120310	Creative writing–fiction	Engl	309B	4Q	U	
120310	Fr comp: writng & rhetric	Engl	151	5Q	L	
121200	Beginning Greek	Greek	111	4Q	L	
121200	Beginning Greek	Greek	112	4Q	L	
121200	Beginning Greek	Greek	113	4Q	L	
121600	Beginning Latin	Latin	111	4Q	L	
121600	Beginning Latin	Latin	112	4Q	L	
130299	Law of commercial transac	BuLaw	357	4Q	U	
130399	Constit, crim & civil law	LET	120	3Q	L	
130402	Criminal investigation	LET	260	3Q	L	
130700	Law of mgmt process	BuLaw	356	4Q	U	
130799	Law and society	BuLaw	255	4Q	L	
130902	Law of prop and real est	BuLaw	442	4Q	U	
131004	Occup safety and health	SST	120	3Q	L	
131004	Fire safety and fire code	SST	201	3Q	L	
140899	Circulation & pub comm	LMT	102	4Q	L	
150100	Survey of astronomy	PhySc	100	4Q	L	
150316	Principles of biology	Botny	101	4Q	L	
150316	Plant biology	Botny	102	5Q	L	
150323	Principles of biology	Zoolg	101	5Q	L	SL
150323	Introduction to zoology	Zoolg	150	6Q	L	SL
150399	Bioethic prob in biol/med	Zoolg	384	5Q	U	
150399	Biol and future of man	Zoolg	390H	5Q	U	
150399	Human biology	Zoolg	103	5Q	L	
150399	Psychopharmacology	Zoolg	490	5Q	U	
150401	Principles of chem I	Chem	121	3Q	L	
150401	Principles of chem II	Chem	122	3Q	L	
150408	Organic chemistry	Chem	301	3Q	U	
150408	Organic chemistry	Chem	302	3Q	U	
150799	Introduction to physics	Phycs	201	3Q	L	
150799	Introduction to physics	Phycs	202	3Q	L	
150799	Introduction to physics	Phycs	203	3Q	L	
150800	Physical world	PhySc	101	4Q	L	
150899	Physical world	PhySc	121	3Q	L	
150899	Color, light, and sound	PhySc	105	4Q	L	
160300	Basic mathematics	Math	101	4Q	L	
160302	Algebra	Math	113	5Q	L	
160303	Elem topics in math	Math	120	4Q	L	
160303	Elem topics in math	Math	121	3Q	L	
160306	Elem linear algebra	Math	211	4Q	L	
160401	Intro to calculus	Math	163A	4Q	L	
160401	Analytic geom and calc	Math	263A	4Q	L	
160401	Analytic geom and calc	Math	263B	4Q	L	
160401	Intro to calculus	Math	163B	3Q	L	
160499	Intro to math (precalc)	Math	115	5Q	L	
160600	Foundations of geometry	Math	330AB	6Q	U	
160603	Plane analytic geometry	Math	130	4Q	L	
160603	Analytic geom and calc	Math	263A	4Q	L	
160603	Analytic geom and calc	Math	263B	4Q	L	
160603	Analytic geom and calc	Math	263C	4Q	L	
160603	Analytic geom and calc	Math	263D	4Q	L	
160699	Elementary applied math	Math	118	4Q	L	
160701	Finite mathematics	Math	250B	4Q	L	
161101	Intro to bus statistics	QBA	201	4Q	L	
161101	Mathematics in business	BMT	120	4Q	L	
180101	Philosophy of art	Philo	232	3Q	L	
180302	Introduction to ethics	Philo	130	4Q	L	
180303	Bioethic prob in bio/med	Zoolg	384	5Q	U	
180401	Hist of West phil: ancien	Philo	310	5Q	U	
180605	Philosophy of culture	Philo	350	5Q	U	
180609	Philosophy of religion	Philo	260	4Q	L	
180800	Fundamentals of philo	Philo	101	5Q	L	
180800	Introduction to philo	Philo	301	3Q	U	
180904	Islam	Philo	372	4Q	U	VC
190104	Hist and prin of phys ed	H&SS	404	4Q	U	SL
190106	Org and adm of phys ed	H&SS	406	4Q	U	
190200	Kinesiology	H&SS	302	4Q	U	
190200	Kinesiology	Zoolg	352	4Q	U	
190502	Personal and comm health	Hlth	202	4Q	L	
200100	General psychology	Psych	101	5Q	L	
200300	Environmental psychology	Psych	335	5Q	U	
200501	Abnormal psychology	Psych	332	4Q	U	
200508	Psych of adulthood/aging	Psych	374	4Q	U	
200799	Social psych of justice	Psych	337	4Q	U	
200804	Educational psychology	Psych	275	4Q	U	
210302	Fire safety & fire codes	SST	201	3Q	L	
210303	Occup safety and health	SST	120	3Q	L	
210304	Introd to law enforc tech	LET	100	3Q	L	
210304	Const, crim and civil law	LET	120	3Q	L	
210304	Interview & report writg	LET	130	3Q	L	
210304	Criminal investigation	LET	260	3Q	L	
210305	Physical security systems	SST	110	3Q	L	
210305	Occup safety and health	SST	120	3Q	L	
210305	Loss prev in mod retail	SST	210	3Q	L	
210305	Anal of sec needs–survey	SST	220	3Q	L	
210305	Inf and data systems sec	SST	230	3Q	L	
210305	Security administration	SST	240	3Q	L	
210305	Current prob in security	SST	250	3Q	L	
210305	Spec area stud: terrorism	SST	290A	3Q	L	
210305	Spec area stud: law/secur	SST	290B	3Q	L	
210305	Current prob in security	SST	250	3Q	L	
210305	Intro to protective servs	SST	101	3Q	L	
210305	Analytic accounting	SST	260	3Q	L	
210305	Security administration	SST	240	3Q	L	
220201	Prin of macroeconomics	Econ	104	4Q	L	
220201	Prin of microeconomics	Econ	103	4Q	L	
220205	Macroeconomics	Econ	304	4Q	U	
220211	Labor economics	Econ	320	4Q	U	
220213	Microeconomics	Econ	303	4Q	U	
220214	International trade	Econ	340	4Q	U	
220301	Elements of cultural geog	Geog	121	4Q	L	
220305	Elements of physical geog	Geog	101	5Q	L	
220408	Early Christianity	Hist	354	4Q	U	
220421	American hist to 1828	Hist	211	4Q	L	AC
220426	Western civ: Ren to 1648	Hist	101	4Q	L	
220426	Western civ: 1848 to pres	Hist	103	4Q	L	
220426	Western civ: 1648-1848	Hist	102	4Q	L	
220428	Ohio history to 1851	Hist	317A	4Q	U	
220428	Ohio history since 1851	Hist	317B	4Q	U	
220432	Hist of US 1828-1900	Hist	212	4Q	L	AC
220432	Hist of US since 1900	Hist	213	4Q	L	AC
220453	Western civ: 1848-present	Hist	103	4Q	U	
220472	Women in American history	Hist	314	4Q	U	
220511	State politics	PolSc	304	5Q	U	
220602	Criminology	Socio	362	4Q	U	
220606	Intro to sociology	Socio	101	5Q	L	
220609	Elem research techniques	Socio	351	4Q	U	
229900	Intro to women's studies	WomSt	100	4Q	L	

(20) **OKLAHOMA STATE UNIVERSITY**

Dr. Charles E. Feasley
Director of Independent and Correspondence Study Department
001 Classroom Building
Oklahoma State University
Stillwater, Oklahoma 74078
Phone: 405-744-6390

Telecourses are offered. Enrollment on a noncredit basis accepted in credit courses. High school students may enroll in undergraduate courses for credit. Overseas enrollment accepted. Military personnel may enroll through the DANTES program. Minimum period for course completion is thirty days. Maximum period for course completion is one year.

NCES No.	Course Title	Dept.	Course No.	Cred.	Lev.	Specl. Feat.
High School courses						
040101	Accounting IA	Acctg	IA	HF	H	
040101	Accounting IB	Acctg	IB	HF	H	
040601	Business English	BusHS	I	HF	H	
070602	Salesmanship IA	BusHS	IA	HF	H	
070602	Salesmanship IB	BusHS	IB	HF	H	
120307	Mystery fiction	EngHS		HF	H	AC
120307	The short story	EngHS		HF	H	
120307	Science fiction	EngHS		HF	H	
120308	English IA	EngLL	1A	HF	H	
120308	English IB	EngLL	1B	HF	H	
120308	English IIA	EngLL	2A	HF	H	
120308	English IIB	EngLL	2B	HF	H	
120308	English IIIA	EngLL	3A	HF	H	
120308	English IIIB	EngLL	3B	HF	H	
120308	English IVA	EngLL	4A	HF	H	
120308	English IVB	EngLL	4B	HF	H	
121000	French IA	LanHS	1A	HF	H	AC
121000	French IB	LanHS	1B	HF	H	AC
150300	Biology IA	Bio	1A	HF	H	
150300	Biology IB	Bio	1B	HF	H	
160100	Business math IA	MatHS	1A	HF	H	
160100	Business math IB	MatHS	1B	HF	H	
160302	Algebra IA	Algbr	1AA	HF	H	
160302	Algebra IB	Algbr	1B	HF	H	
160302	Algebra IIA	Algbr	2A	HF	H	
160302	Algebra IIB	Algbr	2B	HF	H	
160601	Plane geometry IA	Geom	1A	HF	H	
160601	Plane geometry IB	Geom	1B	HF	H	
160602	Trigonometry	Trig		HF	H	
180302	Technology & change	Philo	I	HF	H	
200505	Self discovery	PCG		HF	H	
220208	Consumer economics IA	SocSt	IA	HF	H	
220208	Consumer economics IB	SocSt	IB	HF	H	
220399	Geography IA	Geog	1A	HF	H	
220399	Geography IB	Geog	1B	HF	H	
220428	Oklahoma history	Hist		HF	H	
220432	American history IA	Hist	1BA	HF	H	
220432	American history IB	Hist	1BA	HF	H	
220433	World history IA	Hist	IA	HF	H	
College courses						
010406	Ecology of agri animals	AnSci	3903	3S	U	
010407	Livestock feeding	AnSci	2123	3S	L	
010500	Principles of horticultur	Hort	1013	3S	L	
010601	Problems in agronomy	Agron	4470	3S	U	
010701	Fundaments of soil scienc	Agron	2124	4S	L	
030300	Music appreciation	Music	2580C	3S	L	AC
030402	Intro theater in Wstn civ	ThArt	2413	3S	L	
030402	Theater history I	ThArt	4453	3S	L	
030402	Theater history II	ThArt	4463	3S	L	
040101	Principles of accounting	Acctg	2103	3S	L	
040106	Principles of accounting	Acctg	2203	3S	L	
040601	Written communication	Bus	3113	3S	U	
040604	Int tech & report writing	Engl	3323	3S	U	
040604	Intro to tech writing	Engl	2333	3S	L	
040904	Intro to management	Mgmt	3013	3S	U	
041001	Marketing	Mktg	3213	3S	U	
041003	Sales management	Mktg	3513	3S	U	
041004	Small-business management	Mktg	4113	3S	U	
041203	Production/operation mgmt	Mgmt	3223	3S	U	
050304	Study of selct Amer films	Engl	3200	3S	U	
050605	Feature writing/news/mag	Journ	4433	3S	U	
060700	Computer programming	CmpSc	2113	3S		CI
060700	Intro BASIC computer prog	CmpSc	2510B	2S	L	CI
060802	Programming in FORTRAN	CmpSc	2113	3S	L	
070100	School in American soc	Culns	2112	3S	L	
070102	Philosophy of education	Educ	3713	3S	U	
070199	History of education	Educ	4123	3S	U	
070401	Human learng in ed psych	Educ	4223	3S	U	
070403	Teaching discipline	Educ	5720	1S	U	
070404	Evaluation: elemen school	Educ	4052	2S	U	
070501	Intl prog/agric educ	AgEd	4713	3S	U	
070511	Trade & industrial educ	IVE	3203	3S	U	
070516	Math for teachers	Math	2413	3S	L	
070516	Structure concepts/teach	Math	2513	3S	L	
070610	Young adult literature	LibSc	4313	3S	U	
070610	Children's literature	LibSc	4023	3S	U	
070702	Effective study skills	Guida	2510A	1S	L	
070811	Spch-lang path for tchrs	SplEd	3213	3S	U	
071203	Educational media	Educ	3122		U	
080603	Thermodynamics	ChemE	2213	3S	L	
080901	Digital electronics	ElecE	2050A	3S	L	
080901	Linear integrated circuit	ElecE	2050D	3S	L	
080903	Elements of elec/electron	ElecE	1103	3S	L	
080904	Fiber optics	ElecE	4050A	3S	U	
080906	Electronic instrum/measur	GnTec	2050C	3S	L	
081000	Technical drawing	EngGr	1153	3S	L	
082303	Radiological safety	NucEg	3233	3S	U	
089900	Elementary dynamics	EngAS	2122	2S	L	
090121	Radiation biology	NucEg	2050B	3S	L	
090504	First aid	HlSci	2602	2S	U	
090901	Personal & comm hlth sci	HlSci	2603	3S	U	
100102	Profitable merch anal	ClTex	4553	3S	U	
100304	Intro to nutrition	HomEc	1113	3S	L	
100601	Child & family developmnt	HomEc	2113	3S	L	
120201	The short story	Lit	3333	3S	U	
120201	Shakespeare	Lit	4723	3S	U	
120201	Period study Am colonial	Engl	2773	3S	L	
120201	Readings in the novel	Lit	4853	3S	U	
120202	Introduction to new media	Lit	3200	3S	U	
120204	Intro to lit & critic wrt	EngLL	2413	3S	L	
120305	English grammar	Engl	4013	3S	U	AC
120307	Intro to technical writng	Engl	2333	3S	L	
120310	Freshman composition I	Engl	1113	3S	L	
120310	Freshman composition II	Engl	1323	3S	L	
120310	Short fiction writing	Engl	3033	3S	U	
120310	Poetry writing	Engl	3043	3S	U	
121000	Elementary French I	Frnch	1115	5S	L	AC
121000	Elementary French II	Frnch	1225	5S	L	AC
121100	Elementary German I	Germn	1115	5S	L	AC
121100	Elementary German II	Germn	1225	5S	L	AC
122500	Elementary Spanish I	Span	1115	5S	L	AC
122500	Elementary Spanish II	Span	1225	5S	L	AC
130799	Business law I	Law	3213	3S	U	
130799	Business law II	Law	3323	3S	U	
150100	Elementary astronomy	Astro	1104	4S	U	
150101	Cosmos	Astro	4010	3S	U	
150202	Descriptive meteorology	Meteo	3033	3S	U	
150301	Biological sciences	Bio	1114	4S	L	
150307	Heredity & man	Zoolg	3123	3S	U	
150408	Organic chemistry	PhySc	2344	4S	L	
150500	General geology	Geol	1014	4S	L	
150600	Intro to oceanography	Ocean	3113	3S	L	
160199	Metric system	Math	4910A	1S	U	
160301	Basic math wth calculator	Math	4910B	2S	U	
160302	Intermediate algebra	Math	1213	3S	L	
160302	College algebra	Math	1513	3S	L	
160306	Elem linear algebra I	Math	3013	3S	U	
160401	Elementary calculus	Math	2713	3S	L	
160401	Calculus I	Math	2265	5S	L	
160602	College algebra & trig	Math	1715	5S	L	
160602	Trigonometry	Math	1613	3S	L	
160606	Differential equations	Math	2613	3S	L	
160802	Elem statistics for bus	Stat	2023	3S	L	
160802	Intermed statistical anal	Stat	3013	3S	U	
180400	Philosophical classics	Philo	1013	3S	L	
180500	Intro critical thinking	Philo	1313	3S	L	
190512	Human sexuality	HomEc	1113	3S	L	
200102	History of psychology	Psych	3273	3S	U	
200199	Intro to psychology	Psych	1113	3S	L	
200502	World of work for adults	CarEd	1112	2S	L	
200507	Excep child psychology	Psych	3202	2S	U	
200599	Psych found of childhood	Psych	3113	3S	U	
200599	Psychology of adolescence	Psych	3213	3S	U	
200700	Social psychology	Psych	3743	3S	U	
210302	Structural fire protectn	FrPro	2143	3S	L	
210302	Fire protection mgt	FrPro	2153	3S	L	
210302	Hydraulic calc of sprklrs	FrPro	3713	3S	U	
210302	Industrial fire pump inst	FrPro	3723	3S	U	
210302	Sprklrs for rack storage	FrPro	3733	3S	U	
220102	Cultural anthropology	Anthr	3353	3S	U	
220201	Intro to macroeconomics	Econ	2013	3S	L	
220201	Intro to microeconomics	Econ	2023	3S	L	
220215	Economics of soc issues	Econ	1113	3S	L	
220300	World regional geography	Geog	2253	3S	L	
220301	Intro to geog behavior	Geog	1113	3S	L	
220305	Physical geography	Geog	1114	4S	L	
220306	Geography of Oklahoma	Geog	3653	3S	U	
220399	Geog of music	Geog	4223	3S	U	
220423	Modern Japan	Hist	3423	3S	U	

NCES No.	Course Title	Dept.	Course No.	Cred.	Lev.	Specl. Feat.
220423	Traditional Japan	Hist	3980A	3S	U	
220426	European hist to 1714	Hist	1613	3S	L	
220426	European hist since 1714	Hist	1623	3S	L	
220428	Oklahoma history	Hist	2323	3S	L	
220432	American history to 1865	Hist	1483	3S	L	
220432	American hist since 1865	Hist	1493	3S	L	
220432	The Great Plains exper	Hist	3980B	3S	U	
220450	Ancient Greece	Hist	3023	3S	U	
220450	Ancient Rome	Hist	3033	3S	U	
220453	Western humanities (mod)	Hum	2203	3S	L	
220501	American government	PolSc	1013	3S	L	
220600	Soc of human sexuality	Socio	4213	3S	U	
220604	Juvenile delinquency	Socio	3523	3S	U	
220605	Soc of American family	Socio	3723	3S	U	
220606	Principles of sociology	Socio	1113	3S	L	
220612	Social ecol & life proc	Socio	4433	3S	U	
220613	Social problems	Socio	2123	3S	L	

Noncredit courses

NCES No.	Course Title	Dept.	Course No.	Cred.	Lev.	Specl. Feat.
020599	Earth-sheltered housing	Arch		NC		
040101	Basic accounting A	Acctg		NC		
040101	Basic accounting B	Acctg		NC		
040601	Business English	Engl		NC		
040604	Tech/report writing	Engl		NC		
050605	Feature writing/news/mag	Journ		NC		
060700	BASIC prog for beginners	CmpSc		NC		
082303	Radiological safety	NucEg		NC		
089900	Hydraulic calc of sprklrs	FrPro		NC		
160301	Intro hand-held calculatr	Math		NC		
210302	Industrial fire pump inst	FrPro		NC		
210302	Sprklrs for rack storage	FrPro		NC		
220499	Genealogical research	Genea		NC		

㉑ **OREGON STATE SYSTEM OF HIGHER EDUCATION**

Dr. Paul A. Wurm
Director
c/o Office of Independent Study
Portland State University
P.O. Box 1491
Portland, Oregon 97207
Phone: 503-464-4865
    800-547-8887 ext. 4865 (out of state)

Credit by examination is available. High school students may enroll in undergraduate courses for credit. Overseas enrollment accepted. Military personnel may enroll through the DANTES program. Minimum period for course completion is three months. Maximum period for course completion is twelve months. A six-month extension is allowed with payment of a $10 fee. VISA and MasterCard are accepted with telephone registration.

NCES No.	Course Title	Dept.	Course No.	Cred.	Lev.	Specl. Feat.
High School courses						
040101	Intro to accounting I	BusAd	1	HF	H	
040101	Intro to accounting II	BusAd	2	HF	H	
040302	Personal finance	BusAd	3	HF	H	
040302	Pers financial decisions	BusAd	4	HF	H	
040601	Business English	Engl	14	HF	H	
120305	English review	Engl	15	HF	H	
120305	10th gr grammar & comp	Engl	3	HF	H	
120305	11th gr grammar & comp	Engl	5	HF	H	
120305	12th gr grammar & comp	Engl	7	HF	H	
120305	Corrective English	Engl	13	HF	H	
120305	9th gr grammar & comp	Engl	1	HF	H	
120307	Tenth-grade literature	Engl	4	HF	H	
120307	11th gr American lit	Engl	6	HF	H	
120307	12 gr English lit	Engl	8	HF	H	
150300	Biology I	Bio	1	HF	H	
150300	Biology II	Bio	2	HF	H	
150900	Earth science I	ErSci	1	HF	H	
150900	Earth science II	ErSci	2	HF	H	
160301	General math I	Math	1	HF	H	
160301	General math II	Math	2	HF	H	
160302	Elements of algebra (A)	Math	3	HF	H	
160302	Elements of algebra (B)	Math	4	HF	H	
160601	Geometry I	Math	5	HF	H	
160601	Geometry II	Math	6	HF	H	
190509	Health education I	Hlth	1	HF	H	

NCES No.	Course Title	Dept.	Course No.	Cred.	Lev.	Specl. Feat.
190509	Health education II	Hlth	2	HF	H	
200199	General psychology	Psych	1	HF	H	
220201	Principles of economics	Econ	1	HF	H	
220432	US history I	Hist	1	HF	H	
220432	US history II	Hist	2	HF	H	
220433	World history I	Hist	3	HF	H	
220433	World history II	Hist	4	HF	H	
220501	Government	Govt	1	HF	H	
229900	Global studies I	GblSt	1	HF	H	
229900	Global studies II	GblSt	2	HF	H	

College courses

NCES No.	Course Title	Dept.	Course No.	Cred.	Lev.	Specl. Feat.
020299	Housing and arch phil	Arch	178	3Q	L	
030501	Basic drawing	Art	291	3Q	L	
040101	Intermed finan acctg I	BusAd	317	4Q	U	
040101	Intermed finan acctg II	BusAd	318	4Q	U	
040101	Intermed finan acctg III	BusAd	319	4Q	U	
040103	Auditing	BusAd	427	4Q	U	
040106	Cost accounting	BusAd	421	4Q	U	
040109	Acctg not-for-profit inst	BusAd	423	3Q	B	
040206	Medical terminology	AllHl	200	3Q	L	
040999	Transportation management	Mgmt	410	3Q	U	
060404	Intro to microcomputers	CmpSc	410	3Q	U	
060705	Intro to FORTRAN	CmpSc	133	4Q	L	
060705	Intro to COBOL	CmpSc	199	4Q	L	
060705	Adv FORTRAN programming	CmpSc	421	4Q	U	
060806	Intro to computer systems	CmpSc	199B	3Q	L	
070404	Indiv curr primary grades	Culns	410	3Q	U	
070506	Calc and comp in elem sch	CmpSc	407	2Q	B	
070509	Health instruction	HlEd	441	3Q	U	
070610	Reading in high school	Educ	469	3Q	U	
080706	Highway materials	CET	229	3Q	L	
120201	World literature	Engl	107	3Q	L	
120201	Contemporary literature	Engl	384	3Q	U	
120201	Contemporary literature	Engl	385	3Q	U	
120307	Survey of English lit	Engl	101	3Q	L	
120307	Survey of English lit	Engl	102	3Q	L	
120307	Survey of English lit	Engl	103	3Q	L	
120307	Shakespeare	Engl	201	3Q	L	
120307	Shakespeare	Engl	202	3Q	L	
120307	Shakespeare	Engl	203	3Q	L	
120307	Survey of American lit	Engl	253	3Q	L	
120307	American fiction	Engl	366	3Q	U	
120310	English composition	Writ	121	3Q	L	
120310	English composition	Writ	122	3Q	L	
120310	English composition	Writ	123	3Q	L	
120310	Short story writing	Writ	324	3Q	U	
120310	Poetry writing	Writ	341	3Q	U	
120310	Poetry writing	Writ	342	3Q	U	
120399	American folklore	Engl	419	3Q	B	
121100	First-year German	Germn	101	4Q	L	
121100	First-year German	Germn	102	4Q	L	
121100	First-year German	Germn	103	4Q	L	
130199	Court procedures	AdJus	460	3Q	U	
130399	Constitutionl crim prcdrs	AdJus	440	3Q	U	
130402	Criminal justice process	AdJus	200	3Q	L	
130403	Juvenile justice process	AdJus	210	3Q	L	
130499	Crimnl law & legal reasng	AdJus	420	3Q	U	
150202	Intro to atmosphere	AtmSc	300	3Q	U	
150202	Weather analysis lab	AtmSc	430	3Q	U	
150500	General geology	Geol	101	3Q	L	
150500	General geology	Geol	102	3Q	L	
150500	General geology	Geol	103	3Q	L	
150500	Geology of Oregon	Geol	352	3Q	U	
150599	Geologic history of life	Geol	301	3Q	U	
150600	Intro to oceanography	Geol	353	3Q	U	
150799	General physics	Phycs	201	3Q	L	
150799	General physics	Phycs	202	3Q	L	
150799	General physics	Phycs	203	3Q	L	
159900	Foundations of phys sci	GenSc	105	3Q	L	
159900	Foundations of phys sci	GenSc	106	3Q	L	
159900	Foundations of phys sci	GenSc	104	3Q	L	
160302	Intermediate algebra	Math	100	4Q	L	
160302	College algebra	Math	101	4Q	L	
160401	Elements of calculus	Math	106	4Q	L	
160401	Calculus	Math	200	4Q	L	
160401	Calculus	Math	201	4Q	L	
160602	Trigonometry	Math	102	4Q	L	
181002	Intro to world religions	Relig	101	3Q	L	
190509	Personal health problems	HlEd	250	3Q	L	
200199	Psych as a social science	Psych	204	3Q	L	
200199	Psych as a natural sci	Psych	205	3Q	L	

NCES No.	Course Title	Dept.	Course No.	Cred.	Lev.	Specl. Feat.
200501	Abnormal psychology	Psych	434	3Q	U	
200504	Developmental psychology	Psych	407	3Q	U	
220102	Native North Americans	Anthr	317	3Q	U	
220102	Native Central Americans	Anthr	318	3Q	U	
220102	Native South Americans	Anthr	318	3Q	U	
220201	Principles of economics	Econ	213	4Q	L	
220201	Principles of economics	Econ	214	4Q	L	
220305	Introductory geography	Geog	105	3Q	L	
220305	Introductory geography	Geog	106	3Q	L	
220305	Introductory geography	Geog	107	3Q	L	
220406	Hist of Western civiliz	Hist	150	3Q	L	
220406	Hist of Western civiliz	Hist	151	3Q	L	
220406	Hist of Western civiliz	Hist	152	3Q	L	
220432	History of United States	Hist	201	3Q	L	
220432	History of United States	Hist	202	3Q	L	
220432	History of United States	Hist	203	3Q	L	
220511	Oregon politics	PolSc	316	3Q	U	

Graduate courses

NCES No.	Course Title	Dept.	Course No.	Cred.	Lev.	Specl. Feat.
070506	Intro AppleWorks for educ	Culns	408A	4Q	G	CI
070506	Computers in education	Culns	410B	4Q	G	CI
070506	LOGO using Logowriter	Culns	410C	4Q	G	CI
070506	Plng for cmptrs in school	Culns	507B	4Q	G	CI
070506	Computers & prblm solving	Culns	507A	3Q	G	CI

Noncredit courses

NCES No.	Course Title	Dept.	Course No.	Cred.	Lev.	Specl. Feat.
120305	Corrective English	Writ	10	NC		
160302	Elements of algebra	Math	10	NC		

㉒ PENNSYLVANIA STATE UNIVERSITY

Dr. David F. Mercer
Director, Department of Independent Learning
128 Mitchell Building
Pennsylvania State University
P.O. Box 3207
University Park, Pennsylvania 16802
Phone: 814-865-5403
         800-458-3617

Telecourses are offered. High school students may enroll in undergraduate courses for credit. Overseas enrollment accepted. Military personnel may enroll through the DANTES program. Minimum period for course completion is one sixth of a course per week. Maximum period for course completion is one year. Only in exceptional cases are gifted high school students permitted to enroll in undergraduate courses for credit. In addition to individual courses, several extended associate degrees are offered through independent learning. Please call or write for additional information. MasterCard and VISA accepted.

NCES No.	Course Title	Dept.	Course No.	Cred.	Lev.	Specl. Feat.
	High School courses					
090709	Modern health	HSSci	001A	HF	H	
090709	Modern health	HlSci	002A	HF	H	
120305	Basic English	HSLng	010	HF	H	
120307	Ninth-grade English	HSLng	001N	HF	H	
120307	Ninth-grade English	HSLng	002N	HF	H	
120307	Tenth-grade English	HSLng	003A	HF	H	
120307	Tenth-grade English	HSLng	004A	HF	H	
120307	Eleventh-grade English	HSLng	005A	HF	H	
120307	Eleventh-grade English	HSLng	006A	HF	H	
120307	Twelfth-grade English	HSLng	007A	HF	H	
120307	Twelfth-grade English	HSLng	008A	HF	H	
120308	Improv of reading skills	HSLng	025	HF	H	
120308	Improv of reading skills	HSLng	026	HF	H	
160302	Elementary algebra	HSMth	001A	HF	H	
160302	Advanced algebra	HSMth	011A	HF	H	
160302	Advanced algebra	HSMth	011B	HF	H	
160302	Modern 4th-year math	HSMth	017	HF	H	
160302	Modern 4th-year math	HSMth	018	HF	H	
160302	Elementary algebra	HSMth	001B	HF	H	
160601	Geometry	HSMth	003A	HF	H	
160601	Geometry	HSMth	004A	HF	H	
160602	Trigonometry	HSMth	007	HF	H	
190699	Driver education	DrvEd	001	HF	H	
220432	American history	HSSSt	005P	HF	H	
220432	American history	HSSSt	006P	HF	H	
220433	World history	HSSSt	003A	HF	H	
220433	World history	HSSSt	004A	HF	H	

NCES No.	Course Title	Dept.	Course No.	Cred.	Lev.	Specl. Feat.
	College courses					
020102	History of landscape arch	LArch	60	3S	L	
030302	Rudiments of music	Music	8	3S	L	AC
030402	Principles of playwriting	Theat	440	3S	U	
030501	Intro visual arts & studi	Art	1	3S	L	
039900	Survey of Western art	ArHis	110	3S	L	
040101	Intro financial acctg	Acctg	101	3S	L	
040111	Managerial accounting	Acctg	104	3S	L	
040114	Introduc federal taxation	Acctg	206	4S	L	
040301	Corporation finance	Finan	301	3S	L	
040301	Fin mgmt of bus entrprise	Finan	305	3S	U	
040302	Personal finance	Finan	108	3S	L	
040306	Security markets	Finan	204	3S	L	
040311	Introduction to finance	Finan	100	3S	L	
040604	Business writing	Engl	202D	3S	L	
040902	Problems of small bus	BusAd	250	3S	L	VC
040903	Intro organizatl behavior	Mgmt	321	3S	U	
040904	Survey of management	Mgmt	100	3S	L	
041007	Business logistics mgmt	BuLog	301	3S	U	
041007	Transport systems	BuLog	304	3S	U	
041104	Industrial relations	LIRel	100	3S	L	AC
041199	Personnel management	Mgmt	341	3S	U	
041299	Intro to quantitative bus	QBA	101	3S	L	
041299	Elementary bus statistics	QBA	102	3S	L	
050101	Advertising and public rl	Commu	240	3S	L	
050699	Law of mass communication	Commu	403	3S	U	
061103	Intro digital systems	CmpuE	271	3S	L	
061103	Intro computers/applic	CmpSc	100	3S	L	
070199	History of education US	EdThP	430	3S	U	
070306	Vocational education	VocEd	1	3S	L	
070306	Safety ed for voc ed teac	IndEd	106	3S	L	
070499	Observ/exp preschl childn	IFS	330A	1S	U	
070499	Observ/exp preschl childn	IFS	330B	3S	L	
070518	Intro to philosophy of ed	EdThP	440	3S	U	
070703	Job placement skills	Agri	100	1S	L	VC
070708	Ed psy for prof effect	EdPsy	020	3S	L	
080703	Fluid flow	CivlE	861	3S	L	
080901	Signals and circuits I	ElecE	251	3S	L	
080901	Signals and circuits II	ElecE	352	3S	U	
080901	Fund electrical circuits	ElecE	101	4S	L	
080901	AC circuits	ElecE	204	2S	L	
080901	Electrical circuits	ElecE	114	3S	L	
081000	Intro engineering graphic	EngGr	10	1S	L	
081000	Engineering design graph	EngGr	11	1S	L	
081000	Spatial analysis	EngGr	103	2S	L	
081100	Mechncs for tech: statics	MecEn	111	3S	L	
081103	Strength & prop of matls	MecEn	213	3S	L	
081104	Dynamics	EMech	12	3S	L	
081104	Statics	EMech	11	3S	L	
081302	Community noise fundamtls	ComDi	297	3S	L	
081302	Community noise fundamtls	ComDi	497	3S	B	
081304	Water pollution control	CivlE	270	3S	U	
081999	Strength of materials	EMech	13	3S	L	
082006	Product design	MecEn	210	3S	L	
082099	Kinematics	MecEn	105	3S	L	
090276	Hlth efts ionizg radiatio	NucEg	497G	4S	U	
090276	Hlth efts ionizg radiatio	NucEg	297G	3S	L	
090603	Intro to health serv org	HPA	101	3S	L	
100223	The profession of dieteti	DSM	100	1S	L	
100309	Nutr component food svcs	Nutri	151	3S	L	
100313	Elementary nutrition	Nutri	150	2S	L	
100313	Diet therp/nutr care dise	Nutri	252	4S	L	
100399	Nutrition of the family	Nutri	251	3S	L	
100399	Qual assur for diete mgmt	DSM	270	3S	L	
100601	Infancy and early childhd	IFS	229	3S	L	
100602	Intro to indiv & fam devl	IFS	129	3S	L	
100602	Family development	IFS	315	3S	U	
100603	Adult development & aging	IFS	249	3S	L	
100699	Field projects	HuDev	395	CV	U	
100699	Spec topics: fam day care	IFS	297F	1S	L	
100701	San/hskpng hlth care facl	DSM	101	3S	L	
100702	Food bev labor cost cntrl	HRIM	337	3S	U	
120101	Intro to language	Ling	10	3S	L	
120202	Masterpieces Wstn lit/Ren	CompL	1	3S	L	
120299	Greek and Roman lit	Class	1	3S	L	
120299	Brazilian lit in trans	Port	456	3S	U	
120299	Spanish lit in trans	Span	231	3S	L	
120305	English language analysis	Engl	100	3S	L	
120307	Amer lit Civ War to WWI	Engl	232	3S	L	
120307	Understanding literature	Engl	001	3S	L	
120310	Basic writing skills	Engl	004	3S	D	

NCES No.	Course Title	Dept.	Course No.	Cred.	Lev.	Specl. Feat.
120310	Rhetoric and composition	Engl	015	3S	L	
120310	Social science writing	Engl	202A	3S	L	
120310	Business writing	Engl	202D	3S	L	
121000	Elementary French I	Frnch	1	4S	L	AC
121000	Elementary French II	Frnch	2	4S	L	AC
121000	Intermediate French	Frnch	3	4S	L	AC
121100	Basic German	Germn	001	4S	L	AC
121100	Basic German	Germn	002	4S	L	AC
121100	Intermediate German	Germn	003	4S	L	AC
122500	Intermediate Spanish	Span	3	4S	L	
129900	Myths and mythologies	CompL	108	3S	L	
130700	Legal envir of business	BuLaw	243	3S	L	
150202	Weather and society	Meteo	002	2S	L	
150202	Tropical meteorology	Meteo	452	3S	U	
150202	Applic of stat to meteoro	Meteo	474	3S	U	
150202	Intro meteorology	Meteo	3	3S	L	
150301	Man and his environment	BioSc	3	3S	L	
150307	Genetics/ecol & evolution	BioSc	2	3S	L	
150399	Physiology	Bio	41	3S	L	
150399	Plants/places and people	Bio	20	3S	L	
150401	Chemical principles	Chem	12	3S	L	
150401	Chemical principles	Chem	13	3S	L	
150408	Organic chemistry	Chem	34	3S	L	
150599	Out of the fiery furnace	EMSci	150	3S	L	VC
150799	General physics	Phycs	203	3S	L	
150799	General physics	Phycs	202	4S	L	
150799	General physics	Phycs	201	4S	L	
150899	Physical science	PhySc	7	3S	L	
160103	Insights into mathematics	Math	36	3S	L	
160199	General view of math	Math	35	3S	L	
160203	Finite mathematics	Math	17	3S	L	
160302	Intermediate algebra	Math	4	3S	L	
160302	College algebra I	Math	5	3S	L	
160302	College algebra II	Math	7	3S	L	
160303	Number systems	Math	200	3S	L	
160306	Elementary linear algebra	Math	18	3S	L	
160401	Techniques of calculus I	Math	110	4S	L	
160401	Techniques of calculus II	Math	111	2S	L	
160401	Calc with analyt geom I	Math	140	4S	L	
160401	Calc with analytc geom II	Math	141	4S	L	
160406	Ordinary diff equations	Math	250	3S	L	
160407	Ord & partial diff equats	Math	251	4S	L	
160499	Matrices	Math	220	2S	L	
160602	Plane trigonometry	Math	6	3S	L	
160801	Elementary statistics	Stat	200	4S	L	
160801	Statistics/educ research	EdPsy	400	3S	B	CI
161299	Technical mathematics	Math	87	5S	L	
161299	Tech math and calculus	Math	88	5S	L	
180404	Existentialism	Philo	102	3S	L	
180499	Basic problems of philos	Philo	001	3S	L	
180501	Critical thinking and arg	Philo	10	3S	L	CI
180502	Elements of symb logic	Philo	12	3S	L	
181304	Jewish/Christian found	Relig	4	3S	L	
181304	Religions of the East	Relig	3	3S	L	
189900	Intro to world religions	Relig	1	3S	L	
189900	Relig in Am lfe & thought	Relig	140	3S	L	
190104	Hist or prin of hl ph ed	ESS	140	3S	L	
190107	Admn hlth/phys ed in schl	ESS	491	2S	U	
190108	Adapted physical educatn	ESS	400	3S	U	
190110	Measurmt eval in hlth/PE	ESS	490	2S	U	
190301	Intramural athletics	ESS	489	3S	U	
190311	Meth prin of ath coaching	ESS	493	2S	U	
190399	Issues in sports medicine	HIEd	297.7	3S	L	
190501	Drugs in society	HIEd	43	1S	L	
190503	Prin healthful living	HIEd	60	3S	L	
190503	Consumer health	HIEd	57	1S	L	
190503	Intr:hlth aspt/hum sexlty	HIEd	046	1S	L	
190503	Consumer health education	HIEd	457	3S	U	
190504	Health and disease	HIEd	19	1S	L	
190509	Lifestyle for better heal	HIEd	15	1S	L	
190509	Education for wellness	HIEd	415	3S	U	
190599	Health aspects of sport	HIEd	5	1S	L	
190599	Internship in health prom	HIEd	495	CV	U	
190706	Leisure in human experien	RecPk	120	3S	L	
200505	Mental health	Psych	37	3S	L	
210103	Public personnel admin	PubAd	496	3S	U	
210499	Child maltreatment	IFS	297E	1S	L	
210599	Funct plan of park	RecPk	434	3S	U	
220101	Cultural anthropology	Anthr	45	3S	L	
220199	Introductory anthropology	Anthr	1	3S	L	
220201	Principles of economics	Econ	14	3S	L	
220202	Hist economic thought	Econ	400	3S	U	

NCES No.	Course Title	Dept.	Course No.	Cred.	Lev.	Specl. Feat.
220204	Intro microecon anal pol	Econ	2	3S	L	
220204	Intro macroecon anal pol	Econ	4	3S	L	
220211	Labor economics	Econ	315	3S	U	
220212	Environmental economics	Econ	428	3S	U	
220301	Human geography	Geog	20	3S	L	VC
220407	History of communism	Hist	142	3S	L	VC
220407	Hist fascism and nazism	Hist	143	3S	L	VC
220426	Western heritage I	Hist	1	3S	L	
220428	Colonial Pennsylvania	Hist	150	3S	L	
220428	History of Pennsylvania	Hist	12	3S	L	VC
220432	Amer civilizatn snc 1877	Hist	21	3S	L	
220432	Amer civilizatn to 1877	Hist	20	3S	L	
220499	Hist of American worker	LlRel	156	3S	L	
220499	Western heritage II	Hist	2	3S	L	
220501	Gov and pol of Am states	PolSc	425	3S	U	
220501	American national govt	PolSc	1	3S	L	
220503	Comparative pol West Eur	PolSc	20	3S	L	
220504	Govt & poltics in mod soc	PolSc	3	3S	L	
220505	International relations	PolSc	14	3S	L	
220511	Amer local govt & admin	PolSc	417	3S	U	
220604	Urbanization of man	SoSci	1	3S	L	
220605	Sociology of the family	Socio	30	3S	L	
220606	Introductory sociology	Socio	1	3S	L	
220607	Introductory social psych	Socio	3	3S	L	
220614	Urban sociology	Socio	15	3S	L	
229900	Intro to American studies	AmSt	100	3S	L	

Noncredit courses

NCES No.	Course Title	Dept.	Course No.	Cred.	Lev.	Specl. Feat.
020101	Plan rdg & arch details	ArchE	1901	NC		
030402	Theater: fund-raising	Theat	5203	NC		
030402	Theater: mgt finan/facilt	Theat	5204	NC		
030402	Theater: audience dvlpt	Theat	5205	NC		
030499	Organizational structure	Theat	5202	NC		
030499	Volunteer & staff dev	Theat	5206	NC		
030499	Directing community theat	Theat	5207	NC		
030699	Craft fair primer	Art	5211	NC		
040604	Technical writing	Engl	5832	NC		
041106	Basic supervision	IndEn	5001	NC		
041106	Advanced supervision	IndEn	5002	NC		
050900	Dynamics volunteer progrm	HuDev	5703	NC		
081000	Engineering graphics	EngGr	5500	NC	L	
081302	Community noise fundamtls	ComDi	5401	NC		
081304	Water pollution control	CivlE	5541	NC		
082501	Petro & naturl gas explor	PNG	952	NC		
082599	Oil & gas production prac	PNG	953	NC		
090276	Hlth efcts ionizing radia	NucEg	5534	NC		
100304	Fat chance: eating & nutr	Nutri	7385	NC		
160301	Basic math	Math	5951	NC		
190799	Beginning stamp collectng	LibAr	5834	NC		
190799	Begin stamp collect/adult	LibAr	5836	NC		
190799	Intermed stamp collect I	LibAr	5837	NC		
190799	Intermed stamp collect II	LibAr	5838	NC		

㉓ PURDUE UNIVERSITY

Jennifer Towler
Coordinator, Self-Directed Learning Programs
Self-Directed Learning Programs
116 Stewart Center
Purdue University
West Lafayette, Indiana 47907
Phone: 317-494-2748

Overseas enrollment accepted.

NCES No.	Course Title	Dept.	Course No.	Cred.	Lev.	Specl. Feat.
	Noncredit courses					
010403	Pest control technology	Entom		NC	V	
090411	Pharmacy correspondence	Pharm		NC	V	
090905	Central service tech trng	RHIM		NC	V	
090905	Central service mgmt & sp	RHIM		NC	V	
100702	Food service mgt & supv	RHIM		NC	V	
100702	Food purchasing & procur	RHIM		NC	V	
100702	Prof cooking & food serv	RHIM		NC	V	
100702	Computer app in food serv	RHIM		NC	V	
100702	Travl & tourism mktg mgmt	RHIM		NC	V	

NCES No.	Course Title	Dept.	Course No.	Cred.	Lev.	Specl. Feat.
220472	Men/women relationships	BGS	210	1S	L	
220499	US labor history	Hist	327	3S	U	
220499	Amer labor hist to 1860	Hist	32796	1S	U	
220499	Amer labor hist 1860-1920	Hist	32797	1S	U	
220499	Amer labor hist 1920-pres	Hist	32798	1S	U	
220500	Intro political science	PolSc	200	3S	U	
220511	Governing the city	BGS	384	1S	U	
220600	Introduction to sociology	Socio	101	3S	L	
220699	Methods of social researc	Socio	375	3S	U	
229900	Seminar in social science	BGS	390	6S	U	
229900	Adv sem in social sci	BGS	396	3S	U	
229900	Machines and society	BGS	381	1S	U	
229900	Women's work	BGS	382	1S	U	
229900	Man against disease	BGS	383	1S	U	

㉔ ROOSEVELT UNIVERSITY

Mr. Arnold Reichler
Director, External Studies Program
College of Continuing Education
430 South Michigan Avenue, Room 124
Roosevelt University
Chicago, Illinois 60605
Phone: 312-341-3866

Enrollment on a noncredit basis accepted in credit courses. Military personnel may enroll through the DANTES program. Maximum period for course completion is six months. Although an external degree per se is not offered, credits earned through correspondence study may be applied to a degree program. Overseas enrollment is restricted to students who have previously taken courses at an American university.

NCES No.	Course Title	Dept.	Course No.	Cred.	Lev.	Specl. Feat.
	College courses					
030600	Pro-seminar	BGS	201	6S	U	
030600	Advanced pro-seminar	BGS	301	3S	U	
030600	Seminar in humanities	BGS	392	6S	U	
030600	Adv seminar humanities	BGS	398	3S	U	
030600	Senior thesis	BGS	399	3S	U	
030600	Study skills	BGS	213	1S	L	
030600	Storyteller's art	BGS	374	1S	U	
050900	Intro to public relations	Journ	202	3S	L	
051108	Communication skills	BGS	212	1S	L	
051399	Television	BGS	371	1S	U	
060199	Bus app IBM PC/XT	CmpSc	341	3S	U	
060705	COBOL programming	CmpSc	213	3S	U	
060705	Adv COBOL programming	CmpSc	219	3S	U	
060705	Advanced BASIC	CmpSc	242	3S	U	
060903	Intro programming tech	CmpSc	202	3S	U	
060904	Systems analysis & design	CmpSc	208	3S	U	
061104	CPSC data processing	CmpSc	101	3S	L	
090602	Health systems adm I	PubAd	351	3S	U	
090702	Adm urban disease problem	PubAd	354	3S	U	
090710	Admin health mgmt II	PubAd	352	3S	U	
120201	Encounters new worlds	BGS	211	1S	L	
120201	Aesthetics	BGS	372	1S	U	
120310	Composition I	Engl	101	3S	L	
120310	Composition II	Engl	102	3S	L	
120310	Composition III	Engl	103	3S	L	
120399	Research skills	BGS	214	1S	L	
150304	Pollution of our environ	BGS	354	1S	U	
150326	Genetics	BGS	353	1S	U	
159900	Seminar natural sciences	BGS	391	6S	U	
159900	Adv sem in natural sci	BGS	397	3S	U	
159900	What is science?	BGS	351	1S	U	
159900	Science and society	BGS	355	1S	U	
159900	Earthquakes	BGS	356	1S	U	
160203	Finite math	Math	116	3S	L	
200100	General psychology	Psych	103	3S	L	
200501	Abnormal psychology	Psych	201	3S	U	
200504	Childhood & adolescence	Psych	254	3S	U	
200509	Personality	Psych	360	3S	U	
200899	Coping with stress	Psych	203	3S	L	
210100	Intro to public admin	PubAd	300	3S	U	
210100	Intro to public admin	PolSc	300	3S	U	
210113	Public policy & admin	PubAd	371	3S	U	
210113	Public policy making	PolSc	372	3S	U	
210304	Adm law enforcement adm	PubAd	345	3S	U	
220305	Physical geography I	Geog	101	3S	L	
220305	Physical geography II	Geog	102	3S	L	
220308	Urban geography	Geog	305	3S	U	
220308	Urban environment	Geog	350	3S	U	
220399	Political geography	Geog	309	3S	U	
220399	Political geography	PolSc	309	3S	U	
220409	American social history	Hist	326	3S	U	
220409	Immigration	Hist	32696	1S	U	
220409	Consumer and technology	Hist	32697	1S	U	
220426	History of Holocaust	Hist	34896	1S	U	
220428	History of Chicago	Hist	307	3S	U	
220428	Chicago history to 1871	Hist	30796	1S	U	
220428	Chicago history 1871-1919	Hist	30797	1S	U	
220428	Chicago history 1920-1987	Hist	30798	1S	U	
220433	Western civ since 1648	Hist	12296	1S	L	
220450	Begin of civilization	Hist	38096	1S	U	
220450	Rise of urban society	Hist	38097	1S	U	
220450	Early civilization	Hist	38098	1S	U	
220450	Urban civilization	Hist	380	3S	U	

㉕ SAINT JOSEPH'S COLLEGE

Ms. Patricia M. Sparks
Dean, External Degree Program
Saint Joseph's College
White's Bridge Road
North Windham, Maine 04062-1198
Phone: 207-892-6766

External degree available through the program. Credit by examination is available. Overseas enrollment accepted. Military personnel may enroll through the DANTES program. Institution offers special arrangements to take courses not listed in this Catalog. Maximum period for course completion is six months.

NCES No.	Course Title	Dept.	Course No.	Cred.	Lev.	Specl. Feat.
	College courses					
040101	Principles of accounting	Bus	Ac101	3S	L	
040101	Principles of accounting	Bus	Ac102	3S	L	
040111	Managerial accounting	Bus	AC204	3S	L	
040902	Operations management	Bus	Mg301	3S	U	
040904	Intro to management	Bus	Mg201	3S	L	
040999	Sales management	Bus	Mk304	3S	U	
041001	Marketing	Bus	Mk201	3S	U	
041004	Marketing management	Bus	Mk401	3S	U	
041099	Retailing	Bus	Mk303	3S	U	
041100	Personnel management	Bus	Mg302	3S	U	
041104	Labor relations	Bus	Mg304	3S	U	
050100	Advertising	Bus	Mk301	3S	U	
070199	History of American ed	Educ	Ed402	3S	U	
070200	Ed administration	Educ	Ed434	3S	U	
070309	Adult learning I	Educ	Ed308	3S	U	
070309	Adult learning I	Educ	Ed309	3S	U	
071100	Measurements & evaluation	Educ	Ed401	3S	U	
090302	Nutrition	HCA	NN202	3S	L	
090601	Financial mgmt in HCA I	HCA	HC441	3S	U	
090601	Financial mgmt in HCA II	HCA	HC442	3S	U	
090602	Am health care systems I	HCA	HC305	3S	U	
090602	Am health care systems II	HCA	HC306	3S	U	
090603	Practicum in health mgt	HCA	HC457	3S	U	
090699	Health care administratio	HCA	HC320	3S	U	
090699	Health care admin II	HCA	NC330	3S	U	
090699	Health care economics	HCA	HC443	3S	U	
090700	Public health I	HCA	HC423	3S	U	
090700	Public health II	HCA	HC424	3S	U	
090703	Environmental health	HCA	ES202	3S	U	
090704	Human ecology	HCA	ES201	3S	U	
090904	Legal aspects of HCA	HCA	HC453	3S	U	
090904	Ethics in health care	HCA	HC455	3S	U	
120307	American literature I	Engl	203	3S	U	
120307	American literature II	Engl	204	3S	U	
120310	English composition I	Engl	106	3S	L	
120310	English composition II	Engl	107	3S	L	
130700	Business law I	Bus	Ba301	3S	U	
130700	Business law II	Bus	Ba302	3S	U	
180400	Intro to philosophy	Philo	201	3S	U	
181002	Comparative religions	Philo	HU302	3S	U	
200100	Intro to psychology	Psych	101	3S	L	
200100	Topics in psychology	Psych	204	3S	U	
200404	Psychology of motivation	Psych	302	3S	U	
200501	Abnormal psychology	Psych	303	3S	U	
200503	Behavior modification	Psych	316	3S	U	
200509	Psychology of personality	Psych	301	3S	U	
200700	Social psychology	Socio	201	3S	U	

NCES No.	Course Title	Dept.	Course No.	Cred.	Lev.	Specl. Feat.
200804	Educational psychology	Educ	Ed301	3S	U	
200901	Industrial psychology	Psych	402	3S	U	
200999	Human relations in bus	Psych	309	3S	U	
220201	Intro to microeconomics	Bus	BA201	3S	L	
220201	Intro to macroeconomics	Bus	BA202	3S	L	
220432	Hist of the United States	Hist	201	3S	L	
220432	Hist of the United States	Hist	202	3S	L	
220433	Western civilization	Hist	101	3S	L	
220433	Western civilization	Hist	102	3S	L	
220601	Modern community	Socio	304	3S	U	
220602	Criminology	Socio	307	3S	L	
220605	The family	Socio	303	3S	U	
220606	Principles of sociology	Socio	201	3S	L	
220613	Social problems	Socio	301	3S	U	

Graduate courses

NCES No.	Course Title	Dept.	Course No.	Cred.	Lev.	Specl. Feat.
090603	Human resources develop	HCA	HS620	3S	G	
090603	Labor relations	HCA	HS630	3S	G	
090699	U.S. health care systems	HCA	HS510	3S	G	
090699	Health services admin	HCA	HS520	3S	G	
090699	Strategic management	HCA	HS530	3S	G	
090699	Organizatnl thery & behvr	HCA	HS540	3S	G	
090699	Applied research paper	HCA	HS570	3S	G	
090699	Financial mgmt in hc adm	HCA	HS600	3S	G	
090699	Economics in health care	HCA	HS610	3S	G	
090699	Medical sociology	HCA	HS640	3S	G	
090699	Marketing hlth care svcs	HCA	HS650	3S	G	
090703	Environmental health	HCA	HS660	3S	G	
090901	Hlth policy, plan & polit	HCA	HS560	3S	G	
090904	Ethic & legl persp hl adm	HCA	HS550	3S	G	

㉖ **SAVANNAH STATE COLLEGE**

Rosemary Banks
Program Specialist, Correspondence Study
Coastal Georgia Center for Continuing Education
Savannah State College Branch
P.O. Box 20436
Savannah, Georgia 31404
Phone: 912-356-2243

Enrollment on a noncredit basis accepted in credit courses. Overseas enrollment accepted. Minimum period for course completion is one quarter. Maximum period for course completion is one year. Savannah State College correspondence courses reflect a sense of obligation to those who cannot undertake resident instruction. Students should meet the minimal requirement of graduation from an accredited high school or have passed the GED. Up to 45 credit quarter hours can be earned. Courses may not be taken to remove deficiencies or after the completion of 135 or more credit hours.

NCES No.	Course Title	Dept.	Course No.	Cred.	Lev.	Specl. Feat.
	College courses					
049900	Introduction to business	Bus	105	5Q	L	
130399	Amer constitutional law	PolSc	311	5Q	U	
160302	College algebra	Math	107	5Q	L	
200599	General psychology	Socio	201	5Q	U	
220399	World of human geography	Socio	111	5Q	L	
220426	US & Afro-Am snc Civ War	Hist	203	5Q	U	
220426	His of early modrn Europe	Hist	331	5Q	U	
220426	History of modern Europe	Hist	332	5Q	U	
220432	US & Afro-Am thr Civ War	Hist	202	5Q	U	
220433	History of world civil	Hist	101	5Q	L	
220433	History of world civil	Hist	102	5Q	L	

NCES No.	Course Title	Dept.	Course No.	Cred.	Lev.	Specl. Feat.
220501	Government	PolSc	200	5Q	U	
220599	Black politics	PolSc	390	5Q	U	
220599	American political proc	PolSc	405	5Q	U	
220699	Introduction to sociology	Socio	201	5Q	U	

㉗ **SOUTHEASTERN COLLEGE OF THE ASSEMBLIES OF GOD**

Thomas G. Wilson
Director
Independent Study by Correspondence
Southeastern College of the Assemblies of God
1000 Longfellow Boulevard
Lakeland, Florida 33801-6099
Phone: 813-665-4404

Credit by examination is available. Overseas enrollment accepted. Institution offers special arrangements to take courses not listed in this Catalog. Minimum period for course completion is two weeks. Maximum period for course completion is one year. Enrollment on a noncredit basis is accepted in all credit courses. High school seniors are permitted to enroll in undergraduate courses for credit. MasterCard/VISA is accepted. An external degree program is available. Southeastern College is a private institution under the sponsorship of the Assemblies of God church.

NCES No.	Course Title	Dept.	Course No.	Cred.	Lev.	Specl. Feat.
	College courses					
059900	Parliamentary procedure	Commu	2111	1S	L	
070199	Philos of Christian educ	Educ	2011	1S	L	
070299	Adm Christian education	Educ	3333	3S	U	
070404	Methods of teaching Bible	Educ	3033	3S	U	
120299	World literature I	Lit	4333	3S	U	
120305	English grammar	Lit	1233	3S	L	
120307	American literature	Lit	3633	3S	U	
120310	English composition	Lit	1133	3S	L	
121200	Greek IA	Lang	2544	4S	L	
121200	Greek IB	Lang	2644	4S	L	
121200	Greek IIA	Lang	3533	4S	U	
121200	Greek IIB	Lang	3633	4S	U	
121300	Hebrew IA	Lang	3144	4S	U	
121300	Hebrew IB	Lang	3244	4S	U	
121300	Hebrew IIA	Lang	4133	3S	U	
121300	Hebrew IIB	Lang	4233	3S	U	
180499	Intro to philosophy	Philo	3233	3S	U	
181002	Comparative religions	Theo	2233	3S	L	
181202	Acts	Theo	2422	2S	L	
181202	Corinthians	Theo	3833	3S	U	
181202	Gospel of John	Theo	4622	2S	U	
181202	Hebrew poetry	Lit	3122	2S	U	
181202	Life of Christ	Theo	2222	2S	L	
181202	New Testament survey	Theo	1233	3S	L	
181202	Old Testament survey	Theo	1133	3S	L	
181202	Pentateuch	Theo	3233	3S	U	
181202	Romans	Theo	4133	3S	U	
181399	Church history I	Theo	3133	3S	U	
181399	Old Testament history I	Theo	2233	3S	L	
181401	Systematic theology I	Theo	2322	2S	L	
181406	Systematic theology II	Theo	2422	2S	L	
181407	Systematic theology III	Theo	3122	2S	U	
181408	Holy Spirit	Theo	3322	2S	U	
181409	Systematic theology IV	Theo	3222	2S	U	
181499	Apologetics	Theo	4123	3S	U	
181499	Introduction to theology	Theo	1122	2S	L	
181499	Hermeneutics	Theo	2622	2S	U	
181499	New Testament theology	Theo	3822	3S	U	
181499	Old Testament theology	Theo	3722	3S	U	
181601	Homiletics I	Theo	3133	3S	U	
181601	Homiletics II	Theo	3233	3S	U	
181602	Pastoral counseling I	Theo	4133	3S	U	
181602	Pastoral counseling II	Theo	4233	3S	U	
181606	Intro to church music	Theo	2011	1S	L	
181607	Pastoral theology I	Theo	3533	3S	U	
181607	Pastoral theology II	Theo	3633	3S	U	
181608	Theology of missions	Theo	2133	2S	L	
181699	Church growth	Theo	4822	2S	U	
181699	Evang work of the church	Theo	1122	2S	L	
200100	Intro to psychology	Psych	1133	3S	L	
220432	American history I	SocSt	4133	3S	U	
220432	American history II	SocSt	4233	3S	U	

㉘ SOUTHERN ILLINOIS UNIVERSITY AT CARBONDALE

Richard C. Crowell
Coordinator, Individualized Learning Program
Division of Continuing Education
Southern Illinois University at Carbondale
Washington Square C
Carbondale, Illinois 62901
Phone: 618-536-7751

Enrollment on a noncredit basis accepted in credit courses. High school students may enroll in undergraduate courses for credit. Overseas enrollment accepted. Students who do not complete a course within the semester that they registered for it may receive an Incomplete. Thereafter, a maximum of one year from issuance of the Incomplete is allowed for completion of the course.

NCES No.	Course Title	Dept.	Course No.	Cred.	Lev.	Specl. Feat.
	College courses					
020505	Structural mechanics I	ConsT	125	3S	L	
020505	Structural mechanics II	ConsT	225	3S	L	
030301	Appl tech information	ATS	416	3U	U	AC
030302	Music understanding	GEC	100	3S	L	AC
030501	Survey of 20th-cen art	ArHis	346	3S	U	SL
030502	Meaning in visual arts	GEC	204	3S	L	
060499	Computer sys applications	Elec	224	3U	L	
070799	Intro technical careers	STC	100	3S	L	
090999	Medical terminology	AllHC	105	2U	L	
110119	Welding blueprint reading	TMTec	183	2S	L	
110199	Const drawing/blueprint	ConsT	102	4S	L	
110303	Intro to electronics	Elec	100	3U	L	
110401	Aircraft electric systems	AMTec	210	2S	L	
110401	Electronics for aviators	AvTec	200	4S	L	
110401	Avionics shop practices	AvTec	203	3S	L	
110601	Primary flight theory	AFMgt	200	3U	L	
120310	Technical writing	STC	102	2S	L	
121000	Intermed French conversat	Frnch	220	2S	L	AC
160302	Intermediate algebra	GED	107	3S	L	
161299	Technical mathematics	STC	105A	2U	L	AC
161299	Technical mathematics	STC	105B	2U	L	AC
180502	Elementary logic	GEC	208	3U	L	AC
210100	Intro public administrat	PolSc	340	3S	U	
210114	Public financial administ	PolSc	443-3	3S	U	
220102	Anthropology	GEB	104	3S	L	AC
220203	Insurance	Finan	327	3U	U	
220208	Consumer problems	ATS	340	3U	U	AC
220305	Understanding the weather	Geog	330	3S	U	
220453	Modern American history	GEB	301	3U	U	AC
220501	Intro Amer govt politics	GEB	114	3S	L	
220503	Politics foreign nations	GEB	250	3S	L	

㉙ SOUTHWEST TEXAS STATE UNIVERSITY

Claudia Cabaniss
Director, Correspondence and Extension Studies
118 Medina Hall
Southwest Texas State University
San Marcos, Texas 78666
Phone: 512-245-2322

Enrollment on a noncredit basis accepted in credit courses. High school students may enroll in undergraduate courses for credit. Overseas enrollment accepted. Minimum period for course completion is forty-five days. Maximum period for course completion is one year. The one-year deadline for course work may be extended once for six months. Correspondence students may write or call for a catalog; books for courses may be ordered by phone or mail also. All courses conducted by correspondence cost $135 each.

NCES No.	Course Title	Dept.	Course No.	Cred.	Lev.	Specl. Feat.
	College courses					
010103	Agricultural marketing	Agri	3351	3S	U	
010107	Farm management	Agri	3317	3S	U	
010199	Intro to ag economics	Agri	2383	3S	L	
010199	Ag resource economics	Agri	4383	3S	U	
030502	Intro to the visual arts	Art	1373	3S	L	
030599	The folk arts of America	Art	2313	3S	L	
030599	Current trends in art	Art	2383	3S	L	

NCES No.	Course Title	Dept.	Course No.	Cred.	Lev.	Specl. Feat.
030599	Spec problems in art/cft	Art	4363	3S	U	
030599	Anct/medieval art hist	Art	4373	3S	U	
030599	History of art III	Art	4383	3S	U	
061199	Programming for teachers	CmpSc	4348	3S	U	
061199	Computers in education	CmpSc	4358	3S	U	
069900	Non-mathematical stats	CmpSc	2328	3S	L	
079900	Early childhood	EdPsy	4311	3S	U	
090699	Medical terminology	HCA	2360	3S	L	
090699	Principles of hosp acctng	HCA	4375	3S	U	
100200	Consumer education	HomEc	1341	3S	L	
100399	Nutr/health/the consumer	HomEc	3362	3S	U	
119900	Special topics in voc ed	VTIE	3313	3S	U	
119900	Tchng voc ed/spec studnts	VTIE	3133A	3S	U	
119900	Usng micrcomputers/voc ed	VTIE	3313B	3S	U	
119900	Teaching entrepreneurship	VTIE	3313C	3S	U	
120299	World literature	Engl	2330	3S	L	
120299	World literature	Engl	2340	3S	L	
120308	The American novel	Engl	3338	3S	U	
120308	The English novel	Engl	3368	3S	U	
120399	Children's literature	Engl	3385	3S	U	
120399	Reading and writing	Engl	1310	3S	L	
120399	Reading and writing	Engl	1320	3S	L	
130699	International law	PolSc	4356	3S	U	
160199	Basic mathematics	Math	1311	3S	L	
160302	College algebra	Math	1315	3S	L	
160401	Calculus I	Math	2471	3S	L	
160401	Calculus II	Math	2472	3S	L	
160406	Differential equations	Math	3323	3S	U	
160602	Plane trigonometry	Math	1317	3S	L	
161101	Math for bus and eco	Math	1319	3S	L	
180500	Elementary logic	Philo	2330	3S	L	
190106	Org and adm of phys educ	PhyEd	4319	3S	U	
200199	Intro to psychology	Psych	1300	3S	L	
200199	History and theory	Psych	4391	3S	U	
200406	Learning and memory	Psych	4342	3S	U	
200501	Abnormal psychology	Psych	3315	3S	U	
200509	Personality	Psych	4316	3S	U	
200799	Social psychology	Psych	3331	3S	U	
200901	Industrial psychology	Psych	3333	3S	U	
220302	Economic geography	Geog	3303	3S	U	
220399	World geography	Geog	1310	3S	L	
220402	Diplomat hist/US fr 1898	Hist	3357	3S	U	
220424	History of England	Hist	3315	3S	U	
220424	Diplomat hist/US to 1898	Hist	3356	3S	U	
220426	Western civilization	Hist	2310	3S	L	
220426	Western civilization	Hist	2320	3S	L	
220501	Principles of Amer govern	PolSc	2310	3S	L	
220501	Functions of Amer govern	PolSc	2320	3S	L	
220602	Criminology	Socio	3343	3S	U	
220604	Juvenile delinquency	Socio	3347	3S	U	
220699	Introduction to sociology	Socio	1310	3S	L	
229900	Intro to crim jus	CrJus	1310	3S	L	
229900	Crime in America	CrJus	2324	3S	L	
229900	The courts and crim procd	CrJus	2350	3S	L	
229900	Correctional sys and prac	CrJus	2355	3S	L	
229900	Community resrces in corr	CrJus	2365	3S	L	
229900	Penology	CrJus	3325	3S	U	
229900	Cr prev: personal and bus	CrJus	3351	3S	U	

㉚ TEXAS TECH UNIVERSITY

Ms. Suzanne Logan
Associate Director, Independent Study by Correspondence
Division of Continuing Education
Texas Tech University
P.O. Box 4110
Lubbock, Texas 79409-2191
Phone: 806-742-1513
  800-MY-COURS

External degree available through the program. Credit by examination is available. Enrollment on a noncredit basis accepted in credit courses. High school students may enroll in undergraduate courses for credit. Overseas enrollment accepted. Military personnel may enroll through the DANTES program. Minimum period for course completion is thirty days. Maximum period for course completion is nine months.

NCES No.	Course Title	Dept.	Course No.	Cred.	Lev.	Specl. Feat.
	High School courses					
010107	Gen agriculture	Agri	1A	1S	H	
010107	Gen agriculture	Agri	1B	1S	H	
030302	Music theory I	Music		1S	H	AC
030399	Music history and lit	Music	1A	1S	H	
040108	Accounting	Acctg	1A	1S	H	
040108	Accounting	Acctg	1B	1S	H	
040599	General business	GenBs	1A	1S	H	
040599	General business	GenBs	1B	1S	H	
040601	Business communications	BuCom	1A	1S	H	
040601	Business communications	BuCom	1B	1S	H	
040902	Personal business managmt	PBM		1S	H	
040999	Bus mgmt & ownership	BuMgt	1A	1S	H	
040999	Bus mgmt & ownership	BuMgt	1B	1S	H	
050606	Journalism	Journ		1S	H	
060199	Computer mathematics I	CpScM	1A	1S	H	
060199	Computer mathematics I	CpScM	1B	1S	H	
060199	Computer mathematics II	CpScM	2A	1S	H	
060199	Computer mathematics II	CpScM	2B	1S	H	
061101	Intro computer programing	CmpSc	1A	1S	H	
061104	Bus data processing	CmpSc	1B	1S	H	
100100	Clothing and textiles	ClTex		1S	H	
100601	Child development	ChDev		1S	H	
100604	Project self-discovery	PeerC	1A	1S	H	
100604	Knowing myself and helpng	PeerC	1B	1S	H	
100604	Intro to high schl manner	Etiq		1S	H	
100699	Family living and parent	FamHS		1S	H	
120305	English I sem 1	EngHS	9A	1S	H	
120305	English I sem 2	EngHS	9B	1S	H	
120305	English II sem 1	EngHS	10A	1S	H	
120305	English II sem 2	EngHS	10B	1S	H	
120305	English III sem 1	EngHS	11A	1S	H	
120305	English III sem 2	EngHS	11B	1S	H	
120305	English IV sem 1	EngHS	12A	1S	H	
120305	English IV sem 2	EngHS	12B	1S	H	
120305	Correlated lang arts I	CorLa	9A	1S	H	
120305	Correlated lang arts I	CorLa	9B	1S	H	
120305	Correlated lang arts II	CorLa	10A	1S	H	
120305	Correlated lang arts II	CorLa	10B	1S	H	
120305	Correlated lang arts III	CorLa	11A	1S	H	
120305	Correlated lang arts III	CorLa	11B	1S	H	
120305	Correlated lang arts IV	CorLa	12A	1S	H	
120305	Correlated lang arts IV	CorLa	12B	1S	H	
121000	French level I	Frnch	1A	1S	H	AC
121000	French level I	Frnch	1B	1S	H	AC
121600	Latin level I	Latin	1A	1S	H	
121600	Latin level I	Latin	1B	1S	H	
122500	Spanish level I	Span	1A	1S	H	AC
122500	Spanish level I	Span	1B	1S	H	AC
122500	Spanish level II	Span	2A	1S	H	AC
122500	Spanish level II	Span	2B	1S	H	AC
130799	Business and consumer law	BusHS		1S	H	
150300	Biology I	Bio	1A	1S	H	
150300	Biology I	Bio	1B	1S	H	
150700	Physics	Phycs	1A	1S	H	
150700	Physics	Phycs	1B	1S	H	
150800	Physical science	PhySc	1A	1S	H	
150800	Physical science	PhySc	1B	1S	H	
160302	Algebra I	Algbr	1A	1S	H	
160302	Algebra I	Algbr	1B	1S	H	
160302	Algebra II	Algbr	2A	1S	H	
160302	Algebra II	Algbr	2B	1S	H	
160302	Pre-algebra	Algbr	1A	1S	H	
160302	Pre-algebra	Algbr	1B	1S	H	
160601	Geometry I	Geom	1A	1S	H	
160601	Geometry I	Geom	1B	1S	H	
160602	Trigonometry	Trig		1S	H	
160603	Analytic geometry	Geom	2A	HF	H	
160699	Informal geometry I	Geom	1A	1S	H	
160699	Informal geometry I	Geom	1B	1S	H	
161202	Fundamentals of math	FOM	1A	1S	H	
161202	Math of consumer econom	MCE	1A	1S	H	
161202	Consumer mathematics	MatHS	1A	1S	H	
161202	Consumer mathematics	MatHS	1B	1S	H	
161202	Fundamentals of math	FOM	1B	1S	H	
161202	Math of consumer econom	MCE	1B	1S	H	
190100	Physical education I	PhyEd	1A	1S	H	
190100	Physical education I	PhyEd	1B	1S	H	
190509	Health education	HlEd		1S	H	
200100	Psychology	Psych		1S	H	

NCES No.	Course Title	Dept.	Course No.	Cred.	Lev.	Specl. Feat.
220100	Anthropology	Anthr		1S	H	
220201	Economics with free enter	Econ		1S	H	
220300	World geography studies	WGS	1A	1S	H	
220300	World geography studies	WGS	1B	1S	H	
220428	Advanced Texas studies	Hist		1S	H	
220432	United States history	USHis	1A	1S	H	
220432	United States history	USHis	1B	1S	H	
220433	World history studies	WHS	2A	1S	H	
220433	World history studies	WHS	2B	1S	H	
220501	United States government	USGov		1S	H	
220600	Sociology	SocHS		1S	H	
	College courses					
010102	Agricultural finance	Agri	3302	3S	U	
010103	Prin of marketing ag prod	AgEco	2306	3S	L	
010104	The agriculture industry	Agri	1111	3S	L	
010704	Soil fertility management	Agri	4335	3S	U	
030302	Intermediate theory	Music	2403	4S	L	CI
030302	Intermediate theory	Music	2404	4S	L	CI
040101	Elementary accounting I	Acctg	2300	3S	L	
040101	Elementary accounting II	Acctg	2301	3S	L	
040301	Corporation finance	Finan	3320	3S	U	
040304	Prin of money/bankg/credt	Finan	3323	3S	U	
040306	Investments	Finan	4324	3S	U	
040601	Managerial communication	Mgmt	3373	3S	U	
040601	Patterns of rpts and corr	BTWri	2309	3S	L	
041001	Introduction to marketing	Mktg	3350	3S	U	
041303	Real estate fundamentals	RlEst	3332	3S	U	
041306	Real estate finance	RlEst	3334	3S	U	
041307	Real estate invest analys	RlEst	4335	3S	U	
050299	Intro to telecommunicatio	Tlcom	3310	3S	U	
050606	Hist of Amer journalism	Journ	3350	3S	U	
050900	Principles of public rela	PubRe	3310	3S	U	
059900	Intro to mass communicatn	MComm	1300	3S	L	
070403	Substitute teaching	TchEd	3100	1S	U	
070403	Improve student behavior	TchEd	3100	1S	U	
070610	Children's literature	Lit	4350	3S	U	
070610	Teaching Engl in sec schs	Engl	4341	3S	U	
070799	Human rel & reality thera	PCG	4357	3S	U	
081104	Statics	CivlE	2301	3S	L	
100304	Nutrition for today	Nutri	1301	3S	L	
100503	Intr housing & interiors	InDes	1380	3S	L	SL
100601	Develop in later childhd	HuDev	3314	3S	U	
100602	Courtship and marriage	MAF	2322	3S	L	
100799	World's wines & spirit bv	RHIM	2312	3S	L	
120200	Short story	EnglL	3331	3S	U	
120201	Masterpieces of lit	EnglL	2301	3S	L	
120201	Masterpieces of lit	EnglL	2302	3S	L	
120204	American novel	EnglL	3326	3S	U	
120305	Essentials of Eng usage	EnglL	1300	3S	L	
120310	Essentials of rhetoric	EngLL	1301	3S	L	
120310	Advanced college rhetoric	EngLL	1302	3S	L	
130799	Business law I	BuLaw	3391	3S	U	
130799	Business law II	BuLaw	3392	3S	U	
139900	Oil & gas law	BuLaw	3395	3S	U	
150500	Man & his earth	Geol	1308	3S	L	
160302	College algebra	Algbr	1320	3S	L	
160399	Fundamentals of mathemat	Math	1300	3S	L	
160401	Intro to math analysis	Math	1330	3S	L	
160401	Intro to math analysis	Math	1331	3S	L	
160401	Analyt geom & calculus II	Math	1552	5S	L	
160401	Calculus II	Math	1351	3S	L	
160401	Calculus II	Math	1352	3S	L	
160401	Calculus III	Math	2350	3S	L	
160602	Trigonometry	Trig	1321	3S	L	
160603	Analytical geometry	Geom	1350	3S	L	
160603	Analyt geom & calculus I	Math	1551	5S	L	
160899	Stat methods in psycholog	Psych	3403	4S	U	
161101	Intro business statistics	Bus	2445	4S	L	
161108	Statistical methods	Stat	2300	3S	U	
180400	Beginning philosophy	Philo	2300	3S	L	
180502	Logic	Philo	2310	3S	L	
190303	Hist sports & recreation	Hist	3338	3S	U	
190500	Patterns of healthful liv	Hlth	1303	3S	L	
190501	Hlth consider & chem dep	HlEd	3308	3S	U	
190503	Consumer health	Hlth	3305	3S	U	
190504	Chron dis/quality of life	HlEd	2201	2S	L	
190504	Reducing risks of disease	HlEd	2202	2S	L	
190701	Process of rec programmng	Rec	3301	3S	U	
190701	Manag leisure servs organ	RecLe	4308	3S	U	
200500	General psychology	Psych	1300	3S	L	
200501	Abnormal psychology	Psych	4305	3S	U	

NCES No.	Course Title	Dept.	Course No.	Cred.	Lev.	Specl. Feat.
200504	Child psychology	ChPsy	2301	3S	L	
200504	Adolescent psychology	Psych	2305	3S	L	
200509	Personality	PsyPe	3306	3S	U	
200509	Mental health	Psych	2302	3S	L	
200599	Psych of human sex behavi	Psych	4300	3S	U	
200599	Stress management	PCG	4357	3S	U	
200700	Intro social psychology	SoPsy	3304	3S	U	
220102	Cultural anthropology	Anthr	2302	3S	L	
220201	Principles of economics I	Econ	2311	3S	L	
220201	Prin of economics II	Econ	2312	3S	L	
220306	Regional geog of world	Geog	2351	3S	L	
220427	Modern Latin America	LatAm	3382	3S	U	
220428	History of Texas	Hist	3310	3S	U	
220432	History of US to 1877	USHis	2300	3S	L	
220432	History of US since 1877	USHis	2301	3S	L	
220433	Western civilization I	WCiv	1300	3S	L	
220433	Western civilization II	WCiv	1301	3S	L	
220501	Amer govt organization	AmGvt	1301	3S	L	
220501	American public policy	PolSc	2302	3S	L	
220600	Introduction to sociology	Socio	1301	3S	L	
220613	Current social problems	Socio	1320	3S	L	

Graduate courses

NCES No.	Course Title	Dept.	Course No.	Cred.	Lev.	Specl. Feat.
070799	Reality therapy & control	PCG	5369	3S	G	
071201	Intro to small comp in'ed	Educ	5318	3S	G	
120399	Language development	SHSci	5323	3S	G	
200599	Stress management	PCG	5369	3S	G	

Noncredit courses

NCES No.	Course Title	Dept.	Course No.	Cred.	Lev.	Specl. Feat.
010102	Agricultural finance	Agri	NC407	NC	D	
010103	Prin of marketing ag prod	AgEco	NC404	NC	D	
010104	The agriculture industry	Agri	NC401	NC	D	
010107	Gen agriculture, part 1	Agri	NC101	NC	D	
010107	Gen agriculture, part 2	Agri	NC104	NC	D	
010704	Soil fertility management	Agri	NC410	NC	D	
030302	Music theory	Music	NC158	NC	D	AC
030302	Inter music theory I	Music	NC536	NC	D	CI
030302	Inter music theory II	Music	NC539	NC	D	CI
040108	Accounting, part 1	Acctg	NC107	NC	D	
040108	Accounting, part 2	Acctg	NC110	NC	D	
040301	Corporation finance I	Finan	NC608	NC	D	
040304	Prin of money, bank & cdt	Finan	NC611	NC	D	
040306	Investments	Finan	NC620	NC	D	
040500	Entrepreneurship: bus pln			NC	D	
040599	General business, part 1	GenBs	NC125	NC	D	
040599	General business, part 2	GenBs	NC128	NC	D	
040601	Business writing	BuCom	NC731	NC	D	VC
040601	Bus communications, pt 1	BuCom	NC737	NC	D	
040601	Bus communications, pt 2	BuCom	NC738	NC	D	
040601	Patterns of rpts & corres	BTWri	NC437	NC	D	
040601	Managerial communication	Mgmt	NC629	NC	D	
040902	Personal bus management	PBM	NC137	NC	D	
040999	Bus managmt & owner, pt 1	BuMgt	NC116	NC	D	
040999	Bus managmt & owner, pt 2	BuMgt	NC119	NC	D	
041001	Intro to marketing	Mktg	NC632	NC	D	
041303	Real estate fundamentals	RlEst	NC614	NC	D	
041306	Real estate finance	RlEst	NC617	NC	D	
041307	Real estate invest analy	RlEst	NC623	NC	D	
050299	Intro to telecommunicatns	Tlcom	NC503	NC	D	
050606	Journalism	Journ	NC179	NC	D	
050606	Hist of American journalm	Journ	NC494	NC	D	
050900	Prins of public relations	PubRe	NC500	NC	D	
059900	Intro to mass communicats	MComm	NC497	NC	D	
061101	Computer literacy	CmpSc	NC139	NC	D	
061101	Intro to comp programming	CmpSc	NC140	NC	D	
061104	Business data processing	CmpSc	NC143	NC	D	
070403	Substitute teaching	TchEd	NC641	NC	D	
070403	Improving student behavio	TchEd	NC644	NC	D	
070610	Teach English in sec sch	Engl	NC446	NC	D	
070610	Children's literature	Lit	NC638	NC	D	
100100	Clothing and textiles	ClTex	NC716	NC	D	
100304	Nutrition for today	Nutri	NC656	NC	D	
100313	Eight steps to basic nutr	Nutri	NC713	NC	D	
100503	Intro to housing & int	InDes	NC650	NC	D	SL

NCES No.	Course Title	Dept.	Course No.	Cred.	Lev.	Specl. Feat.
100600	Divorce decisions			NC	D	
100601	Child development	ChDev	NC167	NC	D	
100601	Developmt in later child	HuDev	NC659	NC	D	
100602	Courtship and marriage	MAF	NC653	NC	D	
100604	Project self discovery	PeerC	NC173	NC	D	
100604	Knowing myself & help oth	PeerC	NC176	NC	D	
100604	Intro to high school mans	Etiq		NC	D	
100699	Family living & parenthd	Famil	NC170	NC	D	
120200	Short story	EnglL	NC443	NC	D	
120201	Masterpieces of lit, pt 1	EnglL	NC431	NC	D	
120201	Masterpieces of lit, pt 2	EnglL	NC434	NC	D	
120204	American novel	EnglL	NC440	NC	D	
120305	Business English	BusEn	NC728	NC	D	
120310	Creative writing			NC	D	
121000	French level I part 1	Frnch	NC161	NC	D	AC
121000	French level II part 2	Frnch	NC164	NC	D	AC
130201	Business and consumer law	Bus	NC113	NC	D	
130799	Business law I	BuLaw	NC596	NC	D	
130799	Business law II	BuLaw	NC599	NC	D	
139900	Oil and gas law	BuLaw	NC602	NC	D	
150300	Biology I part 1	Bio	NC299	NC	D	
150300	Biology I part 2	Bio	NC302	NC	D	
150700	Physics I part 1	Phycs	NC311	NC	D	
150700	Physics I part 2	Phycs	NC314	NC	D	
150800	Physical science part 1	PhySc	NC305	NC	D	
150800	Physical science part 2	PhySc	NC308	NC	D	
160302	Pre-algebra part 1	Algbr	NC281	NC	D	
160302	Pre-algebra part 2	Algbr	NC284	NC	D	
160302	Algebra I part 1	Algbr	NC254	NC	D	
160302	Algebra I part 2	Algbr	NC257	NC	D	
160302	Algebra II part 1	Algbr	NC260	NC	D	
160302	Algebra II part 2	Algbr	NC263	NC	D	
160401	Intro math analysis pt 1	Math	NC512	NC	D	
160401	Intro math analysis pt 2	Math	NC515	NC	D	
160401	Calculus I	Math	NC521	NC	D	
160601	Geometry I part 1	Geom	NC266	NC	D	
160601	Geometry I part 2	Geom	NC269	NC	D	
160602	Trigonometry	Trig	NC287	NC	D	
160603	Analytic geometry	Geom	NC272	NC	D	
160899	Stat methods in psychlgy	Psych	NC572	NC	D	
161101	Intro to business stats	Bus	NC626	NC	D	
161202	Math of consumer eco pt 1	MCE	NC131	NC	D	
161202	Math of consumer eco pt 2	MCE	NC134	NC	D	
161202	Fundamentals of math pt 1	FOM	NC275	NC	D	
161202	Fundamentals of math pt 2	FOM	NC278	NC	D	
180400	Beginning philosophy	Philo	NC542	NC	D	
180502	Logic	Philo	NC545	NC	D	
181202	Intro to New Testament	Relig	NC415	NC	D	
181299	Intro to Old Testament	Relig	NC414	NC	D	
190100	Physical education part 1	PhyEd	NC293	NC	D	
190100	Physical education part 2	PhyEd	NC296	NC	D	
190303	Hist of sports & rec US	Hist	NC488	NC	D	
190500	Patterns of healthful lvg	Hlth	NC455	NC	D	
190501	Risk-take behavior in hth	HlEd	NC464	NC	D	
190504	Chronic dis & quality lfe	HlEd	NC458	NC	D	
190504	Reduce risk of comm disea	HlEd	NC461	NC	D	
190509	General health	HlEd	NC290	NC	D	
190701	Process of rec programmng	Rec	NC467	NC	D	
190701	Manage leisure serv orgs	RecLe	NC470	NC	D	
200500	General psychology	Psych	NC554	NC	D	
200501	Abnormal psychology	Psych	NC578	NC	D	
200502	Re-enter the workplace			NC	D	
200504	Child psychology	ChPsy	NC557	NC	D	
200504	Adolescent psychology	Psych	NC563	NC	D	
200509	Personality	PsyPe	NC569	NC	D	
200509	Mental health	Psych	NC560	NC	D	
200599	Psych of human sex behavr	Psych	NC575	NC	D	
200700	Intro to social psychlgy	SoPsy	NC566	NC	D	
220102	Cultural anthropology	Anthr	NC413	NC	D	
220201	Eco: fund of free ent sys	Econ	NC122	NC	D	
220306	Reg geography of the wrld	Geog	NC449	NC	D	
220427	Modern Latin America	LatAm	NC491	NC	D	
220428	History of Texas	Hist	NC485	NC	D	
220432	US history part 1	USHis	NC323	NC	D	
220432	US history part 2	USHis	NC326	NC	D	
220433	World history studies pt1	WHS	NC329	NC	D	
220433	World history studies pt2	WHS	NC332	NC	D	
220499	Genealogy			NC	D	
220501	United States government	USGov	NC320	NC	D	
220501	American public policy	PolSc	NC551	NC	D	
220600	Intro to sociology	Socio	NC581	NC	D	
220613	Current social problems	Socio	NC584	NC	D	

(31) UNIVERSITY OF ALABAMA

Mr. John C. Burgeson
Director, Independent Study Division
College of Continuing Studies
University of Alabama
P.O. Box 870388
Tuscaloosa, Alabama 35487-0388
Phone: 205-348-7642

Enrollment on a noncredit basis accepted in credit courses. High school students may enroll in undergraduate courses for credit. Overseas enrollment accepted. Military personnel may enroll through the DANTES program. Minimum period for course completion is six weeks. Maximum period for course completion is one year. Two 6-month extensions are available on each course enrollment. The University offers an external degree through New College, not the Independent Study Division; however, credits toward the degree may be earned by correspondence.

NCES No.	Course Title	Dept.	Course No.	Cred.	Lev.	Specl. Feat.
	High School courses					
040104	General business	Bus	1A	HF	H	
040104	General business	Bus	1B	HF	H	
040104	Basic business procedures	Bus	9A	HF	H	
040104	Basic business procedures	Bus	9B	HF	H	
061101	Computer education	CmpSc	9	HF	H	
090101	Modern health	HlSci	1A	HF	H	
120307	Ninth-grade English	Engl	9A	HF	H	
120307	Ninth-grade English	Engl	9B	HF	H	
120307	Tenth-grade English	Engl	10A	HF	H	
120307	Tenth-grade English	Engl	10B	HF	H	
120307	Eleventh-grade English	Engl	11A	HF	H	
120307	Eleventh-grade English	Engl	11B	HF	H	
120307	Twelfth-grade English	Engl	12A	HF	H	
120307	Twelfth-grade English	Engl	12B	HF	H	
120307	Basic grammar review	Engl	13	HF	H	
122500	First yr Spanish I	Span	1A	HF	H	AC
122500	First yr Spanish II	Span	1B	HF	H	AC
150800	Physical science	PhySc	9a	HF	H	
150800	Physical science	PhySc	9b	HF	H	
160301	General mathematics	Math	13A	HF	H	
160301	General mathematics	Math	13B	HF	H	
160302	Algebra I	Math	9A	HF	H	
160302	Algebra I	Math	9B	HF	H	
160302	Algebra II	Math	11A	HF	H	
160302	Algebra II	Math	11B	HF	H	
160304	Unified geometry	Math	10A	HF	H	
160304	Unified geometry	Math	10B	HF	H	
160602	Trigonometry	Math	12	HF	H	
161202	Consumer mathematics	Math	14	HF	H	
220300	World geography	Hist	9B	HF	H	
220403	Economics	Hist	12A	HF	H	
220428	Alabama history	Hist	9A	HF	H	
220432	US history	Hist	11A	HF	H	
220432	US history	Hist	11B	HF	H	
220433	World history	Hist	10A	HF	H	
220433	World history	Hist	10B	HF	H	
220501	US government	PolSc	12B	HF	H	
220600	Sociology	Hist	13	HF	H	
	College courses					
020904	Natural resources of US	GBAdm	332C	3S	U	
030399	Intro to listening	Music	121C	3S	L	
030402	Theatre history	ThArt	451C	3S	U	
030402	Theatre history	ThArt	452C	3S	U	
040301	Business finance	Bus	302C	3S	U	
040305	International finance	Finan	431C	3S	U	
040306	Investments	Bus	414C	3S	U	
040308	Money and banking	Bus	301C	3S	U	
040312	Public finance	Bus	423C	3S	U	
040399	Transportation	Bus	351C	3S	U	
040710	Business risk management	Finan	442C	3S	U	
040712	Personal ins planning	Finan	341C	3S	U	
040905	Organ theory & behavior	Mgmt	300C	3S	U	
041001	Marketing	Mktg	300C	3S	U	
041099	Retail management	Mktg	321C	3S	U	
041099	Sales management	Mktg	338C	3S	U	
041099	Promotional strategy	Mktg	344C	3S	U	
041099	International marketing	Mktg	455C	3S	U	
041099	Marketing research	Mktg	473C	3S	U	
041099	Salesmanship	Mktg	337C	3S	U	
041099	Consumer behavior	Mktg	313C	3S	U	

NCES No.	Course Title	Dept.	Course No.	Cred.	Lev.	Specl. Feat.
041104	Collective bargaining	Mgmt	430C	3S	U	
041199	Intro human resources mgt	Mgmt	301C	3S	U	
041199	Personnel management	Mgmt	310C	3S	U	
041199	Leadership	Mgmt	320C	3S	U	
041301	Real estate appraisal	Finan	432C	3S	U	
041303	Principles of real estate	Finan	331C	3S	U	
041306	Real estate finance	Finan	436C	3S	U	
050499	Intro to mass communica	MComm	101C	3S	L	
050499	Mass media law & regula	MComm	401C	3S	L	
070799	Guidance for teachers	Educ	411C	3S	U	
080699	Process calculations	ChemE	252C	3S	L	
080699	Thermodynamics calculatns	ChemE	253C	3S	L	
100206	Personal finance	ConSc	404C	3S	U	
100299	Consumer protection	ConSc	401C	3S	U	
100313	Intro to human nutrition	HuNut	101C	3S	L	
100313	Child nutrition	HuNut	301C	3S	U	
100401	Decision mkg & fam resour	ConSc	201C	3S	L	
100504	Household equipment	ConSc	240C	3S	L	
100601	Child devel: school age	HuDev	301C	3S	U	
100601	Child devel: adolescence	HuDev	302C	3S	U	
100602	Marriage and the family	HuDev	262C	3S	L	
100699	Human development	HuDev	101C	3S	L	
120299	Greek & Roman mythology	Class	222C	2S	L	
120307	English literature I	EngLL	205C	3S	L	
120307	English literature II	EngLL	206C	3S	L	
120307	American literature I	EngLL	209C	3S	L	
120307	American literature II	EngLL	210C	3S	L	
120307	Major American writers I	EngLL	340C	3S	U	
120307	Major American writers II	EngLL	341C	3S	U	
120307	Contemporary American lit	EngLL	345C	3S	U	
120307	Southern literature	EngLL	347C	3S	U	
120307	Eng Bible as literature	EngLL	363C	3S	U	
120307	Shakespeare	EngLL	366C	3S	U	
120307	The English novel	EngLL	387C	3S	U	
120307	The modern short story	EngLL	390C	3S	U	
120307	The Age of Browning	EngLL	485C	3S	U	
120307	The Age of Hardy	EngLL	486C	3S	U	
120307	Modern British fiction	EngLL	491C	3S	U	
120310	English composition I	Engl	101C	3S	L	
120310	English composition II	Engl	102C	3S	L	
120310	Fiction writing	Engl	301C	3S	U	
120399	Popular culture in Amer	AmSt	322C	3S	L	
121000	Intermediate French I	Frnch	201C	3S	L	
121000	Intermediate French II	Frnch	202C	3S	L	
121100	Elementary German I	Germn	101C	4S	L	AC
121100	Elementary German II	Germn	102C	4S	L	AC
121100	Intermediate German I	Germn	201C	3S	L	AC
121100	Intermediate German II	Germn	202C	3S	L	AC
121100	Intermed scientific Ger I	Germn	209C	3S	L	
121100	Intermed scientific Ger 2	Germn	210C	3S	L	
121100	Ger for reading profic I	Germn	103C	3S	L	
121100	Ger for reading profic II	Germn	104C	3S	L	
121600	Elementary Latin I	Latin	101C	3S	L	
121600	Elementary Latin II	Latin	102C	3S	L	
121600	Intermed Latin reading	Latin	201C	3S	L	
122500	Intermediate Spanish I	Span	201C	3S	L	
122500	Intermediate Spanish II	Span	202C	3S	L	
122500	Advanced grammar & comp	Span	356C	3S	U	
122500	Survey of Spanish lit I	Span	371C	3S	U	
122500	Survey of Spanish lit II	Span	372C	3S	U	
122500	Spanish civilization	Span	364C	3S	U	
130499	Intro to criminal justice	CrJus	100C	3S	L	
130499	Intro to law enforcement	CrJus	220C	3S	L	
130499	Intro to corrections	CrJus	270C	3S	L	
130499	Criminal investigation	CrJus	321C	3S	U	
130499	Intro to private security	CrJus	221C	3S	L	
130499	Org & man con in crim jus	CrJus	330C	3S	U	
130499	Crime prev & control	CrJus	421C	3S	U	
130599	Government & business	LegSt	402C	3S	U	
130799	Law, business & society	LegSt	200C	3S	L	
130999	Real & pers property law	LegSt	407C	3S	U	
140199	Library research	LibSc	140C	2S	L	
150100	Introduction to astronomy	Astro	101C	3S	U	
150103	Introduction to astronomy	Astro	102C	3S	U	
150399	Heredity	Bio	309C	3S	L	
150399	Human reproduction	Bio	210C	2S	L	
150399	Hum anatomy & physiology	Bio	213C	4S	L	
150399	Hum anatomy & physiology	Bio	214C	4S	L	
150399	History of biology	Bio	281C	3S	L	
150399	Medical etymology	Bio	201C	2S	L	
150799	Desc physics non-sci majr	Phycs	115C	3S	L	
150799	Desc physics non-sci majr	Phycs	116C	3S	L	

NCES No.	Course Title	Dept.	Course No.	Cred.	Lev.	Specl. Feat.
160202	Intro to math reasoning	Math	113C	3S	L	
160302	College algebra	Math	109C	3S	L	
160302	High school algebra	Math	001C	1U	L	
160302	Precal, algebra & trig	Math	112C	3S	L	
160302	Intro to college math	Math	120C	3S	L	
160399	Intro college mathematics	Math	111C	3S	L	
160399	Plane geometry	Math	002C	1U	L	
160401	Calculus & analytic geom	Math	126C	4S	L	
160401	Calculus	Math	227C	4S	L	
160401	Introduction to calculus	Math	121C	3S	L	
160403	Analytic geom & calculus	Math	125C	4S	L	
160602	Analytic trigonometry	Math	115C	3S	L	
160801	Statistical methods I	Stat	250C	3S	L	
160801	Statistical methods II	Stat	251C	3S	L	
180302	Ethics	Philo	200C	3S	L	
180599	Intro to deductive logic	Philo	101C	3S	L	
180700	Intro to philosophy	Philo	100C	3S	L	
180902	Intro to New Testament	Relig	112C	3S	L	
181102	Intro religious studies	Relig	100C	3S	L	
190509	Personal health	HlEd	270C	3S	L	
200199	Intro to psychology	Psych	101C	3S	L	
200505	Psychology of adjustment	Psych	207C	3S	L	
209900	Elementary statistic meth	Psych	211C	3S	L	
209900	Applied psychology	Psych	228C	3S	L	
210401	Soc services for delinq	PubAd	308C	3S	U	
210401	Family & child welfare	PubAd	310C	3S	U	
220199	General anthropology I	Anthr	101C	3S	L	
220199	General anthropology II	Anthr	102C	3S	L	
220201	Prin of macroeconomics	Econ	111C	3S	L	
220201	Prin of macroeconomics	Econ	110C	3S	L	
220202	Hist of economic concepts	Econ	450C	3S	U	
220299	Amer economic institution	Econ	160C	3S	L	
220305	Survey of geography	Geog	103C	3S	L	
220306	World regional geography	Geog	105C	3S	L	
220399	Geography of Anglo-Amer	Geog	243C	3S	L	
220399	Geography of West Europe	Geog	246C	3S	L	
220401	Const hist of US to 1877	Hist	323C	3S	U	
220406	Am youth cul 1940s-1950s	AmSt	310C	3S	U	
220408	Hist of Chris chu to 1500	Hist	235C	3S	L	
220408	Hist Chris chu since 1500	Hist	236C	3S	L	
220408	Intro to rel in America	Relig	221C	3S	L	
220421	US hist: colonial period	Hist	220C	3S	L	
220424	England to 1688	Hist	247C	3S	L	
220424	England since 1688	Hist	248C	3S	L	
220427	Colonial Latin American	Hist	237C	3S	L	
220427	Mod Latin Amer since 1808	Hist	238C	3S	L	
220428	Hist of Ala since 1865	Hist	226C	3S	L	
220428	Hist of Alabama to 1865	Hist	225C	3S	L	
220431	Russia to 1894	Hist	361C	3S	U	
220432	The US since 1945	Hist	418C	3S	U	
220432	Western civiliz to 1648	Hist	101C	3S	L	
220432	Western civ since 1648	Hist	102C	3S	L	
220433	Comparative world civiliz	Hist	110C	3S	L	
220453	US Reconstruction	Hist	222C	3S	L	
220499	US in nineteenth century	Hist	221C	3S	L	
220501	Intro to American politic	PolSc	101C	3S	L	
220501	Intro to public policy	PolSc	103C	3S	L	
220509	Pol parties & elections	PolSc	311C	3S	U	
220511	State & local government	PolSc	211C	3S	L	
220599	International relations	PolSc	204C	3S	L	
220599	Public administration	PolSc	206C	3S	L	
220602	Criminology	Socio	301C	3S	U	
220605	The family	Socio	206C	3S	L	
220613	Analysis of social prob	Socio	102C	3S	L	
220615	Minority peoples	Socio	215C	3S	L	
220699	Intro to sociology	Socio	101C	3S	L	
220699	Organ & work in industry	Socio	355C	3S	U	
	Noncredit courses					
220502	Basic citizenship	Hist	99C	NC	H	
220502	Intermediate citizenship	Hist	99B	NC	H	

(32) UNIVERSITY OF ALASKA

Jim Stricks
Director, Center for Distance Education
Room 130, Red Building, College of Rural Alaska
University of Alaska
Fairbanks, Alaska 99775-0900
Phone: 907-474-5353

High school students may enroll in undergraduate courses for credit. Overseas enrollment accepted. Military personnel may enroll through the DANTES program. Minimum period for course completion is two months. Maximum period for course completion is one year.

NCES No.	Course Title	Dept.	Course No.	Cred.	Lev.	Specl. Feat.
	College courses					
030399	Music fundamentals	Music	103	3S	L	
040101	Elementary accounting I	Acctg	101	3S	L	
040101	Elementary accounting II	Acctg	102	3S	L	
040306	Pract guide to mod invest	BusAd	170	3S	L	
041001	Principles of marketing	BusAd	343	3S	U	
041308	Real estate/property law	BusAd	223	3S	L	
050699	Intro to mass communicatn	Journ	101	3S	L	
060700	BASIC programming	CmpSc	106	3S	L	CI
070102	Philosophy of education	Educ	422	3S	U	VC
070102	Human development	Educ	312	3S	U	
070401	Comm in cross-cult clrms	Educ	350	3S	U	VC
070512	Literature for children	Educ	304	3S	U	
070800	Exceptional learner	Educ	375	3S	U	
071100	Measurement & evaluation	Educ	330	3S	U	
071201	Microcomputer applic clrm	Educ	429	3S	U	CI
082500	Fundamentals of petroleum	Petro	101	3S	L	
100313	Science of nutrition	HomEc	203	3S	L	
110601	Private pilot ground schl	Aviat	100	4S	L	LK
120103	Nature of language	Ling	101	3S	L	
120307	Frontier lit of Alaska	Engl	350	3S	U	
120310	Methods of written comm	Engl	111	3S	L	
120310	Intermediate exposition	Engl	211	3S	L	
120310	Technical writing	Engl	314	3S	U	
130701	Business law I	BusAd	331	3S	U	
130702	Business law II	BusAd	332	3S	U	
150304	Natural history of Alaska	Bio	104	3S	L	
160199	Concepts of math I	Math	131	3S	L	
160199	Concepts of math II	Math	132	3S	L	
160302	College algebra	Math	107	3S	L	
160302	Elementary algebra I	Math	075	3S	D	
160302	Elementary algebra II	Math	076	3S	D	
160401	Calculus I	Math	200	4S	L	
160401	Calculus II	Math	201	4S	L	
160602	Trigonometry	Math	108	2S	L	
160802	Elem probability & stats	Stat	301	3S	U	
161299	Basic mathematics	Math	051	3S	D	
200104	Intro to psychology	Psych	101	3S	L	
200504	Developmental psychology	Psych	240	3S	L	
200799	Drugs & drug dependence	Psych	370	3S	U	
220201	Principles of economics I	Econ	201	3S	L	
220201	Principles of economcs II	Econ	202	3S	L	
220299	Alaska economy	Econ	137	3S	L	
220305	Elements of physical geog	Geog	205	3S	L	
220306	Introductory geography	Geog	101	3S	L	
220399	Geography of Alaska	Geog	302	3S	U	
220432	History of the US I	Hist	131	3S	L	
220432	History of the US II	Hist	132	3S	L	
220453	History of Western civ I	Hist	101	3S	L	
220453	History of Western civ II	Hist	102	3S	L	
220499	History of Alaska	Hist	341	3S	U	
220499	Maritime hist of Alaska	Hist	345	3S	U	
220499	Polar exploration & lit	Hist	380	3S	U	
220501	Intro Amer govt & politic	PolSc	101	3S	L	
220603	Population & ecology	Socio	207	3S	L	
220605	Sociology of the family	Socio	242	3S	L	
220613	Social problems	Socio	201	3S	L	
220699	Drugs & drug dependence	Socio	370	3S	U	
220699	Intro to sociology	Socio	101	3S	L	

(33) UNIVERSITY OF ARIZONA

Leslie Dykstra
Program Coordinator, Correspondence/Independent Study
Babcock Building 1201
University of Arizona
1717 East Speedway
Tucson, Arizona 85719
Phone: 602-621-3021

Enrollment on a noncredit basis accepted in credit courses. High school students may enroll in undergraduate courses for credit. Overseas enrollment accepted. Military personnel may enroll through the DANTES program. Minimum period for course completion is six weeks-h.s. courses;

twenty days per unit-college courses. Maximum period for course completion is twelve months.

NCES No.	Course Title	Dept.	Course No.	Cred.	Lev.	Specl. Feat.
	High School courses					
040104	Elementary accounting	Acctg	11A	HF	H	
040104	Elementary accounting	Acctg	11B	HF	H	
099900	Intro to health science	HlEd		HF	H	
100601	Child development	HDFL	A	HF	H	
100601	Child development	HDFL	B	HF	H	
100699	Interpersonal relations	HFL		HF	H	
120310	Vocabulary study	Engl	11-12	HF	H	
120310	Creative writing	Engl		HF	H	
120310	Language and usage	Engl	9A12B	HF	H	
122500	Spanish, first semester	HSLng	A-1	HF	H	
122500	Spanish, second semester	HSLng	A-2	HF	H	
122500	Spanish, third semester	HSLng	B-1	HF	H	
122500	Spanish, fourth semester	HSLng	B-2	HF	H	
150301	Basic life science	Bio	9A	HF	H	
150301	Basic life science	Bio	9B	HF	H	
150900	Basic earth science	Sci	10A	HF	H	
150900	Basic earth science	Sci	10B	HF	H	
160301	General math	Math	9A	HF	H	
160301	General math	Math	9B	HF	H	
160302	Elementary algebra	Math	9C	HF	H	
160302	Elementary algebra	Math	9D	HF	H	
160601	Plane geometry	Math	10A	HF	H	
160601	Plane geometry	Math	10B	HF	H	
160602	Plane trigonometry	Math	11A	HF	H	
161202	Consumer math	Math		HF	H	
200599	Elementary psychology	SocSt	12	HF	H	
220399	World geography	Geog	10A	HF	H	
220399	World geography	Geog	10B	HF	H	
220406	Cultures around the world	Hist	A	HF	H	
220406	Cultures around the world	Hist	B	HF	H	
220420	Black studies	Hist		HF	H	
220428	Arizona history	Hist	11-12	HF	H	
220432	US history	Hist	12	HF	H	
220432	US history to 1865	Hist	11A	HF	H	
220432	US history from 1865	Hist	11B	HF	H	
220432	US/AZ history	Hist	11C	HF	H	
220432	US/AZ history	Hist	11D	HF	H	
220501	Amer political process	Govt	12	HF	H	
220501	US government	Govt	11-12	HF	H	
220511	Arizona government	Govt	11-12	HF	H	
220606	Elementary sociology	SocSt	12	HF	H	
229900	Skills for living	MCE		HF	H	
229900	Free enterprise	SocSt	12	HF	H	
	College courses					
010499	Feeds and feeding	AnSci	4134A	1U	L	
010499	Feeds and feeding	AnSci	4134B	2U	L	
011400	Conserv of nat resources	RNR	4135	3U	L	
030399	Survey of music I	Music	4107	3U	U	
030399	Survey of music II	Music	4108	3U	U	
040101	Principles of accounting	Acctg	4200	3U	L	
040101	Principles of accounting	Acctg	4210	3U	L	
040203	Records management	T&TE	4384	3U	U	
040601	Intro to bus commun	T&TE	4383	3U	U	
041099	Creative advertising	Mktg	4364	3U	U	
041099	Public relations	Mktg	4366	3U	U	
041199	Personnel management	Mgmt	4330	3U	U	
070103	Social found and adminstr	EdFA	4350	3U	U	
090903	Intro to health sci educ	Hlth	4178	3U	U	
090999	International health pblm	Hlth	4433	3U	U	
090999	Safety ed & accident prev	Hlth	4435	3U	U	
100602	Family relations	HomEc	4337	3U	U	
100699	Education for marriage	HomEc	4137	3U	L	
120307	Modern literature	Engl	4261	3U	L	
120308	Major American writers	Engl	4265	3U	L	
121000	Elementary French	Frnch	4101A	2U	L	
121000	Elementary French	Frnch	4101B	2U	L	
121000	Intermediate French	Frnch	4201A	2U	L	
121000	Intermediate French	Frnch	4201B	2U	L	
121100	Elementary German	Germn	4101A	2U	L	AC
121100	Elementary German	Germn	4101B	2U	L	AC
121100	Intermediate German	Germn	4201A	2U	L	AC
122000	Russian, first semester	R&SL	4101A	4U	U	AC
122000	Russian, second semester	R&SL	4101B	4U	U	AC
122000	Russian, third semester	R&SL	4201A	4U	U	AC
122000	Russian, fourth semester	R&SL	4201B	4U	U	AC
122500	Elementary Spanish	Span	4101A	2U	L	
122500	Second-semester Spanish	Span	4101B	2U	L	

NCES No.	Course Title	Dept.	Course No.	Cred.	Lev.	Specl. Feat.
122500	Third-semester Spanish	Span	4201A	2U	L	
122500	Fourth-semester Spanish	Span	4201B	2U	L	
129900	Literature of India	OrStu	4444A	3U	U	
140399	Organization of museums	Anthr	4441	3U	U	
140499	Museum collections mgmt	Anthr	4442	3U	U	
150199	Essentials of astronomy	Astro	4100	3U	U	
150202	Intro meteorology/climate	AtmSc	4171	3U	L	
150316	Plants useful to man	GBio	4412	2U	U	
150321	General plant pathology	PPath	4205	3U	L	
150500	Intro to geology	GeoSc	4101A	3U	L	
150500	Intro to geology	GeoSc	4101B	3U	L	
159900	Insects and man	Entom	4151	3U	L	
160302	Intermediate algebra	Math	4116	3U	L	
160302	College algebra	Math	4117	3U	L	
160401	Calculus	Math	4125A	3U	L	
160401	Elements of calculus	Math	4123	3U	L	CI
160401	Calculus	Math	4125B	3U	L	
160406	Intro to ord dif equat	Math	4254	3U	L	CI
160602	Trigonometry	Math	4118	2U	L	
160899	Intro to statistics	Math	4160	3U	L	
160999	Finite mathematics	Math	4119	3U	L	
180499	Intro to philosophy	Philo	4111	3U	L	
180502	Intro to logic	Philo	4112	3U	L	
180700	Intro to moral & soc phil	Philo	4113	3U	L	
190513	School health education	Hlth	4381	3U	L	
220102	Cultural anthropology	Anthr	4200	3U	L	
220199	Intro to phys anth & arch	Anthr	4101	3U	U	
220199	Prehist peopl of the SW	Anthr	4205	3U	L	
220199	Native peoples of the SW	Anthr	4206	3U	L	
220199	Intro to cult anth & ling	Anthr	4102	3U	U	
220201	Principles of economics	Econ	4201A	3U	L	
220201	Principles of economics	Econ	4201B	3U	L	
220204	Money and banking	Econ	4330	3U	U	
220423	Oriental humanities	OrStu	4140A	3U	L	
220423	Modern Chinese history	OrStu	4476	3U	U	
220423	History of China	OrStu	4375B	3U	U	
220423	Modern Chinese history	OrStu	4476	3U	U	
220423	Modn East Asia, a history	OrStu	4270	3U	U	
220424	History of England	Hist	4117	3U	L	
220424	History of England	Hist	4118	3U	L	
220426	French Revolut & Napoleon	Hist	4420	3U	U	
220432	Intro to hist of Wstn wld	Hist	4101	3U	L	
220432	Intro to hist of Wstn wld	Hist	4102	3U	L	
220432	Hist of the United States	Hist	4106	3U	L	
220432	Hist of the United States	Hist	4107	3U	L	
220432	US: 1945 to present	Hist	4440	3U	U	
220432	History of Am foreign rel	Hist	4449	3U	U	
220432	History of Am foreign rel	Hist	4450	3U	U	
220470	American ethnic history	Hist	4452	3U	U	
220499	History of China	Hist	4375B	3U	U	
220499	Modern Chinese history	Hist	4476	3U	U	
220501	Am national government	PolSc	4102	3U	L	
220505	Intro to internatl relat	PolSc	4150	3U	L	
220511	Am state & local govt	PolSc	4103	3U	L	
220511	Arizona government	PolSc	4214B	1U	L	
220599	Nat & state constitutions	PolSc	4110	3U	L	
220599	Soviet foreign policy	PolSc	4451	3U	U	
220601	Intro to sociology	Socio	4100	3U	L	
220602	Criminology	Socio	4342	3U	U	
220603	World population	Socio	4189	3U	L	
220604	Juvenile delinquency	Socio	4341	3U	U	
220613	American social problems	Socio	4201	3U	L	
220614	Minority rel & urban soc	Socio	4160	3U	L	
220699	Sociology of the family	Socio	4321	3U	U	

(34) **UNIVERSITY OF ARKANSAS**

Mr. William E. Manning
Director, Department of Independent Study
2 University Center
Center for Continuing Education
University of Arkansas
Fayetteville, Arkansas 72701
Phone: 501-575-3647

High school students may enroll in undergraduate courses for credit. Overseas enrollment accepted. Military personnel may enroll through the DANTES program. Minimum period for course completion is three months. Maximum period for course completion is six months.

NCES No.	Course Title	Dept.	Course No.	Cred.	Lev.	Specl. Feat.
	High School courses					
040104	Accounting	Acctg	11A	HF		H
040104	Accounting	Acctg	11B	HF		H
040201	Secretarial office proced	SOP	11A	HF		H
040201	Secretarial office proced	SOP	11B	HF		H
040203	Records management	AdmSc	NL	HF		H
040205	Shorthand	Shthd	12A	HF		H
040205	Shorthand	Shthd	12B	HF		H
040207	Typing	Typg	11A	HF		H
040207	Typing	Typg	11B	HF		H
040601	Business communications	Engl	1 SEM	HF		H
081000	Industrial arts drafting	InArt	12A	HF		H
081000	Industrial arts drafting	InArt	12B	HF		H
120201	World literature	Engl	1STSE	HF		H
120201	World literature	Engl	2NDSE	HF		H
120305	Grammar	Engl	11	HF		H
120305	Grammar	Engl	12	HF		H
120305	Remedial language arts	Engl	1 SEM	HF		H
120305	Advanced language arts	Engl	1 SEM	HF		H
120307	Literature	Engl	11	HF		H
120307	Literature	Engl	12	HF		H
120308	Vocab improv and read dev	Engl	1 SEM	HF		H
120399	Grammar and literature	Engl	9A	HF		H
120399	Grammar and literature	Engl	9B	HF		H
120399	Grammar and literature	Engl	10A	HF		H
120399	Grammar and literature	Engl	10B	HF		H
120399	Grammar and literature	Engl	11A	HF		H
120399	Grammar and literature	Engl	11B	HF		H
120399	Grammar and literature	Engl	12A	HF		H
120399	Grammar and literature	Engl	12B	HF		H
121000	French	ForLg	IA	HF		H
121000	French	ForLg	IB	HF		H
121600	Latin	ForLg	9A	HF		H
121600	Latin	ForLg	9B	HF		H
121600	Latin	ForLg	10A	HF		H
121600	Latin	ForLg	10B	HF		H
122500	Spanish	ForLg	9A	HF		H
122500	Spanish	ForLg	9B	HF		H
129900	Introduction to mythology	Engl	1 SEM	HF		H
150399	Biology	Sci	10A	HF		H
150399	Biology	Sci	10B	HF		H
160301	Remedial arithmetic	Math	I	HF		H
160301	Remedial arithmetic	Math	II	HF		H
160302	Algebra	Math	9A	HF		H
160302	Algebra	Math	9B	HF		H
160302	Advanced algebra	Math	11A	HF		H
160302	Advanced algebra	Math	11B	HF		H
160601	Geometry	Math	10A	HF		H
160601	Geometry	Math	10B	HF		H
161101	Business mathematics	Math	I	HF		H
161101	Business mathematics	Math	II	HF		H
161199	Vocational mathematics	Math	I	HF		H
161199	Vocational mathematics	Math	II	HF		H
190509	Physiology and hygiene	Sci	11B	HF		H
220201	Economics	SocSt	12	HF		H
220302	Commercial geography	SocSt	9A	HF		H
220302	Commercial geography	SocSt	9B	HF		H
220306	United States geography	SocSt	10A	HF		H
220306	United States geography	SocSt	10B	HF		H
220432	United States history	SocSt	11A	HF		H
220432	United States history	SocSt	11B	HF		H
220433	World history	SocSt	10A	HF		H
220433	World history	SocSt	10B	HF		H
220501	American government	SocSt	12A	HF		H
220501	American government	SocSt	12B	HF		H
220502	Civics	SocSt	9A	HF		H
220502	Civics	SocSt	9B	HF		H
220600	Sociology	SocSt		HF		H
	College courses					
010100	Agricultural economics	Agri	2103	3S	L	
010404	Principles of genetics	AnSci	3123	3S	U	
010699	Plant geography	Botny	3513	3S	U	
011400	Conservation of nat resou	Geog	3003	3S	U	
030402	Intro to dramatic art	SpDrA	2223	3S	L	
030499	Origins of modern theater	SpDrA	5753	3S	U	
040101	Principles of acctg I	Acctg	2013	3S	L	
040101	Principles of acctg II	Acctg	2023	3S	L	
040601	Business communications	Mgmt	2323	3S	L	
040904	Intro to management	Mgmt	1033	3S	L	
051104	Parliamentary procedure	SpDrA	2351	1S	L	
051303	Writing for television	SpDrA	4833	3S	U	
070401	Intro to childhood educ	ElEd	1103	3S	L	
070401	Prin & meth in middle sch	SecEd	4043	3S	U	
070404	Teaching science	ElEd	3303	3S	U	
070499	Meth & mat sch & comm rec	Rec	3813	3S	U	
070511	Drafting	VocEd	1603	3S	L	
070511	Industrial design I	VocEd	3603	3S	U	
070511	Industrial safety I	VocEd	2653	3S	L	
070512	Children's literature	ElEd	3273	3S	L	
070512	Reading & other lang arts	ElEd	3333	3S	U	
070516	Teaching math	ElEd	4413	3S	U	
070516	Teaching math	SecEd	4223	3S	U	
070519	Meth & mats phy ed el sch	PhyEd	3373	3S	U	
070522	Teaching of social stud	SecEd	4232	2S	U	
071103	Secon tests & measurement	SecEd	4723	3S	U	
081102	Mechanics of fluids	EngSc	3203	3S	U	
081104	Statics	EngSc	2003	3S	L	
081104	Dynamics	EngSc	3003	3S	U	
081199	Mechanics of materials	EngSc	3103	3S	U	
089900	Engineering statistics	IndEn	3313	3S	U	
089900	Engr economics analysis	IndEn	3413	3S	U	
090599	Personal health & safety	HlEd	1103	3S	L	
100313	Nutrition in health	HomEc	1213	3S	L	
120201	Intro to literature	Engl	1113	3S	L	
120201	Masterpieces Wstrn lit	Engl	1123	3S	L	
120307	Engl lit from beg to 1700	Engl	2113	3S	L	
120307	Engl lit from 1700 to pre	Engl	2123	3S	L	
120310	Composition	Engl	1013	3S	L	
120310	Composition—continuation	Engl	1023	3S	L	
120310	Essay writing	Engl	2013	3S	L	
120310	Intermediate composition	Engl	3003	3S	U	
120399	Vocabulary building	Engl	1153	3S	L	
121000	Elementary French	Frnch	1003	3S	L	
121000	Advanced grammar & comp	Frnch	4003	3S	U	
121000	Elementary French	Frnch	1013	3S	L	
121000	Intermediate French	Frnch	2003	3S	L	
121000	Intermediate French	Frnch	2013	3S	L	
121100	Intro to German	Germn	1003	3S	L	
121100	Intro to German	Germn	1013	3S	L	
121100	Modern German prose	Germn	2003	3S	L	
121600	Vergil's *Aeneid*	Latin	2013	3S	L	
122000	Intro for beginners	Rus	1003	3S	L	
122500	Elementary Spanish	Span	1003	3S	L	
122500	Elementary Spanish	Span	1013	3S	L	
122500	Spanish readings	Span	3063	3S	U	
122500	Intermediate Spanish	Span	2003	3S	L	
122500	Intermediate Spanish	Span	2013	3S	L	
122500	Advanced grammar & comp	Span	4003	3S	U	
150307	Genetics	Botny	3203	3S	U	
150316	Survey of botany	Botny	1013	3S	L	
150317	Bacteria in human affairs	Bact	2003	3S	L	
150399	Nature study	Botny	1022	2S	L	
150900	Man and his environment	Botny	2533	3S	L	
159900	Conservation of nat resou	Zoolg	3133	3S	U	
160199	Patterns in math	Math	1103	3S	L	
160302	College algebra	Math	1203	3S	L	
160401	Calculus I	Math	2555	5S	L	
160401	Calculus II	Math	2565	5S	L	
160401	Calculus III	Math	2573	3S	L	
160408	Finite math	Math	2053	3S	L	
160602	Plane trigonometry	Math	1213	3S	L	
161101	Math of finance	Math	1503	3S	L	
180403	Intro to philosophy	Philo	2003	3S	L	
180599	Logic	Philo	2203	3S	L	
190106	Organ & admin of phy ed	PhyEd	4213	3S	U	
190110	Tests & measure in phy ed	PhyEd	4703	3S	U	
200501	Abnormal psychology	Psych	3023	3S	U	
200503	Applied psychology	Psych	2023	3S	L	
200504	Infancy and early childhd	Psych	3033	3S	U	
200504	Childhood and adolescence	Psych	3093	3S	U	
200599	Exceptional children	Psych	4013	3S	U	
200603	Psychological tests	Psych	4053	3S	U	
200804	Educational psychology	Psych	4033	3S	U	
200902	Personnel psychology	Psych	3043	3S	U	
209900	General psychology	Psych	2003	3S	L	
210403	Problems of child welfare	SoWel	3633	3S	U	
220102	Intro to anthropology	Anthr	2023	3S	L	
220110	Indians of North America	Anthr	3213	3S	U	
220201	Principles of economics I	Econ	2013	3S	L	
220201	Prin of economics II	Econ	2023	3S	L	
220202	Economic dev of the US	Econ	1123	3S	L	

NCES No.	Course Title	Dept.	Course No.	Cred.	Lev.	Specl. Feat.
220300	Emerging nations	Geog	2103	3S	L	
220300	Developed nations	Geog	2203	3S	L	
220302	Economic geography	Geog	2023	3S	L	
220305	Physical geography	Geog	1003	3S	L	
220399	Human geography	Geog	1123	3S	L	
220399	United States & Canada	Geog	3253	3S	U	
220406	Cultural hist of Germany	Germn	2013	3S	L	
220406	Inst ideas of Wstrn man	WCiv	1003	3S	L	
220406	Study of civ 1650-present	WCiv	1013	3S	L	
220421	Col & Rev Amer 1607-1783	Hist	4403	3S	U	
220427	Latin American civilizatn	Span	4223	3S	U	
220432	The Amer Repub 1492-1877	Hist	2003	3S	L	
220432	US as wld power 1877-1965	Hist	2013	3S	L	
220470	American Negro history	Hist	3403	3S	U	
220471	Hist of the Amer Indian	Hist	3103	3S	U	
220501	American national govt	PolSc	2003	3S	L	
220511	State and local govt	PolSc	2203	3S	L	
220599	Intro to political sci	PolSc	1503	3S	L	
220602	Criminology	Socio	3023	3S	U	
220603	Population problems	Socio	3013	3S	U	
220605	Marriage and the family	Socio	2043	3S	L	
220606	General sociology	Socio	2013	3S	L	
220613	Social problems	Socio	2033	3S	L	
220614	Black ghetto	Socio	4123	3S	U	
220614	Urban sociology	Socio	3153	3S	U	
	Noncredit courses					
040203	Business records control	AdmSc	1	NC		
040203	Business records control	AdmSc	2	NC		
041303	Principles of real estate		NC-1	NC		

(35) UNIVERSITY OF CALIFORNIA EXTENSION

Ms. Claire Bluitt
Student Services Supervisor
University of California Extension
2223 Fulton Street
Berkeley, California 94720
Phone: 415-642-4124

Overseas enrollment accepted. Military personnel may enroll through the DANTES program. Minimum period for course completion is four months. Maximum period for course completion is one year. Enrollment on a noncredit basis is accepted in all credit courses. Able high school students are permitted to enroll in undergraduate courses for credit.

NCES No.	Course Title	Dept.	Course No.	Cred.	Lev.	Specl. Feat.
	High School courses					
010599	Horticulture	Agri	AG901		H	
030302	Hist & appreciation music	Music	MU900		H	
030501	Begin drawing & painting	VisAr	A901		H	
049900	General business	Bus	B907		H	
100699	Marriage & family living	HomEc	H903		H	
110504	Photography	VisAr	P900		H	
120202	The short story	Engl	E908		H	
120202	The novel	Engl	E911		H	
120305	Ninth-grade English	Engl	E900		H	
120305	Ninth-grade English	Engl	E901		H	
120305	Tenth-grade English	Engl	E902		H	
120305	Tenth-grade English	Engl	E903		H	
120305	Eleventh-grade English	Engl	E904		H	
120305	Eleventh-grade English	Engl	E905		H	
120305	Twelfth-grade English	Engl	E906		H	
120305	Twelfth-grade English	Engl	E907		H	
120305	Business English	Engl	E912		H	
120305	Basic English	Engl	E915		H	
120308	Improving reading skills	Engl	E913		H	
120310	Composition	Engl	E909		H	
120399	Effective study methods	StSkl	ST900		H	
121000	First-year French	Frnch	F900		H	AC
121000	First-year French	Frnch	F901		H	AC
121000	Second-year French	Frnch	F902		H	AC
121000	Second-year French	Frnch	F903		H	AC
121100	First-year German	Germn	G900		H	AC
121100	First-year German	Germn	G901		H	AC
121100	Second-year German	Germn	G902		H	AC

NCES No.	Course Title	Dept.	Course No.	Cred.	Lev.	Specl. Feat.
121100	Second-year German	Germn	G903		H	AC
121600	First-year Latin	Latin	L900		H	
121600	First-year Latin	Latin	L901		H	
121600	Second-year Latin	Latin	L902		H	
121600	Second-year Latin	Latin	L903		H	
122500	First-year Spanish	Span	S900		H	AC
122500	First-year Spanish	Span	S901		H	AC
122500	Second-year Spanish	Span	S902		H	AC
122500	Second-year Spanish	Span	S903		H	AC
150300	Biology optional lab	Bio	SC903		H	LK
150300	Biology with lab	Bio	SC904		H	
150300	Biology	Bio	SC901		H	
150300	Biology	Bio	SC902		H	
150799	Physics with laboratory	Phycs	SC905		H	
150799	Physics with laboratory	Phycs	SC906		H	
160103	General mathematics	Math	M914		H	
160103	General mathematics	Math	M915		H	
160301	Basic math	Math	M912		H	
160302	Elementary algebra	Math	M900		H	
160302	Elementary algebra	Math	M901		H	
160302	2nd year algebra 1st sem	Math	M908		H	
160302	2nd year algebra 2nd sem	Math	M909		H	
160601	Plane geometry	Math	M904		H	
160601	Plane geometry	Math	M905		H	
160602	Trigonometry	Math	M910		H	
190509	Health science	HlSci	SC900		H	
190603	Driver education	DrvEd	D900		H	
200104	Psychology	Psych	SS911		H	
200201	Economics	Econ	SS909		H	
220399	World geography	Geog	SS901		H	
220399	World geography	Geog	SS902		H	
220432	American history	Hist	SS905		H	
220432	American history	Hist	SS906		H	
220433	World history	Hist	SS903		H	
220433	World history	Hist	SS904		H	
220502	Civics	PolSc	SS900		H	
220606	Sociology	Socio	SS910		H	
	College courses					
030301	Elementary counterpoint	Music	6	3S	L	
030302	Introduction to harmony	Music	5	3S	L	
030501	Two-dimensional design	VisAr	416	2S	U	
030501	Italic lettering	VisAr	424	2S	U	
030501	Beginning drawing	VisAr	5	2S	L	
030502	Fundamental discoveries	VisAr	415	2S	U	
030502	Collage	VisAr	419	2S	U	
030502	Acrylic painting	VisAr	417	2S	U	
030599	Individual study in art	VisAr	457	2S	U	
030603	Intro to modern painting	ArHis	11	1S	L	
030603	Intro to contemporary art	ArHis	13	1S	L	
030603	Ancient art: Egypt	ArHis	152A	4Q	U	
030603	Ancient art: Greece I	ArHis	152E	4Q	U	
030603	Ancient art: Greece II	ArHis	152F	4Q	U	
040101	Acctg: intermediate I	Bus	148	3S	L	
040101	Acctg: intermediate II	Bus	149	3S	L	
040101	Administrative accounting	Bus	125	3S	U	
040101	Intro to accounting II	Bus	2	3S	L	
040101	Accounting: advanced I	Bus	152	3S	U	
040101	Accounting: advanced II	Bus	153	3S	U	
040101	Intro to accounting	Bus	1	3S	L	
040103	Auditing	Bus	126	4S	U	
040106	Cost accounting	Bus	124	3S	U	
040109	Governmental accounting	Bus	131	4S	U	
040114	Federal tax: individuals	Bus	167	3S	U	
040114	Fed tax: partners & corps	Bus	179	3S	U	
040114	Calif personal income tax	Bus	174	1S	U	
040306	Investment management	Bus	430	2S	U	
040601	Business communications	Bus	109	4Q	U	
040703	Pre-retirement planning	Bus	404	1S	U	
040800	Intro to int'l business	Bus	192	3S	U	
040904	Mgmt theory & policy	Bus	158	3S	U	
040904	Finance planning & mgmt	Bus	135	3S	U	
040905	Intro to bus org & mgmt	Bus	492.8	3S	U	
040999	Small business management	Bus	105	3S	U	
040999	Purchasing: basic prin	Bus	453	3S	U	
040999	Mgt of stress & conflict	Bus	454.2	2S	U	
040999	Time management	Bus	491.7	2S	U	
041001	Principles of marketing	Bus	463.3	3S	U	
041103	Mgrs guide to human behav	Bus	490.5	2S	U	
041104	Mgmt of human resources	Bus	173	3S	U	
041104	Labor relations	Bus	451.9	3S	U	
041106	Office mgmt & control	Bus	492.9	3S	U	

NCES No.	Course Title	Dept.	Course No.	Cred.	Lev.	Spec. Feat.
041106	Effective supervision	Bus	411	3S	U	
041199	Effective personnel admin	Bus	424	3S	U	
041203	Production management	Bus	157	3S	U	
041301	Residential appraisal	Bus	408	3S	U	
041303	Real estate principles	Bus	406.8	3S	U	
041305	Real estate economics	Bus	406.9	3S	U	
041306	Real estate finance	Bus	407	3S	U	
041308	Escrows and land titles	Bus	405.8	3S	U	
041308	Real estate law	Bus	405.9	3S	U	
041309	Real estate practice	Bus	406	3S	U	
049900	Purchsng princpls & cases	Bus	453	3S	U	
050601	Editorial workshop	Journ	413	3S	U	
050608	Introduction to news writ	Journ	100	4S	U	
050699	Tech writing	EngAS	412	3S	U	
051303	Screenwriting: story	Film	105A	4S	U	
051303	Screenwriting: script	Film	105B	4S	U	
060404	Intro to microprocessors	CmpSc	400	2S	U	
060502	Concepts of database mgmt	CmpSc	408	3S	U	
060705	Introductory FORTRAN	CmpSc	114	3S	U	
060705	Introductory COBOL	CmpSc	6	3S	L	
060705	Introductory Pascal	CmpSc	13	3S	L	
060705	Intro to program BASIC	CmpSc	11	3S	L	
060904	Systems analysis & design	CmpSc	422	3S	U	
061104	Concepts of data processg	CmpSc	42	3S	U	
070404	Adult ed matls & methods	Educ	355.1	2S	U	
070499	Adult ed principles	Educ	355.4	2S	U	
070506	Computers in elem educ	Educ	391	3S	U	
070512	The reading program	Educ	343	3S	U	
070512	Literature in the schools	Educ	344	3S	U	
070516	Elem curriculum arith/sci	Educ	331	3S	U	
070701	Counseling & guidance	Educ	362.3	3S	U	
080901	Intro to electrical engr	EngAS	40	3S	L	
080999	Designing with oper ampls	EngAS	408	2S	U	
081199	Engineering mechanics	EngAS	36	2S	L	
081200	Digital integrtd circuits	EngAS	480	3S	U	
082602	Surveying engr measuremts	EngAS	4	2S	L	
089900	Intro to control systems	EngAS	171A	4Q	U	
090799	Sound mind sound society	PubHl	406	2S	U	
090799	Alcohol/individ & society	PubHl	178	3S	U	
090799	Alco/social consequences	PubHl	179	2S	U	
100302	Clinical nutrition	NutSc	105A	3S	U	
100311	Survey of nutritional sci	NutSc	12	3S	L	
100313	Nutrition	NutSc	103	3S	U	
100313	The new nutrition	NutSc	107	2S	U	
110502	Fundmnts of graphic desgn	VisAr	438	3S	U	
110504	Photography	Graph	4	2S	L	
120302	English language history	Engl	436	3S	U	
120305	Freshman comp & lit	Engl	2A	3S	L	
120305	Freshman comp & lit	Engl	2B	3S	L	
120305	Intro to language (subjA)	Engl	1	2S	U	
120307	Shakespeare	Engl	117S	4S	U	
120307	American lit 1914 to 1940	Engl	146	4S	U	
120307	The hero and the city	Engl	179	3S	U	
120307	Mystery fiction	Engl	103.9	3S	U	
120307	English novel	Engl	125A	4S	U	
120307	English novel	Engl	125B	4S	U	
120307	American fiction to 1900	Engl	135A	3S	U	
120307	Amer fiction 1900 to pres	Engl	135B	3S	U	
120307	Western novel 19th cent	Engl	152.1	3S	U	
120307	Western novel 20th cent	Engl	152.2	3S	U	
120310	Advanced Engl composition	Engl	119.1	3S	U	
120310	Individ projects writing	Engl	445	2S	U	
120310	Nonfiction writing wrkshp	Engl	428	3S	U	
120310	Writng children's fiction	Engl	422	3S	U	
120399	Gramm & comp/ESL students	Engl	22	3S	L	
120700	Elem Chinese: course I	Chin	3	5S	U	
120700	Elem Chinese: course II	Chin	4	5S	U	
121000	French: elem course I	Frnch	25	3S	L	AC
121000	French: elem course II	Frnch	26	3S	L	AC
121100	Readings: German culture	Germn	137	3S	U	
121100	German: elem course I	Germn	36	3S	U	AC
121100	German: elem course II	Germn	37	3S	U	AC
121100	German: elem course III	Germn	38	3S	L	AC
121100	Intermed German: course I	Germn	39	3S	L	
121400	Elementary Italian I	Ital	15	3S	L	AC
121400	Elementary Italian II	Ital	16	3S	L	AC
122500	Spanish: elem course I	Span	30	3S	L	AC
122500	Spanish: elem course II	Span	31	3S	L	AC
122500	Spanish: elem course III	Span	32	3S	L	AC
122500	Spanish: interm course I	Span	33	3S	L	AC
122500	Span in bus & professions	Span	401	2S	U	AC

NCES No.	Course Title	Dept.	Course No.	Cred.	Lev.	Spec. Feat.
129900	Icelandic lit: part I	Scand	156	2S	U	
129900	Icelandic lit: part II	Scand	157	2S	U	
129900	Elementary mod Icelandic	Scand	180	3S	U	
129900	Intermed modern Icelandic	Scand	181	3S	U	
130799	Intro to business law	Bus	18	3S	L	
130799	Advanced business law	Bus	410.2	2S	U	
139900	The law & Amer legal syst	Law	10	3S	U	
150199	Intro to gen astronomy	Astro	10	4S	L	
150301	Modern biology	Bio	4	3S	L	
150307	Survey of gen genetics	Genet	102	3S	U	
150316	Plant life in California	Botny	113	3S	U	
150316	Plants and civilization	Botny	115	3S	U	
150327	Pest control course br 1	EntSc	401	3S	U	
150327	Pest control course br 2	EntSc	402	3S	U	
150327	Pest control branch 3	EntSc	403	3S	U	
150399	Intro human physiology	Zoolg	1	3S	L	
150401	Introductory chemistry	Chem	25	3Q	L	
150403	Introductory biochemistry	Bioch	105	3S	U	
150408	Organic chemistry prinpls	Chem	18A	2S	L	
150408	Organic chemistry prinpls	Chem	18B	2S	L	
150410	Surface chem/phys-bio sys	Chem	137	3S	U	
150501	Marine geology	Geol	105	4Q	U	
150501	Geology of California	Geol	109	4Q	U	
150501	Intro physical geology	Geol	3	3S	L	
150799	General physics	Phycs	15A	2S	L	
150799	General physics	Phycs	15B	2S	L	
160302	Intermediate algebra	Math	D	2S	L	
160401	Precalculus	Math	9	2S	L	
160499	First-yr anal geom & calc	Math	1.1	3S	L	
160499	First-yr anal geom & calc	Math	1.2	3S	L	
160499	First-yr anal geom & calc	Math	1.3	3S	L	
160602	Plane trigonometry	Math	C	2S	L	
160802	Intro statistical methods	Econ	40	4Q	L	
160803	Intro to statistics	Stat	2	4S	L	
160803	Intro to statistical meth	Stat	40	4Q	L	
161199	Advanced engineering math	Math	119A	3S	U	
161199	Advanced engineering math	Math	119B	3S	U	
161199	Advanced engineering math	Math	119C	3S	U	
161201	Mathematics of finance	Bus	432	3S	U	
180402	History of philosophy	Philo	20A	3S	L	
180403	History of philosophy	Philo	20B	3S	L	
180405	History of Buddhist phil	Philo	169	3S	U	
180700	Individual morality & jus	Philo	2	4S	L	
200501	Abnormal psychology	Psych	127	4Q	U	
200504	Adolescence	Psych	139.1	3S	U	
200799	Psych of communication	Psych	156.1	3S	U	
200799	Social psychology	Psych	160	3S	U	
200799	Psychology of the sexes	Psych	22	3S	U	
209900	General psychology	Psych	1	3S	U	
220106	Intro to physical anthro	Anthr	1	3S	L	
220201	Microeconomics	Econ	1	5Q	U	
220201	Econ principles, problems	Econ	16	3S	U	
220201	Macroeconomics	Econ	3	3S	L	
220211	Labor econ & relations	Econ	148	3S	U	
220214	International economics	Econ	190	4Q	U	
220432	History of the US	Hist	17A	4Q	L	
220432	History of the US	Hist	17B	4Q	L	
220432	Western civilization	Hist	21A	3S	U	
220432	The American West	Hist	189.1	3S	U	
220501	American institutions	PolSc	100	3S	U	
220510	Intro political theory	PolSc	7	3S	L	
220601	Introduction to sociology	Socio	10	3S	L	

Noncredit courses

NCES No.	Course Title	Dept.	Course No.	Cred.	Lev.	Spec. Feat.
010599	Horticulture	Agri	AG901	NC		
020103	Basic interior design	Dsgn	807	NC	U	
020103	Color theory	Dsgn	814	NC		
030302	Elements of music	Music	800	NC		
040601	English for business	Bus	800	NC		
060203	Bus bkkping by computer	CmpSc	802	NC		
069900	Software pkgs for the PC	CmpSc	852	NC		
070703	Career counseling	Bus	810	NC		
081000	Beginning engr drafting	EngAS	800	NC		
089900	Engineering fundamentals	EngAS	843	NC		
090307	Radiologic technology	HlSci	800A	NC		
090307	Radiologic technology	HlSci	800B	NC		
120310	The writer within	Engl	806	NC	U	
120310	Elementary composition	Engl	804	NC		
120310	Magazine article writing	Engl	801	NC		
120310	Advanced article writing	Engl	808	NC		
120310	Short story theory	Engl	816	NC		
120310	Short story writing	Engl	817	NC		

NCES No.	Course Title	Dept.	Course No.	Cred.	Lev.	Specl. Feat.
120310	Writing your own story	Engl	802	NC		
120310	Poetry writing	Engl	815	NC		
120310	Revising your poem	Engl	818	NC		
160302	Elementary algebra	Math	M900	NC		
160302	Elementary algebra	Math	M901	NC		
160399	Entry-level math review	Math	803	NC		
160601	Plane geometry	Math	M904	NC		
160601	Plane geometry	Math	M905	NC		

㊱ UNIVERSITY OF COLORADO AT BOULDER

Dr. John R. Dunn
Program Manager, Independent Study Program
Division of Continuing Education
Box 178, 1221 University
University of Colorado at Boulder
Boulder, Colorado 80309-0178
Phone: 303-492-8756
        800-331-2801 in CO

Telecourses are offered. Enrollment on a noncredit basis accepted in credit courses. High school students may enroll in undergraduate courses for credit. Overseas enrollment accepted. Institution offers special arrangements to take courses not listed in this Catalog. Minimum period for course completion is six weeks. Maximum period for course completion is one year. However, two years are allowed in the case of overseas enrollment or physical disability. Individualized instruction for local residents.

NCES No.	Course Title	Dept.	Course No.	Cred.	Lev.	Specl. Feat.
	High School courses					
030302	Music theory	HSMus	0502	HF	H	
030302	Harmony	HSMus	0701	HF	H	
030302	History & apprec music	HSMus	1101	HF	H	
030502	Beginning drawing & paint	HSArt	0102	HF	H	
040101	Beginning accounting	HSBus	2302	HF	H	
040101	Beginning accounting	HSBus	2402	HF	H	
040299	Office procedures & pract	HSBus	1301	HF	H	
040299	Office procedures & pract	HSBus	1401	HF	H	
040302	Consumer education	HSBus	1901	HF	H	
040601	Business English	HSBus	1101	HF	H	
049900	General business	HSBus	2102	HF	H	
061103	Computer basics	HSCSc	0101	HF	H	
070899	Study skills	HSStS	0101	HF	D	
080999	Basic elec & electronics	HSSci	0901	HF	H	
090119	Health science	HSSci	0102	HF	H	
090119	Health science	HSSci	0202	HF	H	
100699	Personal adj marriage fam	HSHE	1101	HF	H	
120305	Ninth-grade English	HSEng	3102	HF	H	
120305	Ninth-grade English	HSEng	3202	HF	H	
120305	Tenth-grade English	HSEng	3302	HF	H	
120305	Tenth-grade English	HSEng	3402	HF	H	
120305	Eleventh-grade English	HSEng	3502	HF	H	
120305	Eleventh-grade English	HSEng	3602	HF	H	
120305	Twelfth-grade English	HSEng	3702	HF	H	
120305	Twelfth-grade English	HSEng	3802	HF	H	
120305	Basic English	HSEng	0102	HF	H	
120307	The short story	HSEng	0901	HF	H	
120307	Poetry	HSEng	2102	HF	H	
120307	American short story	HSEng	1102	HF	H	
120308	Improvmt of reading skill	HSEng	0401	HF	H	
120310	Composition	HSEng	2302	HF	H	
122500	First year Spanish	HSSpn	0103	HF	H	
122500	First year Spanish	HSSpn	0203	HF	H	
150301	Biology 1	HSSci	0702	HF	H	
150301	Biology 2	HSSci	0802	HF	H	
150301	Biology 3	HSSci	1902	HF	H	
150799	Physics	HSSci	3502	HF	H	
150799	Physics	HSSci	3602	HF	H	
160199	General mathematics	HSMth	0502	HF	H	
160199	General mathematics	HSMth	0602	HF	H	
160301	Basic mathematics 1	HSMth	0103	HF	D	
160301	Basic mathematics 2	HSMth	0202	HF	H	
160302	Beginning algebra	HSMth	3103	HF	H	
160302	Beginning algebra	HSMth	3203	HF	H	
160302	Advanced algebra	HSMth	3502	HF	H	
160302	Advanced algebra	HSMth	3602	HF	H	
160601	Geometry	HSMth	3303	HF	H	
160601	Geometry	HSMth	3403	HF	H	
160602	Pre-calc: trigonometry 1	HSMth	4001	HF	H	
160602	Pre-calc: trigonometry 2	HSMth	4002	HF	H	
160603	Pre-calc: analytic geom	HSMth	3901	HF	H	
161101	Bus & consumer math	HSMth	0901	HF	H	
161101	Bus & consumer math	HSMth	1001	HF	H	
200199	Psychology	HSSSt	0702	HF	H	
200502	Civics 1	HSSSt	0102	HF	H	
220399	World geography	HSSSt	2102	HF	H	
220421	American history	HSSSt	3304	HF	H	
220421	American history	HSSSt	3404	HF	H	
220433	World history	HSSSt	3102	HF	H	
220433	World history	HSSSt	3202	HF	H	
220501	American government 1	HSSSt	3502	HF	H	
220501	American government 2	HSSSt	3602	HF	H	
220502	Civics 2	HSSSt	0103	HF	H	
220599	Modern problems	HSSSt	3702	HF	H	
220606	Sociology	HSSSt	0302	HF	H	
	College courses					
030302	Rudiments of music	Music	1080	3S	L	
030503	Art for elementary teachr	FnArt	3636	3S	U	
040106	Managerial cost accountng	Acctg	3320	3S	U	
040111	Intro to managerial acctg	Acctg	2310	3S	L	
040113	Intro to financial acctg	Acctg	2000	3S	L	
040900	Intro to business	BuPol	1500	3S	L	
070499	Child curriculum planning	ChEd	21	3S	V	
070512	Lit for adolescents	Educ	4322	3S	U	
070512	Children's literature	Educ	4161	3S	U	
070701	Child guidance techniques	ChEd	20	3S	V	
079900	Sp topics: child abuse	Educ	4800	3S	U	VC
081502	Occupational safety mgt	GenEn	4000	3S	U	
090199	Environmental health	PhyEd	2510	3S	L	
100301	Child adm nutrition	ChEd	41	2S	V	
100601	Child development 1	ChEd	10	3S	V	
100601	Child development 2	ChEd	11	3S	V	
120103	Grammar & hist of Eng lan	Engl	4102	3S	U	AC
120304	Studies in lang fiction	Engl	3742	3S	U	
120308	Intro to fiction	Engl	1200	3S	L	
120308	Intro to drama	Engl	1300	3S	L	
120308	Intr to world literat II	Engl	2610	3S	L	
120308	Survey of American lit I	EngLL	3652	3S	U	
120308	Chaucer	Engl	3552	3S	U	
120308	Shakespeare 1	Engl	3562	3S	U	
120308	Shakespeare 2	Engl	3572	3S	U	
120308	Survey of American lit II	Engl	3662	3S	U	
120308	Intr to world literat I	Engl	2600	3S	L	
120308	Contemporary literature	Engl	2530	3S	L	
120310	Intro to creative writing	Engl	1191	3S	L	
120310	Intermediate fiction wksp	Engl	3051	3S	U	
120310	Report writing	Engl	3152	3S	U	
120310	Intro to poetry workshop	Engl	2021	3S	L	
129900	Intro to poetry	Engl	1400	3S	L	
150500	Geological environment	Geol	1030	3S	L	
150500	Geol evolution: Colorado	Geol	1040	3S	L	
160302	College algebra	Math	1010	3S	L	
160499	Analyt geom & calculus I	Math	1300	5S	L	
160499	Analyt geom & calculus II	Math	2300	5S	L	
160602	College trigonometry	Math	1020	2S	L	
160699	College algebra & trig	Math	1100	5S	L	
161299	Math soc sci & business	Math	1070	3S	L	
161299	Calc soc sci & business	Math	1080	3S	L	
180300	Ethics	Philo	1100	3S	L	
180400	Intro to philosophy	Philo	1000	3S	L	
180404	Twentieth-cent philosophy	Philo	4040	3S	U	
181199	Philosophy & religion	Philo	1600	3S	L	
190508	Nutrition and health	Kines	3420	3S	U	
200199	Intro to psychology	Psych	1001	3S	L	
200200	Intro to biopsychology	Psych	2052	3S	L	
200504	Developmental psychology	Psych	4684	3S	U	
200505	Psychology of adjustment	Psych	2303	3S	L	
200508	Child & adolescent psych	Psych	2643	3S	L	
200799	Social psychology	Psych	4406	3S	U	
209900	Stat rsch methods psychol	Psych	2104	4S	L	
220102	Principles of anthro I	Anthr	1030	3S	L	
220102	Principles of anthro II	Anthr	1040	3S	L	
220102	Intro to archaeology	Anthr	2200	3S	L	
220106	Intro to physical anthr I	Anthr	2010	3S	L	
220106	Intro to phys anthr II	Anthr	2020	3S	L	
220201	Prin of microeconomics	Econ	2010	3S	L	
220201	Prin of macroeconomics	Econ	2020	3S	L	
220399	Environ sys climate & veg	Geog	1001	3S	L	

NCES No.	Course Title	Dept.	Course No.	Cred.	Lev.	Specl. Feat.
220399	Env sys landforms & soil	Geog	1011	3S	L	
220428	Hist of Colorado	Hist	2117	3S	L	
220431	Hist of Russia thr 17th c	Hist	4713	3S	U	
220431	Imperial Russia	Hist	4723	3S	U	
220431	Russ Revolution & Sov reg	Hist	4733	3S	U	
220432	Hist of US to 1865	Hist	1015	3S	L	
220432	Hist of US since 1865	Hist	1025	3S	L	
220432	Early American frontier	Hist	4217	3S	U	
220432	Later American frontier	Hist	4227	3S	U	
220499	Hist of Western civiliztn	Hist	1010	3S	L	
220499	Hist of Western civiliztn	Hist	1020	3S	L	
220501	American political system	PolSc	1101	3S	L	
220505	International relations	PolSc	2222	3S	L	
220602	Criminology	Socio	4014	3S	U	
220606	Intro to sociology	Socio	1001	3S	L	
220610	Deviance	Socio	1004	3S	L	
220612	Technology & modernizatio	Socio	4071	3S	U	
220613	Understand social conflic	Socio	1005	3S	L	
	Noncredit courses					
040905	Child adm organ & mgt	ChEd	45	NC	V	
040999	Child adm parents & pers	ChEd	43	NC	V	
041301	Real estate appraisal I	NCRE	21	NC	V	
041303	Real estate prin & pract	NCRE	01	NC	V	
041306	Real estate finance	NCRE	22	NC	V	
041308	Colo rl estate contracts	NCRE	18	NC	V	
041308	Real estate law	NCRE	12	NC	V	
130103	Evidence & investigation	PlEd	10	NC	V	AC
130199	Litigation, civ proc, dis	PlEd	11	NC	V	AC
130999	Probate and property	PlEd	13	NC	V	AC
131599	Legal research	PlEd	12	NC	V	AC

③⑦ UNIVERSITY OF FLORIDA

Dr. Harold Markowitz Jr.
Director, Department of Independent Study by Correspondence
Division of Continuing Education
Department of Independent Study
University of Florida
Gainesville, Florida 32611
Phone: 904-392-1711
        800-327-4218 (out of state)

Enrollment on a noncredit basis accepted in credit courses. High school students may enroll in undergraduate courses for credit. Overseas enrollment accepted. Military personnel may enroll through the DANTES program. Minimum period for course completion is one month. Maximum period for course completion is one year. Registration is completed on the day the forms are received by the program; books are sent the next day from the departmental bookstore. VISA and MasterCard are accepted for all charges. Phone registrations are accepted. There are no out-of-state fees, and tuition is much lower than on campus. This is the single centralized program of independent study by correspondence for Florida's nine public universities.

NCES No.	Course Title	Dept.	Course No.	Cred.	Lev.	Specl. Feat.
	High School courses					
030602	Art/self-instruction I	Art	11A	HF	H	
030602	Art/self-instruction II	Art	11B	HF	H	
040102	Accounting I 1st semester	VocEd	12A	HF	H	
040102	Accounting I 2nd semester	VocEd	12B	HF	H	
120303	English II 1st sem (10th)	Engl	10A	HF	H	
120303	English II 2nd sem (10th)	Engl	10B	HF	H	
120304	Engl III 1st sem (11th)	Engl	11A	HF	H	
120304	Engl III 2nd sem (11th)	Engl	11B	HF	H	
120305	English I 1st sem (9th)	Engl	9A	HF	H	
120305	English I 2nd sem (9th)	Engl	9B	HF	H	
120307	English IV 1st sem (12th)	Engl	12A	HF	H	
120307	English IV 2nd sem (12th)	Engl	12B	HF	H	
150301	Fundamentals of biology 1	Sci	11A	HF	H	
150301	Fundamentals of biology 2	Sci	11B	HF	H	
159900	Fund of environm science	Sci	10A	HF	H	
160302	Algebra II 1st sem	Math	11A	HF	H	
160302	Algebra II 2nd sem	Math	11B	HF	H	
160302	Algebra I 1st sem	Math	10A	HF	H	
160302	Algebra I 2nd sem	Math	10B	HF	H	
160399	Pre-algebra 1st sem	Math	9C	HF	H	
160399	Pre-algebra 2nd sem	Math	9D	HF	H	
160599	Mathematical analysis	Math	12A	HF	H	

NCES No.	Course Title	Dept.	Course No.	Cred.	Lev.	Specl. Feat.
160901	Mathematical analysis	Math	12B	HF	H	
161100	General math I 1st sem	Math	9A	HF	H	
161100	General math I 2nd sem	Math	9B	HF	H	
161201	Business math I 1st sem	Math	11C	HF	H	
161201	Business math I 2nd sem	Math	11D	HF	H	
190506	Personal,soc,family relat	Hlth	11A	HF	H	
190509	Health I life mngt skills	Hlth	12A	HF	H	
200505	Peer couns II self-discov	PeerC	10A	HF	H	
200505	Peer couns:knowing myself	PeerC	9A	HF	H	
220201	Economics	SocSt	12E	HF	H	
220399	World geography 1st sem	SocSt	9A	HF	H	
220399	World geography 2nd sem	SocSt	9B	HF	H	
220432	American history 1st sem	SocSt	11A	HF	H	
220432	American history 2nd sem	SocSt	11B	HF	H	
220433	World history 1st sem	SocSt	10A	HF	H	
220433	World history 2nd sem	SocSt	10B	HF	H	
220501	American government	SocSt	12A	HF	H	
220503	Comparative political sys	SocSt	12C	HF	H	
229900	Humanities to 1500	Hum	12A	HF	H	AC
	College courses					
010199	Prin of food & res econom	AgEcB	3103	4S	U	
010504	Physical landscapes	Geog	2201	3S	L	
010702	General soils	SoilS	3022	4S	U	
019900	Introduction to agronomy	Agron	3005c	3S	U	
040710	Risk mgmt and insurance	Insur	3015	3S	U	
040903	Organizational behavior	Mgmt	3109	3S	U	
041001	Basic marketing concepts	Mktg	3023	3S	U	
041199	Mgmt of labor & ind relat	Mgmt	4407	3S	U	
041199	Concepts of management	Mgmt	3010	3S	U	
041201	Quantit meth of bus decs	QMB	3200	3S	U	
050101	Elements of advertising	Advt	3000	3S	U	
050102	Radio-TV advertising	Advt	4103	3S	U	
050104	Copywriting & visualizatn	Advt	4101	3S	U	
050201	Survey of mass communictn	MComm	1000	2S	L	
050605	Magazine & feature writng	Journ	4300	3S	U	
050800	Writing for mass communic	MComm	2100	3S	L	
050900	Intro to public relations	PubRe	3000	3S	U	
051201	Braille reading & writing	EdVI	4211	3S	U	
070199	History of ed in the US	EdFdn	3514	3S	U	
070520	Educational psychology	EdFdn	3210	3S	U	
071102	Measurement & eval in ed	EdFdn	4430	3S	U	
090255	Case mngt of chil-chr ill	Nrsng	4905A	3S	U	
090255	Communication skills-nurs	Nrsng	4905B	2S	U	
090255	Facil grwth/dev in ill ch	Nrsng	4905C	3S	U	
090255	Prac in case mngt ill ch	Nrsng	4905D	2S	U	
099900	Medical term: hlth profes	MLS	3034	3S	U	AC
100103	Textiles for consumers	ClTex	1401	3S	L	
100304	Man's food	FdSci	2001	2S	L	
100312	The science of nutrition	HuNut	1201	3S	L	
100312	Fund of human nutrition	HuNut	2201	3S	L	
100601	Child grwth & dev:adolesc	ChDev	4240	3S	U	
100601	Child grwth & dev foun yr	ChDev	3220	3S	U	
120202	Amer fict: 1900 to WWII	AmLit	3124	3S	U	AC
120299	Writing about literature	Engl	1102	3S	L	
120299	Brtsh auth: beg-17th cent	EnglL	2011	3S	L	
120303	Language and people	Ling	2000	3S	L	
120305	English grammar	Ling	2340	2S	L	
120307	English novel: 18th cent	EnglL	3112	3S	U	
120307	English novel: 19th cent	EnglL	3122	3S	U	
120307	English novel: 20th cent	EnglL	3132	3S	U	
120307	Brtsh auth:romant to pres	Engl	2020	3S	L	
120310	Beginning fiction writing	CrWri	2110	3S	L	
120310	Expos & argument writing	Engl	1101	3S	L	
120310	Techn writ & bus communic	Engl	3213	3S	U	
120310	Advanced exposition	Engl	3310	3S	U	
120310	Beginning poetry writing	CrWri	2300	3S	L	
121100	Beginning German 1	Germn	1120	4S	L	
121100	Beginning German 2	Germn	1121	3S	L	
121100	Beginning German 3	Germn	1122	3S	L	
130799	Business law problems	BuLaw	4200	4S	U	
130799	Business law	BuLaw	4100	3S	U	
150199	Discovering the universe	Astro	1002	3S	L	
150401	Chemistry for lib studies	Chem	1020	3S	L	
150599	Expl the geological sci	Geol	1000	3S	L	
150599	Physical geology	Geol	2015	3S	L	
160302	Basic college algebra	Math	1102	3S	L	
160305	Precalculus: alg & trig	Math	1142	4S	L	
160602	College trigonometry	Math	2114	2S	L	
160603	Analyt geometry & calc 1	Math	3311	4S	U	
160603	Analyt geometry & calc 2	Math	3312	4S	U	
160802	Stat proc for behav sci	Stat	4122	4S	U	

NCES

No.	Course Title	Dept.	Course No.	Cred.	Lev.	Specl. Feat.
180301	Ethical iss & life choice	Philo	2630	3S	L	
180599	Intro to philosophy	Philo	2010	3S	L	
180902	The Christian tradition	Relig	3505	3S	U	
181103	Religion in America	Relig	2120	3S	L	
181104	Introduction to religion	Relig	2000	3S	L	
181201	Intro to Old Testament	Relig	2210	3S	L	
181202	Intro to New Testament	Relig	2240	3S	L	
190599	Contemporary health sci	HlEd	2100	3S	L	
200199	Applied psychology	Psych	3101	3S	U	
200199	General psychology	Psych	2013	3S	L	
200504	Developmental psychology	DePsy	3003	3S	U	
200509	Personality	PsyPe	4004	3S	U	
200799	Social psychology	SoPsy	4004	3S	U	
200901	Industrial psychology	Psych	4004	3S	U	
220102	Cultural anthropology	Anthr	2410	3S	L	
220105	Language and culture	Anthr	2610	3S	L	
220199	Bio anthrop: human evolut	Anthr	3511	3S	U	
220201	Basic economics I	Econ	2013	3S	L	
220201	Basic economics II	Econ	2023	3S	L	
220202	Economic history of US	AmHis	3370	3S	U	
220299	Economic concepts & inst	Econ	2000	3S	U	
220302	Conservation of resources	Geog	3370	3S	U	
220306	The face of Florida	Geog	3271	3S	U	
220409	Urban America since 1879	AmHis	4463	3S	U	
220426	19th-century Europe:surve	EuHis	3004	3S	U	
220426	20th-century Europe:surve	EuHis	3005	3S	U	
220428	Florida to 1845	AmHis	3422	3S	U	
220428	Florida since 1845	AmHis	3423	3S	U	
220431	Russia to Nicholas I	EuHis	3571	3S	U	
220431	Hist of Russia, 1825-pres	EuHis	3572	3S	U	
220432	United States to 1877	AmHis	2010	3S	L	
220432	United States since 1877	AmHis	2020	3S	L	
220432	Labor history of the US	AmHis	3501	3S	U	
220432	American civilization	AmHis	1000	3S	L	
220450	Ancient & mediev civiliza	EuHis	2100	3S	L	
220453	Modern world to 1815	Hist	1023	3S	L	
220453	Modern world since 1815	Hist	1030	3S	L	
220453	Hitler's Third Reich	EuHis	4465	3S	U	
220499	World War II, 1931-1945	Hist	4244	3S	U	
220501	American federal govt	PolSc	2041	3S	L	
220505	International relations	IntRe	2002	3S	L	
220511	Am state & local govt	PolSc	2112	3S	L	
220602	Criminology	CJC	3011	3S	U	
220602	Law enforcement	CJC	3101	3S	U	
220602	Corrections	CJC	3301	3S	U	
220602	Intro to criminal justice	CJC	2020	3S	L	
220605	Marriage & the family	Socio	2430	3S	L	
220606	Principles of sociology	Socio	2000	3S	L	
220614	Urban sociology	Socio	3410	3S	U	
229900	Law and society	IntSt	4900	3S	U	

Noncredit courses

No.	Course Title	Dept.	Course No.	Cred.
010902	Principles of silvicultur	Fores	2	NC
010999	Introduction to forestry	Fores	1	NC
011202	Guidelines for bird mgt	PstCn	3	NC
040707	Life & health insurance	Insur	6	NC
040709	Prop & liability insur	Insur	7	NC
040799	Bail & bail bonds ins	Insur	3	NC
040799	Industrial fire in Fla	Insur	4	NC
040799	Motor veh phys damage ins	Insur	5	NC
040902	Condominium assoc mgt-FL	Condo	1	NC
041106	Intro to princ of superv	Suprv	1	NC
041106	Supervisory communication	Suprv	2	NC
041106	Writ communic for suprvs	Suprv	7	NC
041199	Supervisory leadership	Suprv	3	NC
041199	Managing problem employee	Suprv	4	NC
041199	Working better with boss	Suprv	5	NC
041199	Job productivity	Suprv	6	NC
070703	Princp of a job search	CaRes	1	NC
081304	Water treatment operat	WtrTr	1	NC
081304	Wastewatr trtment plt opr	WWTrt		NC
081399	Activated sludge skills	WWTrt	1	NC
100205	Condominium Act (Florida)	Condo	2	NC
100702	Dietary manager course	DtMgt	1	NC
150327	Guide for struct fumigat	PstCn	1	NC
150327	Contr of subterr termites	PstCn	2	NC
190508	Nutrition in diet modif	DtMgt	2	NC

㊳ **UNIVERSITY OF GEORGIA**

Dr. Ernestine M. Copas
Associate Director for Academic Credit
Georgia Center for Continuing Education
University of Georgia
Athens, Georgia 30602
Phone: 404-542-6400

Enrollment on a noncredit basis accepted in credit courses. High school students may enroll in undergraduate courses for credit. Overseas enrollment accepted. Minimum period for course completion is six weeks. Maximum period for course completion is one year. The persons to contact are Dr. Mary R. Baine (404-542-3243) for high school courses, Mr. Edward S. Weeks (404-542-3243) for college courses, and Dr. Helen H. Mills (404-542-1756) for noncredit courses.

NCES

No.	Course Title	Dept.	Course No.	Cred.	Lev.	Specl. Feat.
High School courses						
120305	English 10: semester 1	Engl		HF	H	
120305	English 11: semester 1	Engl		HF	H	
120305	English 12: semester 1	Engl		HF	H	
120307	English 10: semester 2	Engl		HF	H	
120307	English 11: semester 2	Engl		HF	H	
120307	English 12: semester 2	Engl		HF	H	
121000	French I: semester 1	ForLg		HF	H	AC
121000	French I: semester 2	ForLg		HF	H	AC
121000	French II: semester 1	ForLg		HF	H	AC
121000	French II: semester 2	ForLg		HF	H	AC
122500	Spanish I: semester 1	ForLg		HF	H	AC
122500	Spanish I: semester 2	ForLg		HF	H	AC
122500	Spanish II: semester 1	ForLg		HF	H	AC
122500	Spanish II: semester 2	ForLg		HF	H	AC
160302	Algebra I: semester 1	Math		HF	H	
160302	Algebra I: semester 2	Math		HF	H	
160302	Algebra II: semester 1	Math		HF	H	
160302	Algebra II: semester 2	Math		HF	H	
160601	Geometry: semester 1	Math		HF	H	
160601	Geometry: semester 2	Math		HF	H	
220201	Intro to economics: sem 1	Econ		HF	H	
220201	Intro to economics: sem 2	Econ		HF	H	
220432	US history: semester 1	Hist		HF	H	
220432	US history: semester 2	Hist		HF	H	
220433	World history: semester 1	Hist		HF	H	
220433	World history: semester 2	Hist		HF	H	
220501	American gov: semester 1	Govt		HF	H	
220501	American gov: semester 2	Govt		HF	H	
College courses						
010599	Horticultural science	Agri	300	5Q	U	
010603	Agricultural entomology	Agri	374	5Q	U	
030502	Ancient and medieval art	ArHis	287	5Q	L	
030502	Renaissance to 18th cent	ArHis	288	5Q	L	
030502	19th and 20th century art	ArHis	289	5Q	L	
030502	Appreciatn of visual arts	Art	300	5Q	U	
040101	Principles of acctg I	Acctg	110	5Q	L	
040101	Principles of acctg II	Acctg	111	5Q	L	
040114	Tax I	Acctg	540	4Q	U	
040201	Office practice and proc	BOEd	506	5Q	U	
040201	Principles of office mgmt	BOEd	507	5Q	U	
040301	Financial management	Finan	330	5Q	U	
040306	Investments	Finan	431	5Q	U	
040399	American financial system	Finan	452	5Q	U	
040601	Writing for business	Engl	302Q	5Q	U	
040902	Small-business management	Mgmt	554	5Q	U	
040903	Manage and organ behavior	Mgmt	351	5Q	U	
041001	Principles of marketing	Mktg	360	5Q	U	
041005	Principles of advertising	Mktg	351Q	5Q	U	
041005	Principles of retailing	Mktg	560	5Q	U	
041199	Human resources mgt	Mgmt	443Q	5Q	U	
041203	Operations analysis	Mgmt	371Q	5Q	U	
049900	Business law II	LegSt	576	5Q	U	
049900	Business law I	LegSt	370	5Q	U	
050699	Jrnlsm in secondry school	Journ	566	5Q	U	
050699	Law of communication	Journ	504	5Q	U	
051199	Psych of speech communic	Spch	466	5Q	U	
070505	Business communication	BOEd	401	5Q	U	
070509	Effects of drug use & abu	HlEd	521	5Q	U	
070520	Learning and motivation	EdPSF	304	5Q	U	
070520	Psych of early childhood	EdPSF	401	5Q	U	
070520	Adolescent psychology	EdPSF	305	5Q	U	
070602	Career dev for life plan	EdGS	399	3Q	U	

NCES No.	Course Title	Dept.	Course No.	Cred.	Lev.	Specl. Feat.
090899	Clinical medicine	VetSc	561	CV	U	
100206	Prin of family finance	FMHCS	364	5Q	U	
100312	Nutrition and fitness	FND	251Q	5Q	L	
100503	Interior design	InDes	381Q	5Q	U	
100601	Intro to child developmnt	ChFam	395	5Q	U	
100602	The family	ChFam	461	5Q	U	
100604	Interper rel & marriage	ChFam	393	5Q	U	
120201	Western world lit I	Engl	250Q	5Q	L	
120201	Western world lit II	Engl	251Q	5Q	L	
120299	Children's literature	Engl	455Q	5Q	U	
120303	Derivatives frm Grk & Ltn	CILL	310	5Q	U	
120305	Composition part I	Engl	101	5Q	L	
120305	Composition part II	Engl	102	5Q	L	
120307	English lit to 1700	Engl	231G	5Q	L	
120307	English lit after 1700	Engl	232G	5Q	L	
120307	Survey of American lit	Engl	307Q	5Q	U	
120307	Southern literature	Engl	320Q	5Q	U	
120307	Modern novel	Engl	409Q	5Q	U	
120307	Early American literature	Engl	470T	5Q	U	
120399	Mythology in classicl lit	CILL	150	5Q	L	
121000	Elementary French	Frnch	101	5Q	L	AC
121000	Elementary French	Frnch	102	5Q	L	AC
121000	Elementary French	Frnch	103	5Q	L	AC
121000	Intermediate French	Frnch	104	5Q	L	
121100	Elementary German I	Germn	151Q	5Q	L	AC
121100	Elementary German II	Germn	152Q	5Q	L	AC
121100	Intermediate German I	Germn	153Q	5Q	L	
121100	Intermediate German II	Germn	252Q	5Q	L	AC
121100	Commercial German	Germn	357Q	5Q	U	
121600	Elementary Latin I	CILL	101	5Q	L	AC
121600	Elementary Latin II	CILL	102	5Q	L	AC
121600	Elementary Latin III	CILL	103	5Q	L	
121600	Readings in Latin poetry	CILL	304	5Q	U	
121600	Golden age of Latin lit	CILL	204	5Q	L	
122500	Elementary Spanish I	Span	151Q	5Q	L	AC
122500	Elementary Spanish II	Span	152Q	5Q	L	AC
122500	Elementary Spanish III	Span	251Q	5Q	L	AC
122500	Intermediate Spanish II	Span	252Q	5Q	L	AC
150202	Meteorology	Geog	492Q	5Q	U	
150304	Ecology	Bio	350	5Q	U	
150307	Genetics	Bio	440Q	5Q	U	
160199	Finite mathematics I	Math	101Q	5Q	L	
160203	Finite mathematics	Math	155Q	5Q	L	
160302	Fundamentals of algebra	Math	103Q	5Q	L	
160401	Analyt geom & calculus I	Math	166Q	5Q	L	
160602	Trigonometry	Math	112Q	5Q	L	
160801	Elementary statistics	Math	240Q	5Q	L	
160802	Stat analysis for bus	MgtSc	312	5Q	U	
180302	Introduction to ethics	Philo	305	5Q	U	
180502	Intro to deductive logic	Philo	110	5Q	L	
180800	Intro to philosophy	Philo	101	5Q	L	
181002	Intro to West rel traditn	Relig	115	5Q	L	
181002	Intro to maj rel perspect	Relig	116	5Q	L	
190501	Effcts drug use and abuse	Educ	521	5Q	U	
200199	Elementary psychology	Psych	101	5Q	L	
200501	Abnormal psychology	Psych	423	5Q	U	
200504	Soc & personality develop	Psych	259	5Q	L	
200504	Intro to child developmnt	Psych	395	5Q	U	
200509	Theories of personality	Psych	451	5Q	U	
200599	Psych of sex & sex deviat	Psych	326	5Q	U	
200599	Psychology of speech comm	Psych	466	5Q	U	
200799	Social psychology	Psych	371Q	5Q	U	
210199	Prin of public admin	PolSc	341Q	5Q	L	
210304	Intro to crim justice adm	PolSc	204	5Q	L	
220102	Cultural anthropology	Anthr	405	5Q	U	
220107	Intro to social anthro	Anthr	102	5Q	L	
220201	Prin of macroeconomics	Econ	107	5Q	L	
220201	Prin of microeconomics	Econ	106	5Q	L	
220202	Hist of economic thought	Econ	473Q	5Q	U	
220207	Econ development of US	Econ	233	5Q	L	
220211	Labor economics	Econ	386	5Q	U	
220299	Government and business	Econ	478Q	5Q	U	
220301	Intro to human geography	Geog	101	5Q	L	
220302	Economic geography	Geog	358	5Q	U	
220305	Earth science survey	Geog	104	5Q	L	
220406	Classical culture: Greece	ClCiv	120	5Q	L	
220406	Classical culture: Rome	ClCiv	121	5Q	L	
220426	Early modern Western civ	Hist	121	5Q	L	
220426	Modern Western civiliztn	Hist	122	5Q	L	
220428	History of Georgia	Hist	470Q	5Q	U	
220432	American history to 1865	Hist	251	5Q	L	
220432	American hist since 1865	Hist	252	5Q	L	

NCES No.	Course Title	Dept.	Course No.	Cred.	Lev.	Specl. Feat.
220501	American government	PolSc	101	5Q	L	
220501	National security policy	PolSc	375Q	5Q	U	
220503	Comp European polit sys	PolSc	310Q	5Q	U	
220503	Comparative forgn policy	PolSc	490Q	5Q	U	
220503	Soviet pol & forgn policy	PolSc	480Q	5Q	U	
220504	Contemp Amer forn policy	PolSc	455Q	5Q	U	
220505	Internat polit & organ	PolSc	210Q	5Q	L	
220506	Minority politics	PolSc	356Q	5Q	U	
220511	State and local governmnt	PolSc	350Q	5Q	U	
220604	Juvenile delinquency	Socio	307	5Q	U	
220605	Marriage and family	Socio	103Q	5Q	L	
220605	The family	Socio	461	5Q	U	
220606	Introductory sociology	Socio	105	5Q	L	
220607	Social psychology	Socio	371Q	5Q	U	
220607	Personality & soc struct	Socio	427	5Q	U	
220613	Contemporary soc problems	Socio	160	5Q	L	
220699	Sociology of occupations	Socio	485	5Q	U	

Noncredit courses

NCES No.	Course Title	Dept.	Course No.	Cred.	Lev.	Specl. Feat.
040300	Prof financ planner cert	ConEd		NC	L	VC
040300	Prof Financ Planner Cert	ConEd		NC	L	VC
041100	Directional management	ConEd		NC	L	VC
041103	Interpersonal Skills Cert	ConEd		NC	L	
090399	Gardening for handicapped	ConEd		NC	H	VC
090800	Practice vet med videos	VetSc		NC	B	VC
100601	Child Caregiver Certifica	ConEd		NC	H	VC
100603	Basics in Gerontology Cer	ConEd		NC	H	
100702	Dietary Manager Certifica	ConEd		NC	H	
110699	Towing and Recovery Cert	ConEd		NC	H	VC

㊴ UNIVERSITY OF IDAHO

Ms. Julie E. Rinard
State Coordinator, Correspondence Study in Idaho
Correspondence Study in Idaho
University of Idaho
Continuing Education Building, Room 116
Moscow, Idaho 83843
Phone: 208-885-6641

Enrollment on a noncredit basis accepted in credit courses. High school students may enroll in undergraduate courses for credit. Overseas enrollment accepted. Military personnel may enroll through the DANTES program. Maximum period for course completion is one year.

NCES No.	Course Title	Dept.	Course No.	Cred.	Lev.	Specl. Feat.
High School courses						
090115	Health education	Hlth	I	HF	H	
100202	Consumer economics	ConEd	I	HF	H	
120305	Lit and composition	FrEng	I	HF	H	
120305	Lit, comp and grammar	SoEng	I	HF	H	
120307	Lit and composition	FrEng	II	HF	H	
120307	Lit, comp and grammar	SoEng	II	HF	H	
120307	American lit and comp	JrEng	I	HF	H	
120307	American lit and comp	JrEng	II	HF	H	
120307	English lit and comp	SrEng	I	HF	H	
120307	English lit and comp	SrEng	II	HF	H	
120308	Reading	Read	I	HF	H	
150300	Biology	Bio	I	HF	H	
150300	Biology	Bio	II	HF	H	
150900	Earth science	ErSci	I	HF	H	
150900	Earth science	ErSci	II	HF	H	
160301	General mathematics	GnMth	I	HF	H	
160301	General mathematics	GnMth	II	HF	H	
160302	Algebra	Algbr	I	HF	H	
160302	Algebra	Algbr	II	HF	H	
160604	Geometry	Geom	I	HF	H	
160604	Geometry	Geom	II	HF	H	
220432	American history	AmHis	I	HF	H	
220432	American history	AmHis	II	HF	H	
220433	World history	WHS	I	HF	H	
220501	American government	AmGvt	I	HF	H	
220511	State and local govt	Govt	II	HF	H	
220600	Sociology	Socio	I	HF	H	
College courses						
010107	Princ of farm/ranch mgmt	AgEco	C278	4S	L	
010199	Ag in its soc/econ envir	AgEco	C101	3S	L	
010901	Pub relations-nat resourc	Fores	C400	2S	U	

NCES No.	Course Title	Dept.	Course No.	Cred.	Lev.	Specl. Feat.
030302	Survey of music	Music	C100	3S	L	AC
040101	Principles of accounting	Acctg	C201	3S	L	
040101	Intermediate accounting	Acctg	C304	4S	U	
040101	Intermediate accounting	Acctg	C305	4S	U	
040111	Managerial accounting	Acctg	C202	3S	L	
040203	Local govt records mgmt	BusEd	C312	2S	U	
041001	Marketing	Bus	C321	3S	U	
041303	Fundamntls of real estate	RlEst	C201	3S	L	
041306	Real estate finance	Bus	C465	3S	U	
041308	Real estate law	Bus	C464	3S	U	
050199	Promotional strategy	Bus	C420	3S	U	
060799	Digital computer prog	Engin	C131	2S	L	
070309	Devel/org of extension ed	AgEd	C248	2S	L	
070309	Intro to adult education	VocEd	C473	3S	U	
070309	Psych of adult learners	VocEd	C474	3S	U	
070507	Contemporary education	Educ	C468	3S	U	
070512	Elementary language arts	Educ	C338	3S	U	
070515	Elem school science meths	Educ	C344	3S	U	
070522	Social studies methods	Educ	C421	3S	U	
070803	Ed of exceptional child	SplEd	C275	3S	U	
070803	Behavioral principles	SplEd	C323	3S	U	
081000	Engineering graphics	Engin	C101	2S	L	
081000	Engineering graphics	Engin	C102	2S	L	
081102	Fluid mechanics	EngSc	C320	3S	U	
081104	Statics	EngSc	C210	3S	L	VC
081104	Dynamics	EngSc	C220	3S	L	
081200	Mechanics of materials	EngSc	C340	3S	U	
082699	Elementary surveying	Engin	C201	3S	L	AC
090799	El microbio/pub health	Bact	C154	3S	L	
100202	Consumer education	ConEd	C471	3S	U	
100699	Contemp family relations	HomEc	C440	3S	U	
120305	Composition	Engl	C101	3S	L	
120305	Composition	Engl	C102	3S	L	
120307	The novel for nonmajors	Engl	C321	3S	U	
122500	Elementary Spanish	Span	C101	4S	L	AC
122500	Elementary Spanish	Span	C102	4S	L	AC
130700	Legal envir of business	Bus	C265	3S	L	
130700	Business law	Bus	C466	3S	U	
130700	Business law	Bus	C366	3S	U	
140200	Introduction to museology	Anthr	C324	3S	U	
140303	Mgmt of small libraries	LibSc	C425	4S	U	
140305	Museum administration	Anthr	C419	3S	U	
140307	Use of the school library	LibSc	C422	2S	U	
140401	Cataloging & classificat	LibSc	C420	4S	U	
140408	Acquisition & collect dev	LibSc	C421	3S	U	
140804	Intro to reference work	LibSc	C423	3S	U	
150304	General ecology	Bio	C331	3S	U	
150399	Man and the environment	Bio	C200	3S	L	
150700	General physics	Phycs	C114	3S	L	
150799	General physics	Phycs	C113	3S	L	
160203	Finite math	Math	C111	4S	L	
160301	Math for elem teachers	Math	C135	3S	L	
160301	Math for elem teachers	Math	C136	3S	L	
160302	College algebra	Math	C140	3S	L	
160401	Survey of calculus	Math	C160	4S	L	
160602	Analytic trigonometry	Math	C179	2S	L	
160603	Analytic geom and calc I	Math	C180	4S	L	
160801	Intro to statistics	Math	C252	3S	L	
180300	Ethics	Philo	C101	3S	L	
180401	History of ancient philo	Philo	C309	3S	U	
180403	History of modern philo	Philo	C310	3S	U	
200104	Intro to psychology	Psych	C100	3S	L	
200501	Abnormal psychology	Psych	C311	3S	U	
200504	Developmental psychology	Psych	C205	3S	L	
200504	Per/social devel in child	Psych	C309	3S	U	
200509	Psychology of personality	Psych	C310	3S	U	
200599	Human sexuality	Psych	C210	2S	L	
200599	Cognitive development	Psych	C409	3S	U	
200603	Meas and eval in psych	Psych	C402	3S	U	
200799	Social psychology	Psych	C320	3S	U	
209900	Statistical methods	Psych	C300	3S	U	
209900	Profes issues and ethics	Psych	C495	3S	U	
210102	Public administration	PolSc	C441	3S	U	
210110	Politics and energy	PolSc	C155	1S	L	
210111	Politics and pollution	PolSc	C152	1S	L	
220100	Study of man	Anthr	C301	3S	U	
220201	Principles of economics	Econ	C151	3S	L	
220201	Principles of economics	Econ	C152	3S	L	
220204	Money and banking	Econ	C403	3S	U	VC
220423	History of the Far East	Hist	C470	3S	U	
220424	History of England	Hist	C271	3S	L	
220424	History of England	Hist	C272	3S	L	

NCES No.	Course Title	Dept.	Course No.	Cred.	Lev.	Specl. Feat.
220428	Idaho and the Pacific NW	Hist	C423	3S	U	
220432	Intro to US history	Hist	C111	3S	L	
220432	Intro to US history	Hist	C112	3S	L	
220450	History of civilization	Hist	C101	3S	L	
220450	History of civilization	Hist	C102	3S	L	
220501	US govt: structure & func	PolSc	C101	3S	L	
220501	US govt: policies & issue	PolSc	C102	3S	L	
220511	American state government	PolSc	C275	3S	L	
220511	American local government	PolSc	C276	3S	L	
220599	Local govt purchasing	PolSc	C253	2S	L	
220602	Intro to criminal just ad	CrJus	C201	3S	L	
220604	Juvenile delinquency	Socio	C330	3S	U	
220608	Rural sociology	Socio	C310	3S	U	
220612	Introduction to soc ser	Socio	C140	3S	L	
220613	Social problems	Socio	C230	3S	L	
220699	Introduction to sociology	Socio	C110	3S	L	

Graduate courses

NCES No.	Course Title	Dept.	Course No.	Cred.	Lev.	Specl. Feat.
209900	Profes issues and ethics	Psych	C595	3S	G	

Noncredit courses

NCES No.	Course Title	Dept.	Course No.	Cred.	Lev.	Specl. Feat.
080900	Elem electrical theory	ElecE	C010	NC	L	
160303	Remedial mathematics	Math	C50	NC	L	

㊵ **UNIVERSITY OF ILLINOIS**

Dr. Robert W. Batchellor
Head, Guided Individual Study
University of Illinois
302 East John Street, Suite 1406
Champaign, Illinois 61820
Phone: 217-333-1321

Enrollment on a noncredit basis accepted in credit courses. High school students may enroll in undergraduate courses for credit. Overseas enrollment accepted. Military personnel may enroll through the DANTES program. Minimum period for course completion is six weeks. Maximum period for course completion is nine months.

NCES No.	Course Title	Dept.	Course No.	Cred.	Lev.	Specl. Feat.
	College courses					
040101	Principles of acctg I	Acctg	X201	3S	L	
040101	Principles of acctg II	Acctg	X202	3S	L	
040101	Intermediate accounting	Acctg	X211	3S	U	
040106	Cost accounting	Acctg	X221	3S	U	
040109	Governmental accounting	Acctg	X361	3S	U	
040304	Money, credit, & fin mkts	Finan	X258	3S	U	
040601	Bus & admin communication	BTWri	X251	3S	U	
040604	Report writing	BTWri	X272	3S	U	
040800	Intro to internationl bus	BusAd	X382	3S	L	
040800	International management	BusAd	X384	3S	U	
040800	Japanese managemt systems	BusAd	X294	3S	U	
040800	International marketing	BusAd	X370	3S	U	
040900	Intro to management	BusAd	X247	3S	U	
040901	Business policy	BusAd	X389	3S	U	
040999	Purchasing management	BusAd	X199	3S	L	
041001	Principles of marketing	BusAd	X202	3S	U	
050100	Introduction to advertisg	Advt	X281	3S	U	
050104	Advert creative strategy	Advt	X382	3S	U	
050199	Advert in contemp society	Advt	X393	3S	U	
070516	Math for elem teachers	Math	X201	5S	U	
070700	Indiv counslg & group wrk	EdPsy	X199	3S	L	
070799	Mental hyg & the school	EdPsy	X312	2S	U	
071102	Const & use of tests	EdPsy	X391	4S	U	
081000	Engineering graphics	GenEn	X103	3S	L	
081104	Analyt mechanics-statics	TAM	X150	2S	L	
081104	Engr mechanics I–statics	TAM	X152	3S	L	
081104	Engr mech II–dynamics	TAM	X212	3S	U	
081199	Elem mech of solids	TAM	X221	3S	U	
090299	Patient education	HlEd	X394	3S	U	
090504	First aid	HlEd	X199	2S	L	
090700	Intro to public health	HlEd	X101	3S	L	
100601	Child dev for elem teachr	EdPsy	X236	3S	U	
120307	Introduction to drama	EngLL	X102	3S	L	
120307	Masterpieces of Amer lit	EngLL	X116	3S	L	
120307	Intro to Shakespeare	EngLL	X118	3S	L	
120307	Modern short story	EngLL	X246	3S	U	
120307	American fiction	EngLL	X249	3S	U	

NCES No.	Course Title	Dept.	Course No.	Cred.	Lev.	Spec. Feat.
120307	Masterpieces of Engl lit	Engl	X115	3S	L	
120307	The British novel	Engl	X247	3S	U	
120310	Principles of composition	Rhet	X105	4S	L	
120310	Advan narrative writing	Rhet	X205	3S	U	
121000	Elementary French	Frnch	X101	4S	L	AC
121000	Elementary French	Frnch	X102	4S	L	AC
121000	Intermediate French I	Frnch	X103	4S	L	AC
121000	Intermediate French II	Frnch	X104	4S	L	AC
121000	Intro Fr lit 17th-18th ce	Frnch	X209	3S	U	
121000	Intro Fr lit 19th-20th ce	Frnch	X210	3S	U	
121100	Elementary German	Germn	X101	4S	L	
121100	Elementary German	Germn	X102	4S	L	
121100	Intermediate German	Germn	X103	4S	L	
121100	Intermediate German	Germn	X104	4S	L	
121600	Elementary Latin	Latin	X101	4S	L	
121600	Elementary Latin	Latin	X102	4S	L	
121600	Intermediate Latin	Latin	X103	4S	L	
121600	Intro to Latin literature	Latin	X104	4S	L	
122000	First-year Russian	Rus	X101	4S	L	AC
122000	First-year Russian	Rus	X102	4S	L	
122000	Second-year Russian	Rus	X103	4S	L	
122000	Second-year Russian	Rus	X104	4S	L	
122000	19th-cent Rus lit in tran	Rus	X315	3S	L	
122500	Elementary Spanish	Span	X101	4S	L	
122500	Elementary Spanish	Span	X102	4S	L	
122500	Reading & writing Spanish	Span	X123	4S	L	
122500	Reading & writing Spanish	Span	X124	4S	L	
122500	Span lit: Mid Age-18th c	Span	X240	3S	U	
122500	Span lit: 19th cen to pre	Span	X241	3S	U	
122500	Spanish-Amer literature	Span	X242	3S	U	
150700	Gen phys: mech heat matte	Phycs	X123	4S	L	
150700	Gen phys: elec mag atm nu	Phycs	X124	4S	L	
160302	College algebra	Math	X112Z	5S	L	
160302	College algebra	Math	X112	3S	L	
160306	Elem linear alg with appl	Math	X125	3S	L	
160401	Calc & analyt geom I	Math	X120	5S	L	
160401	Calc & analyt geom II	Math	X132	3S	L	
160401	Calc & analyt geom III	Math	X242	5S	L	
160406	Differ eq & orthog funct	Math	X285	3S	U	
160602	Plane trigonometry	Math	X114	2S	L	
160800	Descriptive statistics	Psych	X233	3S	U	
160800	Inferential statistics	Psych	X234	2S	U	
161100	Finite math: bus & soc sc	Math	X124	3S	L	
161100	Calculus-bus and soc sci	Math	X134	4S	L	
161101	Economic statistics I	Econ	X172	3S	L	
161103	Intro econ-bus statistics	Econ	X171	3S	L	
161108	Statistical meth in psych	Psych	X235	5S	U	
190500	Contemporary health	HlEd	X100	3S	L	
190501	Drug use and abuse	HlEd	X243	3S	U	
190502	Public health practice	HlEd	X310	4S	U	
190503	Health prog development	HlEd	X210	3S	U	
190504	Intro to epidemiology	HlEd	X274	2S	U	
190509	Found of health behavior	HlEd	X204	3S	U	
190512	Human sexuality	HlEd	X206	3S	U	
190515	Sexuality prog developmnt	HlEd	X225	2S	U	
190515	Hlth & safety ed elem sch	HlEd	X312	3S	U	
190599	Patient education	HlEd	X394	3S	U	
200100	Intro to psychology	Psych	X100	4S	L	AC
200401	Behavior modification	Psych	X337	3S	U	
200403	Cognitive psychology	Psych	X224	3S	U	
200406	Psy of learning & memory	Psych	X248	3S	U	
200501	Abnormal psychology	Psych	X238	3S	U	
200509	Psychology of personality	Psych	X250	3S	U	
200700	Intro to social psychol	Psych	X201	3S	U	
200804	Educational psychology	EdPsy	X211	3S	U	
200901	Industrial psychology	Psych	X245	3S	U	
220102	Intro to cultural anthro	Anthr	X103	4S	L	
220105	Intro to linguistic anthr	Anthr	X270	3S	U	
220201	Introduction to economics	Econ	X101	4S	L	
220202	Hist of econ thought	Econ	X306	3S	U	
220206	Intro to public finance	Econ	X214	3S	U	
220207	Comparative econ systems	Econ	X255	3S	U	
220305	Physical geography I	Geog	X102	4S	L	
220305	Physical geography II	Geog	X103	3S	L	
220401	Const dev of US to 1865	Hist	X369	3S	U	
220401	Const dev of US snce 1865	Hist	X370	3S	U	
220426	Hist of West civ to 1660	Hist	X111	4S	L	
220426	Hist of West civ fr 1660	Hist	X112	4S	L	
220432	US history to 1877	Hist	X151	4S	L	
220432	US history 1877 to pres	Hist	X152	4S	L	
220432	US in 20th century	Hist	X262	3S	U	
220500	Intro to political sci	PolSc	X100	3S	L	
220501	American government	PolSc	X150	3S	L	
220503	Intro to compar politics	PolSc	X240	3S	U	
220505	International relations	PolSc	X280	3S	U	
220510	Contemp political theory	PolSc	X396	3S	U	
220511	Municipal government	PolSc	X305	3S	U	
220600	Introduction to sociology	Socio	X100	3S	L	
220612	Stratification & soc clas	Socio	X223	3S	U	
220613	Family violence	Socio	X242	3S	U	
220613	Alcohol and society	Socio	X241	3S	U	
220699	Collective behavior	Socio	X240	3S	U	

㊶ UNIVERSITY OF IOWA

Leonard Kallio
Acting Assistant Director, Guided Correspondence Study
Center for Credit Programs
116 International Center
University of Iowa
Iowa City, Iowa 52242
Phone: 319-335-2575
        800-272-6430 in IA

External degree available through the program. Enrollment on a noncredit basis accepted in credit courses. High school students may enroll in undergraduate courses for credit. Overseas enrollment accepted. Military personnel may enroll through the DANTES program. Minimum period for course completion is two weeks per credit hour. Maximum period for course completion is nine months. Telecourses are offered within Iowa by a sister program, Off-Campus Courses and Programs.

NCES No.	Course Title	Dept.	Course No.	Cred.	Lev.	Spec. Feat.
	College courses					
030302	Introduction to music	Music	259	3S	L	AC
030401	Basic playwriting	Theat	4962	3S	L	
030401	Advanced playwriting	Theat	49167	3S	B	
030501	Calligraphy I	Art	1Y140	3S	B	
040301	Intro financial mgmt	Bus	6F100	3S	B	
040306	Investments	Bus	6F111	3S	B	
040502	Entrepreneurship new bus	Bus	6F127	3S	B	
040502	Managing new or small bus	Bus	6F128	3S	B	
040708	General insurance	Finan	6F102	3S	B	
040903	Organizational behavior	Bus	6K160	3S	B	
050605	News-ed lab;free-lnc writ	Journ	19170	3S	B	
051104	Organizational leadership	ComSt	36C43	3S	L	
051199	Parliamentary procedure	ComSt	36C42	1S	L	
059900	Spec proj in mass comm	JMC	19180	CV		
070199	Human abilities	Educ	7P102	3S	B	
070401	Intro to education	Educ	7S101	3S	B	
070404	Methods early child ed	Educ	7E157	3S	B	
070404	Classroom management	Educ	7E170	CV	B	
070512	Lit for adolescents	Educ	7S193	3S	B	
070512	Methods high sch reading	Educ	7S194	3S	B	
070800	Exceptional persons	Educ	7U130	3S	B	
070801	Spec ed erly chldhd tchrs	Educ	7E138	3S	B	
070801	Mthds tchg presch handic	Educ	7U120	3S	B	
070803	Education of the gifted	Educ	7U137	3S	B	
070803	Education of the gifted	Educ	7C137	3S	B	
070806	Mental retardation	Educ	7U135	3S	B	
071202	Intro instr des & techn	Educ	7W120	3S	B	
081000	Lettering	EngAS	58105	1S	B	
081000	Mechanical drawing	EngAS	58105	2S	B	
081505	Qual control & eng stats	Engin	56162	3S	U	
090117	Pathology	Nrsng	96120	4S	B	
090302	Diet therapy	HomEc	17147	3S	B	
090904	Intro biomedical ethics	Relig	32163	3S	B	SL
100313	Nutrition	HomEc	17142	3S	B	
100602	Parent-child relshps	HomEc	17114	3S	B	
120107	Language and society	Ling	10311	3S	L	
120202	Maj 19th-cent Brit works	EngLL	877	3S	L	
120202	Amer works before 1900	EngLL	864	3S	L	
120202	Chaucer	EngLL	8120	3S	B	
120202	Shakespeare	EngLL	8122	3S	B	
120202	Pop lits detective fictn	EngLL	8142	3S	B	
120202	Sci fiction hist survey	EngLL	8182	3S	B	
120202	Women in literature	EngLL	8161	3S	U	
120202	Chan concept women in lit	EngLL	8169	3S	B	
120299	Amer music rock and roll	AmSt	4575	3S	L	
120299	American autobiography	AmSt	45190	3S	B	

NCES No.	Course Title	Dept.	Course No.	Cred.	Lev.	Specl. Feat.
120305	Greek & Lat for vocab bld	Class	20101	2S	B	
120305	Med & tech terminology	Class	20103	2S	B	
120307	Lit & cult 20th-cent Amer	EngLL	8106	3S	B	
120307	Eng novel Scott to Butler	EngLL	8133	3S	B	
120307	Lit of African peoples	Engl	1298	3S	L	AC
120307	Prose by women writers	Engl	8188	3S	B	
120307	Interpret of literature	Engl	8G1	3S	L	
120310	Expository writing	EngLL	8W10	3S	L	
120310	Creative writing	EngLL	8W23	3S	L	
120310	Fiction writing	EngLL	8W151	3S	B	
120310	Advanced fiction writing	EngLL	8W161	3S	B	
120310	Writing for bus & indus	EngLL	8W113	3S	B	
120310	Adv fiction writing II	EngLL	8W162	3S	B	
120310	Writng for sciences-biomd	Engl	8W112	3S	B	
120310	Rhetoric	Rhet	103	4S	L	
120310	Poetry writing	Engl	8W152	3S	B	
120310	Tech & sci writing	Engl	8W15	3S	L	
120310	Wrtg for sci (biomedical)	Engl	8W112	3S	B	
120310	Wrtg for bus & industry	Engl	8W113	3S	B	
120700	Chinese I	Asian	391	4S	L	AC
120700	Chinese II	Asian	392	4S	L	AC
121000	Elementary French	Frnch	91	4S	L	AC
121000	Elementary French	Frnch	92	4S	L	AC
121100	Elementary German I	Germn	1311	3S	L	AC
121100	Elementary German II	Germn	1312	3S	L	AC
121600	Elementary Latin	Class	201	4S	L	AC
121600	Elementary Latin	Class	202	4S	L	
122000	First year Russian I	Rus	411	4S	L	
122100	First-year Sanskrit	Asian	3921	4S	L	AC
122500	Elementary Spanish I	Span	351	4S	L	AC
122500	Elementary Spanish II	Span	352	4S	L	AC
122500	Intermediate Spanish I	Span	3511	3S	L	
122500	Intermediate Spanish II	Span	3512	3S	L	
122500	Intens elem readg Spanish	Span	357	3S	L	
150401	Principles of chemistry	Chem	413	3S	L	
150599	Introduction to geology	Geol	125	4S	L	LK
150599	Evolution of the earth	Geol	126	3S	L	
160302	Basic algebra I	Math	22M1	3S	L	
160302	Basic algebra II	Math	22M2	3S	L	
160306	Intro linear algebra	Math	22M27	4S	L	
160308	Elements of group theory	Math	22M50	3S	L	
160399	Finite mathematics	Math	22M10	4S	L	
160401	Calculus I	Math	22M25	4S	L	
160401	Calculus II	Math	22M26	4S	L	
160401	Engineering calculus I	Math	22M35	4S	L	
160401	Quantitative methods	Math	22M17	4S	L	
160401	Introduction to calculus	Math	22M11	4S	L	
160405	Fund props spaces & funcs	Math	22555	3S	L	
160601	Foundations of geometry	Math	22M70	3S	L	
160601	Basic geometry	Math	22M3	3S	L	
160602	Trigonometry	Math	22M5	3S	L	
160603	Elementary functions	Math	22M19	3S	L	
160802	Intro to stat methods	Educ	7P143	3S	B	
161107	Intro to biostatistics	PvMed	63161	3S	B	
161107	Math for biol sciences	Math	22M15	4S	L	
181104	Religion and society	Relig	322	3S	L	
181199	Religion & women	Relig	32111	3S	B	
181199	Lit & phil tht Holocaust	Relig	32148	3S	B	
181199	Quest for human destiny	Relig	322	3S	L	
181199	The Jewish experience	Relig	32120	3S	B	
181301	World of Old Testament	Relig	32105	3S	B	
181302	World of New Testament	Relig	32122	3S	B	
181399	Ind studies in relig (UG)	Relig	32195	3S	U	
190299	Human anatomy	PhyEd	2753	3S	L	
190702	Aging & leisure	LeiSt	10416	3S	B	
190799	Contemp issues rec & leis	LeiSt	10414	3S	B	
190799	Hlth promo corp hosp priv	LeiSt	10413	3S	B	
200199	Elementary psychology	Psych	311	CV	L	AC
200501	Abnormal psychology	Psych	31163	3S	B	
200503	Behavior modification	Psych	31170	3S	B	
200506	Death and dying	Relig	32193	2S	B	AC
200799	Intro to social psych	Psych	3115	3S	L	
200804	Ed psych & measurement	Educ	7P75	3S	L	
200804	Educational psychology	Educ	7P131	3S	B	
200804	Adolescent & young adult	Educ	7P133	3S	B	
200805	Socialization sch child	Educ	7P109	3S	B	
200901	Psych in bus & industry	Psych	3119	3S	L	
210404	Intro to social work	SocWk	4222	4S	L	
210405	Sexual hlth in later life	SocWk	42199	3S	B	
210499	Individual study aging	SocWk	42191	CV	B	
210499	Perspectives on aging	SocWk	42184	3S	B	
220101	Intro Midwest prehistory	Anthr	11320	3S	L	

NCES No.	Course Title	Dept.	Course No.	Cred.	Lev.	Specl. Feat.
220101	Biblical archaeology	Relig	32103	1S	B	SL
220101	Midw prehistory emph Iowa	Anthr	11320	3S	L	
220102	Intro study cult & soc	Anthr	1133	4S	L	
220102	Anthro & contemp world	Anthr	11310	3S	L	
220102	Women in rural societies	WomSt	13115	3S	B	
220107	Women's roles cross-cult	Anthr	156	3S	B	
220201	Prncples microeconomics	Econ	6E1	4S	L	
220201	Prncples macroeconomics	Econ	6E2	4S	L	
220201	Microeconomics	Econ	6E103	3S	B	
220201	Macroeconomics	Econ	6E105	3S	B	
220216	Problems in urban econ	Econ	6E137	3S	B	
220301	Intro to human geography	Geog	441	4S	L	
220308	Urban geography	Geog	44135	3S	B	
220402	US in world affairs 1900	Hist	16151	3S	B	
220408	Relig & occult in antiqty	Relig	20113	3S	B	
220423	Civilizations of Asia	Hist	165	3S	L	
220423	Civilizations of Asia	Asian	3956	3S	L	
220426	West civztn to 1792	Hist	161	3S	L	
220426	West civztn since 1792	Hist	162	3S	L	
220426	20th-cent Europe Nazi era	Hist	16135	3S	B	
220426	19th-cent Eur: imper era	Hist	16134	3S	B	
220428	History of Iowa to 1900	Hist	16137	3S	B	
220432	Amer history 1492-1877	Hist	16A61	3S	L	
220432	Amer history 1877-present	Hist	16A62	3S	L	
220432	Contemp US 1940-present	Hist	16168	3S	B	
220432	Great Plains	Hist	16134	3S	B	
220432	New Deal/new era 1920-40	Hist	16167	3S	B	
220432	US in wrld afrs 1900-1975	Hist	16152	3S	B	
220451	Vietnam War in his persp	Hist	1611	3S	L	
220452	Medieval civilization	Hist	16110	3S	B	
220499	Prbs women & soc in past	Hist	1615	3S	L	
220511	Munic govt & politics	PolSc	30111	3S	B	
220511	American state politics	PolSc	30113	3S	B	
220511	Urban administration	PolSc	30121	3S	B	
220511	Iowa govmt & politics	PolSc	30112	CV	B	
220599	Ind study in pol science	PolSc	30190	CV	B	
220602	Sociology of corrections	Socio	34145	3S	B	
220602	Socio of law & crim just	Socio	34182	3S	B	
220602	Criminology	Socio	34140	3S	B	
220603	World population problems	Socio	34174	3S	B	
220604	Juvenile delinquency	Socio	34141	3S	B	
220605	American family	Socio	34161	3S	B	AC
220606	Intro to socio principles	Socio	341	3S	L	AC
220606	Intro to socio problems	Socio	342	3S	L	
220606	Contemporary socio theory	Socio	34191	3S	B	

Graduate courses

NCES No.	Course Title	Dept.	Course No.	Cred.	Lev.	Specl. Feat.
070199	Cogn differential psych	Educ	7P202	3S	G	
070701	Intro rehabil services	Educ	7C241	2S	G	
071103	Educ measurement & eval	Educ	7P257	3S	G	
180999	Rdgs in Asian religions	Relig	32265	2S	G	
181299	Rdg Jewish/Chrstn scripts	Relig	32260	2S	G	
181399	Rdgs theol & rel thought	Relig	32263	2S	G	
181399	Ind studies in relig grad	Relig	32290	3S	G	
181599	Rdgs in religious ethics	Relig	32264	2S	G	
190107	Phys ed program planning	PhyEd	28260	3S	G	

Noncredit courses

NCES No.	Course Title	Dept.	Course No.	Cred.	Lev.	Specl. Feat.
090104	Interp card arrhythmias I	Nrsng	90676	NC	V	
090104	Interp card arrhythm II	Nrsng	90677	NC	V	
160199	Building math confidence	ConEd	MC2	NC	D	
160301	Practical math review	Math	SI30	NC	D	

④② **UNIVERSITY OF KANSAS**

Ms. Nancy R. Colyer
Director, Independent Study
Division of Continuing Education
University of Kansas
Lawrence, Kansas 66045-2606
Phone: 913-864-4792

Enrollment on a noncredit basis accepted in credit courses. High school students may enroll in undergraduate courses for credit. Overseas enrollment accepted. Maximum period for course completion is nine months.

NCES No.	Course Title	Dept.	Course No.	Cred.	Lev.	Specl. Feat.
	High School courses					
100604	Project self-discovery			HF	H	
120308	Short story reluct readrs			HF	H	
200502	Career planning			HF	H	
220501	American government			HF	H	
	College courses					
030399	Intro to jazz	Music	298	3S	L	AC
040101	Financial accounting	Bus	240	4S	L	
040111	Managerial accounting	Bus	241	3S	L	
040601	Business communication	Bus	355	3S	U	
040903	Organizational behavior	Mgmt	443	3S	U	
040999	Prod/operations managemnt	Mgmt	423	3S	U	
041105	Personnel management	Mgmt	544	3S	U	
041106	Supervisory management	Mgmt	343	3S	U	
050199	Elements of advertising	Journ	240	3S	L	
050608	Reporting I	Journ	350	3S	U	
051102	Intercultural communicatn	ComSt	246	3S	U	
051103	The loving relationship	ComSt	455	3S	U	
051103	Life shaping	ComSt	459	2S	U	AC
051110	Speech and lang develop	SHSci	566	3S	U	VC
051110	Survey of comm disorders	SHSci	261	3S	L	VC
051110	Communication disorders	SHSci	761	3S	U	VC
070404	Teaching reading in sec s	Culns	429	3S	U	AC
070404	Teach read content areas	Culns	351	3S	U	
070404	Teach lit for young adult	Culns	630	3S	U	
070699	Educ in multicultural soc	Culns	210	3S	U	
070699	Multicultural education	Culns	705	3S	U	
070810	Manage behavior problems	SplEd	798	3S	U	
070810	Manage behav prob comput	SplEd	798	3S	U	CI
070899	Psych exceptional child	SplEd	725	3S	U	
070899	Psych excep child: comput	SplEd	725	3S	U	CI
080101	Space dynamics	AeSpE	655	3S	U	
100601	Intro child behav & devel	HDFL	160	3S	L	
100601	Intro child behav & devel	HDFL	432	3S	U	
100601	Children and television	HDFL	325	3S	U	
100602	Marriage & family relatns	HDFL	288	3S	L	
100604	Analysis evryday behavior	HDFL	180	3S	L	
100699	Prin nutr & health in dev	HDFL	220	3S	L	
100699	Prin of env design & fam	HDFL	102	3S	L	
100699	Theories of human develop	HDFL	480	3S	U	
120201	Greek and Roman myth	Class	148	3S	L	
120201	Greek and Roman myth	Class	348	3S	U	
120305	Composition & literature	Engl	101	3S	L	
120305	Composition & literature	Engl	102	3S	L	
120305	Grammar & usage composit	Engl	325	3S	U	
120307	Shakespeare	Engl	332	3S	U	
120307	Literature for children	Engl	466	3S	U	
120307	American literature I	Engl	320	3S	U	
120307	American literature II	Engl	322	3S	U	
120307	Dir readings: Hemingway	Engl	495	CV	U	
120307	Directed readings: Cather	Engl	495	CV	U	
120307	Kansas literature	Engl	570	3S	U	AC
120307	Intro to fiction	Engl	209	3S	U	
120307	Recent popular fiction	Engl	325	3S	U	
120310	Technical writing	Engl	362	3S	U	
120310	Creative writing: fiction	Engl	351	3S	U	
120399	Grk & Lat elem in Eng lge	Class	232	3S	L	
120399	Grk & Lat elem in Eng lge	Class	332	3S	U	
121000	Elementary French I	Frnch	110	5S	L	VC
121000	Elementary French II	Frnch	120	5S	L	VC
121100	Elementary German I	Germn	104	5S	L	AC
121100	Elementary German II	Germn	108	5S	L	AC
121600	Elementary Latin	Latin	104	5S	L	AC
121600	Latin reading & grammar	Latin	108	5S	L	
121600	Epic poetry of Golden Age	Latin	316	3S	U	
122500	Elementary Spanish I	Span	104	5S	L	AC
122500	Spanish reading course	Span	100	3S	L	
122500	Intermediate Spanish I	Span	212	3S	L	
122500	Elementary Spanish II	Span	108	5S	L	
150202	Unusual weather	Meteo	320	3S	U	
150202	Introductory meteorology	Meteo	105	3S	L	
150202	Introductory meteorology	Meteo	105	5S	L	
150301	Human reprod bio & behav	Bio	303	3S	U	
150399	Human physiology	Bio	305	3S	U	
150399	Principles of biology	Bio	104	3S	L	
160299	Modern elementary math	Math	110	3S	L	
160302	Algebra	Math	101	3S	L	
160302	Intermediate algebra	Math	002	3S	L	
160302	Intro algebra	Math	000	3S	L	
160401	Calculus I	Math	115	3S	L	

NCES No.	Course Title	Dept.	Course No.	Cred.	Lev.	Specl. Feat.
160401	Calculus II	Math	116	3S	L	
160408	Precalculus math	Math	104	5S	L	
160602	Trigonometry	Math	103	2S	L	
160603	Calculus I	Math	121	5S	L	
180404	Intro to philosophy	Philo	140	4S	L	
180599	Intro to logic A	Philo	148	3S	L	CI
180905	History of Judaism	Relig	320	3S	U	VC
181199	The loving relationship	Relig	475	3S	U	
181202	Understanding the Bible	Relig	124	3S	L	
190311	Coaching of basketball	HPE&R	252	2S	L	
190311	Coaching of track & field	HPE&R	390	2S	L	
190505	Environmental health	HPE&R	649	3S	U	
190512	AIDS and STDs: facts	HPE&R	713	3S	U	VC
190599	Personal & commun health	HPE&R	260	3S	L	
200199	General psychology	Psych	104	3S	L	
200408	Cognitive psychology	Psych	318	3S	U	
200499	Brain, mind, behavior	Psych	440	3S	U	
200599	Psych of adolescence	Psych	626	3S	U	
200599	Children and television	Psych	325	3S	U	
200599	The mind	Psych	390	3S	U	VC
200799	Social psychology	Psych	260	3S	L	
200804	Educational psychology	EPR	300	3S	U	
200805	Comm and class management	EPR	310	3S	U	
220106	Intro physical anthropol	Anthr	104	4S	L	
220106	Intro physical anthropol	Anthr	304	4S	U	
220201	Introductory economics	Econ	104	4S	L	
220305	Intro physical geography	Geog	104	3S	L	
220399	Environmental conservatn	Geog	304	3S	U	
220409	Childhood and youth Amer	Hist	606	3S	U	AC
220426	Inside Hitler's Germany	Hist	341	3S	U	
220432	Hist US through Civil War	Hist	128	3S	L	
220433	Hist US since Civil War	Hist	129	3S	L	
220433	World history: introd	Hist	100	3S	L	
220470	Black exper in Americas	AfrSt	106	3S	U	
220471	Hist of American Indian	Hist	619	3S	U	
220499	History of art	ArHis	100	3S	L	
220499	History of Kansas	Hist	620	3S	U	
220499	Intro to art history	ArHis	300	3S	U	
220499	Impressionism	ArHis	535	3S	U	
220501	Intro to US politics	PolSc	110	3S	L	
220503	Intro to compar politics	PolSc	150	3S	L	
220507	Library res political sci	PolSc	190	1S	L	
220606	Elements of sociology	Socio	104	3S	L	
220613	Sociology of aging	Socio	523	3S	U	
220699	Socio prob & Amer values	Socio	160	3S	L	

④③ UNIVERSITY OF KENTUCKY

Dr. Earl Pfanstiel
Director, Independent Study Program
Room 1, Frazee Hall
University of Kentucky
Lexington, Kentucky 40506-0031
Phone: 606-257-3466

Enrollment on a noncredit basis accepted in credit courses. High school students may enroll in undergraduate courses for credit. Overseas enrollment accepted. Military personnel may enroll through the DANTES program. Minimum period for course completion is eight weeks. Maximum period for course completion is one year. A four-month extension may be requested; the fee is $25.

NCES No.	Course Title	Dept.	Course No.	Cred.	Lev.	Specl. Feat.
	High School courses					
040101	Accounting I first half	BusHS	01	HF	H	
040101	Accounting I second half	BusHS	02	HF	H	
049900	Business math second half	BusHS	04	HF	H	
049900	Business law	BusHS	06	HF	H	
049900	Gen business first half	BusHS	07	HF	H	
049900	Gen business second half	BusHS	08	HF	H	
049900	Business math first half	BusHS	03	HF	H	
059900	Mass media/print/radio/TV	EngHS	21	HF	H	
100602	Family studies first hf	FamHS	60	HF	H	
100602	Family studies second hf	FamHS	61	HF	H	
120305	Grammar grade 9	Engl	13	HF	H	
120305	Grammar grade 10	Engl	15	HF	H	
120305	Grammar grade 11	Engl	17	HF	H	
120305	Grammar grade 12	Engl	19	HF	H	

NCES No.	Course Title	Dept.	Course No.	Cred.	Lev.	Specl. Feat.
120307	Literature grade 9	Engl	14	HF	H	
120307	Literature grade 10	Engl	16	HF	H	
120307	Literature grade 11	Engl	18	HF	H	
120307	Literature grade 12	Engl	20	HF	H	
121000	French I, II, III, IV	LanHS	26	1U	H	
121100	German I, II	LanHS	24	1U	H	
121600	Latin I, II	LanHS	23	1U	H	
122500	Spanish I, II, III, IV	LanHS	25	1U	H	
150300	Gen biology first half	SciHS	50	HF	H	
150300	Gen biology second half	SciHS	51	HF	H	
150900	Earth science first half	SciHS	52	HF	H	
150900	Earth science second half	SciHS	53	HF	H	
160301	General math II first hlf	MatHS	29	HF	H	
160301	Gen math I first half	MatHS	70	HF	H	
160301	Gen math I second half	MatHS	71	HF	H	
160301	General math II second hf	MatHS	30	HF	H	
160302	Algebra I first half	MatHS	31	HF	H	
160302	Algebra I second half	MatHS	32	HF	H	
160302	Algebra II first half	MatHS	33	HF	H	
160302	Algebra II second half	MatHS	34	HF	H	
160401	Precalculus first half	MatHS	37	HF	H	
160401	Precalculus second half	MatHS	38	HF	H	
160601	Plane geometry first half	MatHS	35	HF	H	
160601	Plane geometry second hf	MatHS	36	HF	H	
160602	Trigonomety	MatHS	39	HF	H	
190509	Personal-community health	Hlth	27	HF	H	
190509	Pers-comm hlth second hf	Hlth	28	HF	H	
200502	Psychology	Psych	43	HF	H	
220399	World geog first half	Geog	39	HF	H	
220399	World geog second half	Geog	40	HF	H	
220432	US history first half	Hist	41	HF	H	
220432	US history second half	Hist	42	HF	H	
220433	World civilization 1st hf	SocSt	46	HF	H	
220433	World civilization 2nd hf	SocSt	47	HF	H	
220502	Civics first half	SocSt	48	HF	H	
220502	Civics second half	SocSt	49	HF	H	
220601	Sociology first half	SocHS	44	HF	H	
220601	Sociology second half	SocHS	45	HF	H	

College courses

NCES No.	Course Title	Dept.	Course No.	Cred.	Lev.	Specl. Feat.
010199	Economics of food and agr	Agri	101	3S	L	
010402	Agri animal science	Agri	106	4S	L	
010407	Agri feeds and feeding	Agri	380	3S	U	
010604	Agri plant science	Agri	104	4S	L	
010607	Field crop production	Agri	386	3S	U	
010703	Soil science management	Agri	366	3S	U	
010901	Elements of forestry	Fores	100	2S	L	
030303	Introduction to music	Music	200	3S	L	
040101	Principles of accounting	Acctg	201	3S	L	
040101	Prin of accounting II	Acctg	202	3S	L	
040205	Theory of shorthand I	BOEd	112	3S	L	
040207	Beginning typewriting	BOEd	117	3S	L	
040301	Corporate finance	Finan	300	3S	U	
040902	Business management	Mgmt	300	3S	U	
040903	Organizational behavior	Mgmt	410	3S	U	
041003	Marketing management	Mktg	300	3S	U	
041104	Personnel and industrial	Mgmt	320	3S	U	
049900	Law, business and society	Mgmt	340	3S	U	
049900	Business law I	Mgmt	341	3S	U	
049900	Business law II	Mgmt	441	3S	U	
070516	Math for elem teachers I	Math	201	3S	L	
070516	Math for elem teachers II	Math	202	3S	L	
089900	Engineering tech writing	Engl	204	3S	L	
100103	Clothing awareness select	HomEc	337	3S	U	
100199	Introduction to textiles	HomEc	120	3S	L	
100399	Food nutrition for man	HomEc	101	3S	L	
100499	Personal/family finance	HomEc	251	3S	L	
100602	Individual marriage & fam	HomEc	252	3S	L	
110503	Basic engineering graphcs	Graph	105	2S	L	
120201	Western lit Greeks–1660	Engl	261	3S	L	
120201	Western lit 1660–present	Engl	262	3S	L	
120201	Lit Old Testament	Engl	270	3S	L	
120201	Lit New Testament	Engl	271	3S	L	
120201	Shakespeare survey	Engl	425	3S	U	
120201	American lit 1800-1860	Engl	451	3S	U	
120201	American lit 1860-1900	Engl	452	3S	U	
120201	Women in literature	Engl	375	3S	U	
120303	English lit survey I	Engl	221	3S	L	
120303	English lit survey II	Engl	222	3S	L	

NCES No.	Course Title	Dept.	Course No.	Cred.	Lev.	Specl. Feat.
120310	Freshman composition	Engl	101	3S	L	
120310	Advanced freshman comp	Engl	102	3S	L	
120310	Writing for industry	Engl	203	3S	L	
120399	Etymology	Engl	201	3S	L	
120399	Medical terminology	CILL	131	3S	L	
121000	Elementary French I	Frnch	101	3S	L	
121000	Elementary French II	Frnch	102	3S	L	
121000	Intermediate French I	Frnch	201	3S	L	
121000	Intermediate French II	Frnch	202	3S	L	
121100	Elementary German I	Germn	111	3S	L	
121100	Elementary German II	Germn	112	3S	L	
121200	Beginning Greek	Greek	151	3S	L	
121200	Intermediate German I	Germn	201	3S	L	
121200	Intermediate German II	Germn	202	3S	L	
121600	Elementary Latin I	Latin	101	3S	L	
121600	Elementary Latin II	Latin	102	3S	L	
122500	Elementary Spanish I	Span	141	3S	L	
122500	Elementary Spanish II	Span	142	3S	L	
122500	Intermediate Spanish I	Span	241	3S	L	
122500	Intermediate Spanish II	Span	242	3S	L	
150199	Descriptive astronomy I	Astro	191	3S	L	
150199	Descriptive astronomy II	Astro	192	3S	L	
150301	Human biology	Bio	110	3S	L	
150306	Evolution	Bio	508	3S	U	
150307	Principles of genetics	Bio	404	3S	U	
150311	Principles of microbiol	Bio	108	3S	L	
150316	Plant biology	Bio	106	3S	L	
150323	Animal biology	Bio	104	3S	L	
150399	Animal-plant microbiology	Bio	103	3S	L	
150399	Economic botany	Bio	465	3S	U	
160302	Remedial algebra	Math	108R	3S	L	
160302	College algebra	Math	109	3S	L	
160401	Calculus I: integral	Math	113	4S	L	
160401	Calculus II: differential	Math	114	4S	L	
160401	Elementary calculus	Math	123	3S	L	
160602	Trigonometry	Math	112	2S	L	
160801	Descriptive statistics	Stat	292	1S	L	
160899	Probability	Stat	293	1S	L	
160899	Sampling and inference	Stat	294	1S	L	
161101	Mathematics of finance	Math	121	3S	L	
180399	Introductory ethics	Philo	130	3S	L	
180405	Asian philosophy	Philo	343	3S	U	
180501	Elementary logic	Philo	120	3S	L	
180700	Intro to philosophy	Philo	100	3S	L	
200199	Intro to psychology	Psych	100	4S	L	
200501	Abnormal psychology	Psych	533	3S	U	
200504	Developmental psychology	Psych	223	3S	L	
200901	Industrial psychology	Psych	502	3S	U	
200902	Personnel psychology	Psych	503	3S	U	
210401	Social welfare	SocWk	222	3S	L	
210402	Social work profession	SocWk	322	4S	U	
220201	Principles of economics I	Econ	260	3S	L	
220201	Prin of economics II	Econ	261	3S	L	
220204	Monetary economics	Econ	485	3S	U	
220305	Soils, vegetation, land	Geog	132	3S	L	
220306	Regional geography	Geog	152	3S	L	
220309	Weather, climate, water	Geog	130	3S	L	
220399	Environmental geography	Geog	210	3S	L	
220399	Human geography	Geog	252	3S	L	
220424	British people I	Hist	202	3S	L	
220424	British people II	Hist	203	3S	L	
220426	History of Europe to 1713	Hist	104	3S	L	
220426	Europe 1713 to present	Hist	105	3S	L	
220428	History of Kentucky	Hist	240	3S	L	
220432	US history through 1865	Hist	108	3S	L	
220432	US history since 1865	Hist	109	3S	L	
220432	US history since 1939	Hist	566	3S	U	
220432	Civil War 1860-1877	Hist	464	3S	U	
220432	History of the Old South	Hist	578	3S	U	
220501	American government	PolSc	101	3S	L	
220507	Political parties	PolSc	470	3S	U	
220511	State government	PolSc	255	3S	L	
220511	Municipal government	PolSc	452	3S	U	
220601	The community	Socio	220	3S	L	
220602	Criminology	Socio	437	3S	U	
220604	Juvenile delinquency	Socio	538	3S	U	
220605	The family	Socio	409	3S	U	
220606	Introductory sociology	Socio	101	3S	L	
220609	Relations in administratn	Socio	542	3S	U	
220609	Dimensions of aging	Socio	528	3S	U	
220610	Deviant behavior	Socio	436	3S	U	
220613	Modern social problems	Socio	152	3S	L	

(44) UNIVERSITY OF MICHIGAN

Mr. Andrew W. Storey
Director, Independent Study
Extension Service
University of Michigan
200 Hill Street
Ann Arbor, Michigan 48104
Phone: 313-764-5306

Credit by examination is available. Enrollment on a noncredit basis accepted in credit courses. High school students may enroll in undergraduate courses for credit. Overseas enrollment accepted. Minimum period for course completion is eight weeks. Maximum period for course completion is one year.

NCES No.	Course Title	Dept.	Course No.	Cred.	Lev.	Specl. Feat.
	High School courses					
040205	Beginning shorthand	BusEd	016N	HF	H	
	College courses					
019900	The environ & the citizen	NatSc	485	2S	B	
019900	The environ & the citizen	NatSc	486	2S	B	
030399	Topics in Amer cult: jazz	AmCul	301	3S	L	
040101	Principles of accounting	Acctg	271	3S	L	
050299	Tech & prof writing	Hum	498	3S	U	
050399	Intro to film	Spch	220	3S	L	
070512	Tchng Engl as a for lang	Educ	D4481	2S	B	
120304	Lit & cult of Ireland	Engl	317	3S	L	
120304	Contemporary Am novel	Engl	434	3S	U	
120307	Great Books	GrBks	201	3S	L	
120399	Teach Eng as a forgn lang	Educ	D448	3S	B	
120399	Major American authors	Engl	475	3S	U	
120399	Contemporary poetry	Engl	441	3S	U	
121000	First special rdg course	Frnch	111	4S	B	
121000	Second special rdg course	Frnch	112	4S	B	
121100	First special rdg course	Germn	111	4S	B	
121100	Second special rdg course	Germn	112	4S	B	
129900	Asia through fiction	AsiSt	441	3S	L	
160602	Analyt geom & calculus I	Math	115	4S	L	
160602	Analyt geom & calculus II	Math	116	3S	L	
209900	Intro to psychology	Psych	172	4S	L	
209900	Psychology of aging	Psych	459	3S	U	
209900	Intro to behavior modific	Psych	474	3S	B	
220201	Principles of economics	Econ	201	4S	L	
220499	Pales & Arab-Israeli conf	Hist	592	3S	B	
229900	Intro to women's studies	WomSt	240	4S	L	
229900	Cross-disci studies	WomSt	342	3S	L	
229900	Women and the arts	WomSt	344	3S	L	
	Noncredit courses					
019900	The environ & the citizen	NatSc	485	NC		
019900	The environ & the citizen	NatSc	486	NC		
040601	Pract wrtg for business	BuCom	I	NC		
050605	Writing nonfiction	Journ	1	NC		
050605	Wrtg fiction for mags	Journ	2	NC		
070512	Tchng Engl as a for lang	Educ	04481	NC		
119900	Fire service inst traing	FrPro	I	NC		
120307	Great Books	GrBks	201	NC		

(45) UNIVERSITY OF MINNESOTA

Ms. Deborah L. Hillengass
Acting Director, Department of Independent Study
45 Wesbrook Hall
University of Minnesota
77 Pleasant Street, SE
Minneapolis, Minnesota 55455
Phone: 612-624-0000
          800-234-6564

Credit by examination is available. Telecourses are offered. Enrollment on a noncredit basis accepted in credit courses. High school students may enroll in undergraduate courses for credit. Overseas enrollment accepted. Military personnel may enroll through the DANTES program. Institution offers special arrangements to take courses not listed in this Catalog. Maximum period for course completion is one year-correspondence courses; six months-video courses. Courses in which credit units are given as 'V' are available for certificate credit.

NCES No.	Course Title	Dept.	Course No.	Cred.	Lev.	Specl. Feat.
	High School courses					
040101	Accounting A	Bus	9813	HF	H	
040101	Accounting B	Bus	9814	HF	H	
040205	Shorthand A	Bus	9901	HF	H	
049900	General business A	Bus	9823	HF	H	
049900	General business B	Bus	9824	HF	H	
129900	Ninth-grade English A	Engl	9831	HF	H	
129900	Ninth-grade English B	Engl	9832	HF	H	
129900	Tenth-grade English A	Engl	9833	HF	H	
129900	Tenth-grade English B	Engl	9834	HF	H	
129900	Eleventh-grade English A	Engl	9835	HF	H	
129900	Eleventh-grade English B	Engl	9836	HF	H	
129900	Twelfth-grade English A	Engl	9847	HF	H	
129900	Twelfth-grade English B	Engl	9848	HF	H	
129900	Straight thinking	Engl	9839	QT	H	
129900	Youth in conflict	Engl	9840	QT	H	
129900	Meaning/self-discov–lit	Engl	9841	QT	H	
129900	Practical writing	Engl	9842	QT	H	
129900	Advanced composition	Engl	9845	HF	H	
129900	Comparative mythology	Engl	9844	QT	H	
129900	Contemp lit and problems	Engl	9843	HF	H	
129900	Black American experience	Engl	9924	QT	H	
129900	American dream and drama	Engl	9846	HF	H	
129900	Creative writing	Engl	9849	HF	H	
150399	Biology A	Bio	9801	HF	H	
150399	Biology B	Bio	9802	HF	H	
160199	Math for consumer: basics	Math	9881	QT	H	
160199	Math for consumer:banking	Math	9882	QT	H	
160199	Math for consumer:spendng	Math	9883	QT	H	
160199	Math for consumer:problms	Math	9884	QT	H	
160302	Elementary algebra A	Math	9892	HF	H	
160302	Elementary algebra B	Math	9893	HF	H	
160302	Higher algebra A	Math	9885	HF	H	
160302	Higher algebra B	Math	9886	HF	H	
160601	Geometry A	Math	9887	HF	H	
160601	Geometry B	Math	9888	HF	H	
160602	Trigonometry	Math	9876	QT	H	
209900	General psychology A	Psych	9941	HF	H	
209900	General psychology B	Psych	9942	HF	H	
220432	American history B	Hist	9923	HF	H	
220432	American history A	Hist	9922	HF	H	
220433	World history A	Hist	9920	HF	H	
220433	World history B	Hist	9921	HF	H	
220501	Probs of Amer democracy A	PolSc	9911	HF	H	
220501	Probs of Amer democracy B	PolSc	9912	HF	H	
	College courses					
010103	Agriculture mkts & prices	Agri	1400	4Q	L	
010499	Principles of beekeeping	AnSci	0004C	3V	L	
010499	Horse production	AnSci	1600	4Q	L	
010504	Home landscape design	Hort	1010	4Q	L	
010504	Residential landscp desig	Hort	3030	4Q	U	
011400	Conserv of nat resources	Fores	1201	3Q	L	
029900	The meaning of place	AmSt	3920	4Q	U	VC
029900	The meaning of place	AmSt	5920	4Q	B	VC
029900	The meaning of place	Arch	5956	4Q	B	VC
030302	Ear trng & sight singing	Music	1501	4Q	L	
030302	Music appreciation	Music	5950	4Q	U	AC
030402	Hist of American theatre	Theat	5186	4Q	U	AC
030499	Playwriting	Theat	5115	4Q	U	AC
030500	Intro to visual arts	ArHis	1001	4Q	L	VC
040101	Principles of acctg I	Acctg	1024	3Q	L	
040101	Principles of acctg II	Acctg	1025	3Q	L	
040101	Accounting fundamentals I	GColl	1540	4Q	L	
040101	Acct fundamentals II	GColl	1542	4Q	L	
040111	Managerial accounting	Acctg	1051	4Q	L	
040114	Income tax accounting	Acctg	5135	4Q	U	
040302	Consumer problems	Bus	1731	4Q	L	AC
040601	Intro to business commun	Comp	1031	2Q	U	VC
040703	Estate planning	GColl	3583	4Q	U	
040710	Risk mgmt and insurance	Insur	3100	4Q	U	
040800	International business	BuMgt	3004	4Q	U	
041001	Marketing: introduction	GColl	1551	5Q	L	
041001	Principles of marketing	Mktg	3000	4Q	U	
041100	Personnel administration	GColl	3560	4Q	U	
041106	Applied supervision	GColl	3602	4Q	U	
049900	Intro to modern business	Bus	1511	5Q	L	
049900	Government and business	BuMgt	3005	4Q	U	
050600	Intro to mass communicatn	Journ	1001	2Q	L	
050606	History of journalism	Journ	5601	4Q	U	
050699	Communic & public opinion	Journ	5501	4Q	U	

NCES No.	Course Title	Dept.	Course No.	Cred.	Lev.	Specl. Feat.
050699	Magazine writing	Journ	3173	4Q	U	AC
051109	Efficient reading	Rhet	1147	3Q	L	
060404	Microprocessors	ElecE	3352	4Q	U	
070299	Personal time management	Educ	5110	2Q	U	AC
071199	Intro to statistics	Educ	3220	3Q	U	
071199	Statistics	GColl	1454	5Q	L	
079900	How to study	GColl	1085	2Q	U	
079900	Multidisc aspects aging	Educ	5440	4Q	U	VC
080000	Deformable body mechanics	AeSpE	3016	4Q	U	
080399	Amer architecture to 1860	AmSt	3970	4Q	U	
081502	Indust rel: manpower mgmt	IndRe	3012	4Q	U	
081599	Work measurment standards	IEOR	0103	5V	L	
081599	Supervision I	IndRe	0001C	3V	L	
081599	Indust rel: labor mktg	IndRe	3002	4Q	U	
081999	Soils engineering	EngAS	0001C	4V	L	
081999	Concrete materials	EngAS	0302C	3V	L	
090118	Intelligent self medicat	Pharm	3001	2Q	U	
090199	Aspects phys disability	HSU	5008	4Q	U	VC
090199	Multidisc aspects aging	HSU	5009	4Q	U	VC
090706	Child abuse & neglect	PubHl	5642	3Q	U	VC
100301	Tech of food processing	FdScN	1102	4Q	L	
100602	Parent-child relationship	GColl	1722	4Q	L	
100602	Minority families	FSocS	3240	4Q	U	
100602	Family stress & coping	FSocS	5240	3Q	U	VC
100604	Parenting: altern for 80s	FSocS	5240	4Q	U	AC
100604	American families in tran	FSocS	5230	4Q	U	AC
100699	Human sexual behavior	FSocS	5001	5Q	U	
120201	European folk tales	Engl	5414	4Q	U	AC
120299	Ellery Queen detect stor	AmSt	1920	4Q	L	AC
120299	Tech terms–science med	Class	1048	3Q	L	
120299	Magic/witchcraft/occult	Class	1019	4Q	L	AC
120299	Religion: Greek & Helleni	Class	3071	4Q	U	AC
120299	Madness/dev behav Greece	Class	5005	4Q	U	AC
120299	Intro to mod lit: poetry	Engl	1017	4Q	L	
120299	Intro to mod lit: drama	Engl	1019	4Q	L	
120299	Shakespeare I	Engl	3241	4Q	U	
120299	Shakespeare II	Engl	3242	4Q	U	
120299	American literature I	Engl	3411	4Q	U	
120299	American literature II	Engl	3412	4Q	U	
120299	American literature III	Engl	3413	4Q	U	
120299	20th-century Engl novel	Engl	5153	4Q	U	
120299	Afro-American literature	Engl	1816	3Q	L	
120299	Reading short stories	GColl	1371	3Q	L	
120299	Philosophy through lit	GColl	3352	4Q	U	
120299	Humanities in mod world I	Hum	1101	4Q	L	
120299	Hum in modern world II	Hum	1002	4Q	L	
120299	Hum in modern world III	Hum	1103	4Q	L	
120299	Hum in modern world IV	Hum	1104	4Q	L	
120299	European heritage: Greece	Hum	1111	4Q	L	
120299	European heritage: Rome	Hum	1113	4Q	L	
120299	Mod sci fiction & fantasy	Engl	1020	4Q	L	AC
120299	Survey English lit I	Engl	3111	4Q	U	
120299	Survey English lit III	Engl	3113	4Q	U	
120299	American short story	Engl	3455	4Q	U	
120299	Am lit:major fig & themes	Engl	1016	4Q	L	
120299	Survey English lit II	Engl	3112	4Q	U	
120307	Celtic world	Engl	3910	4Q	U	AC
120310	Fiction writing	Engl	3101	4Q	U	AC
120310	Journal & memoir writing	Engl	5109	4Q	U	AC
120310	Writing practice I	Comp	1011	5Q	L	
120310	Writing about literature	Comp	3011	4Q	U	
120310	Writing in the humanities	Comp	3012	4Q	U	
120310	Writing about science	Comp	3015	4Q	U	
120310	Writing for arts	Comp	3013	4Q	U	
120310	Writing for social scienc	Comp	3014	4Q	U	
120310	Tech writing for engineer	Comp	3031	4Q	U	
120310	Writing for business	Comp	3032	4Q	U	
120700	Religions in East Asia	EAsLL	1032	4Q	L	
121000	Beginning French I	Frnch	1101	5Q	L	AC
121000	Beginning French II	Frnch	1102	5Q	L	AC
121000	Beginning French III	Frnch	1103	5Q	L	AC
121000	French literary texts	Frnch	3104	5Q	U	
121100	Beginning German I	Germn	1101	5Q	L	AC
121100	Beginning German II	Germn	1102	5Q	L	AC
121100	Beginning German III	Germn	1103	5Q	L	
121100	Intermediate German	Germn	1301	5Q	L	
121100	Ger lit: Heinrich Böll	Germn	3610	4Q	U	
121200	Beginning classical Greek	Greek	1101	5Q	L	
121400	Beginning Italian I	Ital	1101	5Q	L	AC
121600	Beginning Latin I	CILL	1101	5Q	L	
121600	Beginning Latin II	CILL	1102	5Q	L	
121600	Beginning Latin III	CILL	1103	5Q	L	
121600	Cicero	CILL	3105	5Q	U	
121600	Vergil: *Aeneid*	CILL	3106	5Q	U	
121600	Latin readings	CILL	1104	5Q	L	
121800	Beginning Norwegian I	Norw	1101	5Q	L	AC
121800	Beginning Norwegian II	Norw	1102	5Q	L	AC
122000	Beginning Russian I	Rus	1101	5Q	L	AC
122000	Beginning Russian II	Rus	1102	5Q	L	AC
122000	Beginning Russian III	Rus	1103	5Q	L	AC
122000	Scientific Russian I	Rus	1221	5Q	L	
122000	Scientific Russian III	Rus	1223	2Q	L	AC
122500	Beginning Spanish I	Span	1101	5Q	L	AC
122500	Beginning Spanish II	Span	1102	5Q	L	AC
122500	Beginning Spanish III	Span	1103	5Q	L	AC
122500	Intermediate Spanish	Span	1104	5Q	L	AC
122500	Reading and composition	Span	1105	5Q	L	AC
122500	Civ: pre-Columb to 1825	Span	1502	4Q	L	AC
122600	Beginning Swedish I	Swed	1101	5Q	L	AC
122600	Beginning Swedish II	Swed	1102	5Q	L	AC
129900	Beginning Polish I	Plsh	1101	5Q	L	AC
129900	Modern Judaism	JwSt	3126	4Q	U	
129900	The Holocaust	JwSt	3521	4Q	U	AC
129900	Tales of H C Andersen	Scand	3602	4Q	U	AC
130202	Law of contracts & agency	Law	3058	4Q	U	
130703	Partner corp & real prope	Law	3078	4Q	U	
130907	Personal prop wills & est	Law	3088	4Q	U	
139900	Law in society	GColl	1235	5Q	L	
139900	Practical law	GColl	1534	5Q	L	
150102	Solar astronomy	GColl	1161	5Q	L	
150300	General biology	Bio	1009	5Q	L	LK
150304	Intro to ecology	EnvD	3001	4Q	U	
150401	Principles of chemistry	GColl	1166	5Q	I	
150700	General physics	Phycs	1104	4Q	L	
150700	General physics	Phycs	1105	4Q	L	
150700	General physics	Phycs	1106	4Q	L	
150799	Introduction to physics	Phycs	1041	4Q	L	
150799	Introduction to physics	Phycs	1042	4Q	L	
150799	General physics	Phycs	1281	4Q	L	
150799	General physics	Phycs	1291	4Q	L	
150799	General physics	Phycs	1271	4Q	L	
150800	Changing physical world	Phycs	1003	4Q	U	VC
160199	Precalculus	Math	1201	5Q	L	
160304	College alg/analyt geom	Math	1111	5Q	L	
160306	Linear alg & lin diff equ	Math	3221	5Q	U	
160401	Intro to calculus	Math	1142	5Q	L	
160402	Analysis IV	Math	3211	5Q	U	
160406	Differential equations	Math	3066	4Q	U	
160412	Analysis I	Math	1211	5Q	L	
160412	Analysis II	Math	1221	5Q	L	
160412	Analysis III	Math	1231	5Q	L	
160602	Trigonometry	Math	1008	3Q	L	
180399	Ethics	GColl	1355	4Q	L	
180501	Logic	Philo	1001	3Q	L	
180999	Religions of East Asia	Relig	1032	4Q	L	
181004	Wmn in contemp Amer relig	AmSt	5123	4Q	B	
181103	Women and religion	WomSt	5123	4Q	L	
200102	Abnormal psychology	Psych	3604	4Q	U	
200504	Psych of human developmnt	Psych	1283	5Q	U	
200504	Maturity and aging	ChPsy	3304	4Q	U	
200504	Infancy	ChPsy	3302	4Q	U	
200507	Aspects phys disability	PMR	5445	4Q	U	
200509	Intro to personality	Psych	3101	4Q	U	
200599	Child psychology	Psych	1301	4Q	L	
200599	Adolescent psychology	Psych	5303	4Q	U	
200599	Multidisc aspects aging	ChPsy	5305	4Q	U	VC
209900	General psychology	Psych	1001	5Q	L	
220102	Intro to soc & cult anthr	Anthr	1102	5Q	L	
220102	Culture and personality	Anthr	5141	4Q	U	
220199	Indians of North America	Anthr	3211	5Q	U	
220199	Human origins	Anthr	1101	5Q	L	
220201	Principles of macroeconom	Econ	1102	4Q	L	
220201	Principles of microeconom	Econ	1101	4Q	L	
220204	Money and banking	Econ	3701	4Q	U	
220299	Macroeconomic theory	Econ	3102	4Q	U	
220299	Economic security	Econ	5534	4Q	U	
220306	Geog of US and Canada	Geog	3101	4Q	U	
220306	Geography of Minnesota	Geog	3111	4Q	U	
220306	Geog of South America	Geog	3121	4Q	U	
220306	Geography of USSR	Geog	3181	4Q	U	
220306	Minnesota resources	Geog	3841	4Q	U	
220399	Environmental problems	Geog	3355	4Q	U	
220409	Roman realities	Class	3970	4Q	U	AC
220409	Famous figrs in ancie bio	Class	5006	4Q	B	VC

NCES No.	Course Title	Dept.	Course No.	Cred.	Lev.	Spec. Feat.
220423	Asian civilizations	Hist	3452	4Q	U	
220423	Asian civilizations	Hist	3453	4Q	U	
220423	Asian civilizations	Hist	3451	4Q	U	
220426	English history	Hist	3151	4Q	U	
220426	English history	Hist	3152	4Q	U	
220426	Dipl hist Eur: 19th-20th	Hist	5284	4Q	U	
220426	Dipl hist Eur: 19th-20th	Hist	5285	4Q	U	
220426	Dipl hist Eur: 19th-20th	Hist	5286	4Q	U	
220426	Europe during World W II	Hist	3224	4Q	U	AC
220432	American history	Hist	1301	4Q	L	
220432	American history	Hist	1302	4Q	L	
220450	Ancient civilization I	Hist	1051	3Q	L	
220450	Ancient civilization II	Hist	1052	3Q	L	
220450	Ancient civilization III	Hist	1053	3Q	L	
220450	Readings in ancient civ	Hist	1062	2Q	L	
220450	Readings in ancient civ	Hist	1063	2Q	L	
220450	Ancient Near East I	Hist	5051	3Q	U	
220453	Intro mod European hist	Hist	1001	4Q	L	
220453	Intro mod European hist	Hist	1002	4Q	L	
220453	Intro mod European hist	Hist	1003	4Q	L	
220501	American govt & politics	PolSc	1001	5Q	L	
220507	Political parties	PolSc	5737	4Q	U	
220599	Govt & pol of Sov Union	PolSc	5471	4Q	U	
220599	Govt & pol–African count	PolSc	5478	4Q	U	
220599	Chinese govt and politics	PolSc	5473	4Q	U	
220601	American community	Socio	1002	4Q	L	
220602	Elements of criminology	Socio	3103	4Q	U	
220603	World population problems	Socio	3551	4Q	U	
220607	Intro to soc psychology	Socio	5201	4Q	U	
220699	Introduction to sociology	Socio	1001	4Q	L	
220699	Death and dying	Socio	5960	4Q	U	
220699	Soc of law & soc control	Socio	3102	4Q	U	
220699	Analytical social theory	Socio	5701	4Q	U	
220699	Multidisc aspects aging	Socio	5960	4Q	U	VC

Noncredit courses

NCES No.	Course Title	Dept.	Course No.	Cred.	Lev.	Spec. Feat.
120310	Preparatory composition	Commu	0011	NC		
120310	Grammar review	GColl	0402	NC		
120310	Independent writing	Commu	0017	NC		
121000	French for grad students	Frnch	0001	NC		
122500	Spanish for grad students	Span	0221	NC		
160302	Intermediate algebra	GColl	0631	NC	L	
160399	Basic mathematics	Math	0001	NC		
160399	Basic mathematics	Math	0002	NC		
160399	Basic mathematics	Math	0003	NC		
160399	Basic mathematics	Math	0004	NC		

(46) UNIVERSITY OF MISSISSIPPI

Ms. Dorothy H. Parks
Coordinator, Department of Independent Study
Center for Public Service and Continuing Studies
E. F. Yerby Center, Room 2
University of Mississippi
University, Mississippi 38677
Phone: 601-232-7313

Telecourses are offered. High school students may enroll in undergraduate courses for credit. Overseas enrollment accepted. Military personnel may enroll through the DANTES program. Minimum period for course completion is six weeks. Maximum period for course completion is one year. Enrollment on a noncredit basis accepted in some credit courses.

NCES No.	Course Title	Dept.	Course No.	Cred.	Lev.	Spec. Feat.
	College courses					
030302	Music literature I	Music	101	3S	L	AC
030399	Opera	Music	203	1S	L	AC
030402	Survey of theatre history	ThArt	327	3S	U	
030402	Survey of theatre history	ThArt	328	3S	U	
030502	Art appreciation	Art	281	3S	L	
030602	Mat and tech of painter	Art	105	1S	L	
040101	Intro to accounting prin	Acctg	201	3S	L	
040101	Intro to accounting prin	Acctg	202	3S	L	
040199	Administrative accounting	Acctg	301	3S	U	
040206	Office procedures	OfAdm	351	3S	U	
040308	Money and banking	Econ	303	3S	U	
040308	Money and banking	Finan	303	3S	U	
040601	Business communication	GenBs	271	3S	L	
040799	Risk and insurance	Finan	341	3S	U	

NCES No.	Course Title	Dept.	Course No.	Cred.	Lev.	Spec. Feat.
041001	Marketing principles	Mktg	351	3S	U	
041099	Buyer-seller comm	Mktg	354	3S	U	
041099	Intro to retailing	Mktg	361	3S	U	
041301	Real estate valuatn & app	Finan	353	3S	U	
041306	Real est fin & mort bankg	Finan	355	3S	U	
041309	Principles of real estate	Finan	351	3S	U	
050199	Intro to advertising	Mktg	353	3S	U	
050699	School publications	SecEd	528	3S	U	
050699	Intro to advertising	Journ	385	3S	U	
050699	School publications	Journ	399	3S	U	
051110	Anat & phys spch/hear mec	ComDi	205	3S	L	
061103	Computer science survey	CmpSc	103	3S	L	
070512	Children's lit, K-8	LibSc	301	3S	U	
070520	Psychology of adolescence	Educ	309	3S	U	
070522	Science in the elem sch	ElEd	303	3S	U	
070522	Soc studies in the el sch	ElEd	401	3S	U	
070599	Arith in the elem school	ElEd	403	3S	U	
070602	Career education	Culns	300	3S	U	
070610	Found of elem reading	Read	300	3S	U	
070610	Tchng rdng in elem school	Read	415	3S	U	
070610	Diagnostic tchng of readg	Read	417	3S	U	
070610	Readg in the sec school	Read	429	3S	U	
070701	Principles of guidance	Educ	539	3S	U	
070799	Psyc of human grwth & dev	Educ	333	3S	U	
070800	Survey of except children	SplEd	201	3S	L	
100313	Nutrition	HomEc	311	3S	U	
100601	Child development	ElEd	305	3S	U	
100601	Child care and developmnt	HomEc	321	3S	U	
100602	Marriage and family rel	HomEc	325	3S	U	
100699	Human sexuality	HomEc	435	3S	U	
100700	Institution equipment	HomEc	464	3S	U	
120199	Anat & phys spch/hear mch	Ling	205	3S	L	
120299	Shakespeare	Engl	301	3S	U	
120299	Shakespeare	Engl	302	3S	U	
120299	Backgro of Am lit culture	Engl	403	3S	U	
120299	Am novel before 1914	Engl	573	3S	U	
120299	Am novel after 1914	Engl	574	3S	U	
120299	Survey of English lit	Engl	308	3S	U	
120299	Survey of English lit	Engl	309	3S	U	
120299	Sur of Am lit to Civ War	Engl	303	3S	U	
120299	Sur Am lit since Civ War	Engl	304	3S	U	
120299	Faulkner's fiction	Engl	466	3S	U	
120299	Intro to literature	Engl	200	3S	L	
120302	Hist of the English lang	Engl	406	3S	U	
120302	Hist of the English lang	Ling	406	3S	U	
120305	Advanced English grammar	Engl	401	3S	U	
120305	Advanced English grammar	Ling	401	3S	U	
120307	Masterworks of Engl lit	Engl	205	3S	L	
120307	Masterworks of Engl lit	Engl	206	3S	L	
120310	English composition	Engl	101	3S	L	
120310	English composition	Engl	102	3S	L	
120310	Advanced composition	Engl	321	3S	U	
120700	Outdoor recreation	Rec	432	3S	U	
121000	Second-year French	Frnch	201	3S	L	AC
121000	Second-year French	Frnch	202	3S	L	AC
121000	Elementary French	Frnch	101	3S	L	AC
121000	Elementary French	Frnch	102	3S	L	AC
121100	Elementary German	Germn	101	3S	L	AC
121100	Elementary German	Germn	102	3S	L	AC
121100	Second-year German	Germn	201	3S	L	
121100	Second-year German	Germn	202	3S	L	
121600	Intro to Latin	Latin	101	3S	L	
121600	Intro to Latin	Latin	102	3S	L	
121600	Intermediate Latin	Latin	202	3S	L	
121600	Latin review and reading	Latin	203	3S	L	
121600	Intermediate Latin	Latin	201	3S	L	
122000	Elementary Russian	Rus	101	3S	L	AC
122000	Elementary Russian	Rus	102	3S	L	AC
122500	Elementary Spanish	Span	101	3S	L	AC
122500	Elementary Spanish	Span	102	3S	L	AC
122500	Second-year Spanish	Span	201	3S	L	
150102	Descriptive astronomy	Astro	101	3S	L	
150102	Descriptive astronomy	Astro	102	3S	L	
150399	Survey of biology I	Bio	102	3S	L	
150399	Survey of biology II	Bio	104	3S	L	
150499	Environmental chemistry	Chem	201	3S	L	
150499	Environmental chemistry	Chem	202	3S	L	
150799	Phys of sound and music	Phycs	111	1S	L	AC
150799	Phys of light color art	Phycs	112	1S	L	
150899	Physical science	Phycs	105	3S	L	
160299	Math for elem teachers I	Math	245	3S	L	
160299	Math for elem teachers II	Math	246	3S	L	

NCES No.	Course Title	Dept.	Course No.	Cred.	Lev.	Specl. Feat.
160302	College algebra	Math	121	3S	L	
160401	Unif calc & analyt geom	Math	261	3S	L	
160401	Unif calc & analyt geom	Math	262	3S	L	
160401	Unif calc & analyt geom	Math	263	3S	L	
160401	Unif calc & analyt geom	Math	264	3S	L	
160406	Elem differential equatns	Math	353	3S	U	
160499	Elem math analysis I	Math	267	3S	L	
160499	Elem math analysis II	Math	268	3S	L	
160602	Trigonometry	Math	123	3S	L	
160899	Elem statistics	Math	175	3S	L	
180399	Business ethics	Philo	327	3S	U	
180499	History of philosophy	Philo	301	3S	U	
180499	History of philosophy	Philo	302	3S	U	
180599	Logic	Philo	203	3S	L	
180609	Phil of religion	Philo	307	3S	U	
180700	Phil of contemporary soc	Philo	102	3S	L	
180999	World religions	Relig	205	3S	L	
181299	New Testament thought	Relig	306	3S	U	
190509	Personal and comm health	PhyEd	191	3S	L	
190511	Safety education	PhyEd	507	3S	U	
190599	First aid	PhyEd	203	3S	L	
190700	Rec needs of spl populatn	Rec	184	3S	L	
190700	Hist & foundtns of rec	Rec	194	3S	L	
200804	Educational psychology	Educ	307	3S	U	
220201	Principles of economics	Econ	201	3S	L	
220201	Principles of economics	Econ	202	3S	L	
220299	Economic fluctuations	Econ	509	3S	U	
220402	Am diplomacy to 1898	Hist	315	3S	U	
220402	Am diplomacy since 1898	Hist	316	3S	U	
220409	Reform movement in the US	Hist	331	3S	U	
220426	Modern Europe to 1660	Hist	151	3S	L	
220426	Modern Europe since 1660	Hist	152	3S	L	
220428	Miss 1540 to the present	Hist	311	3S	U	
220432	The US to 1877	Hist	105	3S	L	
220432	The US since 1877	Hist	106	3S	L	
220472	Women's movemnt in the US	Hist	332	3S	U	
220472	Women in the South	Hist	333	3S	U	
220499	Women in the South	SouSt	303	3S	U	
220599	Criminal investigation	PolSc	333	3S	U	
220602	Criminology	Socio	431	3S	U	
220604	Juvenile delinquency	Socio	333	3S	U	
220615	The prison community	Socio	421	3S	U	
	Noncredit courses					
121100	PhD German	Germn	95	NC	L	

47 **UNIVERSITY OF MISSOURI–COLUMBIA**

Dr. Roger G. Young
Director
Center for Independent Study
University of Missouri–Columbia
136 Clark Hall
Columbia, Missouri 65211
Phone: 314-882-6431

Telecourses are offered. Enrollment on a noncredit basis accepted in credit courses. High school students may enroll in undergraduate courses for credit. Overseas enrollment accepted. Military personnel may enroll through the DANTES program. Maximum period for course completion is nine months. There is provision for one 3-month extension per course.

NCES No.	Course Title	Dept.	Course No.	Cred.	Lev.	Specl. Feat.
	High School courses					
010499	Functional horsemanship	Agri		HF	H	
010500	Introductory horticulture	Agri		1U	H	
019900	Agriculture	Agri		1U	H	
030599	Art I	Art		HF	H	
040104	Bookkeeping	BusEd		1U	H	
040207	Typing/keyboarding	BusEd		1U	H	
040299	Clerical practice	BusEd		HF	H	
041099	Retailing	BusEd		HF	H	
049900	Introduction to business	BusEd		1U	H	
049900	Sales fundamentals	BusEd		1U	H	
049900	You & the world of work	BusEd		HF	H	
049900	You & the world of work	PerDv		HF	H	
050600	Intro to journalism	Engl		HF	H	
061101	Computer literacy	BusEd		HF	H	

NCES No.	Course Title	Dept.	Course No.	Cred.	Lev.	Specl. Feat.
061101	Computer literacy	Math		HF	H	
070703	Career planning	PerDv		HF	H	
070799	Planning for college	PerDv		HF	H	
081000	General drafting	InArt		1U	H	
081000	Technical drafting	InArt		HF	H	
100202	Consumer econ: econ envir	BusEd		HF	H	
100202	Econ: making decisions	BusEd		HF	H	
100313	Fund of nutrition	HomEc		HF	H	
100601	Parenting child dev	PerDv		HF	H	
100602	Pers adj dating marriage	PerDv		HF	H	
100604	Project self-discovery	PerDv		HF	H	
120305	Ninth-grade English	Engl		1U	H	
120305	Tenth-grade English	Engl		1U	H	
120305	Eleventh-grade English	Engl		1U	H	
120305	Twelfth-grade English	Engl		1U	H	AC
120305	Grammar spell and vocab	Engl		HF	H	
120307	Contemp Afro-Amer prose	Engl		HF	H	
120307	Eng lit thru Shakespeare	Engl		HF	H	
120307	Man and myth	Engl		HF	H	
120307	Search for iden thru lit	Engl		HF	H	
120307	Shrt stry reluc readers	Engl		HF	H	
120307	Readings in Amer novel	Engl		HF	H	
120307	Afro-Amer lit: early year	Engl		HF	H	
120308	Reading & study skills	Engl		HF	H	
120399	Thnkng clear: mkng sense	Engl		HF	H	
121000	French I	Lang		1U	H	AC
122500	Spanish I	Lang		1U	H	AC
130799	Consumer & business law	BusEd		HF	H	
139900	You and the law	Civcs		HF	H	
150300	Survey of living world	Sci		HF	H	
150401	Chemistry	Sci		1U	H	
150599	Environmental geology	Sci		HF	H	
150599	Underground world caves	Sci		HF	H	
150700	Physics	Sci		1U	H	
150900	Aerospace: space explor	Sci		HF	H	
159900	Conserv of nat resources	Sci		HF	H	
159900	Spec topics life science	Sci		HF	H	
160301	General mathematics	Math		1U	H	
160302	Algebra I	Math		1U	H	
160302	Algebra II	Math		1U	H	
160399	General mathematics II	Math		1U	H	
160401	Precalculus	Math		1U	H	
160601	Geometry	Math		1U	H	
160602	Trigonometry	Math		HF	H	
160899	Fund of stat and probabil	Math		HF	H	
161101	Business mathematics	Math		HF	H	
181002	World religions	Relig		HF	H	
190500	Health	HPE&R		HF	H	
190509	Fitness for well-being	HPE&R		HF	H	
190600	Driver education	DrvEd		HF	H	AC
200100	Psych: found human behavr	Psych		HF	H	
200100	Personal & social psych	Psych		HF	H	
200500	Psych everyday topics	Psych		HF	H	
220100	Anthropology	Anthr		HF	H	
220109	Indians of Missouri	Anthr		HF	H	
220200	Economics making decision	Econ		HF	H	
220399	World geography	Geog		HF	H	
220428	Missouri history	Hist		HF	H	
220432	Amer history to 1865	Hist		HF	H	
220432	Amer history since 1865	Hist		HF	H	
220433	World history to Am Revol	Hist		HF	H	
220433	World hist since Am Revol	Hist		HF	H	
220452	Medieval history	Hist		HF	H	
220501	American government	Govt		HF	H	
220505	International relations	Govt		HF	H	
220509	Civics: natl/state/local	Civcs		HF	H	
220509	Civics: polit proc/prob	Civcs		HF	H	
220600	Sociology	Socio		HF	H	
229900	Contemporary world	SocSt		HF	H	
	College courses					
010500	Basic home horticulture	Hort	20	3S	L	
030399	Intro symphonic music	Music	2	3S	L	VC
040101	Accounting I	Acctg	36	3S	L	
040101	Accounting I	Acctg	36	3S	L	VC
040111	Accounting II	Acctg	37	3S	L	
040111	Accounting II	Acctg	37	3S	L	VC
040311	Principles of finance	Finan	123	3S	L	
040500	Entrepreneurship	BusAd	392	3S	B	VC
040904	Fundamentals of mgmt	Mgmt	202	3S	B	
041001	Principles of marketing	Mktg	204	3S	B	
041100	Personnel management	Mgmt	310	3S	B	

NCES No.	Course Title	Dept.	Course No.	Cred.	Lev.	Specl. Feat.
050606	Hist & prin of journalism	Journ	309	3S	B	
050699	High school journalism	Journ	380	2S	B	
060799	Intro to BASIC	CmpSc	371	3S	B	VC
070199	Hist found Amer education	EdFdn	B351	3S	B	
070309	Org & admin of adult ed	AEdSF	K420	3S	B	
070503	Art activ in elem school	CuIns	T230	2S	B	
070509	Elements of health educ	HPE&R	H65	2S	L	
070516	Algebra for elem teachers	Math	7	3S	L	
070516	Geometry for el teachers	Math	8	3S	L	
070519	Org & adm of PE programs	HPE&R	H279	2S	B	
070520	Learning & instruction	EdPsy	A205	2S	B	
070520	Adolescent psychology	EdPsy	A208	2S	B	
070520	Intro educ meas & eval	EdPsy	A280	2S	B	
070520	Found educ & psych meas	EdPsy	A380	3S	B	
070520	Changing wld-chang class	EdPsy	489X	3S	B	VC
070520	Coping student prob	EdPsy	489W	3S	B	VC
070610	Teaching of reading	CuIns	T315	3S	B	
070610	Teach reading comp	CuIns	T410	3S	B	VC
070699	Photography for teachers	CuIns	T373	3S	B	VC
070800	Educ of exceptional indiv	SplEd	L339	3S	B	
070806	Intro mental retardation	SplEd	330	3S	B	
070806	Intro mental retardation	SplEd	330	3S	B	
070899	Psych educ excep indiv	SplEd	313	3S	B	VC
071102	Educational statistics I	EdRes	R370	3S	B	
079900	Problems	ExtEd	400	CV	B	
081000	Gen engineering drawing	EngGr	11	3S	L	
081103	Mech of materials	EMech	110	3S	L	
081104	Engr mech: dynamics	EMech	150	2S	L	
081104	Engr mech: dynamics	EMech	160	3S	L	
081104	Engineer mechan-statics	EMech	50	3S	L	
090602	Amer health-care system	HSMgt	210HM	3S	B	
120299	Classical mythology	Class	60	3S	L	
120299	Intro to folklore	Lit	185	3S	L	
120299	Womens exp in mod fiction	Lit	101	3S	L	
120299	Women in pop culture	WomSt	201	3S	B	
120299	Lit New Testament	Lit	124	3S	L	
120299	Women's exper mod fiction	WomSt	101	3S	L	
120307	Literary types	Lit	12	3S	L	
120307	Afro-American literature	Lit	104	3S	L	
120307	Intro to Shakespeare	Lit	135	3S	L	
120307	American literature	Lit	175	3S	L	
120307	Eng lit: beging to 1784	Lit	201	3S	U	
120307	Gothic fiction	Lit	101	3S	L	
120310	Fundamentals of comp	Comp	10	3S	L	
120310	Technical writing	Comp	161	3S	L	
120310	Exposition & argument	Comp	20	3S	L	
120310	Creative writing: poetry	Engl	70	3S	L	
121000	Elementary French I	Frnch	1	5S	L	AC
121000	Elementary French II	Frnch	2	5S	L	AC
121000	Elem French III	Frnch	3	3S	L	AC
121600	Elementary Latin I	CILL	1	5S	L	
122500	Elementary Spanish I	Span	1	5S	L	AC
122500	Elementary Spanish II	Span	2	5S	L	AC
122500	Elementary Spanish III	Span	3	3S	L	AC
130700	Intro to business law	Mgmt	254	3S	B	
150101	Cosmos	Astro	11	3S	L	VC
150202	Introductory meteorology	AtmSc	50	3S	L	
150327	Insects in environment	Entom	101	3S	L	
150599	Physical geology	Geol	2	4S	L	LK
150799	Mechanical universe	Phycs	275	3S	B	VC
150900	Earth science II	Geol	56	3S	L	VC
160199	Basic concepts mod math	Math	12	3S	L	
160302	Basic algebra	Math	3	2S	L	
160302	College algebra	Math	10	3S	L	
160302	Fund algebra II	Math	002B	2S	L	VC
160401	Analytic geom & calculus	Math	80	5S	L	
160401	Calculus II	Math	175	5S	L	
160401	Calculus III	Math	201	5S	B	
160401	Elements of calculus	Math	61	3S	L	
160602	Trigonometry	Math	9	2S	L	
160802	Elementary statistics	Stat	31	3S	L	
180501	Intro to logic	Philo	10	3S	L	
180800	General intro to philo	Philo	1	3S	L	
190703	Problems	RecPA	300	CV	B	
200100	General psychology	Psych	1	3S	L	
200300	Environmental psychology	Psych	312	3S	B	
200406	Human learning	Psych	212	3S	B	
200504	Child development	EdPsy	A207	2S	B	
200599	Child psychology	Psych	170	3S	L	
200599	Adolescent psychology	Psych	271	3S	U	
200599	Brain mind & behavior	Psych	101	3S	L	VC
200901	Industrial psychology	Psych	212	3S	B	

NCES No.	Course Title	Dept.	Course No.	Cred.	Lev.	Specl. Feat.
200906	Human factors	Psych	311	3S	B	
210100	Intro to public admin	PolSc	310	3S	B	
210401	Social welfare soc work	SocWk	125	3S	L	
220201	Fund of microeconomics	Econ	2	3S	L	
220299	Fund of macroeconomics	Econ	1	3S	L	
220299	Intro American economy	Econ	40	3S	L	VC
220305	Physical geography 1	Geog	111	3S	L	
220305	Physical geography	Geog	112	3S	L	
220306	Reg & nations of world I	Geog	1	3S	L	
220306	Reg & nations of world II	Geog	2	3S	L	
220306	Geography of Missouri	Geog	125	3S	L	
220407	Age of ascendancy	Hist	173	3S	L	
220424	Britain 1688 to present	Hist	106	3S	L	
220428	History of Missouri	Hist	210	3S	B	
220432	Foundations Western civ	Hist	1	3S	L	
220432	American history to 1865	Hist	3	3S	L	
220432	American hist since 1865	Hist	4	3S	L	
220432	Period of Amer Revolution	Hist	364	3S	B	
220450	Roman culture	Class	116	3S	L	
220499	Mod West civilization	Hist	112	3S	L	
220499	Vietnam: television hist	Hist	101	3S	L	VC
220501	American government	PolSc	1	3S	L	
220505	International relations	PolSc	55	3S	L	
220509	Politics Third World	PolSc	350	3S	B	
220510	Amer political thought	PolSc	360	3S	B	
220511	State government	PolSc	102	3S	L	
220599	Intro to political sci	PolSc	11	3S	L	
220599	Congress legislative pol	PolSc	316	3S	B	VC
220599	Constitution: del balance	PolSc	320	3S	B	VC
220599	US defense policy	PolSc	335	3S	B	
220602	Criminology	Socio	211	3S	B	VC
220606	Intro to sociology	Socio	1	3S	L	
220608	Rural sociology	RuSoc	1	3S	L	
220614	Urban sociology	RuSoc	216	3S	B	
220615	Sociology of aging	Socio	322	3S	B	
220699	Social justice soc policy	SocWk	303	3S	B	
220699	Sociology of aging	Socio	322	3S	B	VC
229900	Intro to peace studies	Socio	50	3S	L	

Graduate courses

NCES No.	Course Title	Dept.	Course No.	Cred.	Lev.	Specl. Feat.
070309	Prog devlpmt & evaluation	ExtEd	403	3S	G	
070400	Secondary school curric	CuIns	T445	3S	G	
070404	Fund of ext tchng of adul	ExtEd	406	3S	G	
070506	Intro tchrs microcomputer	CuIns	306	3S	G	VC
070506	Microcomputers	CuIns	308	3S	G	VC
070610	Issues & trends reading	CuIns	T420	3S	G	
220432	Sp topic recent Amer hist	Hist	400	3S	G	
220699	Social justice soc policy	SocWk	303	3S	G	

Noncredit courses

NCES No.	Course Title	Dept.	Course No.	Cred.	Lev.	Specl. Feat.
080799	City and county planning	PolSc		NC		
090103	Clinical lab tests	Nrsng		NC		
090201	Ischemic coron artery dis	Nrsng		NC		
090214	Mgmt peptic ulcer gastro	Nrsng		NC		
090299	Recogn & treat anx dis	Nrsng		NC		
090302	Enteral parenteral n supp	Nrsng		NC		
090307	Cancer chemotherapy	Nrsng		NC		
090403	Nurses guide to immuniz	Nrsng		NC		
090403	Prac look substance abuse	Nrsng		NC		
090404	Drug intera clinical set	Nrsng		NC		
090408	Pharmacotherapeutics	Nrsng		NC		
090499	Psychotherapeutic drugs	Nrsng		NC		
090499	Rational use of diuretics	Nrsng		NC		
090499	Drugs used in the eye	Nrsng		NC		
090599	Poisonings part I	Nrsng		NC		
090599	Poisonings part II	Nrsng		NC		
090601	Con princ effect nur mgmt	Nrsng		NC		
090699	Comm skills nurs mgmt	Nrsng		NC		
099900	Hypertension part I	Nrsng		NC		
099900	Hypertension part II	Nrsng		NC		
099900	Hlth care needs older wom	Nrsng		NC		
099900	Alt conven med care	Nrsng		NC		
099900	Arthritis drug therapy	Nrsng		NC		
099900	Elderly a holistic appr	Nrsng		NC		
181002	Major world religions	Relig		NC		
181202	Intro to the Old Testmnt	Relig		NC		
181202	Life & letters of Paul	Relig		NC		
210303	Hazardous materials	PubAf		NC	L	
210304	Criminal investigation	PubAf		NC		
210304	Law enforcemnt patrol pro	PubAf		NC		
210399	Narcotics/law enforcement	PubAf		NC		
210503	So you're a park bd memb	PubAd		NC		

(48) UNIVERSITY OF NEBRASKA–LINCOLN

Mr. Monty E. McMahon
Director, Independent Study Program, Division of Continuing
Studies
269 Nebraska Center for Continuing Education
University of Nebraska–Lincoln
33rd and Holdrege Streets
Lincoln, Nebraska 68583-0900
Phone: 402-472-1926

External degree available through the program. Enrollment on a noncredit basis accepted in credit courses. High school students may enroll in undergraduate courses for credit. Overseas enrollment accepted. Military personnel may enroll through the DANTES program. Minimum period for course completion is five weeks. Maximum period for course completion is one year. The Independent Study Program also offers an accredited high school diploma program.

NCES No.	Course Title	Dept.	Course No.	Cred.	Lev.	Specl. Feat.
High School courses						
010599	Horticulture	Agri	00901	HF	H	AC
010599	Horticulture	Agri	01101	HF	H	AC
019900	General agriculture	Agri	00102	HF	H	
019900	General agriculture	Agri	00202	HF	H	
030302	Beginning piano	Music	00101	HF	H	
030302	Intermediate piano	Music	00301	HF	H	
030302	Harmony	Music	00701	HF	H	
030302	Music theory	Music	00502	HF	H	
030399	History & apprec of music	Music	01101	HF	H	
030501	General art	Art	00102	IIF	H	LK
030501	Advanced drawing	Art	00701	HF	H	LK
030501	Advanced watercolor	Art	00901	HF	H	LK
040101	Beginning accounting	BusEd	02302	HF	H	
040101	Beginning accounting	BusEd	02402	HF	H	
040205	Beginning shorthand	BusEd	01502	HF	H	AC
040205	Begining shorthand	BusEd	01602	HF	H	AC
040207	Typing with one hand	BusEd	00102	HF	H	
040207	Beginning typing	BusEd	00302	HF	H	
040207	Beginning typing	BusEd	00402	HF	H	
040207	Advanced typing	BusEd	00502	HF	H	
040207	Advanced typing	BusEd	00602	HF	H	
040299	Office proced & practice	BusEd	01301	HF	H	
040299	Office proced & practice	BusEd	01401	HF	H	
040699	Business English	BusEd	01101	HF	H	
049900	General business	BusEd	02102	HF	H	
061103	Computer BASICS	CmpSc	00101	HF	H	
079900	Effective methds of study	StSkl	00101	HF	H	
090199	Health science	Sci	00102	HF	H	
090199	Health science	Sci	00202	HF	H	
100104	Clothing construction	HomEc	00702	HF	H	
100699	Persl adju, marriage, fam	HomEc	01101	HF	H	
109900	Etiquette	HomEc	00101	HF	H	
109900	General homemaking	HomEc	00302	HF	H	
109900	General homemaking	HomEc	00402	HF	H	
110412	Small engine care/operatn	IndEd	00503	HF	H	
110412	Small engine maint/repair	IndEd	00602	HF	H	
110413	Automotive mechanics	IndEd	00701	HF	H	
110504	Photography	Photo	00102	HF	H	LK
119900	General shop	IndEd	00101	HF	H	
119900	General shop	IndEd	00201	HF	H	
120305	Basic English 1	Engl	00102	HF	H	
120305	Basic English 2	Engl	00202	HF	H	
120307	The short story	Engl	00901	HF	H	
120307	American short story	Engl	01102	HF	H	
120307	Poetry	Engl	02102	HF	H	
120307	General literature	Engl	00504	HF	H	
120307	General literature	Engl	00703	QT	H	
120310	Composition: basic expos	Engl	02302	HF	H	
120399	Eleventh-grade English	Engl	03502	HF	H	
120399	Eleventh-grade English	Engl	03602	HF	H	
120399	Twelfth-grade English	Engl	03702	HF	H	
120399	Twelfth-grade English	Engl	03802	HF	H	
120399	Ninth-grade English	Engl	03102	HF	H	
120399	Ninth-grade English	Engl	03202	HF	H	
120399	Tenth-grade English	Engl	03302	HF	H	
120399	Tenth-grade English	Engl	03402	HF	H	
121000	First-year French	Lang	00203	HF	H	AC
121000	Second-year French	Lang	00301	HF	H	AC
121000	Second-year French	Lang	00402	HF	H	AC
121000	First-year French	Lang	00103	HF	H	AC
121100	First-year German	Lang	00101	HF	H	AC
121100	First-year German	Lang	00201	HF	H	AC
121100	Second-year German	Lang	00301	HF	H	AC
121100	Second-year German	Lang	00401	HF	H	AC
121600	First-year Latin	Lang	00101	HF	H	
121600	First-year Latin	Lang	00201	HF	H	
121600	Second-year Latin	Lang	00301	HF	H	
121600	Second-year Latin	Lang	00401	HF	H	
121600	Third-year Latin	Lang	00501	HF	H	
121600	Third-year Latin	Lang	00601	HF	H	
122500	Second-year Spanish	Lang	00302	HF	H	AC
122500	Second-year Spanish	Lang	00402	HF	H	AC
122500	First-year Spanish	Lang	00103	HF	H	AC
122500	First-year Spanish	Lang	00203	HF	H	AC
150300	Basic biology	Sci	00702	HF	H	
150300	Basic biology	Sci	00802	HF	H	
150399	Advanced biology	Sci	01901	HF	H	LK
150399	Advanced biology	Sci	02001	HF	H	LK
150401	Chemistry	Sci	03101	HF	H	LK
150401	Chemistry	Sci	03201	HF	H	LK
150700	Gen physics (calc-based)	Sci	05102	HF	H	
150700	Gen physics (calc-based)	Sci	05202	HF	H	
150704	Bsc electrcty & electrncs	Sci	00901	HF	H	LK
150799	Physics	Sci	03502	HF	H	LK
150799	Physics	Sci	03602	HF	H	LK
150800	Physical science	Sci	01301	HF	H	LK
150800	Physical science	Sci	01401	HF	H	LK
160301	Basic mathematics 1	Math	00103	HF	H	
160301	Basic mathematics 2	Math	00202	HF	H	
160302	Beginning algebra	Math	03103	HF	H	
160302	Beginning algebra	Math	03203	HF	H	
160302	Advanced algebra	Math	03501	HF	H	
160302	Advanced algebra	Math	03601	HF	H	
160399	General mathematics	Math	00502	HF	H	
160399	General mathematics	Math	00602	HF	H	
160601	Geometry	Math	03403	HF	H	
160601	Geometry	Math	03303	HF	H	
160602	Precalculus: trigonometry	Math	04002	HF	H	
160603	Analytic geom & calculus	Math	05101	HF	H	
160603	Analytic geom & calculus	Math	05201	HF	H	
160699	Precal analytic geo & alg	Math	03901	HF	H	
161299	Business & consumer math	Math	00901	HF	H	
161299	Business & consumer math	Math	01001	HF	H	
190699	Driver education	DrvEd	00102	HF	H	
200199	Psychology	SocSt	00702	HF	H	
220201	Economics	BusEd	02704	HF	H	
220208	Consumer education	BusEd	01901	HF	H	
220399	World geography	SocSt	02102	HF	H	
220399	World geography	SocSt	02202	HF	H	
220432	American history	SocSt	03304	HF	H	
220432	American history	SocSt	03404	HF	H	
220433	World history	SocSt	03102	HF	H	
220433	World history	SocSt	03202	HF	H	
220501	American government	SocSt	03502	HF	H	
220501	American government	SocSt	03602	HF	H	
220502	Civics	SocSt	00103	HF	H	
220606	Sociology	SocSt	00302	HF	H	
229900	Modern problems	SocSt	03702	HF	H	
College courses						
020103	Interior design	InDes	130X	3S	L	LK
030599	Intro art history & crit	Art	167X	3S	L	
040101	Intermediate accounting	Acctg	313X	3S	L	
040101	Introductory accounting	Acctg	201X	3S	L	
040101	Introductory accounting	Acctg	202X	3S	L	
040111	Managerial accounting	Acctg	308X	3S	U	
040311	Finance	Finan	361X	3S	U	
040708	Principles of insurance	Econ	307X	3S	U	
040708	Principles of insurance	Finan	307X	3S	U	
040902	Operatns & resourcs mgmt	Mgmt	331X	3S	U	
040999	Administrative policy	Mgmt	435X	3S	B	
041001	Marketing	Mktg	341X	3S	U	
041001	Marketing	Mktg	341X	3S	U	CI
041199	Personnel administration	Mgmt	361X	3S	U	
041200	Elem quantitative methods	Econ	245X	3S	L	
041200	Elem quantitative methods	Mgmt	245X	3S	L	
041301	Real estate appraisal	RlEst	441X	3S	U	
041303	Real estate prin & prac	Finan	382X	3S	U	
041303	Real est princ & practice	RlEst	382X	3S	U	
041304	Real estate management	RlEst	345X	3S	U	
041306	Real estate finance	Finan	482X	3S	U	
041306	Real estate finance	RlEst	482X	3S	U	
041307	Real estate investments	RlEst	439X	3S	U	

NCES No.	Course Title	Dept.	Course No.	Cred.	Lev.	Specl. Feat.
050401	Adv broadcast writing	Bdcst	474X	3S	U	
070404	Tchng soc stud in ele sch	Culns	307X	3S	U	
081503	Intro indust decisn modls	IMSE	206X	3S	U	
090504	Emergency health care	HPE&R	170X	3S	L	
090999	Elements health promotion	HPE&R	101X	3S	L	
100313	Introduction to nutrition	HNFSM	151X	3S	L	
100699	Human devel & the family	HuDev	160X	3S	L	
120301	Composition	Engl	150X	3S	L	
120301	Composition	Engl	254X	3S	L	
120307	Twentieth-century fiction	Engl	205BX	3S	L	
120307	Shakespeare	Engl	230AX	3S	L	
120310	Business writing	Engl	255X	3S	L	
120310	Special topics in writing	Engl	258X	2S	L	
129900	Scientific Greek & Latin	Class	116X	2S	L	
150304	Principles of ecology	BioSc	320X	3S	U	
150799	Elementary gen physics	Phycs	141X	4S	L	
150799	Elementary gen physics	Phycs	142X	4S	L	
150799	General physics	Phycs	211X	4S	L	
150799	General physics	Phycs	212X	4S	L	
150799	Elementary gen physics	Phycs	141X	5S	L	LK
150799	Elementary gen physics	Phycs	142X	5S	L	LK
160302	Algebra	Math	100X	2S	L	
160302	Algebra	Math	101X	2S	L	
160602	Trigonometry	Math	102X	2S	L	
160603	Analyt geom & calculus I	Math	106X	5S	L	
160603	Analyt geom & calculus II	Math	107X	5S	L	
160603	Analyt geom & calc III	Math	208X	4S	L	
180599	Elementary logic	Philo	110X	3S	L	
180609	Philosophy of religion	Philo	265X	3S	L	
200199	Elementary psychology II	Psych	171X	3S	L	
200199	Elementary psychology I	Psych	170X	3S	L	
200599	Psychosocl aspcts alchlsm	Psych	222X	3S	L	
200804	Learning in the classroom	EdPsy	362X	3S	U	
200804	Psychology for education	EdPsy	261X	3S	L	
220201	Principles of economics	Econ	211X	3S	L	
220201	Principles of economics	Econ	212X	3S	L	
220299	Statistics	Econ	215X	3S	L	
220301	Intro human geography	Geog	140X	3S	L	
220302	Intro economic geography	Geog	120X	3S	L	
220306	Geography of US	Geog	271X	3S	L	
220426	History early mod Europe	Hist	212X	3S	L	
220426	Western civ since 1715	Hist	101X	3S	L	
220426	West civ to 1715	Hist	100X	3S	L	
220428	Nebraska history	Hist	359X	3S	U	
220432	American history to 1877	Hist	201X	3S	L	
220432	Amer history after 1877	Hist	202X	3S	L	
220452	History of Middle Ages	Hist	211X	3S	L	
220501	American government	PolSc	100X	3S	L	
220507	Polit prties & elctn camp	PolSc	230X	3S	L	
220599	Contemporary foreign govt	PolSc	104X	3S	L	
220599	Intro to public admin	PolSc	210X	3S	L	
220602	Delinquency and crime	Socio	209X	3S	L	
220605	Marriage and the family	Socio	225X	3S	L	
220606	Intro to sociology	Socio	153X	3S	L	
220613	Social problems	Socio	201X	3S	L	

Noncredit courses

NCES No.	Course Title	Dept.	Course No.	Cred.	Lev.	Specl. Feat.
041308	Settlement Procedures Act	RlEst	1X	NC	V	
041308	Fair-housing laws	RlEst	2X	NC	V	
041308	Truth-in-lending Act	RlEst	3X	NC	V	
041309	Contracts & agen relation	RlEst	4X	NC	V	
041309	Legal documents in rl est	RlEst	5X	NC	V	
041309	Closing rl est transactn	RlEst	6X	NC	V	
089900	Field insp & plan review	BlgIn	1X	NC	V	
160302	Algebra	Math	90X	NC	L	

(49) UNIVERSITY OF NEVADA–RENO

Ms. Catharine D. Sanders
Director, Independent Study by Correspondence
Division of Continuing Education
333 College Inn
University of Nevada–Reno
Reno, Nevada 89557
Phone: 702-784-4652

Overseas enrollment accepted. Military personnel may enroll through the DANTES program. Minimum period for course completion is two–eight weeks. Maximum period for course completion is one year. An external degree, the Bachelor of General Studies degree, is offered. Enrollment in undergraduate courses is available to high school students approved for concurrent registration in the University Superior Student Program by the University's Office of Admissions and Records.

NCES No.	Course Title	Dept.	Course No.	Cred.	Lev.	Specl. Feat.
High School courses						
061101	Computer literacy I	CmpSc	1	HF	H	
150301	Introductory biology I	Bio	1	HF	H	
150301	Introductory biology II	Bio	2	HF	H	
160401	High school calculus I	Math	1	HF	H	
160401	High school calculus II	Math	2	HF	H	
College courses						
040101	Introductory accounting I	Acctg	C201	3S	L	
040101	Introduct accounting II	Acctg	C202	3S	L	
040999	Exec planning hskpng oper	HoAdm	C312	3S	U	
040999	Organ theory appl svc ind	HoAdm	C407	3S	U	
040999	Convention management	HoAdm	C385	3S	U	
041006	Hotel marketing I	HoAdm	C380	3S	U	
049900	Orientation to hotel ind	HoAdm	C101	3S	L	
049900	Front office operations	HoAdm	C114	3S	L	
049900	International tourism	HoAdm	C449	3S	U	
049900	Food-service operations I	HoAdm	C260	3S	L	
050605	Magazine writing	Journ	C418	2S	U	
050800	Corporate communications	Journ	C335	3S	U	
069900	Computer logic design	CmpSc	C333	3S	U	
070403	Sci tchg & dev of reasng	Culns	C4811	3S	U	
070403	Five teaching skills	Culns	C4812	1S	U	
070599	Curric dev in envirnml ed	Culns	C449	3S	U	
070899	Ed of the exceptnl child	Culns	C443	3S	U	
090999	Medical terminology	CILSc	C111	1S	L	
100313	Human nutrition	HomEc	C121	3S	L	
100601	Child development	HomEc	C131	3S	L	
100699	Chld & fmls: multi-eth so	HomEc	C438	CV	U	
120307	Introduction to fiction	Engl	C244	2S	L	
120307	Intro to literature	Engl	C131	2S	L	
120399	Vocabulary and meaning	Engl	C181	2S	L	
120399	Introduction to drama	Engl	C253	3S	L	
120399	Introduction to poetry	Engl	C261	CV	L	
120399	Oral Engl for non-native	Engl	C10	3S	L	
121000	Elementary French I	Frnch	C101	4S	L	
121000	Elementary French II	Frnch	C102	4S	L	
121000	Reading French I	Frnch	C205	2S	L	
121000	Reading French II	Frnch	C209	2S	L	
121100	Reading German I	Germn	C205	2S	L	
121100	Reading German II	Germn	C209	2S	L	
121400	Elementary Italian I	Ital	C101	4S	L	
121400	Elementary Italian II	Ital	C102	4S	L	
121400	Second-year Italian	Ital	C203	3S	L	AC
121400	Second-year Italian	Ital	C204	3S	L	AC
122500	Elementary Spanish I	Span	C101	4S	L	
122500	Elementary Spanish II	Span	C102	4S	L	
122500	Reading Spanish I	Span	C205	2S	L	
122500	Reading Spanish II	Span	C209	2S	L	
150323	General zoology	Bio	C160	3S	L	
150399	General biology	Bio	C103	3S	L	
160302	Intermediate algebra	Math	C101	3S	L	
160302	College algebra	Math	C110	3S	L	
160399	Algebra and trigonometry	Math	C115	4S	L	
160401	Elements of calculus I	Math	C211	3S	L	
160602	Plane trigonometry	Math	C102	2S	L	
160603	Analytic geometry	Math	C140	3S	L	
161101	Mathematics of finance	Math	C210	3S	L	
161199	Math of casino games	HoAdm	C436	3S	U	
161299	Math for information age	Math	C105	3S	L	
169900	Elementary school math I	Math	C173	3S	L	
169900	Elementary school math II	Math	C174	3S	L	
200501	Abnormal psychology	Psych	C441	3S	U	
200508	Psychology of adolescence	Psych	C234	3S	L	
200508	Child psychology	Psych	C233	3S	L	
200509	Personality	Psych	C435	3S	U	
200804	Educational psychology	Psych	C321	3S	U	
209900	Introductory psychology	Psych	C101	3S	L	
220101	Introdctn to archaeology	Anthr	C202	3S	L	
220199	Introdctn to anthropology	Anthr	C101	3S	L	
220199	Intr to hum evol & prehis	Anthr	C102	3S	L	
220299	Princpls of statistics I	Econ	C261	3S	L	
220299	Princpls of statistics II	Econ	C262	3S	L	
220299	Prin of microeconomics	Econ	C102	3S	L	
220299	Prin of macroeconomics	Econ	C101	3S	L	
220301	Intro to cultural geog	Geog	C106	3S	L	
220424	England & the British Emp	Hist	C393	3S	U	
220424	England & the Brit Emp II	Hist	C394	3S	U	

NCES No.	Course Title	Dept.	Course No.	Cred.	Lev.	Specl. Feat.
220426	European civilization	Hist	C105	3S	L	
220426	European civilization	Hist	C106	3S	L	
220428	Nevada history	Hist	C217	3S	L	
220501	Prin of Amer const govt	PolSc	C103	3S	L	
220511	Constitution of Nevada	PolSc	C100	1S	L	
220606	Principles of sociology	Socio	C101	3S	L	
220613	Social problems	Socio	C102	3S	L	
229900	Intro to women's studies	WomSt	C101	3S	L	
	Noncredit courses					
070199	Legal foundations of educ	Educ	CA	NC		
090118	Pharmacology by home sty	Nrsng		NC		
161202	Fund of the metric system	Math	CC	NC		D
220502	Citizenship for new Amer	PolSc	CA	NC		D

(50) **UNIVERSITY OF NEW MEXICO**

Terry Dominguez
Director, Independent Study Through Correspondence
University of New Mexico
1634 University Boulevard, NE
Albuquerque, New Mexico 87131
Phone: 505-277-2931

Overseas enrollment accepted. Minimum period for course completion is two months. Maximum period for course completion is one year.

NCES No.	Course Title	Dept.	Course No.	Cred.	Lev.	Specl. Feat.
	College courses					
040601	Business communications	BusEd	265	3S	L	
070512	Tchng of reading elem sch	ElEd	331	3S	U	
070516	Math for elem sch tchrs I	Math	111	3S	L	
070516	Math for elem sch tchs II	Math	112	3S	L	
090255	Nurs pathophysiology I	Nrsng	239	3S	L	
090255	Nurs pathophysiology II	Nrsng	240	3S	L	
090799	Personal & comm health	HlEd	171	3S	L	
090799	Fund human sexuality	HlEd	212	3S	L	
120302	History of Engl language	Engl	445	3S	U	
120307	Children's literature	ElEd	443	3S	U	
120307	Survey of early Engl lit	Engl	294	3S	L	
120307	Survey of later Engl lit	Engl	295	3S	L	
120307	American literature	Engl	296	3S	L	
120310	Writing standard English	Engl	100	3S	L	
120310	Expository writing	Engl	220	3S	L	
120399	Writing, reading in expos	Engl	101	3S	L	
120399	Writing, reading lit	Engl	102	3S	L	
122500	Elementary Spanish	Span	101	3S	L	
122500	Elementary Spanish	Span	102	3S	L	
122500	Intermediate Spanish	Span	201	3S	L	
122500	Intermediate Spanish	Span	202	3S	L	
122500	Advanced grammar & comp	Span	301	3S	U	
122500	Advan comp & conversation	Span	302	3S	U	
140199	Fundamentals of lib sci	LibSc	424	3S	U	
140804	Classification & catalog	LibSc	427	3S	U	
150100	Intro to astronomy	Astro	101	3S	L	
150599	Physical geology	Geol	101	3S	L	
150599	Historical geology	Geol	102	3S	L	
160302	Intermediate algebra	Math	120	3S	L	
160302	College algebra	Math	121	3S	L	
160302	Algebra & trigonometry	Math	150	4S	L	
160401	Calculus I	Math	162	4S	L	
160401	Calculus II	Math	163	4S	L	
160401	Calculus III	Math	264	4S	L	
160499	Vector analysis	Math	311	3S	U	
160700	Intro to prob & statistic	Math	145	3S	L	
170102	Military hist of the US	Hist	375	3S	U	
180599	Introduction to logic	Philo	156	3S	L	
189900	Intro to philoso problems	Philo	110	3S	L	
200501	Abnormal psychology	Psych	332	3S	U	
200799	Social psychology	Psych	271	3S	L	
200799	General psychology I	Psych	101	3S	L	
200799	General psychology II	Psych	102	3S	L	
220201	Principles & problems	Econ	200	3S	L	
220201	Principles of economics	Econ	201	3S	L	
220204	Money and banking	Econ	315	3S	L	
220428	History of New Mexico	Hist	360	3S	U	
220428	Hist of SW, Span period	Hist	380	3S	U	
220432	Hist of US to 1877	Hist	161	3S	L	
220432	Hist of US since 1877	Hist	162	3S	L	

NCES No.	Course Title	Dept.	Course No.	Cred.	Lev.	Specl. Feat.
220433	Western civilization	Hist	101	3S	L	
220433	Western civilization	Hist	102	3S	L	
220599	The political world	PolSc	110	3S	L	
220599	American politics	PolSc	200	3S	L	
220606	Introduction to sociology	Socio	101	3S	L	
220613	Social problms: sel topcs	Socio	211	3S	L	
220614	The urban community	Socio	351	3S	U	

(51) **UNIVERSITY OF NORTH CAROLINA**

Mr. Norman H. Loewenthal
Associate Director for Independent Study
Division of Extension and Continuing Education
Abernethy Hall, CB #3420
University of North Carolina
Chapel Hill, North Carolina 27599-3420
Phone: 919-962-1106

Credit by examination is available. Telecourses are offered. Enrollment on a noncredit basis accepted in credit courses. High school students may enroll in undergraduate courses for credit. Overseas enrollment accepted. Military personnel may enroll through the DANTES program. Institution offers special arrangements to take courses not listed in this Catalog. Minimum period for course completion is eight weeks. Maximum period for course completion is nine months. This is an interinstitutional program within the consolidated University of North Carolina (UNC) system. The institutional code precedes the course number: A—Appalachian State University; C—UNC at Chapel Hill; E—East Carolina University; G—UNC at Greensboro; S—North Carolina State University; T—Western Carolina University; W—Winston-Salem State University; and Z—Elizabeth City State University.

NCES No.	Course Title	Dept.	Course No.	Cred.	Lev.	Specl. Feat.
	College courses					
010406	Poultry production	AnSci	S200	3S	L	
030302	Fundamentals of music	Music	C21	3S	L	AC
030302	Intro to music	Music	C40	3S	L	AC
030599	History of Western art	ArHis	C31a	3S	L	
030599	History of American art	ArHis	S203	3S	L	
040101	Acctg I concepts fin rept	Acctg	S210	3S	L	
040101	Basic accounting princip	Bus	C71	3S	L	
040101	Prin of accounting I	Acctg	G201	3S	L	
040101	Prin of accounting II	Acctg	G202	3S	L	
040111	Elem management account	Bus	C72	3S	L	
040111	Acctg II intro mgerl acct	Acctg	S220	3S	L	
040601	Business writing	Engl	C32	3S	L	
040601	Business writing	Engl	C32a	2S	L	
041001	Principles of marketing	Mktg	A3050	3S	U	
041303	Real estate prin & prac	RlEst	A2850	3S	L	
061001	Computer literacy	CmpSc	S100	2S	L	
070100	School and society	Educ	S344	3S	U	
080901	Electrical circuits I	ElecE	S211	3S	L	
090115	Intro to human nutrition	Nutri	C50	3S	L	
090602	Mgmt of health resources	HCA	W460	3S	U	
090699	Long-term care for aging	HCA	C176	3S	U	
090699	Long-term care admin II	HCA	C177	3S	U	
119900	Technology and change	IntSt	W4604	3S	U	
120301	Social dialects	Spch	C153	3S	U	
120305	English grammar	Engl	C36	3S	L	
120307	Contemporary literature	Engl	C24	3S	L	
120307	Shakespeare	Engl	C58	3S	L	
120307	Amer lit: beginning-1865	Engl	C81	3S	L	
120307	Brit lit Chaucer to Pope	Engl	C20	3S	L	
120310	English comp & rhetoric	Engl	C1	3S	L	
120310	Composition & rhetoric	Engl	S111	3S	L	
120310	English comp & rhetoric	Engl	C2	3S	L	
120310	Composition & reading	Engl	S112	3S	L	
120310	Introduction to fiction	Engl	C23W	3S	L	
120310	Advanced creative writing	Engl	C35	3S	L	
120310	Advanced poetry writing	Engl	C35P	3S	L	
120310	Foundation composition	Engl	T300	3S	L	
120310	Writing for bus & indus	Engl	E3880	3S	U	
120310	Creative writing	Engl	C34	3S	L	
120399	Fund of Eng as a 2nd lang	Engl	T416	3S	U	
121000	Elementary French	Frnch	C1	4S	L	AC
121000	Beginning French	Frnch	G102a	4S	L	AC
121100	Elementary German	Germn	C1	3S	L	AC
121100	Elementary German	Germn	C2	3S	L	AC
121100	Intermediate German	Germn	C3	3S	L	

NCES No.	Course Title	Dept.	Course No.	Cred.	Lev.	Spec. Feat.
121100	Intermediate German	Germn	C4	3S	L	
121400	Elementary Italian	Ital	C1	3S	L	AC
121400	Elementary Italian	Ital	C2	3S	L	AC
121400	Intermediate Italian	Ital	C3	3S	L	AC
121400	Intermediate Italian	Ital	C4	3S	L	AC
121600	Intermediate Latin	Latin	C3	3S	L	
121600	Intermediate Latin	Latin	C4	3S	L	
121600	Elementary Latin	Latin	C1	3S	L	AC
121600	Elementary Latin	Latin	C2	3S	L	
122000	Elementary Russian	Rus	C1	3S	L	
122000	Elementary Russian	Rus	C2	3S	L	
122000	Intermediate Russian	Rus	C3	3S	L	
122000	Intermediate Russian	Rus	C4	3S	L	
122500	Intermediate Spanish	Span	C3	3S	L	
122500	Intermediate Spanish	Span	C4	3S	L	
129900	Medical word form & etym	Class	C25	3S	L	
129900	Word formation & etymol	Class	C26	3S	L	
140804	Research skills	LibSc	E1000	1S		
150199	Conceptual astronomy	Phycs	G203	3S	L	LK
150316	Plants and life	Bio	C10	3S	L	
150401	Gen descriptive chem I	Chem	C11	3S	L	
150401	Gen descriptive chem II	Chem	C21	3S	L	
150401	Intro to chemical concept	Chem	C10	2S	L	
150401	General chemistry I	Chem	G111	3S	L	
150401	General chemistry II	Chem	G114	3S	L	LK
150500	Introductory geology/lab	Geol	C11	4S	L	LK
150500	General physical geology	ErSci	S101	3S	L	
150599	Geol of the nat'l parks	Geol	E1800	4S	L	
150600	Surv coastal marine envmt	Ocean	E2125	2S	L	
150700	General physics	Phycs	S204	3S	L	
150700	General physics	Phycs	S207	3S	L	
150899	Gen environmental science	EnvSc	Z101	3S	L	
160302	Algebra & trigonometry	Math	S111	4S	L	
160401	Analytic geom & calc I	Math	S141	4S	L	
160401	Analytic geom & calc II	Math	S241	4S	L	
160401	Analytic geom & calc III	Math	S242	4S	L	
160401	Elements of calculus	Math	S113	4S	L	
160601	Trig & analytic geometry	Math	C30	3S	L	
160601	Pre-calculus	Math	Z118	3S	L	
160800	Basic statistics	Stat	Z251	3S	L	
160899	Intro stat for engineers	Stat	S361	3S	U	
161101	Mathematics of finance	Math	S122	3S	L	
161199	Calc for bus & social sci	Math	C22	3S	L	
170102	American military history	Hist	C77	3S	L	
180300	Introduction to ethics	Philo	C22	3S	L	
180499	Main problems in phil	Philo	C20	3S	L	
180502	Introd symbolic logic	Philo	C21	3S	L	
181201	Intro to Old Test lit	Relig	C21	3S	L	
181202	Intro to New Test lit	Relig	C22	3S	L	
190700	Intro to recreation	Rec	S152	3S	L	
190700	Intro to comm recreation	Rec	C10	3S	L	
200100	General psychology	Psych	C10	3S	L	AC
200100	Intro to psychology	Psych	S200	3S	L	AC
200501	Abnormal psychology	Psych	G341	3S	U	
220100	General anthropology	Anthr	C41	3S	L	
220102	Cultural anthropology	Anthr	S252	3S	L	
220102	Cultural anthropology	Anthr	G213	3S	L	
220201	Economics I	Econ	S201	3S	L	
220201	Intermediate microecon	Econ	S301	3S	L	
220217	Econ & bus statistics	Econ	S350	3S	L	
220301	Cultural geography	Geog	G105	3S	L	
220305	Physical geography	Geog	C10	3S	L	
220305	Intro to environ geog	ErSci	S208	3S	L	
220306	Landscapes of US & Canada	Geog	C57	3S	L	
220402	US foreign relations-1914	Hist	C143	3S	U	
220402	US foreign rel 1914-pres	Hist	C144	3S	U	
220421	Amer history to 1865	Hist	C21	3S	L	AC
220424	English history to 1688	Hist	C44	3S	L	
220424	English hist since 1688	Hist	C45	3S	L	
220426	Mod Europ hist 1500-1815	Hist	C48	3S	L	
220426	Mod Europ hist since 1815	Hist	C49	3S	L	
220428	North Carolina 1524-1835	Hist	C161	3S	U	
220428	North Carolina 1835-pres	Hist	C162	3S	U	
220431	Hist of Russia 1861-pres	Hist	C31	3S	L	
220432	Amer history since 1865	Hist	C22	3S	L	
220432	United States 1845-1914	Hist	S243	3S	L	
220433	The world since 1945	Hist	C15	3S	L	
220450	Ancient history	Hist	C41	3S	L	
220450	Ancient world to 180 AD	Hist	S207	3S	L	
220499	Hist of Western civ I	Hist	C11	3S	L	
220499	Hist of Western civ II	Hist	C12	3S	L	
220499	Western civ since 1400	Hist	S205	3S	L	

NCES No.	Course Title	Dept.	Course No.	Cred.	Lev.	Spec. Feat.
220501	Intro to govern in the US	PolSc	C41	3S	L	
220501	Amer national govt	PolSc	Z301	3S	U	
220501	Intro to American govt	PolSc	S201	3S	U	
220505	US foreign policy	PolSc	T334	3S	U	
220510	Clas & medie poli thought	PolSc	C63	3S	L	
220511	State & local gov in US	PolSc	C42	3S	L	
220511	State and local govt	PolSc	S202	3S	L	
220599	Urban politics	PolSc	W3371	3S	U	
220599	European politics	PolSc	C52	3S	L	
220602	Criminology	Socio	S306	3S	U	
220602	Crime and delinquency	Socio	C23	3S	L	
220604	Juvenile delinquency	Socio	S425	3S	U	
220605	Sociology of family	Socio	S204	3S	L	
220605	Family & society	Socio	C30	3S	L	
220605	Marriage & family	Socio	G355	3S	U	
220605	The family	Socio	Z401	3S	U	
220606	American society	Socio	C10	3S	L	
220606	Intro to sociology	Socio	Z201	3S	L	
220606	Intro to sociology	Socio	G211	3S	L	
220699	Black-white relat in US	Socio	C22	3S	L	
220699	Population problems	Socio	C21	3S	L	
220699	Corrections & penology	Socio	G413	3S	U	
220699	Population problems	Socio	G339	3S	U	

Noncredit courses

NCES No.	Course Title	Dept.	Course No.	Cred.	Lev.	Spec. Feat.
079900	Family day care mgmt	FamDC	C1	NC		V
079900	Buildg qual in fam daycar	FamDC	C2	NC		V
090200	Marketing for dent pract	DOP	CMKT	NC		V
120310	Engl composition & gramm	Engl	CO	NC		D
160302	Contemporary algebra	Math	CR	NC		D

⑤② **UNIVERSITY OF NORTH DAKOTA**

Ms. Rebecca Monley
Director
Department of Correspondence Study
University of North Dakota
Box 8277, University Station
Grand Forks, North Dakota 58202
Phone: 701-777-3044

Telecourses are offered. Enrollment on a noncredit basis accepted in credit courses. High school students may enroll in undergraduate courses for credit. Overseas enrollment not accepted. Maximum period for course completion is one year. Television courses, however, must be completed within the semester they are offered (one extra month is allowed).

NCES No.	Course Title	Dept.	Course No.	Cred.	Lev.	Spec. Feat.
	College courses					
030502	Intro to under of art	VisAr	110	3S	L	
030502	Art history survey	VisAr	210	3S	L	
040101	Elements of accounting	Acctg	200	3S	L	
040101	Elements of accounting	Acctg	201	3S	L	
040106	Cost accounting I	Acctg	305	3S	U	
040203	Records management	BVEd	315	3S	U	
040311	Principles of finance	Finan	310	3S	U	
040601	Business communications	BVEd	320	3S	U	
040904	Principles of management	Mgmt	300	3S	U	
040999	Production management	Mgmt	301	3S	U	
041001	Principles of marketing	Mktg	301	3S	U	
041099	Salesmanship	Mktg	204	2S	L	
041100	Personnel management	Mgmt	302	3S	U	
041301	Real estate appraisal	Finan	324	3S	U	
041303	Principles of real estate	Finan	320	3S	U	
041306	R estate finance & invest	Finan	321	3S	U	
050100	Advertising and sales pro	Mktg	302	3S	U	
060705	Programming in BASIC	CmpSc	105	2S	L	
060705	Computer programming I	CmpSc	160	4S	L	
061103	Introduction to computers	CmpSc	101	2S	L	
061103	Intro to computer lab	CmpSc	101L	1S	L	
070306	Philosophy of voc ed	BVEd	444	3S	U	
070800	Career/voc ed of excep ch	Educ	421	3S	U	
070899	Prescriptive teaching	Educ	318	3S	U	
081000	Engineering graphics	Engin	101	2S	L	
081000	Descriptive geometry	Engin	102	2S	L	
081599	Industrial safety	IndTc	440	2S	U	
090118	Elements of pharmacology	Pharm	204	3S	L	
090303	Int occupational therapy	OccTh	200	2S	L	
099900	Medical terminology	OccTh	205	1S	L	

NCES No.	Course Title	Dept.	Course No.	Cred.	Lev.	Specl. Feat.
100313	Fundamentals of nutrition	HomEc	240	3S	L	
100313	Geriatric nutrition	HomEc	495	2S	U	
120299	American Indian lit	EngLL	367	3S	U	
120307	Survey of English lit	EngLL	301	3S	U	
120307	Survey of English lit	EngLL	302	3S	U	
120307	Survey of American lit	EngLL	303	3S	U	
120307	Survey of American lit	EngLL	304	3S	U	
120307	Shakespeare	EngLL	315	3S	U	
120308	Introduction to fiction	EngLL	211	2S	L	
120310	Composition I	Engl	101	3S	L	
120310	Composition II	Engl	102	3S	L	
120310	Composition III	Engl	203	2S	L	
120310	Technical & business writ	Engl	209	2S	L	
120310	Creative writing	Engl	305	2S	L	
121000	Beginning French	CILL	101	4S	L	AC
121000	Beginning French	CILL	102	4S	L	AC
121000	Second-year French	CILL	201	4S	L	AC
121000	Second-year French	CILL	202	4S	L	AC
121000	Third-year French	CILL	301	3S	U	
121000	Third-year French	CILL	302	3S	U	
121100	Beginning German	CILL	101	4S	L	AC
121100	Beginning German	CILL	102	4S	L	AC
121600	First-year college Latin	CILL	101	4S	L	AC
121600	First-year college Latin	CILL	102	4S	L	AC
121800	Beginning Norwegian	CILL	101	4S	L	AC
121800	Beginning Norwegian	CILL	102	4S	L	
121800	Second-year Norwegian	CILL	201	4S	L	
121800	Second-year Norwegian	CILL	202	4S	L	
122500	Beginning Spanish	CILL	101	4S	L	AC
122500	Beginning Spanish	CILL	102	4S	L	AC
122500	Second-year Spanish	CILL	201	4S	L	AC
122500	Second-year Spanish	CILL	202	4S	L	AC
130799	Business law I	Acctg	315	3S	U	
130799	Business law II	Acctg	316	3S	U	
160302	College algebra	Math	103	3S	L	
160302	Intermediate algebra	Math	102	3S	L	
160302	College algebra	Math	103	5S	L	
160401	Calculus I	Math	211	4S	L	
160401	Calculus II	Math	212	4S	L	
160401	Calculus III	Math	213	4S	L	
160602	Trigonometry	Math	105	2S	L	
181002	World religions	Relig	203	3S	L	
181099	Introduction to religion	Relig	101	3S	L	
181502	Contemporary moral issues	Relig	205	2S	L	
181599	Death and dying	Relig	345	2S	U	
181599	Intro to humanities	Hum	101	4S	L	
200100	Intro to psychology	Psych	101	3S	L	
200501	Abnormal psychology	Psych	370	3S	U	
220201	Principles of econ I	Econ	201	3S	L	
220201	Principles of econ II	Econ	202	3S	L	
220301	Cultural geography	Geog	151	3S	L	
220306	World regional geography	Geog	161	3S	L	
220306	Geography of Canada	Geog	362	3S	U	
220306	Geography of North Dakota	Geog	369	3S	U	
220426	Western civ to 1500	Hist	101	3S	L	
220426	Western civ since 1500	Hist	102	3S	L	
220428	History of North Dakota	Hist	220	3S	U	
220501	American government I	PolSc	101	3S	L	
220501	American government II	PolSc	102	3S	L	
220602	Criminology	Socio	252	3S	L	
220605	The family	Socio	335	3S	U	
220606	Introduction to sociology	Socio	101	3S	L	
220607	Social psychology	Socio	361	4S	U	
220608	Rural sociology	Socio	331	3S	U	
220699	Aging	Socio	352	3S	U	

NCES No.	Course Title	Dept.	Course No.	Cred.	Lev.	Specl. Feat.
	Noncredit courses					
040101	Accounting fundamentals I	Acctg		NC		
040101	Accounting fund II	Acctg		NC		
041304	Real estate management			NC		
090699	Long-term-care admin			NC		
100309	School food service	SFS		NC		
100313	Nutrit for dietary persnl	DtMgt		NC		
100702	Dietary managers course	DtMgt		NC		
129900	ESO reading course			NC		
160301	Elem concepts of math	Math		NC		
181599	Relig values in marriage	Relig		NC		
220599	Naturalization course	PolSc		NC		

(53) UNIVERSITY OF NORTHERN COLORADO

Dr. Nancy L. Reddy
Assistant Director, Independent Study
Division of Statewide Programs, Frasier Hall #11
University of Northern Colorado
Greeley, Colorado 80639
Phone: 303-351-2944

Telecourses are offered. Enrollment on a noncredit basis accepted in credit courses. Overseas enrollment accepted. Institution offers special arrangements to take courses not listed in this Catalog. Minimum period for course completion is three weeks. Maximum period for course completion is one year.

NCES No.	Course Title	Dept.	Course No.	Cred.	Lev.	Specl. Feat.
	College courses					
070899	Hndcpd stu in reg clsrm	EdSE	410	2S	U	AC
100504	Cnsmr aspct of hshld equi	FND	308	3S	U	
131101	Environmnt, politcs & law	EnvSt	205	2S	L	
150300	Biological science	Bio	100	3S	L	
160102	Intro to history of math	Math	464	2S	U	
160302	Intermediate algebra	Math	123	3S	L	
160602	Plane trigonometry	Math	125	3S	L	
220202	History of econ thought	Econ	470	3S	U	
220204	Money and banking	Econ	202	3S	L	
220306	World geography	Geog	100	3S	L	
220306	Colorado	Geog	350	3S	U	
220501	National govt of the US	PolSc	100	3S	L	
220501	President and bureaucracy	PolSc	302	3S	U	
220503	Soviet politics	PolSc	412	3S	U	
220511	Colorado politics	PolSc	203	3S	L	
	Graduate courses					
070899	Seminar in mainstreaming	SplEd	506	3S	G	AC
	Noncredit courses					
131800	Colorado criminal statuts	LawEn	102	NC	L	
229900	Law enforcement supervisn	LawEn	100	NC	L	

(54) UNIVERSITY OF NORTHERN IOWA

Dr. James E. Bodensteiner
Director of Credit Programs
Guided Correspondence Study Program
University of Northern Iowa
Cedar Falls, Iowa 50614
Phone: 319-273-2121

Overseas enrollment accepted. Military personnel may enroll through the DANTES program. Minimum period for course completion is two weeks per credit hour. Maximum period for course completion is one year. The program's telecourses are available in Iowa only. High school students may enroll in a lower-level college course if they are seniors, in the upper quarter of their class, and endorsed by their principal.

NCES No.	Course Title	Dept.	Course No.	Cred.	Lev.	Specl. Feat.
	College courses					
040101	Principles of acctng I	Acctg	12030	3S	L	
040101	Principles of acctng II	Acctg	12031	3S	L	
070199	History of education	Educ	26134	3S	B	
070404	Methods in elem science	Educ	21142	2S	B	
070404	Social studies elem sch	Educ	21143	2S	B	
070404	Group eval techniques	Educ	25181	3S	B	
070504	Intro to business	Bus	15010	3S	L	
100313	Basic nutrition	HomEc	31030	2S		
120307	Modern drama	EngLL	62115	3S	B	
120307	20th-cent British novel	EngLL	62120	3S	B	
120307	British novel thru Hardy	EngLL	62156	3S	B	
120307	Lit for young adults	EngLL	62165	3S	B	
120307	Intro to literature	EngLL	62031	3S	L	
120310	Intro to college writing	Engl	62005	3S	L	
150599	Fundamentals of geology	Geol	87128	4S	B	
160103	Metric system measurement	Math	80136	2S	B	
160803	Fund of statistical meth	Math	80172	3S	B	
181104	Religions of the world	Relig	64124	3S	B	
181104	Individual readings relig	Relig	64189	CV	B	
190509	Personal health	Hlth	41015	2S	L	
190509	Consumer health	Hlth	41164	2S	L	

NCES No.	Course Title	Dept.	Course No.	Cred.	Lev.	Specl. Feat.
200199	Intro to psychology	Psych	40008	3S	L	
200499	Psychology of aging	Psych	40173	3S	B	
200804	Child psychology	Educ	20100	2S	B	
200804	Development of young chld	Educ	20109	3S	B	
200804	Psych of adolescence	Educ	20116	2S	B	
200804	Social psychology educ	Educ	20140	3S	B	
220299	Econ for general educ	Econ	92024	3S	U	
220305	Communicatng through maps	Geog	97050	2S	L	
220306	Regional geog Middle East	Geog	97150	3S	B	
220308	Urban geography	Geog	97132	3S	U	
220399	World geography	Geog	97025	3S	U	
220399	Political geography	Geog	97170	3S	B	
220423	Foreign area stdy: India	Hist	68125	3S	U	
220423	Foreign area stdy-Mideast	Hist	68127	3S	L	
220426	Modern Europe to 1815	Hist	96054	3S	L	
220426	Modern Europe since 1815	Hist	96055	3S	L	
220428	History of Iowa	Hist	96130	3S	B	
220432	US history to 1877	Hist	96014	3S	U	
220432	US history since 1877	Hist	96015	3S	U	
220432	Recent US history	Hist	96116	3S	B	
220432	The black in US history	Hist	96122	3S	B	
220432	US foreign relations	Hist	96138	3S	B	
220472	Women's studies: intro	Hist	68040	3S	L	
220499	Humanities I	Hist	68021	4S	U	
220499	Humanities II	Hist	68022	4S	U	VC
220501	Intro to Amer politics	PolSc	94014	3S	U	
220601	Principles of sociology	Socio	98058	3S	U	
220602	Corrections & punishment	Socio	98126	3S	B	
220604	Juvenile delinquency	Socio	98127	3S	L	
220605	The family	Socio	98105	2S	U	
220610	Social deviance & control	Socio	98123	3S	B	
220613	Social problems	Socio	98060	3S	U	
220615	Minority group relations	Socio	98130	3S	B	

(55) UNIVERSITY OF OKLAHOMA

Mr. Hugh Harris
Director
Independent Study Department
University of Oklahoma
1700 Asp Avenue, Room B-1
Norman, Oklahoma 73037
Phone: 405-325-1921

Enrollment on a noncredit basis accepted in credit courses. High school students may enroll in undergraduate courses for credit. Overseas enrollment accepted. Military personnel may enroll through the DANTES program. Minimum period for course completion is four–six weeks. Maximum period for course completion is one year. All students may have one 6-month extension per course for an additional fee, which is $20 in the case of a course taken for college credit, $10 for a high school course, and $20 for a course taken on a noncredit basis.

NCES No.	Course Title	Dept.	Course No.	Cred.	Lev.	Specl. Feat.
	High School courses					
011400	Conservatn nat resources	SocSt		HF	H	
030501	Calligraphy	Art	A	HF	H	LK
030501	Beginning drawing	Art	C	HF	H	
030501	Drawing II	Art	E	HF	H	
030502	Art understanding	Art	D	HF	H	
040104	Bookkeeping	Acctg	A	HF	H	LK
040104	Bookkeeping	Acctg	B	HF	H	LK
040207	Begin type for one hand	Typg	AH	HF	H	
040207	Typewrit first yr fir sem	Typg	A	HF	H	
040207	Typewrit first yr sec sem	Typg	B	HF	H	
040207	Typewrit second yr fir se	Typg	C	HF	H	
040207	Typewrit second yr sec se	Typg	D	HF	H	
040302	General business	Bus	A	HF	H	
040302	General business	Bus	B	HF	H	
040604	Business Engl second sem	Engl	L	HF	H	
040604	Business Engl first sem	Engl	K	HF	H	
050605	Creative prose writing	Journ		HF	H	
061101	Computer literacy	CmpSc		HF	H	VC
070702	Tools for learning	StSkl		HF	H	
080100	Aerospace education	Aero	A	HF	H	
080100	Aerospace education	Aero	B	HF	H	
100100	Clothes	HomEc	B	HF	H	
100300	Food	HomEc	E	HF	H	
100501	Home furnishings	HomEc	F	HF	H	
100600	Relationships child grow	HomEc	A	HF	H	
100600	Etiquette-mannrs fr today	HomEc		HF	H	
120300	Engl ninth-gr first sem	Engl	A	HF	H	
120300	Engl ninth-gr second sem	Engl	B	HF	H	
120300	Engl tenth-gr first sem	Engl	C	HF	H	
120300	Engl tenth-gr second sem	Engl	D	HF	H	
120300	Engl eleventh-gr fir sem	Engl	E	HF	H	
120300	Engl twelfth-gr fir sem	Engl	G	HF	H	
120300	Engl twelfth-gr sec sem	Engl	H	HF	H	
120300	Vocabulary building-bi sc	StSkl	A	HF	H	
120300	Vocabulary building-coll	StSkl	B	HF	H	
120305	Basic English grammar	Engl		HF	H	
120310	Advanced composition	Engl	J	HF	H	
121000	French first-yr first sem	Frnch	A	HF	H	AC
121000	French first-yr second se	Frnch	B	HF	H	AC
121000	French second-yr first se	Frnch	C	HF	H	AC
121000	French second-yr sec sem	Frnch	D	HF	H	AC
121100	German first yr first sem	Germn	A	HF	H	AC
121100	German first yr sec sem	Germn	B	HF	H	AC
121100	German second yr fir sem	Germn	C	HF	H	AC
121100	German second yr sec sem	Germn	D	HF	H	AC
121600	Latin first-yr first sem	Latin	A	HF	H	
121600	Latin first-yr second sem	Latin	B	HF	H	
121600	Latin second-yr first sem	Latin	C	HF	H	
121600	Latin second-yr second se	Latin	D	HF	H	
122500	Spanish first-yr fir sem	Span	A	HF	H	AC
122500	Spanish first-yr sec sem	Span	B	HF	H	AC
122500	Spanish second-yr fir sem	Span	C	HF	H	AC
122500	Spanish second-yr sec sem	Span	D	HF	H	AC
140100	Use of the library	LibSc		HF	H	
150300	Biology first sem	Bio	A	HF	H	
150300	Biology second sem	Bio	B	HF	H	
160301	General math first sem	Math	K	HF	H	
160301	General math second sem	Math	M	HF	H	
160302	Algebra first sem	Math	A	HF	H	
160302	Algebra second sem	Math	B	HF	H	
160302	Algebra third sem	Math	E	HF	H	
160302	Algebra fourth sem	Math	F	HF	H	
160400	Pre-calc & analytic geom	Math	H	HF	H	
160601	Modern geometry first sem	Math	C	HF	H	
160601	Modern geometry sec sem	Math	D	HF	H	
160602	Trigonometry	Math	G	HF	H	
161201	Business mathematics	Math	L	HF	H	
190500	Investigating your health	Sci	C	HF	H	
200100	Psychology	Psych		HF	H	
220201	Basic economics	Econ	C	HF	H	
220300	World geography first sem	WGS	A	HF	H	
220300	World geography sec sem	WGS	B	HF	H	
220428	Oklahoma history	Hist	O	HF	H	
220432	American hist first sem	AmHis	E	HF	H	
220432	American hist second sem	AmHis	F	HF	H	
220433	World history first sem	WHS	J	HF	H	
220433	World history second sem	WHS	K	HF	H	
220501	American government	AmGvt		HF	H	
220502	Problems of democracy	Dem		HF	H	
220600	Sociology	Socio		HF	H	
	College courses					
030300	Understanding of music	Music	1113	3S	L	AC
030400	History of the theater I	Drama	2713	3S	L	
030400	History of the theater II	Drama	2723	3S	L	
040101	Fund financial acct	Acctg	2113	3S	L	
040106	Cost accounting	Acctg	3313	3S	U	
040108	Intermed accounting I	Acctg	3113	3S	U	
040108	Intermed accounting II	Acctg	3123	3S	U	
040109	Governmental accounting	Acctg	3323	3S	U	
040111	Fund managerial acct	Acctg	2123	3S	L	
040301	Business finance	Finan	3303	3S	U	
040302	Personal finance	Finan	1203	3S	L	
040304	Fncl intermediaries/mkts	Finan	3403	3S	U	
040604	Business report writing	BuCom	3113	3S	U	
040604	Adv business communicatn	BuCom	3223	3S	U	
040904	Prin orgn and management	Mgmt	3013	3S	U	
041001	Intro to marketing	Mktg	3013	3S	U	
041100	Personnel management	Mgmt	3513	3S	U	
041303	Real estate principles	Finan	3503	3S	U	
050301	Intro to advertising	Journ	2303	3S	L	
050605	Prof writ: magazine writ	Journ	3534	4S	U	
050605	Prof writing: the novel	Journ	4514	4S	U	
050605	Prof writing: fundamental	Journ	3504	4S	U	
050605	Prof writ: appr to fictio	Journ	3514	4S	U	

NCES No.	Course Title	Dept.	Course No.	Cred.	Lev.	Specl. Feat.
050606	History of journalism	Journ	4803	3S	U	
050900	Prin of public relations	Journ	3413	3S	U	
070503	Public school art	Art	3142	2S	U	
070505	Supvsn sec sch publicat	Journ	4703	3S	U	
070512	Lang arts elem/middl schs	Educ	4253	3S	U	
070512	Teaching of English	Engl	4913	3S	U	
070516	Math in elem/mid schools	Educ	4152	2S	U	
070516	Arith for elem teach I	Math	2213	3S	L	
070516	Arith for elem teach II	Math	3213	3S	U	
070522	Social stud elem/mid schs	Educ	4323	3S	U	
070800	Educ exceptional children	Educ	3412	2S	U	
070808	Adaptive phy ed program	PhyEd	3882	2S	U	
080703	Hydrology	CivlE	5843	3S	U	
080900	Electrical science	Engin	2613	3S	L	
081102	Fluid mechanics	Engin	3223	3S	U	
081103	Rigid-body mechanics	Engin	2113	3S	L	
081104	Thermodynamics	Engin	2213	3S	L	
081199	Strength of materials	Engin	2153	3S	L	
081500	Intro to industrial engrg	IndEn	2011	3S	L	
081503	Fund of engrg economy	Engin	4223	3S	U	
081900	Struct and prop materials	Engin	2313	3S	L	
100100	Textiles	HuDev	2443	3S	L	
100109	Sociodynamics of fashion	HuDev	3452	2S	U	
100313	Elementary nutrition	HuDev	1823	3S	L	
120201	Classical mythology	ClCul	2383	3S	L	
120201	World lit to 1700	Engl	2433	3S	L	
120201	The Bible as literature	Engl	2453	3S	L	
120201	Mod Brit and cont drama	Engl	4433	3S	U	
120201	World lit since 1700	Engl	2443	3S	L	
120201	Soviet lit in English	MLang	3533	3S	U	
120201	Russian lit in translatn	Rus	2003	3S	L	
120201	Mythology and folklore	MLang	3043	3S	U	
120300	Latin derivatives	ClCul	1412	2S	L	
120300	Medical vocabulary	ClCul	2412	2S	L	
120302	Hist of English language	Engl	4133	3S	U	
120305	Prin English comp I	Engl	1113	3S	L	
120305	Prin English comp II	Engl	1213	3S	L	
120307	Engl lit 1375 to 1700	Engl	2543	3S	L	
120307	Engl lit 1700 to present	Engl	2653	3S	L	
120307	American lit to Civil War	Engl	2773	3S	L	
120307	Amer lit since Civil War	Engl	2883	3S	L	
120307	Shakespeare hist & comed	Engl	4523	3S	U	
120307	Shakespeare trag & poems	Engl	4533	3S	U	
120307	American drama	Engl	4813	3S	U	
120307	Ethnic literature	Engl	2023	3S	L	
120307	Intro to Shakespeare	Engl	2513	3S	L	
121000	French civilization	Frnch	4313	3S	U	
121000	Beginning French I	Frnch	1115	5S	L	AC
121000	Beginning French II	Frnch	1225	5S	L	AC
121000	Sur Frnch lit to 1800	Frnch	4153	3S	U	
121000	Sur Frnch lit 19th-20th c	Frnch	4163	3S	U	
121000	Intermediate French I	Frnch	2113	3S	L	AC
121000	Intermediate French II	Frnch	2223	3S	L	AC
121000	French convers & culture	Frnch	2133	3S	L	AC
121000	French convers & lit	Frnch	2243	3S	L	AC
121000	Advanced Frnch compositn	Frnch	3423	3S	U	
121100	Beginning German I	Germn	1115	5S	L	AC
121100	Beginning German II	Germn	1225	5S	L	AC
121100	Hist German lit to 1750	Germn	4153	3S	U	
121100	Begin German for read I	Germn	1013	3S	L	
121100	Begin German for read II	Germn	1023	3S	L	
121100	Intermediate German I	Germn	2113	3S	L	
121100	Intermediate German II	Germn	2223	3S	L	
121100	Scientific German I	Germn	3013	3S	U	
121100	Hist German lit from 1750	Germn	4163	3S	U	
121100	Scientific German II	Germn	3123	3S	U	
121100	German comp and convers	Germn	2323	3S	L	
121200	New Testament Greek	Greek	2123	3S	L	
121300	Beginning Hebrew I	Hebr	1114	4S	L	
121300	Beginning Hebrew II	Hebr	1214	4S	L	
121300	Intermediate Hebrew	Hebr	2113	3S	L	
121600	Beginning Latin I	Latin	1115	5S	L	
121600	Beginning Latin II	Latin	1215	5S	L	
121600	Advanced poetry—Vergil	Latin	3213	3S	U	
121600	Interm prose—Cicero Orat	Latin	2113A	3S	L	
121600	Interm prose—Livy	Latin	2113C	3S	L	
121600	Interm prose-Cicero essay	Latin	2113B	3S	L	
122000	Beginning Russian I	Rus	1115	5S	L	AC
122000	Beginning Russian II	Rus	1225	5S	L	AC
122000	Scientific Russian I	Rus	3023	3S	U	
122000	Scientific Russian II	Rus	3213	3S	U	
122000	Begin business Russian	Rus	3023	3S	U	
122000	Advan business Russian	Rus	3123	3S	U	
122500	Spanish civilization	Span	4313	3S	U	
122500	Beginning Spanish I	Span	1115	5S	L	AC
122500	Beginning Spanish II	Span	1225	5S	L	AC
122500	Sur Sp-Am lit 1888-pres	Span	4103	3S	U	
122500	Sur Spanish lit to 1700	Span	4153	3S	U	
122500	Sur Spanish lit from 1700	Span	4163	3S	U	
122500	Spanish reading I	Span	2113	3S	L	
122500	Spanish reading II	Span	2223	3S	L	
122500	Spanish composition	Span	2423	3S	L	
122500	Advan Spanish composition	Span	3423	3S	U	
122500	Surv Sp/Amer lit to 1888	Span	4093	3S	U	
122500	First yr Spanish review	Span	1235	5S	L	AC
130400	Elementary criminal law	PolSc	4813	3S	U	
130402	Criminal legal procedure	PolSc	4803	3S	U	
130700	Legal environ of business	BuLaw	3323	3S	U	
130900	Real property	BuLaw	4613	3S	U	
140307	Children's literature	LibSc	4303	3S	U	LK
150100	General astronomy	Astro	1504	4S	L	
150400	Chemis for nonsci majors	Chem	1614	4S	L	
150408	Organic chemistry I	Chem	3053	3S	U	LK
150408	Organic chemistry II	Chem	3153	3S	U	LK
150500	Phy geol for sci/eng majs	Geol	1114	4S	L	LK
150500	Hist geol for sci/eng maj	Geol	1124	4S	L	
160302	Intermediate algebra	Math	0123	3S	D	
160302	College algebra	Math	1513	3S	L	
160306	Linear algebra	Math	3333	3S	U	
160401	Calculus I	Math	1823	3S	L	
160401	Calculus II	Math	2423	3S	L	
160401	Calculus III	Math	2434	3S	L	
160602	Trigonometry	Math	1612	2S	L	
160603	Analytic geometry	Math	1812	2S	L	
160802	Elements of statistics	Econ	2843	3S	L	
160802	Elementary statistics	Math	3703	3S	U	
161101	Calculus I:bus/life/so sc	Math	1743	3S	L	
161101	Math for bus/life/soc sci	Math	1443	3S	L	
161101	Calculus for bus/life/soc	Math	2123	3S	L	
180100	Aesthetics: beauty and ar	Philo	3053	3S	U	
180300	History of ethics	Philo	3253	3S	U	
180401	Hist Greek and Roman phil	Philo	3313	3S	U	
180402	Hist medieval philosophy	Philo	3323	3S	U	
180403	Hist modern philosophy	Philo	3333	3S	U	
180500	Introduction to logic	Philo	1113	3S	L	
190106	Org & admin health phy ed	PhyEd	4943	3S	U	
190110	Tests and meas in phy ed	PhyEd	4923	3S	U	
190200	Kinesiology	PhyEd	3713	3S	U	
190308	Theory coaching/athl mgt	PhyEd	2022	2S	L	
190311	Theory of baseball	PhyEd	3052	2S	U	
190311	Theory of basketball	PhyEd	3072	2S	U	
190311	Theory of track and field	PhyEd	3082	2S	U	
190311	Theory of wrestling	PhyEd	3092	2S	U	
190500	Health education	PhyEd	2913	3S	L	
190501	Drug education	PhyEd	4933	3S	U	
200100	Elements of psychology	Psych	1113	3S	L	
200504	Intro life-span dev psych	Psych	1603	3S	L	
200509	Intro to personality	Psych	1193	3S	L	
200901	Industrial psychology	Psych	3363	3S	U	
210100	Intro public administratn	PolSc	2173	3S	L	
210111	Environmentl conservation	Geog	3253	3S	U	
210304	Intro law enforcement	PolSc	2803	3S	L	
210304	Police administration I	PolSc	3803	3S	U	
210304	Prin criminal investigatn	PolSc	3853	3S	U	
220100	General anthropology	Anthr	1113	3S	L	
220101	Intro to archaeology	Anthr	2113	3S	L	
220101	Archaeology of N America	Anthr	3813	3S	U	
220102	Mythology and folklore	Anthr	3043	3S	U	
220104	High civiliz ancient Amer	Anthr	3893	3S	U	
220201	Principles of economics I	Econ	2113	3S	L	
220201	Principls of economics II	Econ	2123	3S	L	
220214	Intl trade theory/problms	Econ	3613	3S	U	
220300	Human geography	Geog	1103	3S	L	
220306	Prin economic geography	Geog	1213	3S	L	
220306	World geography by region	Geog	2603	3S	L	
220306	Region geography US/Canad	Geog	4913	3S	U	
220402	US diplomat hist to 1900	Hist	3563	3S	U	
220402	US dip hist in 20th cent	Hist	3573	3S	U	
220403	Econ history of US	Econ	1013	3S	L	
220423	East Asian civizn to 1800	Hist	1723	3S	L	
220423	Mod East Asia since 1800	Hist	1733	3S	L	
220424	England to 1603	Hist	2313	3S	L	
220424	England since 1603	Hist	2323	3S	L	
220426	Europe 1500 to 1815	Hist	1223	3S	L	

NCES No.	Course Title	Dept.	Course No.	Cred.	Lev.	Specl. Feat.
220426	Europe since 1815	Hist	1233	3S	L	
220427	Hispanic Amer 1492-1810	Hist	2613	3S	L	
220427	Hispanic Amer 1810-pres	Hist	2623	3S	L	
220428	History of Oklahoma	Hist	3393	3S	U	
220432	United States 1492-1865	Hist	1483	3S	L	
220432	United States 1865-pres	Hist	1493	3S	L	
220433	World civilization-1600	Hist	1913	3S	L	
220433	World civilization-1980	Hist	1923	3S	L	
220433	West civilization to 1660	Hist	1613	3S	L	
220433	West civilizat since 1660	Hist	1623	3S	L	
220450	Ancient history	Hist	1033	3S	L	
220450	Hebrew civ in ancie times	ClCul	3413	3S	U	
220450	Hebrew civ in ancie times	Hist	3413	3S	U	
220500	Intro to political sci	PolSc	1603	3S	L	
220501	Govt of the United States	PolSc	1113	3S	L	
220505	Intro to internatl relat	PolSc	2503	3S	L	
220505	US diplomat hist to 1900	PolSc	3563	3S	U	
220507	American polit parties	PolSc	2403	3S	L	
220511	State government	PolSc	2303	3S	L	
220511	Urban govt and politics	PolSc	3313	3S	U	
220511	Government of Oklahoma	PolSc	3303	3S	U	
220605	The family	Socio	3723	3S	U	
220606	Intro to sociology	Socio	1113	3S	L	
220610	Sociology: crime & delinq	Socio	3523	3S	U	

Noncredit courses

NCES No.	Course Title	Dept.	Course No.	Cred.	Lev.	Specl. Feat.
040604	Review of English usage	BuCom	3000	NC	D	
050402	Tech writing for prof'ls	BTWri		NC	D	
050605	Creative prose writing	Journ		NC	D	
050605	Prof writ I fundamentals	Journ		NC	D	
050605	Prof writ II appr fiction	Journ		NC	D	
050605	Prof writ III the novel	Journ		NC	D	
050605	Prof writ IV nonfiction	Journ		NC	D	
070702	Tools for learning	StSkl		NC	D	VC
110503	Calligraphy	Art		NC	D	
110503	Drawing fundamentals	Art		NC	D	
110503	Drawing methods	Art		NC	D	
120300	Vocabulary bldg-hi sch	StSkl	A	NC	D	
120300	Vocabulary bldg for coll	StSkl	B	NC	D	
120305	English review	Engl		NC	D	
120305	Basic English grammar	Engl		NC	D	
120310	Advanced composition	Engl		NC	D	
160302	Basic algebra for college	Math		NC	D	
160400	Pre-calc & analytic geom	Math		NC	D	
220502	Citizenship for aliens	Citz		NC	D	

(56) UNIVERSITY OF SOUTH CAROLINA

Ms. Sylvia A. Brazell
Director, Student Support Services
Telecommunications Instruction and Independent
Learning
University of South Carolina, 915 Gregg Street
Columbia, South Carolina 29208-0422
Phone: 803-777-2188

Telecourses are offered. High school students may enroll in undergraduate courses for credit. Overseas enrollment accepted. Military personnel may enroll through the DANTES program. Minimum period for course completion is one–two months. Maximum period for course completion is one year. Tuition is the same for in-state and out-of-state enrollments. Enrollment on a noncredit basis is accepted in all courses. A free catalog may be obtained from Independent Learning.

High School courses

NCES No.	Course Title	Dept.	Course No.	Cred.	Lev.	Specl. Feat.
040299	Office proc & practices	BusAd	BE013	HF	H	
040299	Office proc & practices	BusAd	BE014	HF	H	
040901	General business I	BusAd	BE021	HF	H	
100604	Etiquette	HomEc	HE001	HF	H	
120300	Basic English I	Engl	EN001	HF	H	
120300	Basic English 2	Engl	EN002	HF	H	
120399	Ninth-grade English I	Engl	EN031	HF	H	
120399	Ninth-grade English II	Engl	EN032	HF	H	
120399	Tenth-grade English I	Engl	EN033	HF	H	
120399	Tenth-grade English II	Engl	EN034	HF	H	
120399	Eleventh-grade English I	Engl	EN035	HF	H	
120399	Eleventh-grade English II	Engl	EN036	HF	H	
120399	Twelfth-grade English I	Engl	EN037	HF	H	

NCES No.	Course Title	Dept.	Course No.	Cred.	Lev.	Specl. Feat.
120399	Twelfth-grade English II	Engl	EN038	HF	H	
120399	Business English	Engl	BE011	HF	H	
150301	Basic biology I	Sci	S1015	HF	H	
150301	Basic biology II	Sci	S1016	HF	H	
150800	Physical science	Sci	SI013	HF	H	
150800	Physical science	Sci	SI014	HF	H	
160302	Beginning algebra I	Math	MA031	HF	H	
160302	Beginning algebra II	Math	MA032	HF	H	
160302	Advanced algebra I	Math	MA035	HF	H	
160302	Advanced algebra II	Math	MA036	HF	H	
160401	Precalculus: geo and alg	Math	MA039	HF	H	
160401	Precalculus: trigonometry	Math	MA040	HF	H	
160601	Geometry I	Math	MA033	HF	H	
160601	Geometry II	Math	MA034	HF	H	
160602	Trigonometry	Math	MA037	HF	H	
161201	Business & consumer math	Math	MA009	HF	H	
161201	Business & consumer math	Math	MA010	HF	H	
161299	Basic math I	Math	MA001	HF	H	
161299	Basic math 2	Math	MA002	HF	H	
190599	Health science I	Sci	S1001	HF	H	
190599	Health science II	Sci	S1002	HF	H	
200104	Psychology	SocSt	SS007	HF	H	
220201	Economics	SocSt	BE027	HF	H	
220305	World geography I	SocSt	SS021	HF	H	
220305	World geography II	SocSt	SS022	HF	H	
220432	American history I	SocSt	SS033	HF	H	
220432	American history II	SocSt	SS034	HF	H	
220433	World history I	SocSt	SS031	HF	H	
220433	World history II	SocSt	SS032	HF	H	
220501	American government	SocSt	SS035	HF	H	
220501	American government	SocSt	SS036	HF	H	
220502	Civics	SocSt	SS001	HF	H	
220606	Sociology	SocSt	SS003	HF	H	

College courses

NCES No.	Course Title	Dept.	Course No.	Cred.	Lev.	Specl. Feat.
040101	Fundamentals of acctg	BusAd	C-225	3S	L	
040101	Fundamentals of acctg	BusAd	C-226	3S	L	
040103	Auditing I	BusAd	C-438	4S	U	
040106	Cost/managerial acctg I	BusAd	C-432	3S	U	
040108	Financial accounting I	BusAd	C-431	4S	U	
040108	Financial accounting II	BusAd	C-433	4S	U	
040108	Financial accounting III	BusAd	C-436	3S	U	
040109	Govern & nonprofit acctg	BusAd	C-533	3S	U	
040114	Tax I	BusAd	C-434	3S	U	
040301	Commer bank prac & policy	BusAd	C-465	3S	U	
040399	Commer & central banking	BusAd	C-301	3S	U	
040710	Prin of risk & insurance	BusAd	C-341	3S	U	
040904	Prin of management	BusAd	C-371	3S	U	
040999	Retailing management	BusAd	C-552	3S	U	
041001	Marketing	BusAd	C-350	3S	U	
041005	Mktg communicatns & strat	BusAd	C-455	3S	U	
041099	Buyer behavior	BusAd	C-351	3S	U	
041303	Intro real est & urb dev	BusAd	C-366	3S	U	
070401	Organ & curr middle sch	Educ	C-451	3S	U	
070509	Health educ elem schools	HlEd	C-331	3S	U	
070512	Lang arts in elem school	Educ	C-507	3S	U	
070515	Science in elem school	Educ	C-515	3S	U	
070516	Basic concepts elem math	Math	C-501	3S	U	
070516	Basic concepts elem math	Math	C-502	3S	U	
070520	Intro to educ psychology	Educ	C-335	3S	U	
070803	Psych of exceptnl child	Psych	C-528	3S	U	
070805	Spec learn disab sch chil	Psych	C-531	3S	U	
090710	Personal & commun health	HlEd	C-221	3S	L	
090999	Women and their bodies	WomSt	J-113	3S	L	VC
100206	Personal finance	BusAd	C-369	3S	U	
100312	Geriatric nutrition	Nrsng	J-524	3S	U	VC
120103	Vocabulary & semantics	Engl	C-452	3S	U	
120201	The short story	Engl	C-435	3S	U	
120205	Studies in literary theor	Engl	C430a	3S	U	
120302	Develop of English lang	Engl	C-453	3S	U	
120307	Composition & literature	Engl	C-102	3S	L	
120307	American literature	Engl	C-287	3S	L	
120307	Chaucer	Engl	C-401	3S	U	
120307	Shakespeare's tragedies	Engl	C-405	3S	U	
120307	Shakespeare's comedies	Engl	C-406	3S	U	
120307	Children's literature	Engl	C-431	3S	U	
120307	Adolescent literature	Engl	C-432	3S	L	
120307	Fiction	Engl	C-282	3S	L	
120307	English literature II	Engl	C-290	3S	L	
120307	English literature I	Engl	C-289	3S	L	
120307	Drama	Engl	C-284	3S	L	
120307	Poetry	Engl	C-286	3S	L	

NCES No.	Course Title	Dept.	Course No.	Cred.	Lev.	Specl. Feat.
120307	Modern American lit	Engl	J-423	3S	U	VC
120310	Composition	Engl	C-101	3S	L	
120310	Writer's workshop	Engl	J-603	3S	U	VC
121000	Intro French	ForLg	C-102	3S	L	AC
121000	Intro French	ForLg	C-101	4S	L	AC
121600	Intro Latin	ForLg	C-101	4S	L	
121600	Intro Latin	ForLg	C-102	3S	L	
122500	Intro Spanish	ForLg	C-101	3S	L	AC
122500	Intro Spanish	ForLg	C-102	3S	L	AC
130202	Survey of commercial law	BusAd	C-324	3S	U	
130202	Commercial law I	BusAd	C-437	3S	U	
130202	Commercial law II	BusAd	C-439	3S	U	
140199	Jump over the moon	LibIn	J-523	3S	U	VC
150100	Descriptive astronomy IA	Astro	C111A	1S	L	
150100	Descriptive astronomy II	Astro	C-112	3S	L	
150100	Descriptive astronomy IIA	Astro	C112A	1S	L	
150100	Descriptive astronomy I	Astro	C-111	3S	L	
150310	Oceans and man	MarSc	C-210	3S	L	
150700	General physics I lab	Phycs	C201L	1S	L	AC
150700	General physics II	Phycs	C-202	3S	L	AC
150700	General physics I	Phycs	C-201	3S	L	AC
160199	Precalculus mathematics	Math	C-115	4S	L	
160199	Intro to elementary math	Math	C-100	3S	L	VC
160302	Basic college mathematics	Math	C-111	3S	L	
160401	Calc for b adm & soc sci	Math	C-122	3S	L	
160701	Finite mathematics	Math	C-170	3S	L	
160803	Elementary statistics	Math	C-201	3S	L	
180499	Hist of modern philosophy	Philo	C-202	3S	L	
180501	Intro to logic I	Philo	C-110	3S	L	
180599	Intro to philosophy	Philo	C-102	3S	L	
190105	Phil & prin of physica ed	PhyEd	C-232	3S	L	
190106	Organ & admin of phy educ	PhyEd	C-553	3S	U	
190110	Measuremnt & eval phy edu	PhyEd	C-545	3S	U	
190311	Foundations of coaching	PhyEd	C-302	3S	U	
190311	Scientific bases for coac	PhyEd	C-303	3S	U	
200104	Intro to psychology	Psych	C-101	3S	L	
200501	Abnormal psychology	Psych	C-410	3S	U	
200504	Abnorm behavior in childn	Psych	C-510	3S	U	
200504	Psych of child developmnt	Psych	C-520	3S	U	
200505	Psychology of adjustment	Psych	C-103	3S	L	
200599	Psychology of marriage	Psych	C-301	3S	U	
200599	Human sexual behavior	Psych	C-300	3S	U	
200599	Psych of adolescence	Psych	C-521	3S	U	
210101	Intro to public admin	GovIS	C-370	3S	U	
210103	Public financial admin	GovIS	C-571	3S	U	
210199	Public personnel managemt	GovIS	C-572	3S	U	
220201	Principles of economics	BusAd	C-221	3S	L	
220201	Principles of economics	BusAd	C-222	3S	L	
220211	Labor economics	BusAd	C-506	3S	U	
220299	Gov policy toward bus	BusAd	C-379	3S	U	
220303	Man's impact on environmt	Geog	C-343	3S	U	
220305	Intro to weather & clim	Geog	C-202	4S	L	
220306	Geog of North America	Geog	C-424	3S	U	
220426	Intro European civilizat	Hist	C-101	3S	L	
220426	Intro European civilizat	Hist	C-102	3S	L	
220426	Cont Europe WWI to WWII	Hist	C-317	3S	U	AC
220426	Europe from WWII to prese	Hist	C-318	3S	U	AC
220428	Hist of SC 1670-1865	Hist	C-341	3S	U	
220428	Hist of SC since 1865	Hist	C-342	3S	U	
220432	Hist of US discov to pres	Hist	C-201	3S	L	
220432	Hist of US discov to pres	Hist	C-202	3S	L	
220432	Civ War & reconstruction	Hist	C-404	3S	U	
220432	Rise of indust America	Hist	C-405	3S	U	
220432	US history since 1945	Hist	C-407	3S	U	
220499	Amer South comes of age	Hist	J-641	3S	U	VC
220501	American national govt	GovIS	C-201	3S	L	
220501	Contem US foreign policy	GovIS	C-341	3S	U	
220504	Comparative politics	GovIS	C-316	3S	U	
220504	Ideology & world politics	GovIS	C-430	3S	U	
220504	US & world prob: perspctv	GovIS	C-101	3S	L	
220504	US & world prob: perspctv	GovIS	C-102	3S	L	
220505	International relations	GovIS	C-315	3S	U	
220599	The Vietnam War	GovIS	J-501	3S	U	VC
220601	Socio of delin youth beha	Socio	C-350	3S	U	
220602	Sociology of crime	Socio	C-353	3S	U	
220606	Introductory sociology	Socio	C-101	3S	L	
220610	Socio of deviant behavior	Socio	C-323	3S	U	
220613	Intro to social problems	Socio	C-340	3S	U	
220699	Sociology of sex roles	Socio	C-301	3S	U	
220699	Sociology of leisure	Socio	C-365	3S	U	

NCES No.	Course Title	Dept.	Course No.	Cred.	Lev.	Specl. Feat.
Noncredit courses						
040306	Personal invest stock mkt	BusAd	C-004	NC		
041303	Fundmntls of real estate	BusAd	C-002	NC		
041304	Prin of real estate mgt	BusAd	C-003	NC		

57 **UNIVERSITY OF SOUTH DAKOTA**

Director, Extended Studies
Independent Study Division
University of South Dakota
414 East Clark
Vermillion, South Dakota 57069
Phone: 605-677-5281

Telecourses are offered. Enrollment on a noncredit basis accepted in credit courses. High school students may enroll in undergraduate courses for credit. Overseas enrollment accepted. Military personnel may enroll through the DANTES program. Minimum period for course completion is three–six weeks. Maximum period for course completion is one year. Students are allowed to submit only four assignments per week.

NCES No.	Course Title	Dept.	Course No.	Cred.	Lev.	Specl. Feat.
High School courses						
030502	Beg drawing and painting	Art	01H	HF	H	LK
040101	Beginning accounting 1	BusEd	23H02	HF	H	
040101	Beginning accounting 2	BusEd	24H02	HF	H	
040207	Beginning typing 1	BusEd	03H02	HF	H	
040207	Beginning typing 2	BusEd	04H02	HF	H	
040207	Advanced typing	BusEd	05H02	HF	H	
049900	General business 1	BusEd	21H02	HF	H	
049900	Business English	BusEd	11H01	HF	H	
070899	Effective methods of stdy	StSkl	01H01	HF	H	
090199	Health science 1	HlSci	01H01	HF	H	
090199	Health science 2	HlSci	02H02	HF	H	
100104	Clothing construction	HomEc	07H02	HF	H	
100604	Personal adjustment	HomEc	11H01	HF	H	
100701	Etiquette	Etiq	01H01	HF	H	
100701	General homemaking 1	HomEc	03H02	HF	H	
100701	General homemaking 2	HomEc	04H02	HF	H	
120299	General literature 1	Engl	05H03	QT	H	
120299	General literature 2	Engl	06H02	QT	H	
120305	Ninth-grade English 1	Engl	31H02	HF	H	
120305	Ninth-grade English 2	Engl	32H02	HF	H	
120307	Tenth-grade English 1	Engl	33H02	HF	H	
120307	Tenth-grade English 2	Engl	34H02	HF	H	
120307	Eleventh-grade English 1	Engl	35H02	HF	H	
120307	Eleventh-grade English 2	Engl	36H02	HF	H	
120307	Twelfth-grade English 1	Engl	37H02	HF	H	
120307	Twelfth-grade English 2	Engl	38H02	HF	H	
120307	The short story	Engl	09H01	HF	H	
120308	Improvemnt of rdg skill 1	Engl	03H01	HF	H	
120310	Composition	Engl	23H02	HF	H	
120399	Basic English	Engl	01H02	HF	H	
121000	Beginning French 1	ForLg	01H02	HF	H	AC
121000	Beginning French 2	ForLg	02H01	HF	H	AC
121000	Second-year French 1	ForLg	03H01	HF	H	AC
121000	Second-year French 2	ForLg	04H01	HF	H	AC
121100	Beginning German 1	ForLg	01H01	HF	H	AC
121100	Beginning German 2	ForLg	02H01	HF	H	AC
121100	Second-year German 1	ForLg	03H01	HF	H	AC
121100	Second-year German 2	ForLg	04H01	HF	H	AC
122500	Beginning Spanish 1	ForLg	01H02	HF	H	AC
122500	Beginning Spanish 2	ForLg	02H02	HF	H	AC
122500	Second-year Spanish 1	ForLg	03H02	HF	H	AC
122500	Second-year Spanish 2	ForLg	04H02	HF	H	AC
150300	Basic biology 1	Sci	07H01	HF	H	
150300	Basic biology 2	Sci	08H01	HF	H	
150899	Physical science 1	Sci	13H01	HF	H	LK
150899	Physical science 2	Sci	14H01	HF	H	LK
160301	General mathematics 1	Math	05H02	HF	H	
160301	General mathematics 2	Math	06H02	HF	H	
160302	Beginning algebra 1	Math	31H03	HF	H	
160302	Beginning algebra 2	Math	32H02	HF	H	
160302	Advanced algebra 1	Math	35H01	HF	H	
160302	Advanced algebra 2	Math	36H01	HF	H	
160399	Basic mathematics 1	Math	01H03	HF	H	
160399	Basic mathematics 2	Math	02H02	HF	H	
160601	Geometry 1	Math	33H03	HF	H	

NCES No.	Course Title	Dept.	Course No.	Cred.	Lev.	Specl. Feat.
160601	Geometry 2	Math	34H02	HF	H	
161201	Bus and consumer math 1	Math	09H01	HF	H	
161201	Bus and consumer math 2	Math	10H01	HF	H	
200101	Psychology	SocSt	07H02	HF	H	
220201	Economics	BusEd	27H01	HF	H	
220299	Economics	SocSt	27H01	HF	H	
220300	World geography 1	SocSt	21H02	HF	H	
220300	World geography 2	SocSt	22H02	HF	H	
220432	American history 2	Hist	34H02	HF	H	
220432	American history 1	Hist	33H02	HF	H	
220433	World history 1	SocSt	31H02	HF	H	
220433	World history 2	SocSt	32H02	HF	H	
220501	American government 1	Socio	35H02	HF	H	
220501	American government 2	Socio	36H02	HF	H	
220612	Sociology	SocSt	03H02	HF	H	
220613	Modern problems	SocSt	37H01	HF	H	
220699	Personal adjustment	SocSt	11H01	HF	H	

College courses

NCES No.	Course Title	Dept.	Course No.	Cred.	Lev.	Specl. Feat.
040101	Principles of acctg 1	Bus	210	3S	L	
040102	Principles of acctg 2	Bus	211	3S	L	
040601	Professional writing	Engl	300	3S	U	
051109	Communication disorders	Commu	131	3S	L	
070302	Geography for elem tchrs	Educ	162	2S	L	
070302	Teaching art in elem sch	Educ	206	4S	L	
070303	Reading dev in content	Educ	452	3S	U	
070404	Bi-cultural teaching meth	Educ	411	3S	U	
070509	Personal health	Educ	100	3S	L	
070509	First aid	Educ	250	2S	L	
070520	Adol growth & development	Educ	422	3S	U	
070613	Safety education	Educ	450	3S	U	
070701	Guidance in elem schools	Educ	415	3S	U	
120305	English grammar	Engl	203	3S	L	
120307	Intro to literature	Engl	163	3S	L	
120307	Intro to British lit	Engl	221	3S	L	
120307	Intro to British lit 2	Engl	222	3S	L	
120307	American literature 1	Engl	241	3S	L	
120307	American literature 2	Engl	242	3S	L	
120307	Masterpieces of lit 1	Engl	211	3S	L	
120307	Masterpieces of lit 2	Engl	212	3S	L	
120307	Classical mythology	Engl	310	2S	U	
120310	Advanced composition	Engl	200	3S	L	
120310	Composition	Engl	101	3S	L	
121000	First-year French 1	Frnch	101	4S	L	AC
121000	First-year French 2	Frnch	102	4S	L	AC
121000	Practical French	Frnch	201	3S	L	
121000	Read Frnch in arts & sci	Frnch	203	3S	L	
121100	German 1	Germn	101	4S	L	AC
121100	German 2	Germn	102	4S	L	AC
121100	Intermediate German 1	Germn	201	3S	L	AC
121100	Intermediate German 2	Germn	202	3S	L	AC
121200	Greek origins in English	Class	103	2S	L	
121600	Latin literature in trans	Class	363	3S	U	
121600	Latin origins in English	Class	102	2S	L	
121600	Latin refresher & rdg 1	Class	201	3S	L	
121600	Latin refresher & rdg 2	Class	202	3S	U	
121600	Vergil: *The Aeneid*	Class	213	3S	L	
121600	Vergil: *The Aeneid*	Class	214	3S	L	
121600	Writing of Latin 1	Class	301	1S	U	
121600	Writing of Latin 2	Class	302	1S	U	
121600	Classical mythology	Class	361	2S	U	
121600	Roman social institutions	Class	341	2S	U	
122500	Intro to Hispanic culture	Span	202	3S	U	
122500	First year Spanish 1	Span	101	4S	L	AC
122500	First year Spanish 2	Span	102	4S	L	AC
122500	Review of Spanish grammar	Span	201	3S	L	
150199	Astronomy	Astro	203	3S	L	
160103	Foundations of math	Math	351	3S	U	
160199	Modern concepts for el ed	Math	341	3S	U	
160203	Finite mathematics	Math	340	3S	U	
160302	College algebra	Math	111	4S	L	VC
160302	Intro to finite math	Math	112	4S	L	
160306	Linear algebra	Math	315	3S	U	
160401	Elem calculus 1	Math	123	4S	L	
160401	Elem calculus 2	Math	224	4S	L	
160401	Elem calculus 3	Math	225	4S	L	
160406	Differential equations	Math	321	3S	U	
160602	Trigonometry	Math	120	2S	L	
160802	Intro to statistics	Math	381	3S	U	
161199	Calc: mngmt life soc sci	Math	222	4S	L	
190501	Intro to alcholism	Alcho	116	3S	L	
190501	Found prvnt & sbstnc abus	Alcho	316	3S	U	

NCES No.	Course Title	Dept.	Course No.	Cred.	Lev.	Specl. Feat.
200103	General psychology	Psych	101	3S	L	
200509	Personal adjustment	Psych	165	3S	L	
210304	Intro to criminal justice	CrJus	201	3S	L	
210304	Intro to crime & delin	CrJus	250	3S	L	
210304	Criminology	CrJus	351	3S	L	
210304	Penology	CrJus	352	3S	L	
210304	Juvenile delinquency	CrJus	451	3S	L	
220101	Greek art & archaeology	Class	331	3S	U	
220101	South Dakota prehistory	Anthr	320	3S	U	
220101	Roman art & archaeology	ArHis	312	3S	U	
220102	Cultural anthropology	Anthr	100	3S	L	
220201	Prin of economics–macro	Bus	201	3S	L	
220201	Prin of economics–micro	Bus	202	3S	L	
220301	World geography	Geog	100	3S	L	
220428	South Dakota govt and pol	PolSc	315	3S	U	
220432	American history 1	Hist	251	3S	L	
220432	American history 2	Hist	252	3S	L	
220433	Western civilization 1	Hist	121	3S	L	
220433	Western civilization 2	Hist	122	3S	L	
220450	Greek art and archaeology	ArHis	311	3S	U	
220450	Roman art and archaeology	ArHis	312	3S	U	
220501	American government	PolSc	100	3S	L	
220602	Intro to crime and delin	Socio	250	3S	L	
220602	Criminology	Socio	351	3S	U	
220602	Penology	Socio	352	3S	U	
220602	Women, crime, & justice	Socio	491	3S	U	
220602	Female crimnls of the wld	Socio	495	3S	U	
220604	Juvenile delinquency	Socio	451	3S	U	
220605	Courtship & marriage	Socio	280	3S	L	
220606	Intro to sociology	Socio	100	3S	L	
220609	Methods of social res	Socio	310	3S	U	
220613	Social problems	Socio	150	3S	L	
220615	Racial & ethnic relations	Socio	350	3S	U	
220699	Field of social work	Socio	200	3S	L	
220699	Social work practice 2	Socio	330	3S	U	
220699	Issues in social work	Socio	401	3S	U	
220699	Advanced social work prac	Socio	485	3S	U	
220699	Sociology of aging	Socio	458	3S	U	

Noncredit courses

NCES No.	Course Title	Dept.	Course No.	Cred.	Lev.	Specl. Feat.
040101	Accounting: 6 components	Acctg		NC		
041303	Real estate 1			NC		V
041303	Real estate 2			NC		V
041309	Real estate 3			NC		V
150100	Backyard astronomy	Astro		NC		
160199	Math review	Math		NC		
200508	Understanding aging	Psych		NC		
220101	Intro archy of South Dak	Archy		NC		

(58) **UNIVERSITY OF SOUTHERN MISSISSIPPI**

Mr. Billy R. Folkes
Assistant Dean and Director of Independent Study
Division of Lifelong Learning
University of Southern Mississippi
Southern Station Box 5056
Hattiesburg, Mississippi 39406-5056
Phone: 601-266-4197

Enrollment on a noncredit basis accepted in credit courses. High school students may enroll in undergraduate courses for credit. Overseas enrollment accepted. Military personnel may enroll through the DANTES program. Minimum period for course completion is one month. Maximum period for course completion is one year. In addition to the courses offered for academic credit, two special noncredit programs are offered: Citizenship Training and the General Education Development (GED) Preparatory Course.

NCES No.	Course Title	Dept.	Course No.	Cred.	Lev.	Specl. Feat.
	High School courses					
040104	Accounting I 1st half	Bus		HF	H	
040104	Accounting I 2nd half	Bus		HF	H	
040205	Shorthand I 1st half	Bus		HF	H	
040205	Shorthand I 2nd half	Bus		HF	H	
040207	Typewriting I 1st half	Bus		HF	H	
040207	Typewriting I 2nd half	Bus		HF	H	
040207	Typewriting II 1st half	Bus		HF	H	
040207	Typewriting II 2nd half	Bus		HF	H	

NCES No.	Course Title	Dept.	Course No.	Cred.	Lev.	Specl. Feat.
040601	Business communications	Bus		HF	H	
049900	Business dynamics 1st hf	Bus		HF	H	
049900	Business dynamics 2nd hf	Bus		HF	H	
050699	Journalism	Journ		HF	H	
100199	Homemaking II 1st half	HomEc		HF	H	
100313	Homemaking I 2nd half	HomEc		HF	H	
100499	Homemaking II 2nd half	HomEc		HF	H	
100601	Child development	HomEc		HF	H	
100602	Family living	HomEc		HF	H	
100699	Homemaking I 1st half	HomEc		HF	H	
120299	English IV 2nd half	Engl		HF	H	
120305	English I 1st half	Engl		HF	H	
120307	English I 2nd half	Engl		HF	H	
120307	English II 1st half	Engl		HF	H	
120307	English II 2nd half	Engl		HF	H	
120307	English III 1st half	Engl		HF	H	
120307	English III 2nd half	Engl		HF	H	
120310	English IV 1st half	Engl		HF	H	
121000	French I 1st half	Frnch		HF	H	AC
121000	French I 2nd half	Frnch		HF	H	AC
121000	French II 1st half	Frnch		HF	H	AC
121000	French II 2nd half	Frnch		HF	H	AC
122500	Spanish I 1st half	Span		HF	H	AC
122500	Spanish I 2nd half	Span		HF	H	AC
122500	Spanish II 1st half	Span		HF	H	AC
122500	Spanish II 2nd half	Span		HF	H	AC
130799	Business law	Bus		HF	H	
150399	Biology 1st half	Bio		HF	H	
150399	Biology 2nd half	Bio		HF	H	
150401	Chemistry 1st half	Chem		HF	H	
150401	Chemistry 2nd half	Chem		HF	H	
150700	Physics 1st half	Phycs		HF	H	
150700	Physics 2nd half	Phycs		HF	H	
159900	General science 1st half	Sci		HF	H	
159900	General science 2nd half	Sci		HF	H	
160299	Fundamental math I 1st hf	Math		HF	H	
160299	Fundamental math I 2nd hf	Math		HF	H	
160299	Fundamentl math II 1st hf	Math		HF	H	
160299	Fundamentl math II 2nd hf	Math		HF	H	
160302	Algebra I 1st half	Math		HF	H	
160302	Algebra I 2nd half	Math		HF	H	
160302	Algebra II 1st half	Math		HF	H	
160302	Algebra II 2nd half	Math		HF	H	
160601	Geometry 1st half	Math		HF	H	
160601	Geometry 2nd half	Math		HF	H	
161201	Business arithmetic	Bus		HF	H	
169900	Mathematics adv 1st half	Math		HF	H	
169900	Mathematics adv 2nd half	Math		HF	H	
220201	Economics	Econ		HF	H	
220399	Geography	Geog		HF	H	
220432	History US 1877-pres 1st	Hist		HF	H	
220432	History US 1877-pres 2nd	Hist		HF	H	
220433	World history 1st half	Hist		HF	H	
220433	World history 2nd half	Hist		HF	H	
220501	Government United States	PolSc		HF	H	
220511	Governmt MS state & local	PolSc		HF	H	
220699	Sociology	Socio		HF	H	

College courses

NCES No.	Course Title	Dept.	Course No.	Cred.	Lev.	Specl. Feat.
040101	Prin of accounting I	Acctg	201	3S	L	
040101	Prin of accounting II	Acctg	202	3S	L	
040199	Personal finance	Finan	220	3S	U	
040604	Business communications	BusEd	300	3S	U	
040999	Managerial communications	GBAdm	375	3S	U	
041001	Principles of marketing	Mktg	300	3S	U	
041199	Principles of management	Mgmt	360	3S	U	
041301	Residential valuation	REIns	334	3S	U	
041303	Real estate principles	REIns	330	3S	U	
041306	Real estate finance	REIns	432	3S	U	
041308	Real estate law	REIns	340	3S	U	
050605	Feature writing	Journ	301	3S	U	
060201	Introduction to computing	CmpSc	100	3S	L	CI
070516	Math for elem teachers II	Math	310	3S	U	
070516	Math teach jr hi sch math	Math	410	3S	U	
070701	Principles of guidance	Re&Fn	336	3S	U	
081000	Engineering drawing I	IVE	323	3S	U	
081000	Engineering drawing II	IVE	324	3S	U	
090305	Neurology	Ther	454	3S	U	
090305	Pathology	Ther	455	3S	U	
100799	Hospitality industry acct	HRA	480	3S	U	
100799	Legal asp hospitality ind	HRA	481	3S	U	
119900	Engineering economics	IntSt	301	3S	U	

NCES No.	Course Title	Dept.	Course No.	Cred.	Lev.	Specl. Feat.
120201	Shakespeare comedy & trag	Engl	454	3S	U	
120299	Literature of the South	Engl	485	3S	U	
120305	Writing I	Engl	101	3S	L	
120307	Writing II	Engl	102	3S	L	
120310	Poetry writing II	Engl	322	3S	U	
120310	Fiction writing II	Engl	321	3S	U	
120310	Fiction writing III	Engl	421	3S	U	
120310	Poetry writing III	Engl	422	3S	U	
121100	Beginning German I	ForLg	121	3S	L	
121100	Beginning German II	ForLg	122	3S	L	
121100	Intermediate German	ForLg	221	3S	L	
121100	Intermediate German	ForLg	222	3S	L	
130799	Legal environment bus	GBAdm	295	3S	L	
150301	Biological science I	PhySc	106	3S	L	
150301	Biological science II	PhySc	107	3S	L	
150399	History of biology	Bio	400	3S	U	
150399	Zoogeography	Bio	406	3S	U	
150599	Physical geology	Geol	101	3S	L	
150599	Historical geology	Geol	103	3S	L	
150899	Physical science I	PhySc	104	3S	L	
150900	Physical science II	PhySc	105	3S	L	
160103	Finite math bus & soc sci	Math	112	3S	L	
160199	Math for elem teachers I	Math	210	3S	L	
160302	College algebra	Math	101	3S	L	
160401	Calculus I & analyt geom	Math	167	3S	L	
160401	Calculus I & analyt geom	Math	168	3S	L	
160401	Calculus III analytc geom	Math	169	4S	L	
160602	Plane trigonometry	Math	103	3S	L	
180303	Ethics	Philo	356	3S	U	
180599	Introduction to logic	Philo	253	3S	U	
180800	Intro to philosophy	Philo	151	3S	L	
181101	Introduction to religion	Relig	131	3S	L	
181202	The life of Jesus	Relig	335	3S	U	
190106	Organ & admin of PE	PhyEd	426	3S	U	
190311	Org & adm of athletics	CSA	303	3S	U	
190311	Adv tech of coach basktbl	CSA	422	3S	U	
190311	Basic fund coach baskball	CSA	321	3S	U	
190502	Community health	HlEd	321	3S	U	
190509	Personal wellness	HlEd	101	3S	L	
190704	Recreation leadership	Rec	323	3S	U	
200199	General psychology	Psych	110	3S	L	
200408	Psy of personal adjust	Psych	231	3S	U	
200599	Child psychology	Psych	370	3S	U	
200599	Adolescent psychology	Psych	372	3S	U	
210304	Traffic law	CrJus	332	3S	U	
220199	Gen or intro anthropology	Anthr	101	3S	L	
220201	Principles of economics I	Econ	255	3S	L	
220201	Principles economics II	Econ	256	3S	L	
220299	Introduction to economics	Econ	200	3S	L	
220300	Introduction to geography	Geog	102	3S	L	
220306	World regional geography	Geog	101	3S	L	
220306	Geography of US & Canada	Geog	401	3S	U	
220432	United States to 1877	Hist	140	3S	L	
220432	United States since 1877	Hist	141	3S	L	
220433	World civ to AD 1648	Hist	101	3S	L	
220433	World civ since AD 1648	Hist	102	3S	L	
220501	American government	PolSc	101	3S	L	
220509	State & local politics	PolSc	301	3S	U	
220510	Introduction to pol sci	PolSc	220	3S	U	
220602	Intro to criminal justice	CrJus	200	3S	L	
220602	Criminology	Socio	341	3S	U	
220605	Marriage & human sex	Hlth	430	3S	U	
220605	The family	Socio	314	3S	U	
220606	Intro to sociology	Socio	101	3S	L	

(59) **UNIVERSITY OF TENNESSEE, KNOXVILLE**

Dr. Kenneth L. Burton
Executive Director
Center for Extended Learning
420 Communications Building
University of Tennessee
Knoxville, Tennessee 37996-0300
Phone: 615-974-5134

Enrollment on a noncredit basis accepted in credit courses. High school students may enroll in undergraduate courses for credit. Overseas enrollment accepted. Military personnel may enroll through the DANTES program. Institution offers special arrangements to take courses not listed in this Catalog. Maximum period for course completion is one year—

eighteen months. The minimum enrollment time varies from course to course.

NCES No.	Course Title	Dept.	Course No.	Cred.	Lev.	Specl. Feat.
	High School courses					
030501	Art: cartooning I	Art	1HS	HF	H	
030501	Art: cartooning II	Art	2HS	HF	H	
040000	General business	Bus	1HS	HF	H	
040000	General business	Bus	2HS	HF	H	
040104	Accounting	Acctg	1HS	HF	H	
040104	Accounting	Acctg	2HS	HF	H	
040200	Office procedures	OfPro	1HS	HF	H	
040203	Recordkeeping	BusEd	1HS	HF	H	
040601	Bus communication 1st sem	BuCom	1HS	HF	H	
040601	Bus communication 2nd sem	BuCom	2HS	HF	H	
050600	Journalism	Journ	1HS	HF	H	
100206	Consumer ed: pers finance	ConEc	1HS	HF	H	
100313	Foods & nutrition	FdNut	1HS	HF	H	
120300	Tenth-grade English	Engl	3HS	HF	H	
120300	Ninth-grade English	Engl	1HS	HF	H	
120300	Ninth-grade English	Engl	2HS	HF	H	
120305	Ninth-grade lang skills	Engl	F-1H	HF	H	
120305	Tenth-grade lang skills	Engl	S-1H	HF	H	
120305	Eleventh-grade lang skill	Engl	J-1H	HF	H	
120305	Twelfth-grade lang skills	Engl	SR-1H	HF	H	
120307	Tenth-grade English: lit	Engl	4HS	HF	H	
120307	Eleventh-gr Eng: Amer lit	Engl	6HS	HF	H	
120307	Twelfth-gr Eng: Brit lit	Engl	8HS	HF	H	AC
120308	Ninth-grade rdg skills	Engl	F-2H	HF	H	
120308	Eleventh-grade rdg skills	Engl	J-2H	HF	H	
120308	Twelfth-grade rdg skills	Engl	SR-2H	HF	H	
120308	Tenth-grade rdg skills	Engl	S-2H	HF	H	
120310	Eleventh-grade English	Engl	5HS	HF	H	
120310	Twelfth-grade English	Engl	7HS	HF	H	
121000	French I 1st sem	Frnch	1HS	HF	H	AC
121000	French I 2nd sem	Frnch	2HS	HF	H	AC
121000	French II 1st sem	Frnch	3HS	HF	H	AC
121000	French II 2nd sem	Frnch	4HS	HF	H	AC
121600	Latin I 1st sem	Latin	1HS	HF	H	
121600	Latin I 2nd sem	Latin	2HS	HF	H	
121600	Latin II 1st sem	Latin	3HS	HF	H	
121600	Latin II 2nd sem	Latin	4HS	HF	H	
122500	Spanish I 1st sem	Span	1HS	HF	H	AC
122500	Spanish I 2nd sem	Span	2HS	HF	H	AC
122500	Spanish II 1st sem	Span	3HS	HF	H	AC
122500	Spanish II 2nd sem	Span	4HS	HF	H	AC
130700	Business law 1st sem	BuLaw	1HS	HF	H	
130700	Business law 2nd sem	BuLaw	2HS	HF	H	
150000	General science 1st sem	Sci	1HS	HF	H	
150000	General science 2nd sem	Sci	2HS	HF	H	
150300	Biology I 1st sem	Bio	1HS	HF	H	
150300	Biology I 2nd sem	Bio	2HS	HF	H	
160301	Arithmetic 1st sem	Math	9HS	HF	H	
160301	Arithmetic 2nd sem	Math	10HS	HF	H	
160302	Algebra I 1st sem	Math	1HS	HF	H	
160302	Algebra I 2nd sem	Math	2HS	HF	H	
160302	Algebra II 1st sem	Math	3HS	HF	H	
160302	Algebra II 2nd sem	Math	4HS	HF	H	
160601	Geometry: plane 1st sem	Math	5HS	HF	H	
160601	Geometry: plane 2nd sem	Math	6HS	HF	H	
160602	Trigonometry	Math	7HS	HF	H	
161201	Business math 1st sem	BusMa	1HS	HF	H	
161201	Business math 2nd sem	BusMa	2HS	HF	H	
190510	Health education 1st sem	Hlth	7HS	HF	H	
190510	Health education 2nd sem	Hlth	8HS	HF	H	
200100	Psychology 1st sem	Psych	1HS	HF	H	
200100	Psychology 2nd sem	Psych	2HS	HF	H	
200100	Psychology: personality	Psych	3HS	HF	H	
220200	Economics 1st sem	Econ	1HS	HF	H	
220200	Economics 2nd sem	Econ	2HS	HF	H	
220300	World geography 1st sem	Geog	1HS	HF	H	
220300	World geography 2nd sem	Geog	2HS	HF	H	
220432	American history 1st sem	Hist	7HS	HF	H	
220432	American history 2nd sem	Hist	8HS	HF	H	
220433	World history 1st sem	Hist	5HS	HF	H	
220433	World history 2nd sem	Hist	6HS	HF	H	
220501	American govrnmnt 1st sem	AmGvt	1HS	HF	H	
220501	American govrnmnt 2nd sem	AmGvt	2HS	HF	H	
220502	Civics 1st sem	Civcs	1HS	HF	H	
220502	Civics 2nd sem	Civcs	2HS	HF	H	

NCES No.	Course Title	Dept.	Course No.	Cred.	Lev.	Specl. Feat.
220600	General sociology	Socio	1HS	HF	H	
220605	Adjust & marriage prep	Socio	2HS	HF	H	
	College courses					
010100	Natural resource economic	AgEco	470K	3S	U	
010900	Intro to forest, wildlife	Fores	211K	3S	L	
040101	Prin of financial account	Acctg	201K	3S	L	
040101	Intermed finan acct 1st s	Acctg	311K	3S	U	
040101	Intermed finan acct 2nd s	Acctg	312K	3S	U	
040101	Cost & managerial acctg	Acctg	321K	3S	U	
040103	Auditing I	Acctg	401M	3S	U	
040111	Prin of manager account	Acctg	202K	3S	L	
040201	Mgt concep, theory & prac	Bus	315C	3S	U	
040201	Personnel management	Bus	332C	3S	U	
070100	Education in the US	Educ	201C	3S	L	
070100	School in society	Educ	200C	1S	L	
070610	Teaching readng: elem sch	Educ	320C	3S	U	
070610	Teaching readng: seco sch	Educ	321C	3S	U	
070610	Diag/prescr teachg readng	Educ	423C	3S	U	
070800	Ed of exceptional childrn	Educ	250C	3S	L	
080901	Circuits I	ElecE	201K	3S	L	
100313	Introductory nutrition	Nutri	100M	3S	L	
100601	Intro early childhood ed	ChFam	110K	3S	L	
120200	Book & matrls for childrn	LibSv	451M	3S	U	
120200	Book & mtrl, adols & adlt	LibSv	452M	3S	U	
120201	World literature	Engl	270M	3S	L	
120302	Hist of Engl language	Engl	420M	3S	U	AC
120305	Intro to English linguist	Engl	320M	3S	U	
120305	Advanced grammar	Engl	425M	3S	U	
120307	Women in literature	Engl	350M	3S	U	
120307	British lit I	Engl	201K	3S	L	
120307	British lit II	Engl	202K	3S	L	
120307	American lit I	Engl	231K	3S	L	
120307	American lit II	Engl	232K	3S	L	
120307	Intro to Shakespeare	Engl	306K	3S	U	
120310	English composition I	Engl	101K	3S	L	
120310	English composition II	Engl	102K	3S	L	
120310	Technical writing	Engl	280M	3S	L	
120399	Medical & scientif vocab	Engl	300M	3S	U	AC
121000	Elementary French	Frnch	111K	3S	L	
121000	Elementary French	Frnch	112K	3S	L	
121000	Intermediate French	Frnch	211K	3S	L	
121000	Intermediate French	Frnch	212K	3S	L	
121000	Aspects of French lit	Frnch	313K	3S	U	
121000	Frnch for grad students	Frnch	301K	3S	U	
121000	Frnch for grad students	Frnch	302K	3S	U	
121000	History of French lit	Frnch	311K	3S	U	
121000	History of French lit	Frnch	312K	3S	U	
121000	Frnch lit of 16th century	Frnch	411K	3S	U	
121000	Frnch lit of 17th century	Frnch	412K	3S	U	
121000	Frnch lit of 18th century	Frnch	413K	3S	U	
121100	Elementary German	Germn	101K	3S	L	AC
121100	Elementary German	Germn	102K	3S	L	AC
122500	Elementary Spanish	Span	111K	3S	L	AC
122500	Elementary Spanish	Span	112K	3S	L	AC
122500	Intermediate Spanish	Span	211K	3S	L	AC
122500	Intermediate Spanish	Span	212K	3S	L	AC
150401	Chemistry & environment	Chem	111C	3S	L	
150500	Elmnts of geol: physical	Geol	111M	4S	U	LK
150500	Elmnts of geol: historic	Geol	112M	4S	U	LK
160302	Algebraic reasoning	Math	110K	3S	L	
160306	Matrix computations	Math	200K	1S	L	
160401	Calculus A	Math	121K	3S	L	
160401	Calculus B	Math	122K	3S	L	
160401	Calculus I	Math	141K	4S	L	
160401	Calculus II	Math	142K	4S	L	
160401	Calculus III	Math	241K	4S	L	
160406	Differential equations I	Math	231K	3S	L	
161108	Statistics in psychology	Psych	385K	3S	U	
161109	Elem social statistics	Socio	336K	3S	U	
180303	Medical ethics	Philo	345K	3S	U	
180902	Images of Jesus	Relig	326K	3S	U	
181103	Medical ethics	Relig	345K	3S	U	
190502	Death, dying & bereavemnt	Hlth	406K	3S	U	
190503	Consumer health	Hlth	400K	3S	U	
190509	Personal health & wellnss	Hlth	110K	3S	L	
190509	Personal health	Hlth	100C	3S	L	
190511	General safety	Sfty	452K	3S	U	
190512	Human sexuality	ChFam	240K	3S	L	
200100	General psychology	Psych	110K	3S	L	
200200	Biologic basis of behavr	Psych	210K	3S	L	
200500	Behav & experience: human	Psych	220K	3S	L	

NCES No.	Course Title	Dept.	Course No.	Cred.	Lev.	Specl. Feat.
200501	Abnormal psychology	Psych	330K	3S	U	
200504	Child psychology	Psych	300K	3S	U	
200700	Social psychology	Psych	360K	3S	U	
200804	Human grth & devel—child	Educ	203C	3S	L	
200804	Humn grth & devel—adoles	Educ	204C	3S	L	
210304	Phil & ethical issues	CrJus	430C	3S	U	
210304	Criminal justice	CrJus	451K	3S	U	
220100	Human origins	Anthr	110K	3S	L	
220102	Cultural anthropology	Anthr	130K	3S	L	
220201	Princ of econ: microecon	Econ	102C	3S	L	
220201	Intermed macroecon theory	Econ	325C	3S	U	
220201	Princ of econ: macroecon	Econ	101C	3S	L	
220204	Money and banking	Econ	301C	3S	U	
220300	World geography 1st sem	Geog	101K	3S	L	
220300	World geography 2nd sem	Geog	102K	3S	L	
220400	Dev of Western civilizatn	Hist	151K	3S	L	
220400	Dev of Western civilizatn	Hist	152K	3S	L	
220428	History of Tennessee	Hist	449K	3S	U	
220432	History of United States	Hist	251K	3S	L	
220432	History of United States	Hist	251K	3S	L	
220501	US gov & politics	PolSc	101K	3S	L	
220505	International relations 1	PolSc	321M	3S	U	
220505	International relations 2	PolSc	322M	3S	U	
220600	General sociology	Socio	100K	3S	L	
220602	Criminology	Socio	350K	3S	U	
220603	Collect behav & soc movmn	Socio	345K	3S	U	
220603	Sociology of aging	Socio	415K	3S	U	
220604	Juvenile delinquency	Socio	351K	3S	U	
220605	Marriage & family relatns	Socio	208M	3S	L	
220607	Social psychology	Socio	370K	3S	U	
220611	Formal organization	Socio	413K	3S	U	
220613	Social probs & soc chnge	Socio	110K	3S	L	
220614	The city	Socio	363K	3S	U	VC
220614	Urban ecology	Socio	464K	3S	U	
220699	Sociological research	Socio	331K	3S	U	

NCES No.	Course Title	Dept.	Course No.	Cred.	Lev.	Specl. Feat.
	Noncredit courses					
030501	Cartooning I: basic		1	NC		
030501	Cartooning II: advanced		2	NC		
030501	Intr to pencil drawing			NC		
041300	Real estate office mangmt	RIEst		NC	V	
041301	Real estate appraisal	RIEst		NC	V	
061101	Computers			NC		
090404	Tennessee pharmacy laws	Pharm	333	NC	V	
090411	Patnt medcatn prof/phrmct	Pharm	342	NC	V	
090411	Patnt medcatn recrd/nurse	Pharm	343	NC	V	
090411	Geriatric patient care	Pharm	400	NC	U	
090411	Geriatric patient care	Pharm	401	NC	U	
090411	Geriatric patient care	Pharm	402	NC	U	
090411	Geriatric patient care	Pharm	403	NC	U	
090411	Locating a practice	Pharm	404	NC	U	
090411	Prescription pricing syst	Pharm	405	NC	U	
090411	Effective inventry contrl	Pharm	406	NC	U	
090411	Financial planning	Pharm	407	NC	U	
090411	Marketing community pharm	Pharm	408	NC	U	
090411	Home totl parenteral nutr	Pharm	409	NC	V	
090411	Community pharm security	Pharm	410	NC	U	
090411	Automated pharmacy system	Pharm	411	NC	U	
090411	Hospice pharmacy services	Pharm	412	NC	U	
090411	Improv pharm communictns	Pharm	413	NC	U	
100603	Intro to gerontology			NC	V	
100604	Project self-discovery			NC		
120308	How to study			NC		
120310	How to write almost anyth			NC		
120310	Creative writng: articles		1	NC		
120310	Creative writng: stories		2	NC		
120310	Creative writng: poetry		3	NC		
121200	Greek		1	NC		
121200	Greek		2	NC		
121200	Greek		3	NC		
160302	Refresher algebra			NC		
160602	Trigonometry			NC		
161200	Everyday mathematics			NC		
181202	Bible: What does Bble say	Relig	1	NC		
181202	Bible: mighty acts of God	Relig	2	NC		
181202	Bible: What's right	Relig	3	NC		
181202	Bible: New Testament	Relig	4	NC		
181202	Bible: Old Testament	Relig	5	NC		
181202	Bible:What's relig livng?	Relig	6	NC		
181202	Bible: Protestnt denomins	Relig	10	NC		

60 **UNIVERSITY OF TEXAS AT AUSTIN**

Ms. Kathryn R. Allen
Director, Extension Instruction and Materials Center
University of Texas at Austin
P.O. Box 7700
Austin, Texas 78713-7700
Phone: 512-471-5616

Credit by examination is available. High school students may enroll in undergraduate courses for credit. Overseas enrollment accepted. Minimum period for course completion is forty-five days. Maximum period for course completion is nine months.

NCES No.	Course Title	Dept.	Course No.	Cred.	Lev.	Specl. Feat.
	High School courses					
040104	Accounting 1st sem	Acctg		HF	H	
040104	Accounting 2nd sem	Acctg		HF	H	
049900	Personal business mgt	PBM	PBMgt	HF	H	
120302	Junior lit English IIIB	Engl	Eng3B	HF	H	
120305	Senr grammar-comp Eng IVA	Engl	Eng4A	HF	H	
120307	Freshman literature IB	Engl	Eng1B	HF	H	
120307	Sophomore literature IIB	Engl	Eng2B	HF	H	
120307	Junior literature IIIA	Engl	Eng3A	HF	H	
120307	Senior literature IVB	Engl	Eng4B	HF	H	
120307	Lit genre-Arthur legend	Engl	Lit6R	HF	H	
120310	Freshman grammar-comp IA	Engl	EnglA	HF	H	
120310	Soph grammar-comp IIA	Engl	Eng2A	HF	H	
120310	English IV academic comp	Engl		HF	H	
120310	Correlated lang arts IIA	CorLa	CLA2A	HF	H	CI
120310	Correlated lang arts IIB	CorLa	CLA2B	HF	H	CI
120310	Correlated lang arts IIIA	CorLa	CLA3A	HF	H	CI
120310	Correlated lang arts IIIB	CorLa	CLA3B	HF	H	CI
121100	German I 1st sem	Germn	Ger1A	HF	H	AC
121100	German I 2nd sem	Germn	Ger1B	HF	H	AC
121100	German II 1st sem	Germn	Ger2A	HF	H	AC
121100	German II 2nd sem	Germn	Ger2B	HF	H	AC
130799	Business and consumer law	BuLaw		HF	H	
150300	Biology I 1st sem	Bio	Bio1A	HF	H	CI
150300	Biology I 2nd sem	Bio	Bio1B	HF	H	CI
150800	Physical science 1st sem	PhySc	PhS1A	HF	H	LK
150800	Physical science 2nd sem	PhySc	PhS1B	HF	H	LK
160301	Fund of math 1st sem	FOM	FOM1A	HF	H	CI
160301	Fund of math 2nd sem	FOM	FOM1B	HF	H	CI
160302	Algebra I 1st sem	Algbr	Alg1A	HF	H	CI
160302	Algebra I 2nd sem	Algbr	Alg1B	HF	H	CI
160302	Algebra II 1st sem	Algbr	Alg2A	HF	H	
160302	Algebra II 2nd sem	Algbr	Alg2B	HF	H	
160302	Pre-algebra, 1st sem	Math	PALA	HF	H	CI
160302	Pre-algebra, 2nd sem	Math	PALB	HF	H	CI
160402	Elementary analysis	Math	ElAn1	HF	H	
160601	Geometry 1st sem	Geom	Geo1A	HF	H	
160601	Geometry 2nd sem	Geom	Geo1B	HF	H	
160602	Trigonometry one semester	Trig	Trig	HF	H	
161202	Math of cons econ 2nd sem	MCE	MCEB	HF	H	
161202	Math of cons econ 1st sem	MCE	MCEA	HF	H	
161202	Consumer math A	Math	ConMA	HF	H	CI
161202	Consumer math B	Math	ConMB	HF	H	CI
190312	Physical educ I 1st sem	PhyEd	PE1A	HF	H	
190312	Physical educ I 2nd sem	PhyEd	PE1B	HF	H	
190509	Health education I	HlEd	HlEd	HF	H	
220200	Economics	Econ	Econ	HF	H	CI
220301	Wld geog studies 1st sem	WGS	WGSA	HF	H	
220301	Wld geog studies 2nd sem	WGS	WGSB	HF	H	
220432	US history 1st sem	USHis	USHA	HF	H	CI
220432	US history 2nd sem	USHis	USHB	HF	H	
220433	Wld hist studies 1st sem	WHS	WHSA	HF	H	
220433	Wld hist studies 2nd sem	WHS	WHSB	HF	H	
220501	US government	USGov	USGov	HF	H	
220501	Basic US government	USGov	USGov	HF	H	
	College courses					
040604	Bus rpt wrtng behav comm	BuCom	324	3S	U	
040903	Organizational behav admn	Mgmt	336	3S	U	CI
040999	Operations management	Mgmt	335	3S	U	
070199	Psych foundations of educ	EdPsy	332	3S	U	CI
070309	Hum lrn dev: adult years	Culns	371.3	3S	U	
070516	Modern topics elem math I	Math	316K	3S	L	
070516	Modern topics el math II	Math	316L	3S	L	
070516	Struc modern geometry	Math	333L	3S	U	
070899	Orietatn to teachng sp ed	SplEd	101	1S	L	

NCES No.	Course Title	Dept.	Course No.	Cred.	Lev.	Spec. Feat.
070899	Survey of exceptnalities	SplEd	371	3S	U	
100313	Introductory nutrition	HomEc	311	3S	L	CI
120307	Shakespeare: selected ply	Engl	321	3S	U	
120307	American lit 1865 to pres	Engl	338	3S	U	
120307	Intro to lit II black lit	Engl	314L	3S	L	
120307	Mstrwks of lit: British	Engl	316K	3S	L	
120307	Amer lit: begin to 1865	Engl	337	3S	U	CI
120307	Modern short story	Engl	348	3S	U	CI
120307	Masterwks lit: American	Engl	316KA	3S	L	
120310	Rhetoric and composition	Engl	306	3S	L	CI
120310	Literature & composition	Engl	309K	3S	L	
120310	Technical writing	Engl	317	3S	L	
120310	Creative writing	Engl	325	3S	U	
121000	First-year French I	Frnch	506	5S	L	AC
121000	First-year French II	Frnch	507	5S	L	AC
121000	Second-year French I	Frnch	312K	3S	L	AC
121000	Second-year French II	Frnch	312L	3S	L	AC
121100	First-year German I	Germn	506	5S	L	AC
121100	First-year German II	Germn	507	5S	L	AC
121100	Second-year German I	Germn	312K	3S	L	AC
121100	Second-year German II	Germn	312L	3S	L	AC
121200	First-year Greek I	Greek	506	5S	L	
121200	Greek poetry and prose	Greek	312	3S	L	
121200	New Testmnt Gk: The Gospe	Greek	319	3S	L	
121200	Nw Tst Gk: Gsp/Acts/Pl/Ep	Greek	328	3S	U	
121200	First-year Greek II	Greek	507	5S	L	
121600	First-year Latin I	Latin	506	5S	L	
121600	First-year Latin II	Latin	507	5S	L	
121600	Virgil's *Aeneid*	Latin	312K	3S	L	
122200	First-year Czech I	Slav	506	5S	L	AC
122200	First-year Czech II	Slav	507	4S	L	AC
122500	First-year Spanish I	Span	506	5S	L	AC
122500	First-year Spanish II	Span	507	5S	L	AC
122500	Second-year Spanish I	Span	312K	3S	L	AC
122500	Second-year Spanish II	Span	312L	3S	L	
122500	Advanced composition	Span	327	3S	U	
140803	Museum education	ArtEd	376	3S	U	
150103	Introductory astronomy	Astro	302	3S	L	
150302	Cellular & molecular biol	Bio	302	3S	L	
150303	Structure-fnctn organisms	Bio	303	3S	L	
150307	Hered, evol, and society	Zoolg	317	3S	L	
150803	Mechanics	Phycs	301	3S	L	
150899	Gen phys mech heat sound	Phycs	302K	3S	L	
150899	Gen phys elec mag lt nuc	Phycs	302L	3S	L	
150899	Elem phys nontech mech ht	Phycs	609A	3S	L	
150899	Elem phys nontech elec mg	Phycs	609B	3S	L	
160302	College algebra	Math	301	3S	L	CI
160303	First crs theory numbers	Math	328K	3S	U	
160401	Calculus I	Math	808A	4S	L	
160401	Calculus II	Math	808B	4S	L	
160401	Calculus I for bus/econ	Math	403K	4S	L	
160401	Calculus II for bus/econ	Math	403L	4S	L	
160602	Trigonometry	Math	304E	3S	L	
160603	Analytic geometry	Math	305E	3S	L	
160699	Elem fnctns coord geom	Math	305G	3S	L	
161299	Mathematics of investment	Math	303F	3S	L	
180501	Introduction to logic	Philo	312	3S	L	
190512	Human sexuality	HlEd	HE366	3S	U	
200104	Intro to psychology	Psych	301	3S	L	
200403	Stat methds in psychology	Psych	317	3S	L	
200501	Abnormal psychology	Psych	352	3S	U	
200599	Intro child psychology	Psych	304	3S	L	
220102	Cultural anthropology	Anthr	302	3S	L	
220106	Physical anthropology	Anthr	301	3S	L	
220106	Human evolution	Anthr	348	3S	U	
220201	Intro to macroeconomics	Econ	302	3S	L	
220201	Intro to microeconomics	Econ	303	3S	L	
220212	Elem econ of Third World	Econ	316	3S	L	
220301	World of man: intro geog	Geog	305	3S	L	
220424	English civ before 1603	Hist	304K	3S	L	
220424	English civ since 1603	Hist	304L	3S	L	
220432	The US 1492-1865	Hist	315K	3S	L	
220432	The US since 1865	Hist	315L	3S	L	
220452	Westrn civ in med times	Hist	309K	3S	L	
220453	Westrn civ in mdrn times	Hist	309L	3S	L	
220501	American government	Govt	610A	3S	L	
220501	American government	Govt	610B	3S	L	
220504	Intl politics snce 2nd WW	Govt	323M	3S	U	
220505	American foreign relatns	Govt	344	3S	U	
220511	Texas government	Govt	105	1S	L	
220606	Intro to stdy of sociolgy	Socio	302	3S	L	CI
220615	Racial and ethnic rltns	Socio	344	3S	U	
220699	Sex roles	Socio	333K	3S	U	
220699	Nuclear threat	Socio	321K	3S	U	CI

(61) UNIVERSITY OF UTAH

Thomas Kearin
Assistant Dean, Center for Independent Study
Division of Continuing Education Extension Program
1152 Annex Building
University of Utah
Salt Lake City, Utah 84112
Phone: 801-581-6485

Telecourses are offered. Enrollment on a noncredit basis accepted in credit courses. Overseas enrollment accepted. Military personnel may enroll through the DANTES program. Institution offers special arrangements to take courses not listed in this Catalog. Minimum period for course completion is one week per credit hour. Maximum period for course completion is one year.

NCES No.	Course Title	Dept.	Course No.	Cred.	Lev.	Spec. Feat.
	College courses					
030302	Poetry, prose & music	Music	511	3Q	U	
030302	The elements of music	Music	200	3Q	L	
030303	Music fund for elem tchrs	Music	159	2Q	L	
030303	Music ed in elem school	Music	371	3Q	U	
030502	Intro to the visual arts	Art	100	5Q	L	
040101	Elementary accounting	Acctg	221	3Q	L	
040101	Elementary accounting	Acctg	222	3Q	L	
040111	Management accounting	Acctg	350	3Q	U	
040114	Federal tax accounting	Acctg	509	4Q	U	
040114	Federal tax accounting	Acctg	510	4Q	U	
040301	Business finance	Finan	303	4Q	U	
040302	Personal finance	Finan	120	4Q	L	
040306	Investment principles	Finan	336	4Q	U	
040308	Money and banking	Econ	320	3Q	U	
040601	Bus comm & research des	Mgmt	518	4Q	U	
040708	Risk and insurance	Finan	324	4Q	U	
041001	Principles of marketing	Mktg	301	4Q	U	
050103	Principles of advertising	Mktg	350	4Q	U	
050601	The editing process	Commu	301	4Q	U	
050605	Magazine article writing	Commu	451	3Q	U	
051202	Sign language	RecLe	385	3Q	U	VC
070401	Kindergarten/early ch ed	Educ	520	3Q	U	
070404	Storytelling in elem sch	Educ	102	3Q	L	
070404	Tching science in el sch	Educ	449	3Q	U	
070404	Social studies in el sch	Educ	450	3Q	U	
070404	Creative tchg of art elsc	Educ	581-1	3Q	U	
070404	Mathematics in el school	Educ	408	3Q	U	
070404	Language arts in el sch	Educ	430	3Q	U	
070404	Reading as develop prcess	Educ	420	4Q	U	
070404	Tching reading early chil	Educ	421	5Q	U	
070404	Tching reading inter grds	Educ	422	5Q	U	
070404	Tching reading content ar	Educ	558	4Q	U	
070404	Child dev curriculm chge	Educ	624	3Q	U	
070404	Tching reading secon schs	Educ	423	5Q	U	
070404	Gen secondary tching meth	Educ	575	3Q	U	
070404	Art for secondary schs	Art	491	3Q	U	
070404	Math for elementary tchrs	Math	405	4Q	U	
070404	The use of books & librs	EduM	102	2Q	L	
070404	Methods/skills arts/craft	RecLe	320	3Q	U	
070404	Child literature in sch	Educ	440	3Q	U	
070599	Behavior prob in school	Educ	646	3Q	U	
070613	Intro to driver education	HlEd	350	3Q	U	
070613	Organ and admin driver ed	HlEd	351	3Q	U	
070613	Driver ed: internship	HlEd	692	CV	U	
070613	Driver education invd std	HlEd	392	CV	U	
070801	Found of human excptnalty	SplEd	301	3Q	U	
071203	Intro to instruction tech	EduM	561	3Q	U	
071203	Intro to instruction tech	EduM	561	5Q	U	
071203	Prin of graphic communica	EduM	562	4Q	U	
071204	Mgt comput/lrn res center	EduM	565	3Q	U	
071299	Eval and sel of ed media	EduM	503	3Q	U	
081001	Engineering drawing	CivlE	101	2Q	L	
082199	Elements of metallurgy	MetEn	361	3Q	U	
090403	Alcohol and drugs	HlEd	548	3Q	U	
090499	Common medicines	Pharm	370	3Q	U	
090901	Personal health problems	HlEd	101	3Q	U	
090901	School health program	HlEd	312	3Q	U	

NCES No.	Course Title	Dept.	Course No.	Cred.	Lev.	Specl. Feat.
100312	Fundmntls of nutrition	FdNut	144	3Q	U	
120299	Amer lit 1900-1945	Engl	519	5Q	U	
120299	Amer lit since 1945	Engl	520	4Q	U	
120299	Shakespeare: early plays	Engl	540	5Q	U	
120299	American folklore	Engl	573	5Q	U	
120310	Intro to college writing	Writ	101	4Q	L	
122500	Beginning Spanish	Span	101	5Q	L	
129900	First-year Persian	Persi	101	5Q	L	
129900	First-year Persian	Persi	102	5Q	L	
130799	Business law	Mgmt	341	4Q	U	
140199	Cataloging and classifica	EduM	564	4Q	U	
140804	Reference work	EduM	351	4Q	U	
140899	Selection of lib material	EduM	563	4Q	U	
140900	Library work with child	EduM	326	5Q	U	
150199	Popular astronomy	Phycs	106	4Q	L	
150202	Intro to meteorology	Meteo	101	4Q	L	
150300	General biology	Bio	101	5Q	L	
150304	Human ecology	Bio	175	3Q	L	
150307	Human genetics	Bio	335	4Q	U	
150399	Human physiology	Bio	201	5Q	L	
150799	Elementary physics	Phycs	101	5Q	L	
150799	General mechanics sound	Phycs	111	4Q	L	
150799	General heat elec magneti	Phycs	112	4Q	L	
150799	General light modern phy	Phycs	113	4Q	L	
150799	Scien & eng: mechanics	Phycs	171	4Q	L	
150799	Scien & eng: elec magneti	Phycs	172	4Q	L	
150799	Scien & eng: heat/lght/sd	Phycs	173	4Q	L	
150799	Science and soc futurism	Phycs	100	3Q	L	
160302	Intermediate algebra	Math	101	5Q	L	
160302	College algebra	Math	105	5Q	L	
160401	Calculus I	Math	111	4Q	L	
160401	Calculus I	Math	112	4Q	L	
160401	Calculus I	Math	113	4Q	L	
160602	Plane trigonometry	Math	106	5Q	L	
160803	Elementary statistics	Math	107	4Q	L	
190199	Intro to physical educ	ESS	250	2Q	U	
190203	Medical aspects	ESS	283	2Q	L	
190306	Sport psychology	ESS	278	2Q	L	
190511	Home school commun safety	HlEd	304	3Q	U	
190512	Human sexuality	HlSci	300	3Q	U	
190704	The recreation program	RecLe	332	5Q	U	
190709	Outdoor recreation	RecLe	350	3Q	U	
190799	Rec & leisure in mod soc	RecLe	192	5Q	L	
200199	Psychology	Psych	101	5Q	L	
200501	Psych of abnormal behav	Psych	340	4Q	U	
200503	Survey of clinical psych	Psych	332	3Q	U	
200599	Psychology of adolescence	Psych	123	3Q	U	
200603	Elementary statistics	Psych	150	4Q	L	
200799	Social psychology	Psych	341	4Q	U	
220101	Archaeology of Southwest	Anthr	381-3	3Q	U	
220102	Intro to cultural anthro	Anthr	101	5Q	L	
220106	Intro to physical anthro	Anthr	102	5Q	L	
220109	Civiliz of the Aztecs	Anthr	381-1	5Q	U	
220109	Indians of North America	Anthr	302	5Q	U	
220109	Civilization of the Maya	Anthr	381-2	5Q	U	
220201	Economics as social sci	Econ	105	5Q	L	
220202	Economic history of US	Econ	274	4Q	L	
220211	Labor economics	Econ	310	4Q	U	
220301	World cultural geography	Geog	160	5Q	L	
220306	Geography of Utah	Geog	360	5Q	U	
220428	History of Utah	Hist	466	5Q	U	
220432	American civilization	Hist	170	5Q	L	
220450	Hist of civilizat: ancien	Hist	101	5Q	L	
220450	Ancient Greece	Hist	201	4Q	L	
220450	Ancient Rome	Hist	202	4Q	L	
220501	American national govt	PolSc	110	5Q	L	
220505	Intro to intl politics	PolSc	210	5Q	L	
220599	Intro to political sci	PolSc	101	5Q	L	
220606	Intro to sociology	Socio	101	5Q	L	

NCES No.	**Noncredit courses** Course Title	Dept.	Course No.	Cred.	Lev.	Specl. Feat.
040104	Simplified accounting	Acctg	5R	NC		V
040999	Effective writing in bus	Mgmt	7R	NC		V
040999	Retail management	Mgmt	79R	NC		V
041303	Real estate principles	Finan	24	NC		V
071299	Church & synagogue libr	EduM	10R-1	NC		V
160302	Preparatory algebra	Math	50	NC	L	
220502	Naturalization			NC		V

(62) **UNIVERSITY OF WASHINGTON**

Dr. Harry L. Norman
Department Head, Distance Learning
University Extension
University of Washington
5001 25th, NE, GH 23
Seattle, Washington 98195
Phone: 206-543-2350

Enrollment on a noncredit basis accepted in credit courses. High school students may enroll in undergraduate courses for credit. Overseas enrollment accepted. Military personnel may enroll through the DANTES program. Institution offers special arrangements to take courses not listed in this Catalog. Minimum period for course completion is two months. Maximum period for course completion is one year.

NCES No.	Course Title	Dept.	Course No.	Cred.	Lev.	Specl. Feat.
	College courses					
010901	Interp the environment	ForMg	C383	5Q	U	
040601	Basic writ bus commu	BuCom	C305	4Q	U	
040800	Interntnl enviro business	IntBu	C300	3Q	U	
041001	Marketing concepts	Mktg	C301	4Q	U	
041005	Advertising	Mktg	C340	4Q	U	
051201	Beginning Braille	Rehab	C496	3Q	U	
070512	Language learning	Engl	C442	5Q	U	
071103	Basic educ statistics	EdPsy	C490	3Q	U	
081104	Engineering statics	Engin	C210	4Q	L	
090242	Biolog aspects of aging	UConj	C440	3Q	U	SL
090305	Pub sch phys therapy	Rehab	C413b	3Q	U	
090305	Pub sch phys therapy	Rehab	C413c	5Q	U	
100601	Normal devel & atypic inf	Psych	C498	3Q	U	
120103	Intro to linguistic thght	Ling	C200	5Q	L	
120307	Chldrn's lit reconsidered	Engl	C223	5Q	L	AC
120307	Late Renaissance	Engl	C321	5Q	U	
120307	Milton	Engl	C322	5Q	U	
120307	Amer lit: early nation	Engl	C352	5Q	U	
120307	Amer lit: later 19th cent	Engl	C353	5Q	U	
120307	Amer lit: early modern	Engl	C354	5Q	U	
120307	Amer lit: contemp America	Engl	C355	5Q	U	
120307	Shakespeare: survey	Engl	C231	5Q	L	
120307	Shakespeare to 1603	Engl	C314	5Q	U	
120307	Shakespeare after 1603	Engl	C315	5Q	U	
120307	Reading literature	Engl	C200	5Q	L	
120307	The contemporary novel	Engl	C359	5Q	U	
120307	The modern novel	Engl	C340	5Q	U	
120307	Fantasy	Engl	C370	5Q	U	
120307	The Bible as literature	Engl	C309	5Q	U	
120307	Studies in autobiog lit	Engl	C489A	5Q	U	
120307	English novel	Engl	C333	5Q	U	
120310	Beginning verse writing	Engl	C274	5Q	L	
120310	Intermediate verse writng	Engl	C386	5Q	L	
120310	Advanced verse writing	Engl	C422	5Q	U	
120310	Begin short story writing	Engl	C277	5Q	L	
120310	Inter expository writing	Engl	C271	5Q	L	
120310	Advan expository writing	Engl	C379	5Q	U	
120310	Inter short story writing	Engl	C386	5Q	U	
120399	Technical writing	Engin	C331	3Q	U	
120800	Elem Danish	Dan	C101	5Q	L	AC
120800	Elem Danish	Dan	C102	5Q	L	AC
120800	Elem Danish	Dan	C103	5Q	L	AC
121000	Elem French	Frnch	C111	5Q	L	AC
121000	Elem French	Frnch	C112	5Q	L	AC
121000	Elem French	Frnch	C113	5Q	L	AC
121000	Elem French reading	Frnch	C105	5Q	L	
121100	First-year German	Germn	C111	5Q	L	AC
121100	First-year German	Germn	C112	5Q	L	AC
121100	First-year German	Germn	C113	5Q	L	AC
121100	Readings in German lit	Germn	C203	3Q	L	
121100	Basic 2nd-year German	Germn	C201	5Q	L	AC
121100	Inter 2nd-year German	Germn	C202	5Q	L	AC
121300	Biblical Hebrew	Hebr	C400	3Q	U	
121400	Elem Italian	Ital	C111	5Q	L	AC
121400	Elem Italian	Ital	C112	5Q	L	AC
121400	Elem Italian	Ital	C113	5Q	L	AC
121800	Elem Norwegian	Norw	C101	5Q	L	AC
121800	Norwegian contemp novel	Norw	C300	3Q	U	
121800	Elem Norwegian	Norw	C102	5Q	L	AC
121800	Elem Norwegian	Norw	C103	5Q	L	AC
122000	First-year Russian	Rus	C103	5Q	L	AC
122000	First-year Russian	Rus	C101	5Q	L	AC
122000	First-year Russian	Rus	C102	5Q	L	AC

NCES No.	Course Title	Dept.	Course No.	Cred.	Lev.	Specl. Feat.
122500	Cultural bkground lit	Span	C461	5Q	U	
122500	Elem Spanish	Span	C111	5Q	L	AC
122500	Basic grammar review	Span	C122	5Q	L	
122500	Elem Spanish	Span	C112	5Q	L	AC
122500	Elem Spanish	Span	C113	5Q	L	AC
122500	Inter Spanish	Span	C211	5Q	L	AC
122500	Inter Spanish	Span	C212	5Q	L	AC
122500	Advan syntax and comp	Span	C301	5Q	U	
122500	Advan syntax and comp	Span	C302	5Q	U	
122600	Elem Swedish	Swed	C101	5Q	L	AC
122600	Elem Swedish	Swed	C102	5Q	L	AC
122600	Elem Swedish	Swed	C103	5Q	L	AC
130199	Intro to law	OE	C200	5Q	L	
130899	Women and the law	WomSt	C310	5Q	U	
150101	Astronomy	Astro	C101	5Q	L	
150102	The planets	Astro	C150	5Q	L	
150201	Weather	AtmSc	C101	5Q	L	LK
150306	The universe & orig life	Astro	C201	5Q	L	
150401	Chemical science	Chem	C100	5Q	L	
150401	General chemistry	Chem	C140	4Q	L	
150401	General chemistry	Chem	C150	4Q	L	
150600	Survey of oceanography	Ocean	C101	5Q	L	
160306	Elem linear algebra	Math	C205	5Q	L	
160403	Calculus with analyt geom	Math	C124	5Q	L	
160405	Appl of calculus to busin	Math	C157	5Q	L	
160406	Calculus with analyt geom	Math	C125	5Q	L	
160407	Calculus with analyt geom	Math	C126	5Q	L	
160408	Elem diff equations	Math	C238	3Q	L	
160507	Elementary functions	Math	C105	5Q	L	
160802	Basic statistics	Stat	C220	5Q	L	
160802	Basic statistics wth appl	Stat	C301	5Q	U	
160802	Elements of stat methods	Stat	C311	5Q	U	
161101	Appl of algebra to busin	Math	C156	5Q	L	
161299	Math for elem schl tchrs	Math	C170	3Q	L	
180202	Hist intro to philo sci	Philo	C160	5Q	L	
180502	Introduction to logic	Philo	C120	5Q	L	
180700	Phil issues in the law	Philo	C114	5Q	L	
181002	Intro to world religions	Relig	C202	5Q	L	
200501	Deviant personality	Psych	C305	5Q	U	
200504	Normal devel & atypic inf	Psych	C498	3Q	U	
200509	Intro to pers and ind dif	Psych	C205	4Q	L	
200699	Elem psychological stat	Psych	C213	6Q	L	
200702	Social psychology	Psych	C345	5Q	U	
200799	Psych as a social science	Psych	C101	5Q	L	
210501	Adv park & rec mgmt	ForMg	C484	3Q	U	
220102	Intro to anthropology	Anthr	C100	5Q	L	
220107	Principles social anthro	Anthr	C202	5Q	L	
220201	Intro to microeconomics	Econ	C200	5Q	L	
220201	Inter price theory	Econ	C300	5Q	U	
220213	Intro to macroeconomics	Econ	C201	5Q	L	
220302	Economic geography	Geog	C207	5Q	L	
220306	World regions	Geog	C102	5Q	L	
220308	Geography of cities	Geog	C277	5Q	L	
220406	North Amer Ind Pac NW	AInSt	C311	5Q	U	
220428	Hist Washington and NW	Hist	C432	5Q	U	
220505	American foreign policy	PolSc	C321	5Q	U	
220505	Intro to intntl policy	PolSc	C203	5Q	L	
220506	Intro to Amer politics	PolSc	C202	5Q	L	
220507	Politics & mass communic	PolSc	C305	5Q	U	
220510	Intro to politics	PolSc	C101	5Q	L	
220605	The family	Socio	C352	5Q	U	
220606	Survey of sociology	Socio	C110	5Q	L	
220610	Sociology of deviance	Socio	C271	5Q	L	
220610	Socialization	Socio	C347	5Q	U	

Noncredit courses

NCES No.	Course Title	Dept.	Course No.	Cred.	Lev.	Specl. Feat.
160302	Intermediate algebra	Math	C101	NC	H	
160399	Elementary algebra: surve	Math	CA	NC	H	
160399	Elementary algebra: surve	Math	CB	NC	H	
160602	Plane trigonometry	Math	C104	NC	H	

(63) UNIVERSITY OF WISCONSIN–EXTENSION

Ms. Sylvia N. Rose
Director
Independent Study
University of Wisconsin–Extension
432 North Lake Street
Madison, Wisconsin 53706
Phone: 608-263-2055

Telecourses are offered. Enrollment on a noncredit basis accepted in credit courses. Overseas enrollment accepted. Military personnel may enroll through the DANTES program. Gifted high school students are permitted to enroll in undergraduate courses for credit.

NCES No.	Course Title	Dept.	Course No.	Cred.	Lev.	Specl. Feat.
	High School courses					
020402	Architectural drawing	Arch	A88	HF	H	
030302	Beginning music theory I	Music	H30	1U	H	
030302	Beginning music theory II	Music	H31	1U	H	
030599	Basic drawing	VisAr	A20	HF	H	
040104	Basic bookkeeping I	Bus	A30	HF	H	
040104	Basic bookkeeping II	Bus	A31	HF	H	
049900	General business I	Bus	H39	HF	H	
049900	Stocks, bonds & investing	Bus	A69	QT	H	
080400	Automotive mechanics I	EngAS	A60	HF	H	
080400	Automotive mechanics II	EngAS	A61	HF	H	
090799	Personal & family health	HlSci	H30	HF	H	
120305	First-yr high sch Engl I	Engl	H10	HF	H	
120305	First-yr high sch Eng II	Engl	H11	HF	H	
120305	Attack on grammar	Engl	H9	HF	H	
120307	American literature	Lit	H30	HF	H	
120307	American literature	Lit	H31	HF	H	
120310	Second-yr high sch Eng I	Engl	H20	HF	H	
120310	Second-yr high sch Eng II	Engl	H21	HF	H	
120310	Writing & grammar review	Engl	H42	HF	H	
120310	Creative writing	Engl	H45	HF	H	
121000	First-sem high sch French	Frnch	H10	HF	H	
121000	Second-sem high sch Frnch	Frnch	H11	HF	H	
121000	Third-sem high sch French	Frnch	H20	HF	H	
121000	Fourth-sem high sch Frnch	Frnch	H21	HF	H	
121000	Fifth-sem high sch French	Frnch	H30	HF	H	
121000	Sixth-sem high sch French	Frnch	H31	HF	H	
121000	Seventh-sem h s French	Frnch	H40	HF	H	
121000	Eighth-sem high sch Frnch	Frnch	H41	HF	H	
121000	French review	Frnch	A71	HF	H	
121100	First-sem high sch German	Germn	H10	HF	H	
121100	Second-sem high sch Ger	Germn	H11	HF	H	
121100	Third-sem h s German	Germn	H20	HF	H	
121100	Fourth-sem high sch Ger	Germn	H21	HF	H	
121100	Fifth-sem high sch German	Germn	H30	HF	H	
121100	Sixth-sem high sch German	Germn	H31	HF	H	
121100	Eighth-sem high sch Ger	Germn	H41	HF	H	
121600	First-sem high sch Latin	CILL	H10	HF	H	
121600	Second-sem high sch Latin	CILL	H11	HF	H	
121600	Third-sem high sch Latin	CILL	H20	HF	H	
121600	Fourth-sem high sch Latin	CILL	H21	HF	H	
122000	First-sem high sch Russn	Rus	H10	HF	H	
122000	Second-sem h s Russian	Rus	H11	HF	H	
122000	Third-sem h s Russian	Rus	H20	HF	H	
122000	Fourth-sem h s Russian	Rus	H21	HF	H	
122000	Russian conversation/comp	Rus	A70	1U	H	
122000	Fifth-sem h s Russian	Rus	H30	HF	H	
122000	Sixth-sem h s Russian	Rus	H31	HF	H	
122000	Seventh-sem h s Russian	Rus	H40	HF	H	
122000	Eighth-sem h s Russian	Rus	H41	HF	H	
122000	Russian for reading	Rus	A60	HF	H	
122500	First-sem h s Spanish	Span	H10	HF	H	
122500	Second-sem h s Spanish	Span	H11	HF	H	
122500	Third-sem h s Spanish	Span	H20	HF	H	
122500	Fourth-sem h s Spanish	Span	H21	HF	H	
122500	Seventh-sem h s Spanish	Span	H40	HF	H	
122500	Eighth-sem h s Spanish	Span	H41	HF	H	
122500	Fifth-sem h s Spanish	Span	H30	HF	H	
122500	Sixth-sem h s Spanish	Span	H31	HF	H	
150302	General biology I	Bio	H20	HF	H	
150303	General biology II	Bio	H21	HF	H	
160301	Practical arithmetic	MEAS	A52	HF	H	
160302	First-semester algebra	Math	H10	HF	H	
160302	Second-semester algebra	Math	H11	HF	H	
160302	Advanced algebra I	Math	H30	HF	H	
160302	Advanced algebra II	Math	H31	HF	H	
160302	College algebra	Math	H39	HF	H	
160601	Geometry I	Math	H20	HF	H	
160601	Geometry II	Math	H21	HF	H	
160602	Plane trigonometry	Math	H40	HF	H	
161299	Math for electricity I	MEAS	A56	HF	H	
161299	Math for electricity II	MEAS	A57	HF	H	
220299	Contemporary economics	Econ	H40	HF	H	
220305	Physical geography II	Geog	H22	HF	H	
220305	Physical geography I	Geog	H21	HF	H	
220432	US history to 1877	Hist	H30	HF	H	

NCES No.	Course Title	Dept.	Course No.	Cred.	Lev.	Specl. Feat.
220432	US history since 1877	Hist	H31	HF	H	
220472	Quest for equality	SouSt	H30	HF	H	
220501	American govt today	PolSc	H30	HF	H	
	College courses					
010104	Cooperation	Agri	422	3S	L	
010902	Introduction to forestry	Bio	100	2S	L	
030302	Apprec & history of music	Music	101	2S	L	
030302	Apprec & history of music	Music	102	2S	L	
030599	Creative design	Art	131	3S	L	
030699	History of Western art	ArHis	105	4S	L	
040101	Elementary accounting I	Bus	201	3S	L	
040101	Elementary accounting II	Bus	202	3S	L	
040101	Intermediate accounting I	Bus	301	3S	L	
040101	Intermediate acctg II	Bus	302	3S	L	
040106	Cost accounting I	Bus	323	3S	U	
040106	Advanced cost accounting	Bus	413	3S	U	
040109	Governmental accounting	Bus	373	3S	U	
040111	Managerial accounting	Bus	300	3S	L	
040201	Administrative policy	Bus	495	3S	U	
040306	Investments	Bus	322	3S	L	
040306	Principles of finance	Bus	320	3S	U	
040307	Financial management	Bus	427	3S	L	
040400	Management info systems	Bus	210	3S	L	
040903	Organizational behavior	Bus	340	3S	L	
040905	Organization & management	Bus	233	3S	L	
040999	Purchasing & matrls mgmt	Bus	321	3S	U	
040999	Women in management	Bus	334	3S	L	
040999	Managing a small business	Bus	385	3S	L	
041001	Principles of marketing	Bus	311	3S	L	
041001	Promotional policies	Bus	350	3S	L	
041199	Personnel management	Bus	321	3S	L	
049900	Business law	Bus	305	3S	L	
050605	Writing feature articles	Journ	305	3S	L	
050608	Newswriting	Journ	203	3S	L	
050700	Publications design	Journ	207	2S	L	
050900	Public relations	Journ	225	3S	L	
060799	FORTRAN programming	CmpSc	211	2S	U	
070309	Voc tech adult education	Educ	502	2S	L	
070499	School curriculum design	Educ	300	3S	L	
070509	Health info for teachers	Educ	501	3S	L	
070512	Children's literature	Educ	649	3S	L	
070701	Human resource developmnt	Guida	105	1S	L	
070803	Educ Psych of the gifted	EdPsy	501	3S	U	
070899	The exceptional child	Educ	300	3S	L	
070899	Children with handicaps	Educ	496	2S	L	
070902	Human relation-education	Educ	465	3S	L	
070999	Family day care	Educ	481	1S	L	
070999	Asst child care teacher	ChFam	382	1S	L	
070999	Child care teacher	ChFam	381	3S	L	
070999	Admn & orgn of child care	ChFam	479	3S	L	
071099	Child development	EdPsy	320	3S	L	
080799	Critical path network	EngAS	590	2S	L	
081104	Dynamics	EngAS	222	3S	U	
081104	Statics	EngAS	221	3S	U	
081199	Mechanics of materials	EngAS	303	3S	U	
081599	Industrial safety	Sfty	555	3S	L	
081799	Economic analysis—engr	EngAS	312	3S	U	
082099	Intro numerical control	EngAS	428	2S	L	
082199	Intro to materials sci	EngAS	360	3S	L	
090799	Health care in school	Nrsng	470	2S	U	
100206	Consumer education	Bus	344	3S	L	
100601	Development in adolescenc	Educ	321	3S	L	
100604	Human ability & learning	Educ	301	3S	U	
110119	Art & science of welding	EngAS	137	3S	L	
120103	Intro to linguistics	Engl	320	3S	L	
120201	Fantasy & science fiction	Lit	357	3S	L	
120302	Hist of English language	Engl	323	3S	L	
120307	Intro to creative writing	Engl	203	3S	L	
120307	American literature	Engl	212	3S	L	
120307	Shakespearian drama	Engl	217	3S	L	
120307	Shakespearian drama	Engl	218	3S	L	
120307	Saul Bellow	Engl	311	1S	L	
120307	Willa Cather	Engl	312	1S	L	
120307	Doris Lessing	Engl	313	1S	L	
120307	Eudora Welty	Engl	314	1S	L	
120307	Virginia Woolf	Engl	315	1S	L	
120307	Ernest Hemingway	Engl	431	1S	L	
120307	William Faulkner	Engl	433	1S	L	
120307	Graham Greene	Engl	434	1S	L	
120307	The English novel	Engl	460	3S	L	
120307	Camus in translation	Engl	230	1S	L	
120307	De Beauvoir in translation	Engl	231	1S	L	
120307	Colette in translation	Engl	232	1S	L	
120307	Malraux in translation	Engl	260	1S	L	
120307	Thomas Mann	Engl	190	1S	L	
120307	Günter Grass	Engl	191	1S	L	
120307	Scandinavian experience	Engl	295	1S	L	
120310	Technical writing	EngAS	279	3S	L	
120310	Technical writing I	EngAS	273	1S	L	
120310	Technical writing II	EngAS	274	1S	L	
120310	Technical writing III	EngAS	275	1S	L	
120310	Intermediate composition	Engl	201	2S	L	
120310	Intro to creative writing	Engl	203	2S	L	
120399	Freshman English	Engl	102	3S	L	
120500	First-semester Arabic	Hebr	101	4S	L	
120500	Second semseter Arabic	Hebr	102	4S	L	
120800	First semester Danish	Dan	121	4S	L	
120800	Second semester Danish	Dan	122	4S	L	
121000	First-semester French	Frnch	103	4S	L	
121000	Second-semester French	Frnch	104	4S	L	
121000	Third-semester French	Frnch	203	3S	U	
121000	Fourth-semester French	Frnch	204	3S	U	
121000	French-lit: 17th & 18th c	Frnch	221	3S	U	
121000	French-lit: 19th century	Frnch	222	3S	U	
121000	French-lit: 20th century	Frnch	223	3S	U	
121000	Modern French dramatists	Frnch	644	3S	U	
121000	André Malraux	Frnch	360	1S	U	
121000	Camus	Frnch	441	1S	U	
121000	Simone de Beauvoir	Frnch	442	1S	U	
121000	Colette	Frnch	443	1S	U	
121000	Intermediate composition	Frnch	227	2S	U	
121000	Advanced composition	Frnch	324	2S	U	
121000	Business French	Frnch	219	2S	U	
121100	Applied German philology	Germn	662	3S	U	
121100	First-semester German	Germn	101	4S	L	
121100	Second-semester German	Germn	102	4S	L	
121100	Third-semester German	Germn	203	3S	U	
121100	Fourth-semester German	Germn	204	3S	U	
121100	Intro German literature	Germn	221	3S	U	
121100	Intro German literature	Germn	222	3S	U	
121100	The classical period	Germn	302	3S	U	
121100	Contemporary German lit	Germn	305	3S	U	
121100	Goethe's *Faust*	Germn	633	3S	U	
121100	Thomas Mann	Germn	699A	1S	U	
121100	Günter Grass	Germn	699B	1S	U	
121100	Intermediate composition	Germn	223	3S	U	
121100	Intermediate composition	Germn	224	3S	U	
121200	Elementary Greek	Greek	103	4S	L	
121200	Elementary Greek	Greek	104	4S	L	
121200	Plato	Greek	104P	2S	L	
121200	Homer: *The Iliad*	Greek	210	3S	L	
121200	Xenophon & New Testament	Greek	204	3S	L	
121300	First-sem Hebrew—bibl	Hebr	101B	4S	L	
121300	Scnd-sem Hebrew—bibl	Hebr	104	2S	L	
121300	Biblical texts: Esther	Hebr	201	2S	L	
121300	Exodus & Leviticus	Hebr	321	2S	L	
121300	Biblical texts: Joshua	Hebr	322	2S	L	
121300	First-sem Hebrew—modern	Hebr	101M	4S	L	
121300	Scnd-sem Hebrew—modern	Hebr	103	2S	L	
121300	Mod Hebrew conversation	Hebr	225	3S	L	
121300	Sefarad-Spanish Jewry	Hebr	365	3S	U	
121300	Jewish cultural hist I	Hebr	471	3S	L	
121300	Jewish cultural hist II	Hebr	472	3S	L	
121400	First-semester Italian	Ital	103	4S	L	
121400	Second-semester Italian	Ital	104	4S	L	
121400	Third-semester Italian	Ital	203	3S	L	
121600	Elementary Latin	Class	103	4S	L	
121600	Elementary Latin	Class	104	4S	L	
121600	Cicero's *Orations*	Class	203	4S	L	
121600	Vergil	Class	204	4S	L	
121600	Intermediate Latin comp	Class	505	2S	U	
121600	Advanced Latin comp	Class	506	2S	U	
121800	Beginning Norwegian I	Germn	101	4S	L	
121800	Beginning Norwegian II	Germn	102	4S	L	
121900	First-sem Portuguese	Span	101	4S	L	
121900	Second-sem Portuguese	Span	102	4S	L	
122000	First-semester Russian	Rus	101	4S	L	
122000	Second-semester Russian	Rus	102	4S	L	
122000	Third-semester Russian	Rus	203	4S	U	
122000	Fourth-semester Russian	Rus	204	4S	U	
122500	First-semester Spanish	Span	101	4S	L	
122500	Second-semester Spanish	Span	102	4S	L	
122500	Third-semester Spanish	Span	203	4S	U	

NCES No.	Course Title	Dept.	Course No.	Cred.	Lev.	Specl. Feat.
122500	Fourth-semester Spanish	Span	204	4S	U	
122500	Spanish literature	Span	221	3S	U	
122500	Spanish literature	Span	222	3S	U	
122500	Modern Spanish readings	Span	229	3S	U	
122500	Miguel de Unamuno	Span	407	1S	U	
122600	First semester Swedish	Swed	111	4S	L	
122600	Second semester Swedish	Swed	112	4S	L	
122700	First-semester Yiddish	Hebr	101	4S	L	
122700	Second-semester Yiddish	Hebr	102	4S	L	
129900	Greek & Latin medical trm	Class	205	3S	L	
129900	Greek drama in English	Class	313	2S	L	
129900	Classical mythology	Class	370	3S	L	
129900	Engl & Amer lit-19th cent	EnglL	207	3S	L	
129900	Engl & Amer lit-20th cent	EnglL	208	3S	L	
129900	Women in literature	WomSt	250	3S	L	
150201	Global physical environ	EnvSt	120	3S	L	
150202	Weather & climate	EngAS	100	2S	L	
150316	Survey of botany	Bio	100	3S	L	
150401	General chemistry I	EngAS	103	3S	L	
150401	General chemistry II	EngAS	104	3S	L	
150599	General geology	Geol	100	3S	L	
150799	General physics I	EngAS	103	3S	L	
150799	General physics II	EngAS	104	3S	L	
159900	Environmental conservatn	EnvSt	339	3S	L	
160302	Intermediate algebra	Math	101	4S	L	
160302	College algebra	Math	112	3S	L	
160306	Matrix & linear algebra	Math	340	3S	U	
160399	Algebra & trigonometry	Math	114	5S	L	
160406	Differential equations	Math	305	2S	U	
160499	Calculus & analyt geom I	Math	221	5S	U	
160499	Calculus & analyt geom II	Math	222	5S	U	
160499	Calculus & analyt geo III	Math	223	5S	U	
160602	Plane trigonometry	Math	113	2S	U	
160899	Intro statistical methods	Math	301	3S	U	
180199	Intro to philosophy	Philo	101	4S	L	
180301	Introduction to ethics	Philo	241	4S	L	
180502	Beginning logic	Philo	211	4S	L	
189900	Philosophy of religion	Philo	261	4S	L	
190599	Women & their bodies	WomSt	103	3S	L	
200504	Child psychology	Psych	560	3S	L	
200599	Intro to psychology	Psych	202	3S	L	
200701	Intro to socl psychology	Psych	530	3S	L	
210401	Social welfare programs	SocWk	205	3S	L	
210499	Child welfare services	SocWk	462	3S	U	
210499	Social problems of aging	SocWk	422	3S	U	
220102	Intro to anthropology	Anthr	100	3S	L	
220201	Introduction to economics	Econ	101	4S	L	
220201	Prin of macroeconomics	Econ	103	3S	L	
220201	Prin of microeconomics	Econ	104	3S	L	
220214	International economics	Econ	433	3S	U	
220302	Economic geography	Geog	102	3S	L	
220428	History of Wisconsin	Hist	390	3S	L	
220431	Hist of Soviet Russia	Hist	419	3S	U	
220432	American hist 1492-1865	AmHis	101	4S	L	
220432	Amer hist-1865 to present	AmHis	102	4S	L	
220450	Near East and Greece	AnHis	111	3S	L	
220472	Women in American history	Hist	392	4S	L	
220499	Afro-American history	AfAmS	231	3S	L	
220501	American national govt	PolSc	104	3S	L	
220599	Public personnel admin	PolSc	470	3S	U	
220605	Marriage and family	MAF	120	3S	L	
220613	Social problems	Socio	220	3S	L	
220699	Introduction to sociology	Socio	100	3S	L	
220699	Racial & cultural minorit	Socio	224	3S	L	
229900	Soc change & lives-women	WomSt	102	3S	L	
	Noncredit courses					
010104	Cooperatives	Agri	A40	NC	L	
010499	Horse science	AnSci	A50	NC	L	
010902	Eco-sploring	Fores	A10	NC	L	
020402	Architectural drawing	Arch	A88	NC	L	
030599	Basic drawing	VisAr	A20	NC	L	
030599	Painting or drawing	VisAr	A30	NC	L	
030699	History of Western art	ArHis	A15	NC	L	
040101	Intro to accounting I	Bus	A32	NC	L	
040101	Intro to accounting II	Bus	A33	NC	L	
040101	Intermediate accounting I	Bus	A35	NC	L	
040101	Intermediate accting II	Bus	A36	NC	L	
040104	Bookkeeping for bus I	Bus	A30	NC	L	
040104	Bookkeeping for bus II	Bus	A31	NC	L	
040106	Cost accounting I	Bus	A37	NC	U	
040106	Advanced cost accounting	Bus	A38	NC	U	
040109	Governmental accounting	Bus	A373	NC	U	
040111	Managerial accounting	Bus	A34	NC	L	
040201	Administrative policy	Bus	A495	NC	U	
040306	Principles of finance	Bus	A320	NC	L	
040306	Investments	Bus	A322	NC	L	
040307	Financial management	Bus	A427	NC	L	
040400	Management info systems	Bus	A210	NC	L	
040601	Assertiveness in business	Bus	A46	NC	L	
040902	Management-minded supv	Bus	M50	NC	L	
040903	Organizational behavior	Bus	A340	NC	L	
040905	Organization & management	Bus	A233	NC	L	
040999	Women in management	Bus	A334	NC	L	
040999	Managing a small business	Bus	A385	NC	L	
040999	Purchasng & materials mgt	Bus	A436	NC	U	
040999	Intro to service mngmt	Bus	M10	NC	L	
040999	Supv in service mngmt	Bus	M11	NC	L	
040999	Start your own business?	Bus	M16	NC	L	
040999	Managing info & records	Bus	M17	NC	L	
041001	Principles of marketing	Bus	A311	NC	L	
041001	Promotional policies	Bus	A350	NC	L	
041199	Personnel management	Bus	A321	NC	L	
049900	Stocks, bonds & invstmnts	Bus	A69	NC	L	
049900	Business law	Bus	A305	NC	L	
049900	C.P.M. review	Bus	M21	NC	U	
050699	Publicity techniques	Journ	A55	NC	L	
050699	Writing for fun & profit	Journ	A60	NC	L	
050699	Power reading	Journ	A65	NC	L	
050700	Publications design	Journ	A207	NC	L	
060799	Programming the 8086	CmpSc	A111	NC	L	
070699	Intro to child care	ChFam	A40	NC	L	
070699	Family day care	ChFam	A41	NC	L	
080400	Auto mechanics I	EngAS	A60	NC	U	
080400	Auto mechanics II	EngAS	A61	NC	U	
080400	Diesel engines	EngAS	A64	NC	L	
080707	Concrete structures	Engin	A347	NC	U	
081301	Air pollutn & solid waste	EnvSt	A412	NC	L	
081303	Solid waste recycling	EnvSt	A182	NC	L	
081303	Solid waste landfills	EnvSt	A180	NC	L	
081303	Waste to energy	EnvSt	A185	NC	L	
081304	Water & wastewater	EnvSt	A411	NC	L	
081304	Storm & sanitary sewers	EnvSt	A450	NC	L	
081399	Environmental engineering	EnvSt	A410	NC	L	
081399	Occupational health	EnvSt	A413	NC	L	
081399	Environmental engr topics	EnvSt	A413	NC	L	
082001	Intro to refrigeration	EngAS	W97	NC	L	
082001	Air conditioning I	EngAS	V117	NC	L	
082001	Air conditioning II	EngAS	V118	NC	L	
082001	Air conditioning III	EngAS	V119	NC	U	
082003	Steam-plant operation	EngAS	A92	NC	L	
082601	Elementary surveying I	Srvyg	A251	NC	L	
082601	Elementary surveying II	Srvyg	A252	NC	L	
082604	Photogrammetry	Photo	A359	NC	L	
089900	Basic Engr refresher	Engin	A50	NC	U	
089900	Intro to value analysis	EngAS	A361	NC	U	
090999	Counselng for nurse instr	Nrsng	N80	NC	U	
090999	Writng nrsng publications	Nrsng	N85	NC	U	
090999	Adult patient assessment	Nrsng	N60	NC	U	
090999	Interpersonal relations	Nrsng	N70	NC	U	
090999	Management for nurses	Nrsng	N75	NC	U	
100206	Consumer education	Bus	A344	NC	L	
100309	The food server	Rec	A10	NC	L	
110119	Welding & power sources	EngAS	A139	NC	L	
110119	Art of weld inspection I	EngAS	A233	NC	U	
110119	Art of weld inspection II	EngAS	A233	NC	U	
110119	Art of weld inspectn III	EngAS	A234	NC	U	
120305	Attack on grammar	Engl	A12	NC	L	
120310	Creative writing	Engl	A45	NC	L	
120310	Creative writing	Engl	A46	NC	L	
120310	Expository writing	Engl	A53	NC	L	
120310	Intermediate composition	Engl	A63	NC	L	
120310	Writing a nonfiction book	Engl	A64	NC	L	
120399	Vocabulary building	Engl	A51	NC	L	
120399	Manuscript editing	Engl	A52	NC	L	
121000	French for reading-I	Frnch	A60	NC	L	
121000	French for reading-II	Frnch	A61	NC	L	
121000	French review	Frnch	A71	NC	L	
121100	Reading German	Germn	A60	NC	L	
121100	Business German	Germn	A70	NC	L	
121400	Italian for reading	Ital	A60	NC	L	
122000	Russian for reading	Rus	A60	NC	L	
122000	Conversatn & comp in Russ	Rus	A70	NC	L	
122500	Spanish for reading	Span	A60	NC	L	

NCES No.	Course Title	Dept.	Course No.	Cred.	Lev.	Specl. Feat.
129900	Reading Polish I	Plsh	A60	NC	L	
129900	Reading Polish II	Plsh	A61	NC	L	
129900	Engl-American lit-19 cent	Engl	A207	NC	L	
160301	Practical arithmetic	MEAS	A52	NC	L	
160302	Review of college algebra	Math	A39	NC	L	
160401	Review of basic calculus	Math	A42	NC	U	
160401	Review of inter calculus	Math	A43	NC	U	
160401	Review of vector calculus	Math	A45	NC	U	
160601	Geometry I	Math	A20	NC	L	
160601	Geometry II	Math	A21	NC	L	
160602	Review of trigonometry	Math	A40	NC	L	
161299	Math for electricity I	MEAS	A56	NC	L	
161299	Math for electricity II	MEAS	A57	NC	L	
220201	Intro to economics	Econ	A101	NC	L	
220201	Prin of macroeconomics	Econ	A103	NC	L	
220201	Prin of microeconomics	Econ	A104	NC	L	
220214	International economics	Econ	A433	NC	U	
220499	Intro genealogical resrch	Hist	A10	NC	L	

⑥④ UNIVERSITY OF WYOMING

Dr. Heikki I. Leskinen
Coordinator/Associate Professor
Correspondence Study Department
University of Wyoming
Box 3294, University Station
Laramie, Wyoming 82071
Phone: 307-766-5631

Enrollment on a noncredit basis accepted in credit courses. High school students may enroll in undergraduate courses for credit. Overseas enrollment accepted. Military personnel may enroll through the DANTES program. Minimum period for course completion is six weeks. Maximum period for course completion is one year. Contract learning is available in some courses: The student contracts with the professor for a specific grade, which then determines the course requirements/ difficulty level to be met. Use of audiovisual material requires a refundable deposit. The textbook rental service charges $10 a year per book; rentals are made on a first-come, first-served basis. The University Bookstore can be reached at 1-800-228-7232 (in state) or 1-800-423-5809 (out of state). VISA and MasterCard are accepted for book purchases.

NCES No.	Course Title	Dept.	Course No.	Cred.	Lev.	Specl. Feat.
	High School courses					
010902	Intro to forestry	Sci	B1	HF	H	
030502	Introduction to art	Art	A1	HF	H	SL
040104	Bookkeeping I sem 1	Acctg	A1	HF	H	
040104	Bookkeeping I sem 2	Acctg	A2	HF	H	
049900	Business law	Bus	C1	HF	H	
100202	Consumer living	HomEc	C1	HF	H	
100308	Food for everyday life	HomEc	B1	HF	H	
100699	Interpersonal relations	HomEc	A1	HF	H	
120305	Grammar	Engl	A1	HF	H	
120307	American literature	EnglL	B1	HF	H	
120307	English literature	EnglL	C1	HF	H	
120310	Composition	Engl	D1	HF	H	
122500	First-yr Spanish sem 1	Span	A1	HF	H	AC
150304	Environmental science	Sci	C1	HF	H	
150399	Biology	Sci	A1	HF	H	LK
160301	General mathematics	Math	A1	HF	H	
160302	Algebra I sem 1	Math	C1	HF	H	
160302	Algebra II sem 1	Math	E1	HF	H	
160302	Algebra I sem 2	Math	C2	HF	H	
160302	Algebra II sem 2	Math	E2	HF	H	
161201	Business mathematics	Bus	B1	HF	H	
200199	Intr to psychology	SocSt	K1	HF	H	
220215	Economics	SocSt	B1	HF	H	
220432	History of the US sem 1	SocSt	E1	HF	H	
220432	History of the US sem 2	SocSt	E2	HF	H	
220433	World history	SocSt	D1	HF	H	
220501	United States government	SocSt	G1	HF	H	
220613	Social problems	SocSt	J1	HF	H	
	College courses					
010106	Econ of world food & agri	Agri	686	3S	U	
010199	Econ with applic to agr I	Agri	370	3S	L	
010407	Animal nutrition	AnSci	510	5S	U	
010407	Feeds and feeding	AnSci	410	4S	L	
010603	Agricultural entomology	Agri	555	3S	U	

NCES No.	Course Title	Dept.	Course No.	Cred.	Lev.	Specl. Feat.
030302	Introduction to music	Music	300	3S	L	AC
030399	America's ethnic music	Music	312	2S	L	AC
030399	The classical period	Music	611	2S	U	AC
030399	The romantic period	Music	612	2S	U	AC
030402	Intro to theater	ThArt	391	3S	L	
030502	Intro to hist & crit art	ArHis	380	3S	L	
040101	Principles of account I	Acctg	401	3S	L	
040101	Principles of account II	Acctg	402	3S	L	
040904	Management & organization	Mgmt	621	3S	U	
041001	Elements of marketing	Mktg	405	3S	U	
041001	Advertising	Mktg	623	3S	U	
049900	Introduction to business	Bus	300	3S	L	
050605	Journalistic writing	Journ	311	3S	L	
051001	Broadcast fundamentals	Radio	405	3S	L	
051101	Intro to human communcatn	Commu	304	3S	L	
059900	Intr to mass media	Bdcst	300	3S	L	AC
061103	Intro to computer science	CmpSc	301	3S	L	
070199	Issues in contempry educ	Educ	626	2S	U	
070207	Tchr & elemen sch adminis	Educ	621	2S	U	LK
070207	Tchr & second sch adminis	Educ	622	2S	U	LK
070610	Intro to lang & read educ	Educ	510	3S	U	
070610	Reading disabilities	Educ	530	3S	U	VC
070610	Tchg read/content area	Educ	554	2S	U	
071102	Educ tests & measurements	Educ	606	2S	U	
071203	Intro to educ comun & tec	Educ	612	3S	U	
080703	Hydrology	CivlE	680	3S	U	
081104	Statics	EngAS	401	3S	L	AC
081104	Dynamics	EngAS	402	3S	L	AC
100206	Personal finance	HomEc	511	3S	L	
100305	Intr to food science	FdSci	453	3S	L	
100313	Nutrition	HomEc	363	2S	L	
100602	Foundations of marriage	HomEc	542	3S	U	
120305	Freshman English I	Engl	300	3S	L	
120305	Freshman English II	Engl	301	3S	L	
120307	Amer lit: Whitman-Faulkne	EngLL	436	3S	L	
120307	Shakespeare: comedies	EngLL	611	3S	U	
120310	Critical read & writing	Engl	467	3S	L	
120310	Scientific & tech writing	Engl	601	3S	U	
121000	First-year French I	Frnch	301	4S	L	AC
121000	Second-year French	Frnch	420	4S	L	
121100	Second-year German	Germn	420	4S	L	
122500	First-year Spanish I	Span	301	4S	L	AC
122500	First-year Spanish II	Span	302	4S	L	AC
122500	Second-year Spanish	Span	420	4S	L	
130202	Business law I	Bus	431	3S	L	
140307	Admin of sch lib/med cntr	LibSc	634	3S	U	
140401	Cataloging & classficatn	LibSc	638	3S	U	
140408	Selectn of instruc matrls	LibSc	632	3S	U	
140900	Literature for children	LibSc	412	3S	L	
150103	Descriptive astronomy	Astro	302	3S	L	
150403	Food biochemistry	FdSci	672	3S	U	
150501	Introduction to geology	Geol	300	2S	L	LK
160301	Theory of arith I	Math	407	3S	L	
160301	Theory of arith II	Math	408	3S	L	
160302	Precalculus algebra	Math	301	3S	L	
160306	El lin alg & matrix thry	Math	401	3S	L	
160399	Precalculus mathematics	Math	303	5S	L	
160401	Calculus I	Math	311	4S	L	
160401	Calculus II	Math	312	4S	L	
160401	Multivariable calculus	Math	411	4S	L	
160406	Topics in applied math I	Math	418	3S	L	
160602	Precalculus trigonometry	Math	302	3S	L	
160802	Fundmntls of statistics	Stat	405	3S	L	
190502	Personl & communl hlth	Hlth	306	3S	L	
200199	General psychology	Psych	302	4S	L	AC
200503	Alcoholism	Psych	636	3S	U	
200504	The child	Psych	430	3S	L	AC
200504	Exceptional children	Psych	431	2S	L	AC
200599	Drugs and behavior	Psych	421	3S	L	
220102	Expl of cultural diversty	Anthr	302	3S	L	
220106	Human origins	Anthr	301	3S	L	
220201	Prin of macroeconomics	Econ	301	3S	L	
220201	Prin of microeconomics	Econ	302	3S	L	
220205	Intermediate macroecon	Econ	601	3S	U	
220213	Interm microeconomics	Econ	602	3S	L	
220302	Conservation of nat res	Geog	604	3S	U	
220306	Intr world regional geog	Geog	303	3S	L	
220426	Foundation of W Eurpn civ	Hist	310	3S	L	
220426	Hist of Westn Eurpn civza	Hist	311	3S	L	
220427	History of Mexico	Hist	680	3S	U	
220428	History of Wyoming	Hist	360	2S	L	
220428	Hist of the American West	Hist	363	2S	L	AC

NCES No.	Course Title	Dept.	Course No.	Cred.	Lev.	Specl. Feat.
220432	Gen survey of US history	Hist	341	3S	L	
220432	Gen survey of US history	Hist	342	3S	L	
220471	Hist of Indians of the US	Hist	465	3S	L	AC
220501	Gov of the US & Wyo const	PolSc	305	3S	L	
220602	Criminology	Socio	530	3S	U	
220606	Sociological principles	Socio	301	3S	L	
220610	Deviant behavior	Socio	620	3S	U	
220613	Social problems	Socio	305	3S	L	
	Noncredit courses					
050800	Handwriting analysis	GnKno	10	NC		
079900	The school board	Educ	10	NC		LK
160199	Metric system	Math	10	NC		
160399	Precollege mathematics	Math	201	NC		
180901	Buddhism	Relig	10	NC		
180902	Christianity	Relig	11	NC		
180903	Hinduism	Relig	12	NC		
180904	Islam	Relig	13	NC		
180905	Judaism	Relig	14	NC		
220510	Capitalism	PolSc	10	NC		
220510	Communism	PolSc	11	NC		
220510	Socialism	PolSc	12	NC		

(65) UTAH STATE UNIVERSITY

Gary S. Poppleton
Program Administrator, Independent Study Division
Life Span Learning
UMC 5000
Utah State University
Logan, Utah 84322-5000
Phone: 801-750-2131

Telecourses are offered. Enrollment on a noncredit basis accepted in credit courses. High school students may enroll in undergraduate courses for credit. Overseas enrollment accepted. Military personnel may enroll through the DANTES program. Institution offers special arrangements to take courses not listed in this Catalog. Minimum period for course completion is one month. Maximum period for course completion is one year.

NCES No.	Course Title	Dept.	Course No.	Cred.	Lev.	Specl. Feat.
	College courses					
010103	Marketing farm products	AgEco	260	3Q	L	
010103	Farm bsns decision making	AgEco	210	3Q	L	
010107	Farm & ranch management	AgEco	410	3Q	U	
010402	Horse production practice	AnSci	219	3Q	L	
010402	Breeding farm animals	AnSci	456	4Q	U	
010404	Prin of reproduction	AnSci	520	3Q	U	
010406	Lactation of farm animals	AnSci	435	3Q	U	
010407	Animal feeds & feeding	AnSci	245	5Q	L	
010604	Intro to agric plant sci	PlSci	100	4Q	L	
010604	Fruit production	PlSci	450	4Q	U	
010701	General soils	SoilS	358	4Q	U	
010701	Water and environment	SoilS	200	3Q	L	
010801	General fishery biology	WlfSc	350	5Q	U	
011299	Wildlife law enforcement	WlfSc	410	3Q	U	
020102	Intro to landscape archit	LAEP	103	5Q	U	
030502	Survey of Western art	Art	275	3Q	L	
030502	Survey of Western art	Art	276	3Q	L	
030502	Survey of Western art	Art	277	3Q	L	
030602	Exploring art	Art	101	3Q	L	
030602	Typographic design	Art	246	3Q	L	
040101	Introductory accounting	Acctg	201	3Q	L	
040101	Introductory accounting	Acctg	202	3Q	L	
040106	Industrial cost acctg	Acctg	331	4Q	U	
040111	Managerial accounting	Acctg	203	3Q	L	
040201	Intro to business	BusAd	135	3Q	L	
040301	Corporation finance	BusAd	340	4Q	U	
040399	Managing personal finan	BusEd	314	3Q	U	
040502	Entrepren/new venture mgt	BusAd	435	4Q	U	

NCES No.	Course Title	Dept.	Course No.	Cred.	Lev.	Specl. Feat.
040902	Management concepts	BusAd	311	4Q	U	
040902	Administrative sys mgt	BusEd	541	3Q	U	
040902	Small business management	BusAd	235	3Q	L	
040999	Retailing management	BusAd	454	4Q	U	
041001	Fundmntls of marketing	BusAd	350	4Q	U	
041103	Behav dimensions in mgt	BusAd	360	4Q	U	
041203	Operations research	BusAd	308	4Q	U	
050102	Basic advertising design	Art	331	3Q	U	
070516	Math for elem teachers	Math	201	3Q	L	
070516	Math for elem teachers	Math	202	3Q	L	
070516	Math for elem teachers	Math	203	3Q	L	
070522	Teaching social studies	ElEd	420	3Q	U	
070803	Educ of exceptnl children	SplEd	301	3Q	U	
070803	Intro instr for excp chld	SplEd	305	3Q	U	
070803	Ed of gifted & talented	ElEd	584	3Q	U	
070804	Educational audiology	ComDi	528	3Q	U	
070804	Hearing science	ComDi	381	5Q	U	
070805	Developing IEPS	SplEd	535	2Q	U	
070806	Etiology of devel disabil	SplEd	590	3Q	U	
070811	Speech science	ComDi	507	3Q	U	
071103	Measurement & eval in edu	SecEd	604	5Q	U	
071203	Media prod and util el ed	InMed	441	3Q	U	
071203	Media prod & util sec ed	InMed	442	3Q	U	
080505	Soils, water & environmnt	Soils	200	2Q	L	
080703	Water res eng hydraulics	CivEE	352	4Q	U	
080703	Engineering hydraulics	CivEE	553	5Q	U	
080703	Applied hydraulics	CivEE	550	4Q	U	
081102	Elem fluid mechanics	CivEE	350	5Q	U	
081104	Engr mechanics statics	Engin	200	3Q	L	
081104	Engr mechanics dynamics	Engin	202	3Q	L	
090106	Fundmntls of epidemiology	Bio	530	3Q	U	
090111	Personal health	Bio	115	2Q	U	
090113	Communicble disease contr	Bio	512	3Q	U	
090114	Elementary microbiology	Bio	111	4Q	L	
090119	Human physiology	Bio	130	5Q	L	
090301	Phonetics	ComDi	275	3Q	L	
090702	Environmental health	Bio	510	4Q	U	
090702	Insect/rodent vector cont	Bio	413	3Q	U	
090702	Waterborne-disease contrl	Bio	414	3Q	U	
090702	Foodborne-disease control	Bio	516	3Q	U	
100312	Nutrition for people	NFS	122	3Q	U	
100312	Human nutrition	NFS	540	3Q	U	
120299	Children's literature	Engl	416	3Q	U	
120299	Lit for adolescents	Engl	417	3Q	U	
120305	Elements of grammar	Engl	109	3Q	L	
120305	Grammar	Engl	410	3Q	U	
120308	Intro to short stories	Engl	118	3Q	L	
120310	Writing poetry	Engl	501	3Q	U	
122500	Elem Spanish	Span	101	5Q	L	AC
122500	Elem Spanish	Span	102	5Q	L	AC
122500	Elem Spanish	Span	103	5Q	L	AC
122500	Inter Spanish	Span	201	5Q	L	AC
122500	Inter Spanish	Span	202	5Q	L	AC
122500	Advanced grammar	Span	304	3Q	U	AC
122500	Advanced grammar	Span	305	3Q	U	AC
140499	Cataloging & classificatn	InMed	506	3Q	U	
140499	Use of libraries	InMed	100	3Q	L	
140799	Eval & sel of instr mater	InMed	502	3Q	U	
150301	Biology & the citizen	Bio	101	5Q	L	
150302	General biology	Bio	120	5Q	L	
150304	General ecology	RngSc	384	5Q	U	
150327	Insects affecting man	Bio	190	4Q	L	
150327	Biology of honeybees	Bio	191	2Q	L	
150599	Introductory geology	Geol	101	5Q	L	
160301	Basic mathematics	Math	001	5Q	L	
160302	Elementary algebra	Math	002	5Q	L	
160302	Intro to college algebra	Math	101	5Q	L	
160302	College algebra	Math	105	5Q	L	
160401	Calculus I	Math	215	3Q	L	
160602	Plane trigonometry	Math	106	3Q	L	
160801	Business statistics	BusAd	296	5Q	L	
190510	Dynamic fitness	HPE&R	300	3Q	L	
220201	Economics I	Econ	200	5Q	L	
220201	Economics II	Econ	201	5Q	L	
220208	Microeconomics	Econ	501	4Q	U	
220208	Consumer behavior	BusAd	451	4Q	U	
220432	American civilization	Hist	170	5Q	L	
220452	Civil War & Reconstructn	Hist	438	3Q	U	
220452	Comp civil: anc & medievl	Hist	101	3Q	L	
220453	Comp civilizs: modern	Hist	103	3Q	L	
220453	Comp civs: early modern	Hist	102	3Q	L	
220453	Recent America 1945-pres	Hist	446	3Q	U	

66 WASHINGTON STATE UNIVERSITY

Ms. Ellen L. Krieger
Coordinator, Independent Study
Extended Academic Programs, 202 Van Doren Hall
Washington State University
Pullman, Washington 99164-5220
Phone: 509-335-3557

Telecourses are offered. Enrollment on a noncredit basis accepted in credit courses. High school students may enroll in undergraduate courses for credit. Overseas enrollment accepted. Military personnel may enroll through the DANTES program. Minimum period for course completion is three months. Maximum period for course completion is one year.

NCES No.	Course Title	Dept.	Course No.	Cred.	Lev.	Specl. Feat.
	High School courses					
090101	Basic health	Hlth	1X	HF	H	
150700	Physics first semester	Sci	1X	HF	H	
150700	Physics second semester	Sci	2X	HF	H	
160302	Algebra I first semester	Math	1X	HF	H	
160302	Algebra I second semester	Math	2X	HF	H	
160302	Algebra II first semester	Math	3X	HF	H	
160302	Algebra II second sem	Math	4X	HF	H	
160399	Precalculus first sem	Math	5X	HF	H	
160399	Precalculus second sem	Math	6X	HF	H	
	College courses					
010505	Turfgrass culture	Agron	301X	2S	U	SL
010599	Plants and gardens	Hort	101X	3S	L	SL
010603	Agricultural entomology	Entom	240X	3S	L	SL
010604	Commercial veg crops	Hort	320X	3S	U	
010702	Soils	SoilS	201X	3S	L	
020100	The built environment	Arch	202X	3S	L	
020103	Basic environmntl design	InDes	101X	3S	L	
030399	Survey of music literat	Music	160X	3S	L	AC
040101	Prin of accounting I	Acctg	230X	3S	L	
040101	Prin of accounting II	Acctg	231X	3S	L	
040101	Intermediate accounting I	Acctg	232X	3S	L	
040300	Finance	Finan	325X	3S	U	
040601	Business letter writing	Engl	265X	3S	L	
040710	Risk and insurance	Insur	320X	3S	U	
040903	Organizational behavior	Mgmt	401X	3S	U	
040904	Principles of management	Mgmt	301X	3S	U	
040999	Business strategy/policy	Mgmt	491X	3S	U	
041001	Marketing	Mktg	360X	3S	U	
041099	Consumer behavior	Mktg	367X	3S	U	
041303	Real estate	RlEst	305X	CV	U	
041308	Law of real estate	BuLaw	414X	3S	U	
041309	Real estate administratn	RlEst	406X	3S	U	
059900	Mass communications & soc	Commu	101X	3S	L	
100313	Human nutrition	FdSHN	233X	3S	L	
100399	Nutrition for man	FdSHN	130X	3S	L	
120202	Reading literature	Engl	108X	3S	L	AC
120299	Contemporary Amer fiction	Engl	250X	1S	L	
120299	Native American lit	Engl	341X	3S	U	
120299	Native American lit	AlnSt	341X	3S	U	
120307	English lit to 1750	Engl	209X	3S	L	
120307	English lit 1750 to 1900	Engl	210X	3S	L	
120307	American lit to 1855	Engl	245X	3S	L	
120307	American lit since 1855	Engl	246X	3S	L	
120307	Shakespeare	Engl	305X	3S	U	
120307	Shakespeare	Engl	306X	3S	U	
120307	English Romantic lit	Engl	416X	3S	U	
120307	Victorian literature	Engl	417X	3S	U	
120310	English composition	Engl	101X	3S	L	
120310	Expository writing	Engl	201X	3S	L	
120310	Business communications	Engl	265X	3S	L	
121000	First-semester French	Frnch	101X	4S	L	AC
121000	Second-semester French	Frnch	102X	4S	L	AC
121000	French for travelers	Frnch	103X	1S	L	AC
121100	First-semester German	Germn	101X	4S	L	AC
121100	Second-semester German	Germn	102X	4S	L	AC
122500	First-semester Spanish	Span	101X	4S	L	AC
122500	Second-semester Spanish	Span	102X	4S	L	AC
130400	Criminal law	CrJus	320X	3S	U	
130403	Intro to juvenile justice	CrJus	240X	3S	L	
130699	Law of int'l trade	BuLaw	415X	3S	U	
130799	Law and business I	BuLaw	210X	3S	L	
130799	Law of business organiztn	BuLaw	411X	3S	U	
150700	General physics	Phycs	101X	CV	L	
159900	Principles of conservatn	Zoolg	330X	3S	U	

NCES No.	Course Title	Dept.	Course No.	Cred.	Lev.	Specl. Feat.
160302	Intermediate algebra	Math	101X	3S	L	
160302	Precalculus algebra	Math	107X	3S	L	
160306	Intro linear algebra	Math	220X	2S	L	
160401	Calculus I	Math	171X	4S	L	
160401	Calculus II	Math	172X	4S	L	
160406	Differential equations	Math	315X	3S	U	
160602	Precalculus trigonometry	Math	108X	2S	L	
180302	Ethics in contemp society	Philo	260X	3S	L	
180401	Hum in ancient world	Hum	101X	3S	L	
180405	Phil/religion China/Japan	Philo	315X	3S	U	
180499	Intro to philosophy	Philo	101X	3S	L	
200501	Abnormal psychology	Psych	333X	3S	U	
200504	Developmental psychology	Psych	361X	3S	U	
200509	Intro to personality	Psych	321X	3S	U	
200700	Social psychology	Psych	350X	3S	U	
200703	Productivity/team bldg	EdAdm	323X	3S	U	
209900	Human sexuality	Psych	230X	3S	L	
220107	Human issues int'l dev	Anthr	462X	3S	U	
220201	Contemporary economics	Econ	201X	4S	L	
220201	Fund of macroeconomics	Econ	102X	3S	L	
220201	Fund of microeconomics	Econ	203X	3S	L	
220423	Intro South Asia culture	AsiSt	270X	3S	L	
220423	Intro East Asia culture	AsiSt	275X	3S	L	
220423	History of East Asia	AsiSt	374X	3S	U	
220423	Intro South Asia culture	Hist	270X	3S	L	
220423	Intro East Asia culture	Hist	275X	3S	L	
220423	Pre-mod history East Asia	Hist	374X	3S	U	
220426	Classcl/Christian Europe	Hist	101X	3S	L	SL
220426	Europe since Louis XIV	Hist	102X	3S	L	
220432	American history to 1865	Hist	110X	3S	L	
220432	American hist since 1865	Hist	111X	3S	L	
220450	Hum in ancient world	Hum	101X	3S	L	
220472	History women Amer societ	Hist	298X	3S	L	
220472	History women Amer societ	WomSt	298X	3S	L	
220499	History Pacific Northwest	Hist	422X	3S	U	
220501	Amer national government	PolSc	101X	3S	L	
220505	Human issues in int'l dev	PolSc	462X	3S	U	
220505	International politics	PolSc	222X	3S	L	
220511	State-local government	PolSc	206X	3S	L	
220602	Criminology	Socio	361X	3S	U	
220605	The family	Socio	351X	3S	U	
220606	Intro to sociology	Socio	101X	3S	L	
220607	Social psychology	Socio	350X	3S	U	
220613	Human issues in int'l dev	Socio	462X	3S	U	
220615	Intro women studies	WomSt	200X	3S	L	
220615	The family	WomSt	351X	3S	U	
220699	Sociology of sex roles	Socio	384X	3S	U	
229900	Human sexuality	WomSt	230X	3S	L	
229900	Marital & sex lifestyles	WomSt	150X	3S	L	
229900	Sociology of sex roles	WomSt	384X	3S	U	
	Noncredit courses					
200509	Stress reduction	EdAdm	089X	NC	U	

67 WEBER STATE COLLEGE

Mr. David Barton
Director, Independent Study Program
Continuing Education
Weber State College
Ogden, Utah 84408-4005
Phone: 801-626-6600
    800-848-7770 ext. 6785

External degree available through the program. Credit by examination is available. Enrollment on a noncredit basis accepted in credit courses. High school students may enroll in undergraduate courses for credit. Overseas enrollment accepted. Minimum period for course completion is three months. Maximum period for course completion is one year. Weber State College offers a wide selection of liberal arts courses. An Associate of Sciences degree is available entirely through the Independent Study Program. Specialized courses in the field of health science are also offered through independent study. Bachelor's degrees can be earned solely through independent study in the following areas: health sciences administration, health sciences education, advanced radiological sciences, dental hygiene, and respiratory therapy. Those who are interested in the health sciences should so specify when requesting information.

NCES No.	Course Title	Dept.	Course No.	Cred.	Lev.	Specl. Feat.
	College courses					
010600	Plants in human affairs	Botny	NS101	4Q	L	
020103	Design for living	DisEd	105	4Q	L	
020103	Interior design	InDes	105	4Q	L	
020300	Blueprint reading	DsgnT	117	2Q	L	
030300	Music essentials	Music	169	3Q	L	AC
030302	Introduction to music	Music	HU101	3Q	L	AC
030302	Evolution of jazz	Music	HU102	3Q	L	AC
040100	Elementary accounting I	Acctg	201	3Q	L	
040100	Elementary accounting II	Acctg	202	3Q	L	
040108	Intermediate accounting	Acctg	311	3Q	U	
040111	Managerial accounting	Acctg	230	3Q	L	
040114	Taxation of individuals	Acctg	340	3Q	U	
040300	Personal finance	Finan	101	4Q	L	
040303	Credit and collection	DisEd	218	3Q	L	
040900	Introduction to business	Bus	101	4Q	L	
040900	Management	Mgmt	300	3Q	U	
041000	Fundamental selling	DisEd	114	4Q	L	
041000	Buying methods	DisEd	238	4Q	L	
041001	Distribution principles	DisEd	130	4Q	L	
041001	Visual merchandising	DisEd	140	3Q	L	
041001	Intro to fashion merchand	DisEd	150	5Q	L	
041001	Customer service	DisEd	210	3Q	L	
041002	Merchandising problems	DisEd	116	4Q	L	
041007	Retail merchandising mthd	DisEd	160	4Q	L	
041106	Principles of supervision	DisEd	250	5Q	L	
041300	Real estate	Bus	2410	4Q	L	
049900	Intro to business law	BuLaw	220	4Q	L	
050100	Advertising methods	DisEd	244	5Q	L	
051100	Survey of communication	Commu	110	5Q	L	
059900	Intro mass communication	Commu	HU112	3Q	L	
059900	Mass media society	Commu	328	3Q	U	
060100	Applications in business	CmpSc	170	4Q	L	
060100	College arithmetic	Math	095	3Q	L	
080900	Digital electronics	ElecT	124	5Q	L	CI
090100	Biomedical science core	HISci	111	5Q	L	
090100	Biomedical science core	HISci	112	5Q	L	
090100	Biomedical science core	HISci	113	5Q	L	
090201	Cardiology	RdTec	430	3Q	U	
090202	Dental science teaching	DAsst	405	5Q	U	
090202	Geriatric dental needs	DAsst	410	3Q	U	
090202	Dental hygiene indv rsrch	DAsst	480	CV	U	
090202	Dental science readings	DAsst	483	CV	U	
090259	Imaging pathology I	RdTec	431	4Q	U	
090259	Imaging pathology II	RdTec	440	4Q	U	
090259	Imaging diff diagnosis I	RdTec	442	3Q	U	
090259	Imaging diff diagnosis II	RdTec	444	3Q	U	
090259	Sectional anatomy	RdTec	450	5Q	U	
090259	Radiological internship	RdTec	470	CV	U	
090259	Project in radiology	RdTec	480	CV	U	
090259	Readings in radiology	RdTec	483	CV	U	
090259	Radiology seminar	RdTec	499	CV	U	
090259	Psycho-social medicine	RdTec	300	4Q	U	
090259	Radiation health safety	RdTec	310	3Q	U	
090259	Promotional strategies	RdTec	321	4Q	U	
090259	Advanced patient care	RdTec	325	4Q	U	
090259	Quality assurance	RdTec	340	4Q	U	
090259	Computerized imaging	RdTec	342	4Q	U	
090259	Contemporary imaging I	RdTec	360	4Q	U	
090259	Contemporary imaging II	RdTec	361	4Q	U	
090299	Pathophysiology	HISci	230	4Q	L	
090600	Time management	HCA	320	4Q	U	
090600	Interpersonal skills	HCA	323	4Q	U	
090600	Human resource developmnt	HCA	324	4Q	U	
090600	Admin & supervisor theory	HCA	326	4Q	U	
090600	Health care topics	HCA	480	CV	U	
090600	Directed rdings hlth care	HCA	483	CV	U	
090600	Practicum internship	HCA	489	CV	U	
090600	Seminar in health care	HCA	499	2Q	U	
090601	Hospital organiz & mgmt	HCA	302	4Q	U	
090601	Financ admin in hlth care	HCA	303	4Q	U	
090603	Clinical superv & eval	HCA	317	4Q	U	
090699	Health care systems	HCA	300	4Q	U	
090702	Comnty hlth promotion	HIEd	315	3Q	U	
090799	Patient education	HIEd	319	3Q	U	
090799	Dev of hlth promot prog	HIEd	415	3Q	U	
090799	Foundtns of hlth promot	HIEd	310	3Q	U	
090904	Med-legl aspcts hlth care	HCA	340	4Q	U	
099900	Medical terminology	HISci	101	3Q	L	AC
099900	Training needs analysis	HIEd	321	2Q	U	

NCES No.	Course Title	Dept.	Course No.	Cred.	Lev.	Specl. Feat.
099900	Clinical instruc & eval	HIEd	318	4Q	U	
099900	Occupational community ed	HIEd	330	3Q	U	
099900	Clinical instruction dsgn	HIEd	441	3Q	U	
099900	Clinical instructl skills	HIEd	442	4Q	U	
099900	Clinical instructl eval	HIEd	443	2Q	U	
099900	Health sci ed indep study	HIEd	480	CV	U	
099900	Hlth sci ed directed read	HIEd	483	CV	U	
099900	Pract intrnshp hlth sc ed	HIEd	489	CV	U	
099900	Health sci ed seminar	HIEd	499	2Q	U	
100100	Consumer textiles	DisEd	235	4Q	L	
100206	Plan indiv family finance	ChFam	PD115	3Q	L	
100313	Principles of nutrition	ChFam	PD101	3Q	L	
100601	Human development	ChFam	PD150	5Q	L	
100603	Intro to gerontology	Geron	SS101	5Q	L	
120300	Developmental writing II	Engl	096	3Q	L	
120300	English composition	Engl	101	3Q	L	
120300	English composition II	Engl	102	3Q	L	
120307	Introduction to fiction	Engl	HU232	3Q	L	
120310	English composition	Engl	102	5Q	L	
120310	Fiction writing	Engl	225	3Q	L	
120310	Poetry writing	Engl	326	3Q	U	
120399	Vocabulary building	Engl	107	2Q	L	
129900	Travel & study abroad	Lang	209	3Q	L	
140100	Library research methods	LibSc	340	3Q	L	
150202	Intro to meteorology	Geog	NS113	4Q	L	
150400	Introduction to chemistry	Chem	NS101	5Q	L	
159900	Heredity	Zoolg	230	5Q	L	
160302	First course in algebra	Math	096	5Q	L	
160302	Intermediate algebra	Math	105	5Q	L	
160302	College algebra	Math	107	5Q	L	
160302	Beginning applied algebra	Math	113	5Q	L	
160302	Applied algebra	Math	114	5Q	L	
160302	Applied trigonometry	Math	115	5Q	L	
160800	Statistical analysis I	Stat	260	4Q	L	
160800	Life support logistics	MCE	445	4Q	U	VC
180800	Intro to philosophy	Philo	101	5Q	L	
190100	Fitness for life	PhyEd	108	1Q	L	
190100	Jogging	PhyEd	110	1Q	L	
199900	Personal health	Hlth	101	2Q	L	
200100	Intro to psychology	Psych	SS101	5Q	L	
200505	Psych of adjustment	Psych	SS154	3Q	L	
200509	Theories of personality	Psych	446	3Q	U	
200700	Social psychology	Psych	446	3Q	U	
210100	Intro to public administ	PolSc	370	5Q	U	
210300	Criminal justice	CLEE	SS101	5Q	L	
220100	Introduction anthropology	Anthr	SS101	5Q	L	
220100	Anthropology	Anthr	101	5Q	L	
220201	Economic principles	Econ	101	5Q	L	
220305	Physical geography	Geog	NS101	5Q	L	
220402	Diplomatic history of US	Hist	425	5Q	U	
220420	History of Africa	Hist	374	5Q	U	
220423	History of the Far East	Hist	470	5Q	U	
220426	Twentieth-century Europe	Hist	433	5Q	U	
220428	Utah history	Hist	428	3Q	U	
220429	Hist of the Middle East	Hist	473	5Q	U	
220432	American civilization	Hist	SS170	5Q	L	
220432	Recent America	Hist	319	3Q	L	
220433	World civilization begin	Hist	SS101	4Q	L	
220433	World civilization-1871	Hist	SS102	4Q	L	
220433	World civilization-presnt	Hist	SS103	4Q	L	
220472	Women in American history	Hist	415	3Q	U	
220499	Far Western history	Hist	427	5Q	U	
220501	American national govermt	PolSc	SS110	5Q	L	
220600	Intro to sociology	Socio	SS101	5Q	L	
220613	Social problems	Socio	SS102	5Q	L	
220699	Social stratification	Socio	301	3Q	U	

(68) **WESTERN ILLINOIS UNIVERSITY**

Dr. Joyce E. Nielsen
Director, Independent Study Program
School of Continuing Education, 5 Horrabin Hall
Western Illinois University
Macomb, Illinois 61455
Phone: 309-298-2496

External degree available through the program. Credit by examination is available. Telecourses are offered. Military personnel may enroll through the DANTES program. In exceptional cases, gifted high school students are permitted to enroll in undergraduate courses for credit. Overseas enrollment is not encouraged, but each case is judged on an individual basis. Registration occurs at the beginning of each of three academic terms. Interested readers should request course listings for future terms.

NCES No.	Course Title	Dept.	Course No.	Cred.	Lev.	Specl. Feat.
	College courses					
040301	Business finance	Finan	312	3S	U	
040308	Money, banking and credit	Econ	325	3S	U	
040399	Personal investing	Finan	305	3S	U	
040710	Risk mgmt & insurance	Finan	351	3S	U	
040800	International business	IntBu	317	3S	U	
040903	Organizational behavior	Mgmt	350	3S	U	
040904	Principles of management	Mgmt	349	3S	U	
040999	Management and society	Mgmt	481	3S	U	
040999	Intro to operations mgmt	Mgmt	352	3S	U	
041001	Principles of marketing	Mktg	327	3S	U	
041004	Retailing management	Mktg	343	3S	U	
041005	Advtg & promotional conc	Mktg	331	3S	U	
041099	Consumer market behavior	Mktg	333	3S	U	
041103	Personnel management	Mgmt	353	3S	U	
041303	Principles of real estate	Finan	361	3S	U	
050299	Comp broadcasting systems	CA&Sc	325	3S	U	
051001	Broadcasting and society	CA&Sc	323	3S	U	
100109	Soc psych aspects apparel	HomEc	313	3S	U	
100312	Child nutrition & health	HomEc	303	3S	U	
100313	Intro to nutrition	HomEc	109	3S	L	
100602	Parenting	HomEc	426	3S	U	
100699	Marriage and family	HomEc	321	3S	U	
120299	Personal nonfiction	Engl	400	3S	U	
120305	Modern English grammar	Engl	370	3S	U	
120307	Women and literature	Engl	301	3S	U	
120307	Romantic literature	Engl	320	3S	U	
120310	Writing in humanities	Engl	380	3S	U	
120399	Scientific & tech writing	Engl	381	3S	U	
120399	Modern drama	Engl	360	3S	U	
130803	American law	Hist	303	3S	U	
150103	Astronomy	Geog	325	3S	U	
150303	Human biology	Bio	304	4S	U	
150599	Environmental geology	Geol	375	3S	U	
180301	Moral philosophy	Philo	330	3S	U	
180999	Religion in America	Relig	395	3S	U	
190799	Tourism	Rec	362	3S	U	
190799	Leisure serv for elderly	Rec	452	3S	U	
200799	Fire-related human behavr	Psych	481	3S	U	
210302	Fire protect struc design	InArt	443	3S	U	
210302	Pol & legal fnd fire prot	LEA	485	3S	U	
210302	Adv fire administration	LEA	481	3S	U	
210302	Anlyt appr to fire protec	LEA	482	3S	U	
210302	Psnl mgmt for fire serv	LEA	483	3S	U	
210302	Fire-prvntn organ & mgmt	LEA	484	3S	U	
210302	Disaster & fire def plang	HISci	477	3S	U	
210302	Applic of fire research	Socio	475	3S	U	
210302	Fire dynamics	InArt	475	3S	U	
210302	Incen fire analy & inves	LEA	486	3S	U	
210302	Community and fire threat	Socio	475	3S	U	
210401	Soc serv & welfare policy	Socio	311	3S	U	
210501	Outdoor recreat perspect	Rec	376	3S	U	
220211	Labor instit & pub policy	Econ	340	3S	U	
220299	Intro health economics	Econ	390	3S	U	
220399	Climatology	Geog	327	3S	U	
220399	Population geography	Geog	443	3S	U	
220399	Conserv and mgmt nat res	Geog	426	3S	U	
220426	Germany under Hitler	Hist	438	3S	U	
220432	American history to 1877	Hist	105	3S	L	
220432	American hist since 1877	Hist	106	3S	L	
220432	Business in Am history	Hist	302	3S	U	
220432	US military history	Hist	304	3S	U	
220432	The American West	Hist	308	3S	U	
220432	Am Revol & the new nation	Hist	413	3S	U	
220499	Technology and society	Hist	312	3S	U	
220501	Int to Am govt & politics	PolSc	122	3S	L	
220505	US foreign policy	PolSc	331	3S	U	
220509	Pol systems of W Europe	PolSc	322	3S	U	AC
220599	Supreme Court	PolSc	319	3S	U	
220602	Criminology	Socio	355	3S	U	
220604	Juvenile delinquency	Socio	425	3S	U	
220605	The family	Socio	460	3S	U	
220613	Soc of mental health	Socio	424	3S	U	
220615	Minority peoples	Socio	411	3S	U	
220699	Sex roles	Socio	360	3S	U	

(69) **WESTERN MICHIGAN UNIVERSITY**

Mrs. Geraldine A. Schma
Director, Self-Instructional Programs
Ellsworth Hall, Room B-102
Western Michigan University
Kalamazoo, Michigan 49008-5161
Phone: 616-383-0788

Telecourses are offered. Enrollment on a noncredit basis accepted in credit courses. High school students may enroll in undergraduate courses for credit. Overseas enrollment accepted. Maximum period for course completion is one year.

NCES No.	Course Title	Dept.	Course No.	Cred.	Lev.	Specl. Feat.
	College courses					
010699	Plants of SW Michigan	Bio	599	3S	L	
010699	Trees & shrubs	Bio	599	2S	L	
010699	Economic botany	Bio	599	3S	U	
020699	Connections: tec & change	GenSt	333	2S	L	AC
050299	Mass media: messgs/manip	GnHum	316	4S	U	
050305	Film interpretation	Engl	210	4S	L	
050401	Photography workshop	Educ	550	3S	U	
050402	Technical communication	IndEn	102	3S	L	
050499	Popular literature	GenSt	333	1S	L	
050608	Newswriting	Engl	264	4S	L	
060199	Intro to info processing	Bus	102	3S	L	CI
060199	Intro to computers	CmpSc	105	3S	L	
070306	Prin of vocational educat	VocEd	512	3S	U	
070511	Teach pract arts & voc ed	VocEd	344	3S	L	
070515	Biological sci in elem ed	Bio	107	4S	L	
070599	Course planng & construct	VocEd	342	3S	L	
070603	Coord techniq in co-op ed	VocEd	543	3S	U	
070799	Prin & phil of guidance	CaPlg	580	2S	U	
081504	Operat planning & control	IndEn	326	3S	L	
081505	Quality assurance	IndEn	328	3S	L	
081506	Work analysis	IndEn	305	3S	L	
090199	Medical terminology	MdTrm	301	2S	L	
090303	Hm grth devlment & aging	OccTh	225	3S	L	
090303	Orientat to occup therapy	OccTh	202	3S	L	
090303	Psychiatric conditions	OccTh	436	3S	U	
100299	Time management	ConSc	205	1S	L	
100299	Visual merchandising	ConSc	205	1S	L	
100699	Amer families in transitn	GenSt	333	2S	L	AC
100699	Working: changes/choices	GenSt	333	2S	L	AC
100699	Death & dying: ch/change	GenSt	333	2S	L	AC
120299	The British novel	Engl	544	4S	U	
120299	Children's literature	Engl	282	4S	L	
120308	Personal readg efficiency	Educ	103	2S	L	
120308	Effctv rdg for coll stu	Educ	104	2S	L	AC
120310	Thought & language: expos	Engl	105	4S	L	
120310	Preprofessional writing	Engl	305	4S	L	
120399	Personal vocabulary devel	Educ	502	2S	L	
150300	Biological science	Bio	107	4S	L	
150304	Ecology	Bio	301	4S	L	
150316	Applied botany	Bio	220	4S	L	SL
150316	Medical botany	Bio	599	3S	U	
150399	Environmental biology	Bio	105	3S	L	
150499	History of chemistry	Chem	580	3S	U	
160202	Logic	Philo	520	4S	U	
160301	Computational skills	Math	109	2S	L	
160800	Statistics	Math	366	4S	L	
180399	Medical ethics	Philo	570	1S	U	
180700	Intro to humanities	GnHum	105	4S	L	
180700	American culture	GnHum	302	4S	L	
180700	Depression and war	GnHum	410	4S	U	VC
180700	Civil Rights Movement	GnHum	410	4S	U	VC
181303	Monasticism and reform	MdvSt	500	2S	U	
190108	Beginning bowling	PhyEd	200	1S	L	VC
190108	Beginning golf	PhyEd	200	1S	L	VC
190108	Beginning racquetball	PhyEd	200	1S	L	VC
190108	Beginning tennis	PhyEd	200	1S	L	VC
190108	Intermediate bowling	PhyEd	200	1S	L	VC
190108	Intermediate racquetball	PhyEd	200	1S	L	VC
190108	Intermediate tennis	PhyEd	200	1S	L	VC
190399	Sports and Americans	GenSt	333	3S	L	AC
190504	Healthful living	Bio	599	2S	L	
200501	Abnormal psychology	Psych	250	3S	U	
200508	Child psychology	Psych	160	3S	L	
200599	Intro to human behavior	Psych	150	3S	L	
200599	Brain mind & behavior	Psych	597	3S	U	VC
200599	The mind	Psych	597	3S	U	VC

NCES No.	Course Title	Dept.	Course No.	Cred.	Lev.	Specl. Feat.
200901	Organizational psychology	Psych	344	3S	L	
200901	Industrial psychology	Psych	540	3S	U	
209900	General psychology	Psych	194	3S	L	
209900	Advanced gen psychology	Psych	510	3S	U	
220101	Intro to archeology	Anthr	210	3S	L	
220109	Indians and Eskimos	Anthr	332	3S	L	VC
220199	Prehistory of North Ameri	Anthr	300	3S	L	
220201	Principles of econ: micro	Econ	201	3S	L	
220201	Principles of econ: macro	Econ	202	3S	L	
220204	Money & credit	Econ	420	4S	U	
220204	Price theory	Econ	303	3S	L	
220211	Labor problems	Econ	410	3S	U	
220213	Managerial economics	Econ	400	3S	U	
220299	Contemp econ problems	Econ	100	3S	L	
220306	Geography of Michigan	Geog	311	3S	U	AC
220399	Human geography	Geog	205	3S	L	
220420	Sub-Saharan Africa	GenSt	305	4S	L	VC
220499	Intro to non-Westrn world	GenSt	304	4S	U	
220505	International relations	PolSc	250	4S	U	
220599	Prct appl of mgmt prin	PolSc	270	1S	L	
220599	Soviet & E Europe pol sys	PolSc	344	4S	U	
220601	American society	Socio	100	3S	L	
220602	Criminology	Socio	362	3S	U	
220604	Juvenile delinquency	Socio	564	3S	U	
220606	Principles of sociology	Socio	200	3S	L	
220607	Intro to social psych	Socio	320	3S	L	
220611	Art & society	Socio	570	2S	U	
220615	Intro to social gerontol	Socio	352	3S	U	
220699	Intro to criminal justice	Socio	264	3S	L	
220699	Soc impacts of sci & tech	Socio	171	3S	L	
220699	Computer usage	Socio	182	3S	L	
220699	Amer healthcare system	Socio	495	1S	U	
220699	Organ of healthcare syst	Socio	510	3S	U	
229900	Modern Japanese society	Socio	336	3S	L	AC

⑦⓪ WESTERN OREGON STATE COLLEGE

Susan I. Nisbet
Coordinator, Open Learning Fire Service Program
Division of Continuing Education & Summer Programs
Western Oregon State College
Monmouth, Oregon 97361
Phone: 503-838-1220 ext. 483

Credit by examination is available. Overseas enrollment not accepted. Military personnel may enroll through the DANTES program. Institution offers special arrangements to take courses not listed in this Catalog. Minimum period for course completion is two weeks. Maximum period for course completion is fifteen weeks. The Open Learning Fire Service Program is administered regionally and is open to students at the upper-division level. Instant Replay is a videotape-based system for delivering regularly scheduled upper-division courses throughout the state of Oregon. It is designed for teachers and others.

NCES No.	Course Title	Dept.	Course No.	Cred.	Lev.	Specl. Feat.
	College courses					
070611	1st & 2nd lang acquisitn	Educ	484G	3Q	B	VC
070800	Mng studt beh data & prog	SplEd	423G	3Q	B	VC
071000	Encouraging discrged chld	Educ	462G	3Q	B	VC
071200	Computer literacy in educ	CmpSc	410G	3Q	B	VC
210302	Fire administration	FSA	323	5Q	U	
210302	Anlytc apprch publ fire	FSA	324	5Q	U	
210302	Persnl mngmnt fire servc	FSA	325	5Q	U	
210302	Fire prvntn orgztn & mngt	FSA	326	5Q	U	
210302	Fire related human behvr	FSA	327	5Q	U	
210302	Disastr fire def plng	FSA	328	5Q	U	
210302	Poltcl legal foun of fire	FSA	329	5Q	U	
210302	Fire prtn strct/systems	FSA	330	5Q	U	
210302	Commuty & fire threat	FSA	331	5Q	U	
210302	Incndry fire anlys/invstg	FSA	332	5Q	U	
210302	Applcatns fire research	FSA	333	5Q	U	
210302	Fire dynamics	FSA	334	5Q	U	
210302	Field study	FSA	403	3Q	U	

NCES No.	Course Title	Dept.	Course No.	Cred.	Lev.	Specl. Feat.
210302	Practicum	SoSci	409	3Q	U	
210399	Emrgncy medicl srv admin	FSA	335	3Q	U	
220102	Cultural anthropology	Anthr	312	3Q	U	VC
220308	Seminar urban studies	Geog	407	2Q	U	
220399	Spec stds world affairs	Geog	406	2Q	U	
220399	Practicum	Geog	409	CV	U	

⑦① WESTERN WASHINGTON UNIVERSITY

Janet Howard
Independent Study Coordinator
Continuing Education/Conference Services
Old Main 400
Western Washington University
Bellingham, Washington 98225
Phone: 206-676-3650

Telecourses are offered. Enrollment on a noncredit basis accepted in credit courses. High school students may enroll in undergraduate courses for credit. Overseas enrollment accepted. Institution offers special arrangements to take courses not listed in this Catalog. Maximum period for course completion is one year.

NCES No.	Course Title	Dept.	Course No.	Cred.	Lev.	Specl. Feat.
	College courses					
040101	Prin of financial acctg	Acctg	241	4Q	L	
040101	Prin of financial acctg	Acctg	242	4Q	L	
040109	Fund and governmental acc	Acctg	377	3Q	U	
040111	Prin of managerial acctg	Acctg	243	4Q	L	
070199	Foundations of education	EdFA	411	4Q	U	
070199	History of American educ	EdFA	413	4Q	U	
070199	Global issues/American ed	EdFA	311	4Q	U	
070499	Competencies for certific	Educ	502B	3Q	U	
070899	Intro to exceptional chld	Educ	360	3Q	U	
090902	Traditional Chinese med	SEAS	417A	4Q	U	
100313	Human nutrition	HomEc	250	3Q	L	
119900	Hist and phil of voc ed	Tech	491	3Q	U	
119900	Community/indus resources	Tech	496	1Q	U	
119900	Occupational analysis	Tech	445X	2Q	U	
119900	Safety princip/practices	Tech	488	2Q	U	
120305	Language and exposition	Engl	101	4Q	L	
120307	Survey of American lit	Engl	216	5Q	L	
120307	Contemporary women's lit	Engl	445W	5Q	U	
120310	Journal writing I	Engl	445X	5Q	U	
120310	Journal writing II	Engl	445K	5Q	U	
120310	Creative writing I	Engl	445Y	5Q	U	
120310	Creative writing II	Engl	445M	5Q	U	
160102	Intro to mathematics	Math	151	3Q	L	
160302	College algebra	Math	103	3Q	L	
160302	Intermediate algebra	Math	102	3Q	L	
160302	Algebra appli to bus/econ	Math	155	4Q	L	
160401	Calc with app to bus/econ	Math	156	4Q	L	
160401	Precalculus	Math	105	4Q	L	
160602	Trigonometry	Math	104	3Q	L	
160603	Calc/analytic geometry	Math	124	5Q	L	
160801	Intro to statistics	Math	240	3Q	L	
200199	Intro to psychology	Psych	201	5Q	L	
220110	Intro to cultural anthrop	Anthr	201	5Q	L	
220199	Peoples/subSaharan Africa	Anthr	363	5Q	U	
220403	Econ/unconstrained mkt	Hist	390A	4Q	U	
220403	Economics/constrained mkt	Hist	390B	4Q	U	
220423	Traditional Korea	SEAS	311	5Q	U	
220423	Intro to East Asian civil	Hist	280	5Q	L	AC
220428	History of Pacific NW	Hist	391	3Q	U	
220428	History of Hawaiian Islds	Hist	417C	3Q	U	
220432	American history to 1865	Hist	103	5Q	L	
220432	American history since 1865	Hist	104	5Q	L	
220432	American frontier history	Hist	417X	5Q	U	
220470	Intro to Asian-Amer study	ACS	205	3Q	L	
220470	Comparative minority st	ACS	301	3Q	U	
220605	Sociology of the family	Socio	360	5Q	U	
220606	Intro to sociology	Socio	202	5Q	L	

Use this alphabetical listing to quickly locate the name of any subject-matter area in the Index; then turn to the section of the Index that corresponds to the number following the subject listing. For example, if you are interested in advertising, find Advertising below (Advertising 0501), and then (after carefully reading the key to the Index on its first page) turn to section 0501 of the Index to determine which colleges and universities offer courses in that area.

Abnormal Psychology	200501
Academic Counseling and Guidance	070702
Accounting	0401
Accounting Principles	040101
Accounting Systems	040102
Administration of Health Education	190513
Administration of Libraries and Museums	1403
Administration of Sport	190308
Administrative and Office Services	0402
Administrative Management	210103
Administrative Procedures	040201
Administrative Theory	210101
Adult-Continuing Education Systems	070309
Advertising	0501
Advertising Evaluation	050101
Advertising Media	050102
Advertising Production	050103
Aerodynamics	080101
Aeronautics	080102
Aerospace and Aeronautical Engineering and Technology	0801
Aesthetics	1801
African History	220420
Agency Law	130701
Agricultural Credit and Finance	010102
Agricultural Economics	0101
Agricultural Engineering and Technology	0802
Agricultural Engineering (See 08—Engineering and Engineering Technology)	0102
Agricultural Marketing	010103
Agricultural Organizations	010104
Agricultural Technology	0103
Agriculture and Renewable Natural Resources	01
Agriculture and Renewable Natural Resources	070501
Air-Conditioning, Heating, Ventilation, and Refrigeration Engineering	082001
Aircraft Maintenance	110401
Air-Pollution Control	081301
Algebra	160302
Algebraic Geometry	160304
Algebraic Structures	160305
American Colonial History	220421
American Government	220501
American Military History	170102
Analytic Geometry	160603
Ancient History	220450
Ancient Near East Theology	181301
Ancient Western Philosophy	180401
Animal Anatomy	150324
Animal Diseases, Parasites, and Insects	010403
Animal Genetics	150326
Animal Genetics and Reproduction	010404
Animal Management and Production	010406
Animal Nutrition	010407
Animal or Animal Products Selection and Evaluation	010402
Animal Sciences	0104
Antarctic History	220422
Anthropology	2201

Applications in Computer Science and Data Processing	0601
Applications of Mathematics (General)	1611
Applied Linguistics	120101
Applied Statistics	160802
Appraisal and Valuation	041301
Arabic	1205
Archaeology	220101
Architectural Design	020101
Architectural Drafting	020402
Architectural Engineering and Technology	0803
Architecture and Environmental Design	02
Arithmetic	160301
Arithmetic and Algebra	1603
Arts, Visual and Performing	03
Arts, Visual and Performing	070503
Asian History	220423
Astronomy	1501
Astrophysics	150702
Atmospheric Sciences	1502
Attitudes	200701
Audiology and Speech Pathology	090301
Auditing	040103
Automotive Engineering and Technology	0804
Bacteriology	150317
Banking and Finance	0403
Basic Concepts of Computer Science	061103
Basic Concepts of Data Processing	061104
Basic Health-Care Sciences	0901
Behavior Analysis	200401
Bilingual Education Programs	070611
Biochemistry (See 090102—Biochemistry)	150403
Biological Behavior	150301
Biology	1503
Biopsychology	2002
Bookkeeping	040104
Braille	051201
British History	220424
Buddhism	180901
Business	04
Business	070504
Business and Corporate Finance	040301
Business and Industrial Economics	220213
Business Communication	040601
Business Communication Systems	040602
Business Data Systems	0404
Business Mathematics	161201
Business Policy	040901
Business Report Writing	040604
Business Research Methods	041201
Calculus	160401
Calculus of Variations	160412
Cardiology	090201
Career Development	200502
Career Education	070602
Career Information and Counseling	070703
Cataloging of Collections	140401
Cell Biology	150302
Chemical Engineering and Technology	0806
Chemistry	1504
Child Development	100601
Chinese	1207
Christianity	180902
Christology	181406
Church Administration and Leadership	181607

Citizenship	220502
Civil and Administrative Procedure	1301
Civil Engineering and Technology	0807
Classical Analysis	1604
Climatology	150201
Clinical Chemistry	090103
Clinical Experience	070704
Clinical Health Sciences	0902
Clinical Practices in Health Care and Health Sciences	090905
Clinical Psychology	200503
Clothing and Construction and Alterations	100104
Clothing and Textile Maintenance	100101
Clothing and Textile Merchandising	100102
Clothing and Textiles	1001
Clothing and Textile Selection	100103
Clothing Design	100105
Collection Management	1404
Combined Structures	020505
Command Languages	060701
Commercial Law	1302
Communication	070505
Communication	05
Communication in Architecture and Environmental Design	0204
Communication Networking	050201
Communication Technology	0502
Community-Health Education	190502
Community Medicine	090702
Community Nutrition	100301
Community Psychology	200801
Community Relations	070902
Community Service	0709
Community Sociology	220601
Comparative Economic Systems	220209
Comparative Law	130801
Comparative Literature	120201
Comparative Political Systems	220503
Comparative Religions	181002
Compilers	060802
Computer Applications to Education	071201
Computer Graphics	060102
Computer Hardware	0604
Computer Hardware Systems	0603
Computer Literacy	061101
Computer Operation	060201
Computer Operations and Operations Control	0602
Computer Science and Data Processing	06
Computer Science and Data Processing	070506
Constitutional and Administrative History	220401
Constitutional Law	1303
Construction	1101
Construction and Design Implementation	0203
Consumer Economics	100202
Consumer Economics	220208
Consumer Education	1002
Consumer Finance	040302
Consumer-Health Education	190503
Consumer Mathematics	161202
Consumer Rights and Responsibilities	100205
Contemporary History	220451
Contemporary Western Philosophy	180404
Contemporary World Affairs	220504
Content of Mathematics	160103
Cooperative Education	070603
Copy Preparation	110502
Copywriting	050104
Correctional Services	210301
Cosmology (See 180601—Cosmology)	150101
Cost Accounting	040106
Counseling and Guidance	0707
Counseling Services	070705
Credit and Collections	040303
Criminal Law	1304
Criminal Procedure and Evidence	130402
Criminology	220602
Critical and Persuasive Writing	050602
Cultural Anthropology	220102
Cultural Geography	220301
Curriculum and Instruction—General	0704
Curriculum and Instruction—Programs	0706
Curriculum and Instruction—Subject Matter (Using the Structure of the Classification of Educational Subject Matter)	0705
Dance Choreography	190401
Dance (See 0301—Dance)	1904
Dance (See 1904—Dance)	0301
Danish	1208
Database Management Systems	060502
Database Security	060503
Data Entry	060203
Data-Processing Accounting	040107
Decision Making	100401
Demography and Human Ecology	220603
Descriptive Statistics	160801
Design and Planning	071101
Design and Planning Technology	0202
Developmental Biology	150303
Developmental Psychology	200504
Development of Driving Judgment	190603
Diagnostics	090104
Dialects of the English Language	120301
Dietetics	100302
Dietetics and Nutrition	090302
Differential Geometry	160606
Diplomatic History	220402
Disease Prevention and Control	190504
Distributions (Generalized Functions)	160507
Distributive Education	070604
Drawing	110503
Driver and Safety Education	1906
Driver Education Programs	070613
Drug and Drug-Abuse Information	090403
Drug Regulation and Control	090404
Drugs and Other Substances	190501
Early Christian and Rabbinic Theology	181302
Early Education of the Handicapped	070801
Ecology	150304
Economic Development and International Trade	010106
Economic Geography	220302
Economic Growth and Development	220207
Economic History	220403
Economic Policy	220203
Economics	2202
Economics of Natural Resources	220212
Editorial Processes	050601
Education	07
Education	070507
Educational Administration	0702
Educational Development	0710
Educational Evaluation and Research	0711
Educational Media and Material Production	071203

Educational Media and Resource Centers	071204
Educational Personnel and Staffing	070207
Educational Psychology	200804
Educational, Societal, and Cultural Considerations	0611
Educational Technology and Media	0712
Educational Theory	070102
Electrical	110104
Electrical Engineering and Technology	0809
Electrical Instrumentation	080906
Electrical Power	110303
Electricity	150704
Electromechanical Circuits	080901
Electronics	080903
Elementary Education Systems	070302
Emergency Services	0905
Energy Conversion	082003
Engineering and Construction Surveying	082602
Engineering and Engineering Technology	08
Engineering Mechanics	0811
Engineering Science	0812
English Language and Civilization	120303
English Language and Contemporary Culture	120304
English Language Literature	120307
English Language Structure and Grammar	120305
Entomology	150327
Entrepreneurship	0405
Environmental Design	0201
Environmental Engineering and Technology	0813
Environmental Health Administration	090703
Environmental-Health Education	190505
Environmental Law	131101
Environmental Psychology	2003
Environmental Technology	0206
Epidemiology	090106
Epistemology	1802
Eschatology	181409
Estate Planning	040703
Ethical Principles of Psychology	200101
Ethics	1803
Ethics and Jurisprudence in Health Care and Health Sciences	090904
Ethics of Professions	180303
Ethnology	220104
European History	220426
Evaluation Techniques	041102
Evidence	130103
Evolution	150306
Exercise	190102
Experimental Psychology	2004
Fabric Maintenance and Repair	110406
Family Development	100602
Family-Health Education	190506
Family Medicine	090272
Farm and Ranch Management	010107
Feature and In-Depth Writing	050605
Fields and Waves	080904
Fields of Social Work	210404
Film as Art (See 0503—Film as Communication)	0302
Film as Communication (See 0302—Film as Art)	0503
Financial Institutions	040304
Finite Differences and Functional Equations	160408
Finite Probability	160701
Finite Sets	160203
Finnish	1209
Fire Protection	210302
First Aid	090504

Fisheries	0108
Fisheries Biology	010801
Flight Operations	110601
Fluid Mechanics	081102
Food and Nutrition	1003
Food Habits and Patterns	100304
Food-Production Technology	100305
Food Selection	100308
Food Service	100309
Food-Service Management	100702
Forest Biology	010902
Forest Management and Administration	010901
Forestry	0109
Foundations of Education	0701
Foundations of Probability	160706
Foundations of Psychology	2001
French	1210
Functional Analysis	1605
Gastroenterology	090214
General Accounting	040108
General Botany	150316
General Chemistry	150401
General Dentistry	090202
General Earth-Space Science	1509
General Genetics	150307
General Marketing	041001
General Perspectives of Health Care and Health Sciences	0909
General Physical Sciences	1508
General Zoology	150323
Geography	2203
Geology	1505
Geometrics	160604
Geometry and Topology	1606
Geomorphology	150501
German	1211
Gerontology	100603
Gerontology	090242
Gifted and Talented	070803
God	181401
Governmental and Institutional Accounting	040109
Governmental Regulation of Business	1305
Graphic Arts	1105
Graphics and Drafting for Engineering and Technology	0810
Graph Theory	160204
Greek	1212
Group Games, Contests, and Self-Testing Activities	190103
Group Processes	200702
Group Theory	160308
Health-Care Anatomy	090101
Health Care and Health Sciences	09
Health Care and Health Sciences	070509
Health-Care Delivery Systems	090602
Health-Care Nutrition	090115
Health-Care Physiology	090119
Health Education	1905
Health-Education Instruction	190515
Health Organizations, Standards, and Evaluation	090603
Health Planning	090901
Hearing Handicapped	070804
Hebrew	1213
Hinduism	180903
Historical Geography	220303

Historical Perspectives of Psychology	200102		Judaism	180905
Historical Theology	1813		Juvenile Delinquency	220604
History and Traditions of Philosophy	1804		Juvenile Justice	130403
History of Economics	220202			
History of Film as Communication	050304		Kinesiology	1902
History of Food and Nutrition	100311			
History of Health Care and Health Sciences	090902		Labor and Manpower Economics	220211
History of Leisure Studies	190706		Labor-Management Relations	041104
History of Mathematics	160102		Landscape Architectural Design	020102
History of Physical Education	190104		Landscaping	010504
History of Science	220405		Land Surveying and Subdivision	082601
History of the English Language	120302		Language Analysis	120103
History of Women	220472		Language, Linguistics, and Literature	12
History—Thematic, Area, Period, and Person	2204		Language, Linguistics, and Literature	070512
Home Economics	10		Latin	1216
Home Furnishings	100501		Latin American History	220427
Home Management	1004		Law	13
Home Planning and Interior Design	100503		Law Enforcement	210304
Homiletics	181601		Law of Associations	130702
Hospital and Health-Care Administration	0906		Law of Business and Other Organizations	1307
Hospital Organization and Management	090601		Law of Contracts	130202
Household Equipment	100504		Law of Corporations	130703
Housekeeping Management	100701		Law of State and Local Governments	1318
Housing	1005		Law of Wills and Estates	130907
Housing Planning	020902		Leadership in Leisure Studies	190704
Human Development and Family Studies	1006		Learning Disabled	070805
Human Ecology	090704		Leather and Hide Processing	110205
Human Engineering	200906		Legal History	130803
Human Factors in Industry	081502		Legal Profession	1314
Human Information Processing	200403		Legal Skills	1315
Human Relations	041103		Leisure and Recreation Planning	190703
Hydrology (See 150502—Hydrology)	080703		Leisure Studies	1907
			Libraries and Museums	070514
Industrial and Occupational Safety Services	210303		Libraries and Museums	14
Industrial Arts, Trades, and Technology	070511		Library Administration	140303
Industrial Arts, Trades, and Technology	11		Library and Museum Services and Functions	1408
Industrial Engineering and Technology	0815		Library and Museum User Groups	1409
Industrial-Health Administration	090705		Library Science	1401
Industrial Psychology	200901		Life Insurance	040707
Infectious Diseases	090113		Life Sciences and Physical Sciences	15
Informal Logic	180501		Life Sciences and Physical Sciences	070515
Information and Database Systems	0605		Linear and Multilinear Algebra	160306
Information Communications	0406		Linguistics (Diachronic and Synchronic)	1201
Innovative Communication	0504		Linguistics in Anthropology	220105
Institutional Housekeeping and Food-Service			Literary Aesthetics and Appreciation	120202
Management	1007		Literary Criticism	120204
Instructional Applications	060103		Literary Studies	1202
Instructional Systems Design	071202		Literary Theories	120205
Instruction and Coaching of Sport	190311		Local and State History	220428
Insurance and Risk Management	0407		Logic and Philosophical Methodology	1805
Intellectual and Cultural History	220406		Logic, Sets, and Foundations	1602
Intercultural Communication	051102			
Interior Design	020103		Management	0409
International and Comparative Leisure Studies	190709		Management and Supervision of Curriculum and	
International Banking and Finance	040305		Instruction	070402
International Business	0408		Management Applications	040902
International Economics	220214		Management Science	041202
International Relations	220505		Managerial Accounting	040111
Interpersonal Communication	051103		Manual Communication	051202
Investments and Securities	040306		Manufacturing Engineering and Technology	0817
Islam	180904		Manufacturing (Product Generation)	1102
Italian	1214		Marine Biology	150310
			Marketing	0410
Japanese	1215		Marketing Economics	041002
Journalism	0506		Marketing Functions	041003
Journalism History	050606		Marketing Management	041004

Marketing of Products	041005
Marketing of Services	041006
Marriage and Family	220605
Materials Engineering and Technology	0819
Materials for Libraries and Museums	1407
Materials of Construction	080704
Maternal and Child Health Administration	090706
Mathematical and Statistical Biology	161107
Mathematical and Statistical Psychology	161108
Mathematical and Statistical Sociology	161109
Mathematical Logic	160202
Mathematical Sciences	070516
Mathematical Sciences	16
Mathematical Statistics	160803
Mathematics, General Perspectives	1601
Mathematics of Business and Finance	161101
Mathematics of Economics	161103
Measure and Integration	160403
Measurement and Evaluation in Physical Education	190110
Mechanical Design	082006
Mechanical Engineering and Technology	0820
Mechanics	150803
Medical Hygiene	090111
Medieval History	220452
Medieval Theology	181303
Medieval Western Philosophy	180402
Mediterranean History	220429
Mentally Handicapped	070806
Metallurgical Engineering and Technology	0821
Metaphysics	1806
Meteorology	150202
Methodology	071102
Microbiology	150311
Microbiology	090114
Microprocessors	060404
Military History	1701
Military Sciences	17
Minority Group History	220470
Missiology	181608
Modern History	220453
Modern Theology	181304
Modern Western Philosophy	180403
Monetary and Fiscal Policy	040307
Monetary and Fiscal Theory and Institutions	220204
Money and Banking	040308
Moral and Ethical Issues	181502
Moral and Ethical Studies	1815
Motivation	200404
Museology	1402
Museum Administration	140305
Music	0303
Music in Education	030303
Music Studies	030302
Music Studio and Performance	030301
National Income	220205
Native American	1217
Native American History	220471
Natural-Resource Planning	020904
News Reporting and Writing	050608
Noise-Pollution Control	081302
Nonprint Media	050401
Norwegian	1218
Nuclear Engineering and Technology	0823
Nuclear Medicine	090276
Number Theory	160303
Numerical Analysis	160901

Numerical Analysis and Approximation Theory	1609
Nursing	090255
Nutrition	100313
Nutrition Education	100312
Nutrition Education	190508
Occupational Therapy	090303
Oceanology	1506
Operating Systems	060806
Operations Research	041203
Operations Research (See 041203—Operations Research)	081503
Ordinary Differential Equations	160406
Organic Chemistry	150408
Organizational Communication	051104
Organizational Development and Behavior	040903
Organizational Psychology	200703
Organizational Psychology	200904
Organizational Theory and Behavior	210102
Organization of Marketing	041007
Oriental Philosophy	180405
Ornamental Horticulture	0105
Ornithology	150331
Outdoor Recreation	0110
Paleontology	150504
Partial Differential Equations	160407
Pastoral Care and Counseling	181602
Pastoral Studies	1816
Pathology	090117
Performance Physiology	190203
Personal and Family Finance	100206
Personal Development	100604
Personal-Health Education	190509
Personal Insurance	040712
Personal Moralities	180301
Personnel Management and Administration	0411
Personnel Psychology	200902
Perspectives on Law	1308
Petroleum Engineering	0825
Petroleum Exploration	082501
Pharmaceutical Sciences	0904
Pharmaceutics	090408
Pharmacology	090118
Pharmacy Practices and Management	090411
Phenomenology of Religion	1810
Philosophical Anthropology	180605
Philosophical Foundations	1808
Philosophy of Art	180101
Philosophy of Language	180504
Philosophy of Mathematics	160101
Philosophy of Natural Science	180202
Philosophy of Physical Education	190105
Philosophy of Religion	180609
Philosophy, Religion, and Theology	18
Philosophy, Religion, and Theology	070518
Photogrammetry and Topographic Surveying	082604
Photographic Journalism	050609
Photography	110504
Physical Anthropology	220106
Physical Education	1901
Physical Education Administration	190106
Physical Education Curriculum	190107
Physical Education, Health Education, and Leisure	19
Physical Education, Health Education, and Leisure	070519
Physical Education Instruction	190108

Physical Fitness	190510	Psychology of Learning	200406
Physical Geography	220305	Psychology of Personality	200509
Physically Handicapped	070808	Psychology of the Individual	2005
Physical Therapy	090305	Psychology of Thinking and Problem Solving	200408
Physics	1507	Psychometrics	2006
Physiological Hygiene	090709	Public Address	051107
Plane and Solid Geometry	160601	Public Administration	2101
Planning	0209	Public Administration and Social Services	21
Plant Anatomy and Physiology	010601	Public Education Services and Functions	140803
Plant Genetics and Reproduction	010602	Public Finance	040312
Plant Insects and Control	010603	Public Finance	220206
Plant Management and Production	010604	Public Health	0907
Plant or Plant Products Selection and Evaluation	010607	Public-Health Administration	090710
Plant Pathology	150321	Public-Policy Analysis and Evaluation	210113
Plant Sciences	0106	Public Policy and Natural Resources and Environment	210111
Pneumatology	181408	Public Policy and Science and Technology	210110
Political Behavior	220506	Public Recreation	2105
Political History	220407	Public-Recreation Administration	210503
Political Parties and Public Opinion	220507	Public Relations	0509
Political Science and Government	2205		
Political Structures	220509	Quality Assurance	081505
Political Theory	220510	Quantitative and Nonquantitative Analysis in Public Administration	210114
Populations and Leisure Services	190702	Quantitative Economics	220217
Portuguese	1219	Quantitative Methods	220609
Power Systems	1103	Quantitative Methods	0412
Pragmatic Communication	051106		
Pre-Elementary Education Systems	070301	Radiation Control	082303
Preparation of Food	100314	Radiation Therapy	090307
Principles and Theories of Counseling and Guidance	070701	Radio	0510
Principles and Theories of Curriculum and Instruction	070401	Radio and Public Policy	051001
Principles and Theory of Economics	220201	Radiobiology	090121
Principles and Theory of Evaluation and Research	071103	Radiology	090259
Principles and Theory of Finance	040311	Reading and Language Arts Programs	070610
Principles and Theory of Management	040904	Reading in the English Language	120308
Principles and Theory of Organization	040905	Real Analysis	160402
Principles and Theory of Sociology	220606	Real Estate	0413
Principles of Insurance	040708	Real-Estate Economics	041305
Principles of Real Estate	041303	Real-Estate Finance	041306
Print Media	0507	Real-Estate Investments	041307
Private Ownership	040502	Real-Estate Law	041308
Probability	1607	Real-Estate Practice	041309
Procedure-Oriented Languages	060705	Recordkeeping	040113
Production Planning and Control	081504	Records Management	040203
Product Service (Maintenance)	1104	Recreation Activities	190705
Professional Development	070708	Recreational Environments	210501
Professional Practices in Communication	0508	Recreation Therapy	090308
Professional Practices in Health Care and Health Sciences	090903	Recruitment, Selection, and Separation	041105
Programming Languages	0607	Reference and Retrieval	140804
Programming Systems	0608	Regional Geography	220306
Programming Techniques	060903	Regulation of Employment Relations	1310
Property Insurance	040709	Regulation of the Environment	1311
Property Law	1309	Rehabilitation and Therapy	0903
Property Management	041304	Related Arts	0306
Protective Services	210305	Related Arts and Aesthetic Education	030603
Psychological Programs (Applied and Professional)	2008	Related-Arts Studies	030602
Psychological Sociology	220607	Religion and Culture	181104
Psychological Testing	200603	Religion and Human Experience	1811
Psychology	20	Religion and Personality Studies	181102
Psychology	070520	Religion and Science	181101
Psychology in Economics, Industry, and Government	2009	Religion and Social Issues	181103
Psychology of Adjustment	200505	Religious Education	181603
Psychology of Death	200506	Religious History	220408
Psychology of Disadvantaged Persons (Culturally or Physically Handicapped)	200507	Renewable Natural Resources	0114
Psychology of Identifiable Sets (Women, Blacks, Others)	200508	Resource Management	100402
		Resource Management in Leisure Studies	190701

Rhetorical and Communication Theory	051108
Risk Management	040710
Rural Sociology	220608
Russian	1220
Russian History	220431
Sacred Music	181606
Sacred Writings	1812
Sacred Writings of the Christian Faith	181202
Sacred Writings of the Jewish Faith	181201
Safety and Correctional Services	2103
Safety and Health Law	131004
Safety Education	190511
Sanskrit	1221
School-Library and Media-Center Administration	140307
School Psychology	200805
Secondary Education Systems	070303
Selection and Acquisition of Collections	140408
Sex Education	190512
Shorthand and Transcription	040205
Slavic Languages	1222
Small-Engine Repair	110412
Social and Political Philosophy	1807
Social Anthropology	220107
Social Control and Deviance	220610
Social Economics	220215
Social Environments and Human Behavior	210405
Social Ethics	180302
Social History	220409
Social Institutions	220611
Socially Handicapped	070810
Social Organization and Change	220612
Social Problems	220613
Social Psychology	2007
Social Sciences and Social Studies	070522
Social Sciences and Social Studies	22
Social Welfare	210401
Social Work	2104
Social-Work Methods	210403
Social-Work Practice	210402
Socioeconomic Foundations	070103
Sociolinguistics	120107
Sociology	2206
Sociology of Groups	220615
Sociology of Religion	181004
Sociopsychological Aspects of Clothing and Textiles	100109
Software Methodology	0609
Soil and Water Resources	080205
Soil Chemistry	010701
Soil Classification	010702
Soil Conservation and Land Use	010703
Soil Fertility	010704
Soil Mechanics and Foundations	080706
Soil Sciences	0107
Solar Astronomy	150102
Solid Mechanics	081103
Solid-Waste Control	081303
Soteriology	181407
Spanish	1225
Speaking the English Language	120309
Special Communication	0512
Special Education	0708
Special Functions	160405
Specialized Secretarial Services	040206
Specific Religions	1809
Speech and Hearing Science	051110
Speech Communication	0511

Speech Communication Education	051109
Speech Handicapped	070811
Sport	1903
Sport Activities	190312
Sport History	190303
Sport in Schools and Colleges	190301
Sport Psychology	190306
State and Local Government	220511
Statics and Dynamics	081104
Statistics	1608
Stellar Astronomy	150103
Structural Engineering	080707
Structural Technology	0205
Supervision	041106
Surface Chemistry	150410
Surveying and Mapping	0826
Swedish	1226
Symbolic and Algebraic Manipulation Languages	060707
Symbolic Logic	180502
Systematic Theology	1814
Systems Analysis	060904
Systems of Education	0703
Systems of Psychology	200103
Tax Accounting	040114
Teacher Methods	070404
Teacher Training	070403
Technical Communication	050402
Television	0513
Theater Arts	0304
Theater Arts Studio and Performance	030401
Theater in Education	030403
Theater Studies	030402
Theories in Psychology	200104
Theory and Criticism of Film as Communication	050305
Theory of Computation	0610
Thermodynamics and Kinetics	080603
The Study and Uses of the English Language	1203
Topical Anthropology	220109
Training and Development	041107
Transfer-of-Property Law	130902
Transportation	1106
Transportation Geography	220307
Trigonometry	160602
Turf Grass	010505
Typewriting	040207
United States History	220432
Urban and Rural Economics	220216
Urban Geography	220308
Urban Sociology	220614
User-Oriented Mathematics	1612
Vehicle Maintenance and Repair	110413
Veterinary Medical Sciences	0908
Visual Arts	0305
Visual Arts in Education	030503
Visual-Arts Studies	030502
Visual-Arts Studio and Production	030501
Vocational-Technical Education Systems	070306
Water and Sewage Control	081304
Welding	110119
Welfare and Safety	041108
Wildlife	0112
Wildlife Management	011202

INDEX TO SUBJECT-MATTER AREAS

Key to the Index

This index is based on the classification of educational subject-matter areas prepared by the National Center for Education Statistics (NCES). Listed in alphabetical order are twenty-two broad subject-matter areas, representing major academic disciplines, with more specific areas grouped under them in two levels of subordination. Each main index line has three elements:

- The NCES subject-area identification number, which appears at the left. (NCES numbers also appear in numerical order next to the names of courses in the "Institutions and Correspondence Courses Offered" section, so that the names of courses in an area can be quickly identified in an institution's entry.)
- The name of the subject-matter area.
- The code number for the name of each institution offering one or more courses in the area, plus a code letter for each kind of course the institution offers in that area (E = Elementary, H = High School, C = College, G = Graduate, N = Noncredit). The institution represented by each code number can be identified by a quick glance at the back cover foldout.

Example:

NCES No.	Subject-Matter Area	Institutional Codes
040203	Records Management	5C, 13HN, 16C, 25H

To find the names of specific courses an institution offers in an area, make a note of the NCES number and institutional code number, including the letter code for the kind of course, and identify the institution's name and page number in the Contents, where institutional code numbers and corresponding names are listed in numerical and alphabetical order. Or turn directly to the "Institutions and Correspondence Courses Offered" section, where code numbers and corresponding names are listed numerically and alphabetically at the beginning of institutional entries and—in dictionary fashion—at the top of pages.

(If you have difficulty locating a subject-matter area in this Index, refer first to the Alphabetical Listing of Subject-Matter Areas, which precedes the Index.)

01 AGRICULTURE AND RENEWABLE NATURAL RESOURCES

Agricultural Engineering is listed in the subject-matter area of Engineering and Engineering Technology, but Agricultural Technology is included here. Animal Sciences includes the general care of animals as factors of production. The medical treatment of animals is included in Veterinary Medical Sciences in the subject-matter area of Health Care and Health Sciences. Agricultural Economics is included in this area, but the broad subject matter of Economics is included under Social Sciences and Social Studies. The elements within Plant Sciences are differentiated from similar elements in the area of Life Sciences and Physical Sciences by their emphasis on food and fiber production.

0101 Agricultural Economics 34C, 59C
010102 Agricultural Credit and Finance 30CN
010103 Agricultural Marketing 29C, 30CN, 45C, 65C
010104 Agricultural Organizations 30CN, 63CN
010106 Economic Development and International Trade 64C
010107 Farm and Ranch Management 18H, 29C, 30HN, 39C, 65C
010199 Other Agricultural Economics 14C, 29C, 37C, 39C, 43C, 64C

0102 Agricultural Engineering (See 08—Engineering and Engineering Technology)

0103 Agricultural Technology
010399 Other Agricultural Technology 18H

0104 Animal Sciences 16C
010402 Animal or Animal Products Selection and Evaluation 43C, 65C
010403 Animal Diseases, Parasites, and Insects 23N
010404 Animal Genetics and Reproduction 34C, 65C
010406 Animal Management and Production 6C, 14C, 18H, 20C, 51C, 65C
010407 Animal Nutrition 6CN, 18H, 20C, 43C, 64C, 65C
010499 Other Animal Sciences 33C, 45C, 47H, 63N

0105 Ornamental Horticulture 20C, 47HC
010504 Landscaping 37C, 45C
010505 Turf Grass 6CN, 66C
010599 Other Ornamental Horticulture 35HN, 38C, 48H, 66C

0106 Plant Sciences 13H, 16C, 67C
010601 Plant Anatomy and Physiology 20C
010602 Plant Genetics and Reproduction 4C
010603 Plant Insects and Control 6CN, 38C, 64C, 66C
010604 Plant Management and Production 43C, 65C, 66C
010607 Plant or Plant Products Selection and Evaluation 43C
010699 Other Plant Sciences 34C, 69C

0107 Soil Sciences
010701 Soil Chemistry 20C, 65C
010702 Soil Classification 37C, 66C
010703 Soil Conservation and Land Use 18H, 43C
010704 Soil Fertility 30CN

0108 Fisheries
010801 Fisheries Biology 65C

0109 Forestry 16C, 59C
010901 Forest Management and Administration 39C, 43C, 62C
010902 Forest Biology 37N, 63CN, 64H
010999 Other Forestry 37N

0110 Outdoor Recreation 6CN

0112 Wildlife
011202 Wildlife Management 18H, 37N
011299 Other Wildlife 6C, 65C

0114 Renewable Natural Resources 33C, 34C, 45C, 55H

0199 Other Agriculture and Renewable Natural Resources 18H, 37C, 44CN, 47H, 48H

02 ARCHITECTURE AND ENVIRONMENTAL DESIGN

Subject-matter elements in this area deal with the design of environments as well as the management of construction. Virtually all subject matter related to environmental planning has been included in this subject-matter area. Engineering theory and design involved in building and environmental systems are found in the area of Engineering and Engineering Technology. Elements relating to construction skills can be found in the subject-matter area of Industrial Arts, Trades, and Technology.

0201 Environmental Design 66C
020101 Architectural Design 22N
020102 Landscape Architectural Design 22C, 65C
020103 Interior Design 4HC, 18H, 35N, 48C, 66C, 67C

0202 Design and Planning Technology
020299 Other Design and Planning Technology 21C

0203 Construction and Design Implementation 67C

0204 Communication in Architecture and Environmental Design
020402 Architectural Drafting   63HN

0205 Structural Technology
020505 Combined Structures   28C
020599 Other Structural Technology   20N

0206 Environmental Technology
020699 Other Environmental Technology   69C

0209 Planning
020902 Housing Planning   14C
020904 Natural-Resource Planning   31C

0299 Other Architecture and Environmental Design   45C

03   ARTS, VISUAL AND PERFORMING

Dance is listed in this area as an aesthetic art form. It is also listed in the area of Physical Education, Health Education, and Leisure, where the emphasis is on the physical activity. Film as an artistic medium is included in this area. The knowledge of Film for the transmission of messages is included in the subject-matter area of Communication. Arts Therapy in this subject-matter area should be differentiated from the formalized medical therapy that is included in the area of Health Care and Health Sciences.

0301 Dance (See 1904—Dance)

0302 Film as Art (See 0503—Film as Communication)

0303 Music   20C, 55C, 67C
030301 Music Studio and Performance   4N, 28C, 35C
030302 Music Studies   4HN, 7C, 11HC, 18H, 19C, 22C, 28C, 30HCN, 35HCN, 36HC, 39C, 41C, 45C, 46C, 48H, 51C, 61C, 63HC, 64C, 67C
030303 Music in Education   43C, 61C
030399 Other Music   13C, 14C, 18H, 30H, 31C, 32C, 33C, 42C, 44C, 46C, 47C, 48C, 64C, 66C

0304 Theater Arts   3C, 55C
030401 Theater Arts Studio and Performance   41C
030402 Theater Studies   20C, 22CN, 31C, 34C, 45C, 46C, 64C
030403 Theater in Education   4HC
030499 Other Theater Arts   4C, 14C, 22N, 34C, 45C

0305 Visual Arts   45C
030501 Visual-Arts Studio and Production   13HC, 21C, 22C, 28C, 35HC, 41C, 48H, 55H, 59HN
030502 Visual-Arts Studies   4C, 12C, 13HC, 18H, 19C, 28C, 29C, 35C, 36C, 38C, 46C, 52C, 55H, 57H, 61C, 64HC, 65C
030503 Visual Arts in Education   18H, 36C
030599 Other Visual Arts   4HN, 5C, 13N, 14H, 29C, 35C, 47H, 48C, 51C, 63HCN

0306 Related Arts   24C
030602 Related-Arts Studies   37H, 46C, 65C
030603 Related Arts and Aesthetic Education   4C, 13H, 18H, 35C
030699 Other Related Arts   22N, 63CN

0399 Other Arts, Visual and Performing   4C, 22C

04   BUSINESS

Subject matter that is a part of Distributive Education and Career Education Programs can be found in this area under Marketing. Also, selected subject matter in this classification is applicable to office occupations. Although the knowledge of Economics is an integral part of business, it is listed in the subject-matter area of Social Sciences and Social Studies and not here. The knowledge of the skills involved in many occupational programs is found in this area even though differences may exist in the form and substance of the subject matter as it is presented to students. This is particularly true for elements listed under Administrative and Office Services, such as Typewriting.

0401 Accounting   3C, 9C, 67C
040101 Accounting Principles   5C, 11C, 13C, 14CN, 15C, 16C, 18H, 19C, 20HCN, 21HC, 22C, 25C, 30C, 32C, 33C, 34C, 35C, 36H, 38C, 39C, 40C, 42C, 43HC, 44C, 45HC, 46C, 47C, 48HC, 49C, 51C, 52CN, 54C, 55C, 56C, 57HCN, 58C, 59C, 61C, 63CN, 64C, 65C, 66C, 71C
040102 Accounting Systems   11H, 37H, 57C
040103 Auditing   14C, 21C, 35C, 56C, 59C
040104 Bookkeeping   4H, 14H, 31H, 33H, 34H, 47H, 55H, 58H, 59H, 60H, 61N, 63HN, 64H
040106 Cost Accounting   13C, 14C, 15C, 20C, 21C, 35C, 36C, 40C, 52C. 55C, 56C, 63CN, 65C
040107 Data-Processing Accounting   3C
040108 General Accounting   4C, 13H, 17C, 30HN, 55C, 56C, 67C
040109 Governmental and Institutional Accounting   13C, 21C, 35C, 40C, 55C, 56C, 63CN, 71C
040111 Managerial Accounting   5C, 14C, 19C, 22C, 25C, 36C, 39C, 42C, 45C, 47C, 48C, 51C, 55C, 59C, 61C, 63CN, 65C, 67C, 71C
040113 Recordkeeping   36C
040114 Tax Accounting   4H, 13C, 14C, 16C, 22C, 35C, 38C, 45C, 56C, 61C, 67C
040199 Other Accounting   4H, 46C, 58C

0402 Administrative and Office Services   16C, 59H
040201 Administrative Procedures   14C, 34H, 38C, 59C, 63CN, 65C
040203 Records Management   3C, 14C, 16C, 33C, 34HN, 39C, 52C, 59H
040205 Shorthand and Transcription   4H, 13H, 14HC, 18H, 34H, 43C, 44H, 45H, 48H, 58H
040206 Specialized Secretarial Services   15C, 21C, 46C
040207 Typewriting   4H, 11EHC, 13H, 14HC, 18H, 34H, 43C, 47H, 48H, 55H, 57H, 58H
040299 Other Administrative and Office Services   7C, 13H, 14H, 15C, 16C, 18H, 36H, 47H, 48H, 56H

0403 Banking and Finance   4H, 17C, 38N, 66C, 67C
040301 Business and Corporate Finance   14C, 15C, 17C, 19C, 22C, 30CN, 31C, 38C, 41C, 43C, 55C, 56C, 61C, 65C, 68C
040302 Consumer Finance   13C, 21H, 22C, 36H, 45C, 55HC, 61C
040303 Credit and Collections   67C
040304 Financial Institutions   30CN, 40C, 55C
040305 International Banking and Finance   31C
040306 Investments and Securities   13N, 17C, 22C, 30CN, 31C, 32C, 35C, 38C, 41C, 56N, 61C, 63CN
040307 Monetary and Fiscal Policy   63CN
040308 Money and Banking   7C, 14C, 15C, 17C, 31C, 46C, 61C, 68C
040311 Principles and Theory of Finance   4C, 22C, 47C, 48C, 52C
040312 Public Finance   10C, 13C, 31C
040399 Other Banking and Finance   14C, 17C, 31C, 38C, 56C, 65C, 68C

0404 Business Data Systems   9C, 17C, 63CN

0405 Entrepreneurship   30N, 47C
040502 Private Ownership   4H, 19C, 41C, 65C
040599 Other Entrepreneurship   30HN

05   COMMUNICATION

Film as Communication in this subject-matter area is considered as a means of transmitting messages. In contrast, Film as Art in the area of Arts, Visual and Performing, is considered as an artistic medium. Journalism and Speech Communication are both found in this subject-matter area and not in the area of Language, Linguistics, and Literature with which they are closely related and often reported.

0511   Speech Communication   67C
051102   Intercultural Communication   2C, 4C, 42C
051103   Interpersonal Communication   5C, 13HC, 14C, 19C, 42C
051104   Organizational Communication   34C, 41C
051106   Pragmatic Communication   12C
051107   Public Address   4HC, 13C
051108   Rhetorical and Communication Theory   5C, 19C, 24C, 64C
051109   Speech Communication Education   45C, 57C
051110   Speech and Hearing Science   42C, 46C
051199   Other Speech Communication   2C, 14C, 38C, 41C

0512   Special Communication
051201   Braille   37C, 62C
051202   Manual Communication   19C, 61C
051299   Other Special Communication   2C

0513   Television   19C
051303   Writing for Television   12C, 34C, 35C
051399   Other Television   24C

0599   Other Communication   4C, 10C, 13HC, 19C, 27C, 30CN, 41C, 43H, 64C, 66C, 67C

06   COMPUTER SCIENCE AND DATA PROCESSING

Most of the mathematical logic upon which computer systems are based is included in the subject-matter area of Mathematical Sciences. Knowledge of the engineering design and construction of computing equipment is found in the category of Electrical Engineering and Technology within the subject-matter area of Engineering and Engineering Technology. Knowledge about the ways in which computers and data-processing equipment are utilized can be classified under other subject-matter areas if the emphasis is on the application and not upon the computer or data-processing system.

0601   Applications in Computer Science and Data Processing   9C, 15C, 17C, 67C
060102   Computer Graphics   6CGN
060103   Instructional Applications   4C
060199   Other Applications in Computer Science and Data Processing   4H, 24C, 30H, 69C

0602   Computer Operations and Operations Control
060201   Computer Operation   58C
060203   Data Entry   35N

0603   Computer Hardware Systems

0604   Computer Hardware
060404   Microprocessors   21C, 35C, 45C
060499   Other Computer Hardware   28C

0605   Information and Database Systems   17C
060502   Database Management Systems   35C
060503   Database Security   19C
060599   Other Information and Database Systems   7C

0607   Programming Languages   13N, 20CN, 32C
060701   Command Languages   14C
060705   Procedure-Oriented Languages   13HC, 21C, 24C, 35C, 52C
060707   Symbolic and Algebraic Manipulation Languages   13C
060799   Other Programming Languages   4C, 13C, 39C, 47C, 63CN

0608   Programming Systems   13N
060802   Compilers   20C
060806   Operating Systems   21C

0609   Software Methodology
060903   Programming Techniques   24C
060904   Systems Analysis   24C, 35C

0610   Theory of Computation

0611   Educational, Societal, and Cultural Considerations
061101   Computer Literacy   4H, 13H, 14HN, 15H, 30HN, 31H, 47H, 49H, 51C, 55H, 59N
061103   Basic Concepts of Computer Science   18H, 22C, 36H, 46H, 48H, 52C, 64C
061104   Basic Concepts of Data Processing   13H, 24C, 30HN, 35C
061199   Other Educational, Societal, and Cultural Considerations   29C

0699   Other Computer Science and Data Processing   17C, 29C, 35N, 49C

07   EDUCATION

The subject matter in this area is concerned with the knowledge that is needed to teach and to otherwise carry out the process of education.

0701   Foundations of Education   20C, 51C, 59C
070102   Educational Theory   20C, 32C
070103   Socioeconomic Foundations   33C
070199   Other Foundations of Education   4C, 20C, 22C, 25C, 27C, 37C, 41CG, 47C, 49N, 54C, 60C, 64C, 71C

0702   Educational Administration   25C
070207   Educational Personnel and Staffing   64C
070299   Other Educational Administration   4C, 27C, 45C

0703   Systems of Education
070301   Pre-Elementary Education Systems   4C
070302   Elementary Education Systems   2C, 57C
070303   Secondary Education Systems   2C, 57C
070306   Vocational-Technical Education Systems   22C, 52C, 69C
070309   Adult-Continuing Education Systems   6CGN, 25C, 39C, 47CG, 60C, 63C

0704   Curriculum and Instruction—General   47G
070401   Principles and Theories of Curriculum and Instruction   4C, 13C, 20C, 32C, 34C, 41C, 56C, 61C
070402   Management and Supervision of Curriculum and Instruction   4C
070403   Teacher Training   20C, 30CN, 49C
070404   Teacher Methods   4CG, 20C, 21C, 27C, 34C, 35C, 41C, 42C, 47G, 48C, 54C, 57C, 61C
070499   Other Curriculum and Instruction—General   22C, 34C, 35C, 36C, 63C, 71C

0705   Curriculum and Instruction—Subject Matter (Using the Structure of the Classification of Educational Subject Matter)
070501   Agriculture and Renewable Natural Resources   20C
070503   Arts, Visual and Performing   13C, 47C, 55C
070504   Business   54C
070505   Communication   38C, 55C
070506   Computer Science and Data Processing   21CG, 35C, 47G
070507   Education   39C
070509   Health Care and Health Sciences   11C, 19C, 21C, 38C, 47C, 56C, 57C, 63C
070511   Industrial Arts, Trades, and Technology   20C, 34C, 69C
070512   Language, Linguistics, and Literature   4C, 19C, 32C, 34C, 35C, 36C, 39C, 41C, 44CN, 46C, 50C, 55C, 56C, 62C, 63C
070514   Libraries and Museums   14C

070515 Life Sciences and Physical Sciences 15H, 39C, 56C, 69C
070516 Mathematical Sciences 1C, 4C, 11C, 13C, 15C, 19C, 20C, 34C, 35C, 40C, 43C, 47C, 50C, 55C, 56C, 58C, 60C, 65C
070518 Philosophy, Religion, and Theology 22C
070519 Physical Education, Health Education, and Leisure 34C, 47C
070520 Psychology 2C, 15C, 37C, 38C, 46C, 47C, 56C, 57C
070522 Social Sciences and Social Studies 11C, 34C, 39C, 46C, 55C, 65C
070599 Other Curriculum and Instruction—Subject Matter 4C, 11C, 14C, 46C, 49C, 61C, 69C

0706 Curriculum and Instruction—Programs
070602 Career Education 4C, 20H, 38C, 46C
070603 Cooperative Education 69C
070604 Distributive Education 12C
070610 Reading and Language Arts Programs 2C, 4CGN, 20C, 21C, 30CN, 46C, 47CG, 59C, 64C
070611 Bilingual Education Programs 4C, 70C
070613 Driver Education Programs 4C, 57C, 61C
070699 Other Curriculum and Instruction—Programs 42C, 47C, 63N

0707 Counseling and Guidance 40C
070701 Principles and Theories of Counseling and Guidance 4CN, 15C, 35C, 36C, 41G, 46C, 57C, 58C, 63C
070702 Academic Counseling and Guidance 20C, 55HN
070703 Career Information and Counseling 13H, 19C, 22C, 35N, 37N, 47H
070704 Clinical Experience 13C
070705 Counseling Services 15C
070708 Professional Development 22C
070799 Other Counseling and Guidance 6G, 19C, 28C, 30CG, 31C, 40C, 46C, 47H, 69C

0708 Special Education 2C, 15C, 32C, 41C, 46C, 47C, 52C, 55C, 59C, 70C
070801 Early Education of the Handicapped 14C, 41C, 61C
070803 Gifted and Talented 4C, 39C, 41C, 56C, 63C, 65C
070804 Hearing Handicapped 65C
070805 Learning Disabled 2C, 56C, 65C
070806 Mentally Handicapped 2C, 4C, 41C, 47C, 65C
070808 Physically Handicapped 55C
070810 Socially Handicapped 42C
070811 Speech Handicapped 2C, 20C, 65C
070899 Other Special Education 4C, 6CG, 13C, 15C, 36H, 42C, 47C, 49C, 52C, 53CG, 57H, 60C, 63C, 71C

0709 Community Service 6C
070902 Community Relations 4C, 63C
070999 Other Community Service 63C

0710 Educational Development 70C
071099 Other Educational Development 63C

0711 Educational Evaluation and Research 25C, 32C
071101 Design and Planning 4C
071102 Methodology 40C, 47C, 64C
071103 Principles and Theory of Evaluation and Research 4C, 11C, 34C, 37C, 41G, 62C, 65C
071199 Other Educational Evaluation and Research 4C, 14C, 15C, 45C

0712 Educational Technology and Media 70C
071201 Computer Applications to Education 30G, 32C
071202 Instructional Systems Design 41C
071203 Educational Media and Material Production 20C, 61C, 64C, 65C
071204 Educational Media and Resource Centers 61C

071299 Other Educational Technology and Media 61CN

0799 Other Education 4H, 19C, 29C, 36C, 45C, 47C, 48H, 51N, 64N

08 ENGINEERING AND ENGINEERING TECHNOLOGY

0801 Aerospace and Aeronautical Engineering and Technology 9C, 55H
080101 Aerodynamics 9C, 42C
080102 Aeronautics 19C

0802 Agricultural Engineering and Technology
080205 Soil and Water Resources 65C

0803 Architectural Engineering and Technology
080399 Other Architectural Engineering and Technology 45C

0804 Automotive Engineering and Technology 63HN

0806 Chemical Engineering and Technology
080603 Thermodynamics and Kinetics 20C
080699 Other Chemical Engineering and Technology 31C

0807 Civil Engineering and Technology
080703 Hydrology (See 150502—Hydrology) 22C, 55C, 64C, 65C
080704 Materials of Construction 4C
080706 Soil Mechanics and Foundations 21C
080707 Structural Engineering 4C, 63N
080799 Other Civil Engineering and Technology 47N, 63C

0809 Electrical Engineering and Technology 17C, 39N, 55C, 67C
080901 Electromechanical Circuits 20C, 22C, 35C, 51C, 59C
080903 Electronics 20C
080904 Fields and Waves 20C
080906 Electrical Instrumentation 20C
080999 Other Electrical Engineering and Technology 35C, 36H

0810 Graphics and Drafting for Engineering and Technology 4C, 14HC, 18H, 20C, 22CN, 34H, 35N, 39C, 40C, 41C, 47HC, 52C, 58C, 61C

0811 Engineering Mechanics 22C
081102 Fluid Mechanics 34C, 39C, 55C, 65C
081103 Solid Mechanics 22C, 47C, 55C
081104 Statics and Dynamics 4C, 14C, 22C, 30C, 34C, 39C, 40C, 47C, 55C, 62C, 63C, 64C, 65C
081199 Other Engineering Mechanics 34C, 35C, 40C, 55C, 63C

0812 Engineering Science 35C, 39C

0813 Environmental Engineering and Technology
081301 Air-Pollution Control 63N
081302 Noise-Pollution Control 22CN
081303 Solid-Waste Control 63N
081304 Water and Sewage Control 22CN, 37N, 63N
081399 Other Environmental Engineering and Technology 1C, 37N, 63N

0815 Industrial Engineering and Technology 55C
081502 Human Factors in Industry 36C, 45C
081503 Operations Research (See 041203—Operations Research) 45C, 48C, 55C
081504 Production Planning and Control 69C
081505 Quality Assurance 41C, 69C
081506 Work Measurement 69C
081599 Other Industrial Engineering and Technology 45C, 52C, 63C

0817 Manufacturing Engineering and Technology
081799 Other Manufacturing Engineering and Technology
63C

0819 Materials Engineering and Technology 55C
081999 Other Materials Engineering and Technology 22C,
45C

0820 Mechanical Engineering and Technology
082001 Air-Conditioning, Heating, Ventilation, and
Refrigeration Engineering 63N
082003 Energy Conversion 63N
082006 Mechanical Design 22C
082099 Other Mechanical Engineering and Technology 22C,
63C

0821 Metallurgical Engineering and Technology
082199 Other Metallurgical Engineering and Technology 61C,
63C

0823 Nuclear Engineering and Technology
082303 Radiation Control 20CN

0825 Petroleum Engineering 32C
082501 Petroleum Exploration 22N
082599 Other Petroleum Engineering 22N

0826 Surveying and Mapping
082601 Land Surveying and Subdivision 63N
082602 Engineering and Construction Surveying 35C
082604 Photogrammetry and Topographic Surveying 63N
082699 Other Surveying and Mapping 39C

0899 Other Engineering and Engineering Technology
20CN, 34C, 35CN, 43C, 48N, 63N

09 HEALTH CARE AND HEALTH SCIENCES

Under Basic Health-Care Sciences are those elements of
knowledge that come from the Biological Sciences but whose
emphasis is directed toward the care and treatment of humans and
animals. General knowledge, not specific to the restoration or
preservation of health, is included in the subject-matter area of
Life Sciences and Physical Sciences. Where appropriate, cross-
references are shown in this structure.

Clinical Health Sciences lists those elements of knowledge that
are related to diseases, injuries, or deformities. The list is divided
into five subjectively established categories: (1) knowledge related
to body organs or localized parts of the body, (2) knowledge of
disorders or general conditions of the body, (3) knowledge that is
specific to an age group or type of patient, (4) knowledge of
health care approaches that are not unique to areas of the body or
type of patient but focus instead on the treatment itself, and (5)
knowledge of special-purpose health care and health sciences.

Many of the elements in this subject-matter area can apply to
either humans or animals.

0901 Basic Health-Care Sciences 15H, 67C
090101 Health-Care Anatomy 4H, 31H, 66H
090103 Clinical Chemistry 47N
090104 Diagnostics 41N
090106 Epidemiology 65C
090111 Medical Hygiene 65C
090113 Infectious Diseases 65C
090114 Microbiology (See 150311—Microbiology) 15C, 65C
090115 Health-Care Nutrition 13C, 39H, 51C
090117 Pathology 41C
090118 Pharmacology 13C, 45C, 49N, 52C
090119 Health-Care Physiology 36H, 65C
090121 Radiobiology 20C

090199 Other Basic Health-Care Sciences 15C, 36C, 45C,
48H, 57H, 69C

0902 Clinical Health Sciences 51N
090201 Cardiology 47N, 67C
090202 General Dentistry 67C
090214 Gastroenterology 47N
090242 Gerontology 62C
090255 Nursing 13C, 37C, 50C
090259 Radiology 67C
090272 Family Medicine 4HC
090276 Nuclear Medicine 22CN
090299 Other Clinical Health Sciences 40C, 47N, 67C

0903 Rehabilitation and Therapy
090301 Audiology and Speech Pathology 65C
090302 Dietetics and Nutrition 25C, 41C, 47N
090303 Occupational Therapy 52C, 69C
090305 Physical Therapy 58C, 62C
090307 Radiation Therapy 35N, 47N
090308 Recreation Therapy 13N
090399 Other Rehabilitation and Therapy 13N, 38N

0904 Pharmaceutical Sciences
090403 Drug and Drug-Abuse Information 4HC, 47N, 61C
090404 Drug Regulation and Control 47N, 59N
090408 Pharmaceutics 47N
090411 Pharmacy Practices and Management 23N, 59N
090499 Other Pharmaceutical Sciences 47N, 61C

0905 Emergency Services
090504 First Aid 4C, 20C, 40C, 48C
090599 Other Emergency Services 34C, 47N

0906 Hospital and Health-Care Administration 67C
090601 Hospital Organization and Management 25C, 47N,
67C
090602 Health-Care Delivery Systems 24C, 25C, 47C, 51C
090603 Health Organizations, Standards, and Evaluation 22C,
25CG, 67C
090699 Other Hospital and Health-Care Administration 13C,
25CG, 29C, 47N, 51C, 52N, 67C

0907 Public Health 25C, 40C
090702 Community Medicine 4C, 24C, 65C, 67C
090703 Environmental Health Administration 7C, 25CG
090704 Human Ecology 19C, 25C
090705 Industrial-Health Administration 7C, 19C
090706 Maternal and Child Health Administration 45C
090709 Physiological Hygiene 22H
090710 Public-Health Administration 24C, 56C
090799 Other Public Health 4C, 35C, 39C, 50C, 63HC, 67C

0908 Veterinary Medical Sciences 38N
090899 Other Veterinary Medical Sciences 38C

**0909 General Perspectives of Health Care and Health
Sciences**
090901 Health Planning 13H, 20C, 25G, 61C
090902 History of Health Care and Health Sciences 4C, 71C
090903 Professional Practices in Health Care and Health
Sciences 33C
090904 Ethics and Jurisprudence in Health Care and Health
Sciences 19C, 25CG, 41C, 67C
090905 Clinical Practices in Health Care and Health Sciences
23N
090999 Other General Perspectives of Health Care and Health
Sciences 4HC, 13HC, 28C, 33C, 48C, 49C, 56C,
63N

0999 Other Health Care and Health Sciences 4C, 33H,
37C, 47N, 52C, 67C

13   LAW

14   LIBRARIES AND MUSEUMS

The elements in this subject-matter area represent the substance of knowledge that has been determined to be appropriate to Libraries and Museums.

140305 Museum Administration 39C
140307 School-Library and Media-Center Administration 39C, 55C, 64C
140399 Other Administration of Libraries and Museums 33C

1404 Collection Management
140401 Cataloging of Collections 39C, 64C
140408 Selection and Acquisition of Collections 39C, 64C
140499 Other Collection Management 33C, 65C

1407 Materials for Libraries and Museums
140799 Other Materials for Libraries and Museums 65C

1408 Library and Museum Services and Functions
140803 Public Education Services and Functions 60C
140804 Reference and Retrieval 39C, 50C, 51C, 61C
140899 Other Library and Museum Services and Functions 19C, 61C

1409 Library and Museum User Groups 61C, 64C

1499 Other Libraries and Museums 13H

15 LIFE SCIENCES AND PHYSICAL SCIENCES
The arrangement of elements within the subject-matter category of Biology includes those that could be aggregated into Botany and Zoology as well. To have broken them out would have required another level of coding and two additional digits.

Many of the elements within Biology have been cross-referenced to identical titles in Health Care and Health Sciences. The related elements differ in that the subject matter of Health Care and Health Sciences emphasizes the restoration and preservation of health. Subject matter in Life Sciences and Physical Sciences is not as specific and can be related to a broad range of units of instruction.

1501 Astronomy 3C, 4C, 19C, 20C, 31C, 50C, 55C, 56C, 57N
150101 Cosmology (See 180601—Cosmology) 20C, 47C, 62C
150102 Solar Astronomy 13C, 45C, 46C, 62C
150103 Stellar Astronomy 13C, 14C, 31C, 60C, 64C, 68C
150199 Other Astronomy 13C, 14C, 15C, 33C, 35C, 37C, 43C, 51C, 57C, 61C

1502 Atmospheric Sciences
150201 Climatology 3C, 13C, 62C, 63C
150202 Meteorology 3C, 20C, 21C, 22C, 33C, 38C, 42C, 47C, 61C, 63C, 67C

1503 Biology 4H, 11H, 14HCN, 15H, 18H, 20H, 21H, 30HN, 35H, 39H, 43H, 45H, 47H, 48H, 53C, 55H, 57H, 59H, 60H, 61C, 69C
150301 Biological Behavior 4H, 20C, 22C, 33H, 35C, 36H, 37H, 42C, 43C, 49H, 56H, 58C, 65C
150302 Cell Biology 4C, 60C, 63H, 65C
150303 Developmental Biology 60C, 63H, 68C
150304 Ecology 4HC, 5C, 24C, 32C, 38C, 39C, 45C, 48C, 61C, 64H, 65C, 69C
150306 Evolution 43C, 62C
150307 General Genetics 20C, 22C, 34C, 35C, 38C, 43C, 60C, 61C
150310 Marine Biology 56C
150311 Microbiology (See 090114—Microbiology) 4C, 43C
150316 General Botany 5C, 19C, 33C, 34C, 35C, 43C, 51C, 63C, 69C
150317 Bacteriology 34C
150321 Plant Pathology 33C
150323 General Zoology 19C, 43C, 49C
150324 Animal Anatomy 4H
150326 Animal Genetics 24C
150327 Entomology 18H, 35C, 37N, 47C, 65C
150331 Ornithology 18H

150399 Other Biology 4C, 7C, 13HC, 14C, 19C, 22C, 31C, 34HC, 35C, 39C, 42C, 43C, 45H, 46C, 48H, 49C, 58HC, 61C, 64H, 69C

1504 Chemistry 11H, 17C, 55C, 67C
150401 General Chemistry 4HC, 13H, 18H, 19C, 22C, 35C, 37C, 41C, 45C, 47H, 48H, 51C, 58H, 59C, 62C, 63C
150403 Biochemistry (See 090102—Biochemistry) 35C, 64C
150408 Organic Chemistry 19C, 20C, 22C, 35C, 55C
150410 Surface Chemistry 35C
150499 Other Chemistry 46C, 69C

1505 Geology 20C, 21C, 30C, 33C, 36C, 51C, 55C, 59C
150501 Geomorphology 3C, 35C, 64C
150504 Paleontology 4C
150599 Other Geology 3C, 4C, 13C, 14C, 21C, 22C, 37C, 41C, 47HC, 50C, 51C, 54C, 58C, 63C, 65C, 68C

1506 Oceanology 20C, 21C, 51C, 62C

1507 Physics 13H, 17C, 18H, 30HN, 39C, 40C, 45C, 47H, 48H, 51C, 56C, 58H, 66HC
150702 Astrophysics 3C
150704 Electricity 14N, 48H
150799 Other Physics 4H, 5C, 9C, 13HC, 14C, 19C, 21C, 22C, 31C, 35HC, 36C, 39C, 45C, 46C, 47C, 48HC, 61C, 63C

1508 General Physical Sciences 4C, 17C, 18C, 19C, 30HN, 31H, 45C, 48H, 56H, 60H
150803 Mechanics 60C
150899 Other General Physical Sciences 14HC, 15C, 19C, 22C, 46C, 51C, 57H, 58C, 60C

1509 General Earth-Space Science 4H, 10C, 11C, 13H, 17C, 21H, 33H, 34C, 39H, 43H, 47HC, 58C

1599 Other Life Sciences and Physical Sciences 17C, 21C, 24C, 33C, 34C, 37H, 47H, 58H, 63C, 66C, 67C

16 MATHEMATICAL SCIENCES
Every attempt was made to include in this subject-matter area all subject-matter elements that have their genesis in mathematics. Accordingly, the elements within Probability and Statistics, in particular, will be combined with several other elements in other subject-matter areas.

1601 Mathematics, General Perspectives 20H
160101 Philosophy of Mathematics 4C
160102 History of Mathematics 4C, 5C, 53C, 71C
160103 Content of Mathematics 22C, 35H, 54C, 57C, 58C
160199 Other Mathematics, General Perspectives 4N, 7C, 13HCN, 15H, 20C, 22C, 29C, 32C, 34C, 36H, 38C, 41N, 45HC, 47C, 56C, 57CN, 58C, 64N

1602 Logic, Sets, and Foundations 17C
160202 Mathematical Logic 15C, 31C, 69C
160203 Finite Sets 13C, 22C, 24C, 38C, 39C, 57C
160204 Graph Theory 15C
160299 Other Logic, Sets, and Foundations 42C, 46C, 58H

1603 Arithmetic and Algebra 17C, 19C
160301 Arithmetic 1H, 4HCN, 12C, 14HN, 18H, 20CN, 21H, 22N, 31H, 33H, 34H, 35C, 36H, 39HC, 41N, 43H, 47H, 48H, 52N, 55H, 57H, 59H, 60H, 63HN, 64HC, 65C, 69C

1808 Philosophical Foundations 13C, 19C, 38C, 47C, 58C, 67C

1809 Specific Religions
180901 Buddhism 64N
180902 Christianity 13C, 18H, 31C, 37C, 59C, 64N
180903 Hinduism 64N
180904 Islam 19C, 64N
180905 Judaism 42C, 64N
180999 Other Specific Religions 11C, 41G, 45C, 46C, 68C

1810 Phenomenology of Religion
181002 Comparative Religions 12C, 21C, 25C, 27C, 38C, 47HN, 52C, 62C
181004 Sociology of Religion 45C
181099 Other Phenomenology of Religion 52C

1811 Religion and Human Experience
181101 Religion and Science 15C, 58C
181102 Religion and Personality Studies 31C
181103 Religion and Social Issues 37C, 45C, 59C
181104 Religion and Culture 13C, 37C, 41C, 54C
181199 Other Religion and Human Experience 7C, 36C, 41C, 42C

1812 Sacred Writings
181201 Sacred Writings of the Jewish Faith 37C, 51C
181202 Sacred Writings of the Christian Faith 4C, 11C, 27C, 30N, 37C, 42C, 47N, 51C, 58C, 59N
181299 Other Sacred Writings 4C, 30N, 41G, 46C

1813 Historical Theology
181301 Ancient Near East Theology 41C
181302 Early Christian and Rabbinic Theology 41C
181303 Medieval Theology 69C
181304 Modern Theology 4C, 22C
181399 Other Historical Theology 27C, 41CG

1814 Systematic Theology
181401 God 27C
181406 Christology 11C, 27C
181407 Soteriology 27C
181408 Pneumatology 27C
181409 Eschatology 27C
181499 Other Systematic Theology 27C

1815 Moral and Ethical Studies
181502 Moral and Ethical Issues 52C
181599 Other Moral and Ethical Studies 41G, 52CN

1816 Pastoral Studies
181601 Homiletics 27C
181602 Pastoral Care and Counseling 27C
181603 Religious Education 4C
181605 Worship and Liturgy 4G
181606 Sacred Music 27C
181607 Church Administration and Leadership 4C, 27C
181608 Missiology 4C, 27C
181699 Other Pastoral Studies 27C

1899 Other Philosophy, Religion, and Theology 4C, 11EHCN, 17C, 22C, 50C, 63C

19 PHYSICAL EDUCATION, HEALTH EDUCATION, AND LEISURE

Dance is listed both in Physical Education, Health Education, and Leisure and in Arts, Visual and Performing. As an art form, it is more concerned with aesthetics than with physical movement, although both factors are involved.

Health Education deals with the knowledge that individuals use to maintain good health as members of society. Specific knowledge relating to the restoration and preservation of health is

included in the subject-matter area of Health Care and Health Sciences.

1901 Physical Education 16C, 18H, 30HN, 67C
190102 Exercise 4HCN
190103 Group Games, Contests, and Self-Testing Activities 4H
190104 History of Physical Education 12C, 19C, 22C
190105 Philosophy of Physical Education 56C
190106 Physical Education Administration 12C, 13C, 19C, 29C, 34C, 55C, 56C, 58C
190107 Physical Education Curriculum 22C, 41G
190108 Physical Education Instruction 4C, 6C, 22C, 69C
190110 Measurement and Evaluation in Physical Education 22C, 34C, 55C, 56C
190199 Other Physical Education 4C, 15C, 61C

1902 Kinesiology 19C, 55C
190203 Performance Physiology 61C
190299 Other Kinesiology 41C

1903 Sport
190301 Sport in Schools and Colleges 22C
190303 Sport History 3C, 30CN
190306 Sport Psychology 61C
190308 Administration of Sport 55C
190311 Instruction and Coaching of Sport 13N, 22C, 42C, 55C, 56C, 58C
190312 Sport Activities 18H, 60H
190399 Other Sport 22C, 69C

1904 Dance (See 0301—Dance)
190401 Dance Choreography 4C
190499 Other Dance 4C

1905 Health Education 30CN, 40C, 47H, 55HC
190501 Drugs and Other Substances 10CG, 18H, 22C, 30CN, 38C, 40C, 55C, 57C
190502 Community-Health Education 5C, 7HC, 13C, 14C, 15C, 19C, 40C, 58C, 59C, 64C
190503 Consumer-Health Education 15C, 22C, 30C, 40C, 59C
190504 Disease Prevention and Control 15C, 22C, 30CN, 40C, 69C
190505 Environmental-Health Education 42C
190506 Family-Health Education 18H, 37H
190508 Nutrition Education 36C, 37N
190509 Personal-Health Education 5C, 12C, 13C, 18H, 21HC, 22C, 30HN, 31C, 34H, 35H, 37H, 40C, 43H, 46C, 47H, 54C, 58C, 59C, 60H
190510 Physical Fitness 59H, 65C
190511 Safety Education 5C, 7C, 12C, 14C, 15C, 46C, 59C, 61C
190512 Sex Education 4C, 14C, 20C, 40C, 42C, 59C, 60C, 61C
190513 Administration of Health Education 33C
190515 Health-Education Instruction 11H, 40C
190599 Other Health Education 11C, 12C, 14HC, 15C, 22C, 37C, 40C, 42C, 46C, 56H, 63C

1906 Driver and Safety Education 47H
190603 Development of Driving Judgment 4H, 35H
190699 Other Driver Education 12C, 18N, 22H, 48H

1907 Leisure Studies 46C, 51C
190701 Resource Management in Leisure Studies 5C, 30CN
190702 Populations and Leisure Services 5C, 13C, 41C
190703 Leisure and Recreation Planning 13CN, 47C
190704 Leadership in Leisure Studies 13C, 58C, 61C
190705 Recreation Activities 4C
190706 History of Leisure Studies 22C
190709 International and Comparative Leisure Studies 61C
190799 Other Leisure Studies 13C, 22N, 41C, 61C, 68C

220506 Political Behavior   38C, 62C

220507 Political Parties and Public Opinion   13C, 14C, 42C,
43C, 45C, 48C, 55C, 62C

220509 Political Structures   3C, 4C, 13C, 31C, 47HC, 58C,
68C

220510 Political Theory   13C, 35C, 40C, 47C, 51C, 58C, 62C,
64N

220511 State and Local Government   3C, 4C, 7C, 13C, 15H,
17C, 18H, 19C, 21C, 22C, 24C, 31C, 33HC, 34C,
37C, 38C, 39HC, 40C, 41C, 43C, 47C, 49C, 51C,
53C, 55C, 58H, 60C, 66C

220599 Other Political Science and Government   5C, 7C, 10G,
13C, 15H, 26C, 31C, 33C, 34C, 36H, 39C, 41C,
45C, 46C, 47C, 48C, 50C, 51C, 52N, 56C, 61C, 63C,
68C, 69C

2206 Sociology   3C, 16C, 17C, 18H, 20C, 24C, 30HCN,
31H, 34H, 39H, 40C, 47H, 55H, 59HC, 67C

220601 Community Sociology   4H, 13C, 25C, 33C, 35C,
43HC, 45C, 54C, 56C, 69C

220602 Criminology   2C, 12C, 13C, 14C, 17C, 19C, 25C, 29C,
31C, 33C, 34C, 36C, 37C, 39C, 41C, 43C, 45C, 46C,
47C, 48C, 51C, 52C, 54C, 56C, 57C, 58C, 59C, 64C,
66C, 68C, 69C

220603 Demography and Human Ecology   13C, 17C, 32C,
33C, 34C, 41C, 45C, 59C

220604 Juvenile Delinquency   5C, 12C, 17C, 20C, 22C, 29C,
33C, 38C, 39C, 41C, 43C, 46C, 51C, 54C, 57C, 59C,
68C, 69C

220605 Marriage and Family   2C, 3C, 4C, 5C, 7C, 13C, 14C,
15C, 17C, 20C, 22C, 25C, 31C, 32C, 34C, 37C, 38C,
41C, 43C, 48C, 51C, 52C, 54C, 55C, 57C, 58C,
59HC, 62C, 63C, 66C, 68C, 71C

220606 Principles and Theory of Sociology   5C, 7HC, 8C, 12C,
13C, 15C, 17C, 19C, 20C, 22C, 25C, 33H, 34C,
35H, 36HC, 37C, 38C, 41C, 42C, 43C, 47C, 48HC,
49C, 50C, 51C, 52C, 55C, 56HC, 57C, 58C, 60C,
61C, 62C, 64C, 66C, 69C, 71C

220607 Psychological Sociology   4C, 5C, 22C, 38C, 45C, 52C,
59C, 66C, 69C

220608 Rural Sociology   14C, 39C, 47C, 52C

220609 Quantitative Methods   17C, 19C, 43C, 57C

220610 Social Control and Deviance   3C, 13C, 36C, 43C, 54C,
55C, 56C, 62C, 64C

220611 Social Institutions   14H, 17C, 59C, 69C

220612 Social Organization and Change   8C, 13C, 14H, 20C,
36C, 39C, 40C, 57H

220613 Social Problems   3C, 4C, 12C, 13C, 14C, 17C, 20C,
25C, 30CN, 31C, 32C, 33C, 34C, 36C, 38C, 39C,
40C, 42C, 43C, 48C, 49C, 50C, 54C, 56C, 57HC,
59C, 63C, 64HC, 66C, 67C, 68C

220614 Urban Sociology   10C, 13C, 17C, 22C, 33C, 34C, 37C,
47C, 50C, 59C

220615 Sociology of Groups   2C, 4H, 5C, 31C, 46C, 47C, 54C,
57C, 60C, 66C, 68C, 69C

220699 Other Sociology   1C, 2C, 3C, 4HC, 5C, 11C, 13HC,
14C, 24C, 26C, 29C, 31C, 32C, 33C, 38C, 39C, 40C,
42C, 45C, 47CG, 51C, 52C, 56C, 57HC, 58H, 59C,
60C, 63C, 66C, 67C, 68C, 69C

2299 Other Social Sciences and Social Studies   4C, 10CG,
11E, 13HC, 14H, 19C, 21H, 22C, 24C, 29C, 33H,
37HC, 44C, 47HC, 48H, 49C, 53N, 63C, 66C, 69C